# SPECIAL COLLECTIONS
# IN CHILDREN'S LITERATURE

## AN INTERNATIONAL DIRECTORY
### THIRD EDITION

**Association for Library Service to Children**

compiled and edited by
Dolores Blythe Jones

with the assistance of the
National Planning for Special Collections Committee

American Library Association
Chicago and London
1995

Cover illustration from *Mother Goose in Silhouettes*, cut by Katharine G. Buffum; Boston: Houghton-Mifflin, 1907.

Cover by Tessing Design

Text design by Dianne M. Rooney

Composed by Alexander in Sabon and printed on 50-pound Badger Offset, a p-H neutral stock, and bound in 10-point C1S cover stock by Trade Service Publications

This paper used in this publication meets the minimum requirements of American National Standard for Information Sciences—Permanence of Paper for Printed Library Materials, ANSI Z39.48-1992 ∞

**Library of Congress Cataloging-in-Publication Data**
Special collections in children's literature : an international
   directory / Association for Library Service to Children ; compiled
   and edited by Dolores Blythe Jones ; with the assistance of the
   National Planning for Special Collections Committee. — 3rd ed.
        p.      cm.
     Includes index.
     ISBN 0-8389-3454-4
     1. Children's literature—Library resources—Directories.
   2. Library resources—United States—Directories.   I. Jones,
   Dolores Blythe.   II. Association for Library Service to Children.
   Committee on National Planning for Special Collections.
   Z688.C47S63   1995                                        95-10998
   026.8088'99282—dc20

Printed in the United States of America.

99 98 97 96 95    5 4 3 2 1

*Dedicated to the*
*special collections librarians*
*whose hard work*
*has made this book possible*

*Ride a Cock-Horse to Banbury Cross and a Farmer Went Trotting*
*upon His Grey Mare*
by Randolph Caldecott; London: Routledge [1884].

# ❖❖❖❖❖❖❖ *Contents*

# Contents

 *Foreword*

In 1964 the Association for Library Service to Children of the American Library Association, recognizing the need for coordinating and planning for special collections in the area of literature for children, appointed a Committee on the National Planning for Special Collections of Children's Books. The function of the committee was to identify current collections in the United States and Canada. Questionnaires were sent out to libraries and individuals. Publicity on the project was sent to the various publications in the library and book world. The response was overwhelming and the committee decided to accept R. R. Bowker's offer to publish the results. For two years, Virginia Haviland, Elizabeth Nesbitt, and I met regularly and, with the input of other members of the committee, prepared a manuscript for publication.

The title of the first edition was *Subject Collections in Children's Literature* and included private as well as institutional collections. One hundred and fifty-three collections were included in the 1969 edition.

Due to the interest of researchers, scholars, and librarians, the American Library Association decided to publish a second edition in 1982. With the assistance of Margaret N. Coughlan and Sharyl G. Smith, as well as input from members of the committee, several changes were made. The title became *Special Collections in Children's Literature* to allow for collections in any format—print, illustration, audiovisual materials, foreign translations, etc. Excluded were general browsing collections, private collections, parent-teacher collections, and those in instructional materials centers. Two hundred sixty-eight institutions were included in the second edition.

More than a decade later we have a third edition that includes 300 collections in the United States and 119 collections in forty countries. Such an increase in the number of collections of children's books and related materials shows the value and importance of this specific area of the literary world to the bibliophile, historian, and researcher.

Anyone interested in collecting children's books will want to read Carolyn Clugston Michaels's *Children's Book Collecting* (Library Professional Publications, 1993). In it she covers all aspects of collecting as well as offering a delightful and informative history of children's literature. She lists great collections, private and public; includes a directory of resources; and has a valuable glossary.

Individuals who really care about children's books are usually welcome to see the treasures in a special collection. Researchers and scholars are always welcome to use the materials, but there are a few rules to be followed. A request to the librarian or curator should include a statement of credentials, the nature of the project, previous steps taken and collections investigated, date and approximate time of visit, and how to be reached if time and date are not convenient.

Most historians will agree that children's books are the best source for information on the morals and mores of a period of time or of a country. Even in this technological age of computers and computer games, the printed book is important. The circulation of children's books in public libraries is booming. The appropriate book as a gift to a child is still welcomed. I usually give a book as a gift to a child at Christmas and the response is the same: "This is my best Christmas gift ever!" As Peggy Sullivan said in the second edition in her article, "Collections and Collectors of Children's Books," "it is probably the book we loved the most as children that has been lost, energetically loved to death or left outside in the rain." So it behooves us as librarians to be careful in discarding books and to encourage and publicize the wonderful collections of children's books.

*Carolyn W. Field*
Coordinator Emeritus
The Free Library of Philadelphia

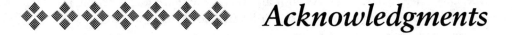 *Acknowledgments*

This publication is an outgrowth of the work of the National Planning for Special Collections Committee of the Association for Library Service to Children of the American Library Association. As such, its publication is the culmination of several years' work, involving a number of committee members. Serenna Day, Karen Nelson Hoyle, Ethel Ambrose, and Mary Beth Dunhouse assisted with the compilation and were part of the formative stage of the project. Other committee members who provided ideas and suggestions were Helen Mullen, Linda Murphy, Corinne Camarata, and Linda Ward Callaghan. We were fortunate to work with ALA Editions editor Bonnie Smothers, who was a rich source of ideas and inspiration. The work of the third edition was not possible without a fine foundation from which to work. That was provided by Carolyn Field and her contributing editors, who worked on the previous two editions of this work. I would like to give special thanks to Jeffrey Garrett, who assisted in locating international collections.

The most important contributors to this volume are the librarians, curators, and directors who provided information on their holdings, without whom this work would not have been possible. With decreasing staffs and increasing demands, the time required to provide us with updated information was precious indeed.

I would like to thank the administration of the University Libraries at the University of Southern Mississippi for their major support of this project and the Children's Library Services Endowment of the Association for Library Service to Children for financial support. Additional support was also received from the staff of the Association for Library Service to Children, especially Eileen Fitzsimons. As with any book, there are many people responsible for its completion. It is our collective hope that this directory of institutions housing materials that are important to the study and appreciation of children's and young adult literature will provide a source of current information for reseachers and others interested in the field.

 *Preface*

This edition includes all institutions and collections covered in preceding editions, with the exception of those who asked to be excluded. The holdings of 82 institutions not included in the second edition have been added. The resulting third edition now includes 300 institutions in the United States whose holdings include materials pertinent to the study of children's and young adult literature. A new feature of this edition is the inclusion of a directory of international collections, describing the holdings of 119 institutions in forty countries. Private collections are not included. The illustrations in this edition come from the holdings of the de Grummond Children's Literature Collection, at the University of Southern Mississippi.

## METHODOLOGY

Questionnaires were sent to all institutions appearing in the second edition, as well as a number of institutions not covered by the preceding editions. In all, 445 questionnaires were mailed to institutions in the United States believed to have holdings of interest to the study of children's and young adult literature. Several follow-up letters were sent to those that did not respond to the first mailing. Institutions listed in the second edition that did not respond to the questionnaire are included in the third edition, using information from the second edition. These institutions are coded with a double asterisk following the institution name in the Directory of United States Collections. In addition, a separate questionnaire was sent to more than 500 institutions in countries throughout the world. Only those institutions that completed the questionnaire are included in this volume.

## ARRANGEMENT

The Directory of United States Collections is arranged alphabetically by state, city, and institution. All collections held by a particular institution are arranged alphabetically following the descriptive information for the institution. For example, Yale University's Beinecke Rare Book and Manuscript Library holds four collections that contain materials pertinent to the study of children's literature. There are separate descriptions and listings for their Special Collections, Cary Collection of Playing Cards, Peter Newell Family Papers, and the Betsy Beinecke Shirley Collection of American Children's Literature. These specific descriptions follow the general information for the Beinecke Library.

Information for each institution includes address, telephone and fax numbers, e-mail and Internet addresses if applicable, the name of a contact person, and the cataloging utility used by the institution. Each collection within an institution is described as specifically as possible, listing any publications that have been produced about that collection. Following the collection description are the subject headings under which that collection is listed in the Subject Listing. For example, the American Popular Literature Collection at Northern Illinois University has entries in the Subject Listing under "Horatio Alger," "Historical," "Oliver Optic," and "Series Books." In most instances, the entry in the Subject Listing provides details that are not present in the Directory. For the most complete information, it is advisable to consult both the Directory and the Subject Listing. The code used for the institution in the Subject Listing follows the institution name in the Directory. An alphabetical listing of these codes is also found on p. xv.

The Subject Listing is arranged alphabetically and includes author, illustrator, and publisher names, as well as genres and subjects important to the study of children's and young adult literature. Information for a specific book title is found under the author of that title. For example, holdings for *Alice in Wonderland* are found under Lewis Carroll. Listed under each subject heading is a code for the institution and a description of its holdings. The descriptions will vary, depending upon how the holdings were reported by the institution. In some cases, exact figures are given for book holdings, while in others, the holdings are described as "substantial" or "extensive." The unit of measurement for holdings of original manuscript and illustrative materials differs across institutions. Therefore, reporting methods include cubic feet, linear feet, and quantities based on number of titles.

It is important to note that many larger collections are not listed under every author, illustrator, or genre that they may hold. For example, it would be impossible to list all of the authors represented in the 85,000 volumes held by the Baldwin Collection. We have only been able to determine their strengths and specialties and provide listings for those areas. It should be assumed that most larger collections are going to hold most of the classic titles, authors, illustrators, and publishers of children's literature.

The codes are derivative of the National Union Catalog (NUC) symbols and reflect the current usage as established in Symbols of American Libraries. A listing of these codes follows this Preface. The codes are arranged alphabetically using the following system: each code consists of units, with each unit containing an uppercase letter or an uppercase and lowercase letter. A code may have as few as one or as many as five units. As an example, the Ohioana Library is represented by the single uppercase letter "O," while the Northern State University in Aberdeen, South Dakota, is represented by "SdAbN." Using the "SdAbN" code as an example, "Sd" is the first unit, representing South Dakota; "Ab" is the second unit, representing the city of Aberdeen; and "N" is the third unit, representing Northern State University. Alphabetization is by units, not individual letters; therefore the code "MoIRC" follows "MWiW" due to the combination of upper- and lowercase letters.

The Directory of International Collections is arranged by country, city, and institution. Information includes address, telephone and fax numbers, e-mail and Internet addresses where applicable, and the name of a contact person. A short description of the collection follows. Holdings of the international collections are not further detailed with specific subject listings as are the United States collections.

 # Institution Abbreviation List

| | |
|---|---|
| AB | Alabama. Birmingham. Birmingham Public Library. |
| AkA | Alaska. Anchorage. Z. J. Loussac Public Library. |
| AkFSD | Alaska. Fairbanks. Fairbanks North Star Borough Public Library. |
| ArCCA | Arkansas. Conway. University of Central Arkansas. |
| ArL | Arkansas. Little Rock. Central Arkansas Library System. |
| ArStC | Arkansas. State University. Arkansas State University. |
| ArU | Arkansas. Fayetteville. University of Arkansas. |
| AzT | Arizona. Tucson. Tucson-Pima Library. |
| AzTeS | Arizona. Tempe. Arizona State University. |
| AzU | Arizona. Tucson. University of Arizona. |
| CAna | California. Anaheim. Anaheim Public Library. |
| CB | California. Berkeley. Berkeley Public Library. |
| CBbWDA | California. Burbank. Walt Disney Archives. |
| CCCla | California. Claremont. The Claremont Graduate School. |
| CCSc | California. Claremont. Scripps College. |
| CF | California. Fresno. Fresno County Public Library. |
| CFLp | California. Fresno. Leo Politi Branch Library. |
| CFlS | California. Fullerton. California State University. |
| CGlen | California. Glen Ellen. Jack London State Historic Park. |
| CL | California. Los Angeles. Los Angeles Public Library. |
| CLob | California. Long Beach. Long Beach Public Library. |
| CLSU | California. Los Angeles. University of Southern California. |
| CLU-C | California. Los Angeles. University of California at Los Angeles. William Andrews Clark Memorial Library. |

| | |
|---|---|
| CLU-S/C | California. Los Angeles. University of California at Los Angeles. Special Collections, UCLA Research Library. |
| CNoS | California. Northridge. California State University, Northridge. |
| COPL | California. Oakland. Oakland Public Library. |
| CP | California. Pasadena. City of Pasadena. |
| CPom | California. Pomona. Pomona Public Library. |
| CRiv | California. Riverside. Riverside City Library. |
| CSahS | California. St. Helena. The Silverado Museum. |
| CSd | California. San Diego. San Diego Public Library. |
| CSf | California. San Francisco. San Francisco Public Library. |
| CSfACA | California. San Francisco. San Francisco Academy of Comic Art. |
| CSfSt | California. San Francisco. San Francisco State University. |
| CSj | California. San Jose. San Jose Public Library. |
| CSmH-A | California. San Marino. The Huntington Library. |
| CSmar | California. San Marcos. California State University, San Marcos. |
| CSt | California. Stanford. Stanford University. |
| CStoC | California. Stockton. University of the Pacific. |
| CU-EDUC | California. Berkeley. University of California at Berkeley. Education-Psychology Library. |
| CoD | Colorado. Denver. Denver Public Library. |
| CoDDB | Colorado. Denver. Denver Botanic Gardens. |
| CoU | Colorado. Boulder. University of Colorado at Boulder. |
| CtH | Connecticut. Hartford. Hartford Public Library. |
| CtHSD | Connecticut. Hartford. Stowe-Day Library. |
| CtHT | Connecticut. Hartford. Trinity College. |
| CtHi | Connecticut. Hartford. Connecticut Historical Society. |
| CtNbT | Connecticut. New Britain. Central Connecticut State University. |
| CtNhHi | Connecticut. New Haven. New Haven Colony Historical Society. |
| CtNhN | Connecticut. New Haven. Southern Connecticut State University. |
| CtNlC | Connecticut. New London. Connecticut College. |
| CtU | Connecticut. Storrs. University of Connecticut. |
| CtY-BR | Connecticut. New Haven. Yale University. Beinecke Rare Book and Manuscript Library. |
| DGU | District of Columbia. Georgetown University. |
| DLC | District of Columbia. Library of Congress. |
| DWP | District of Columbia. District of Columbia Public Library. |
| DeU | Delaware. Newark. University of Delaware. |
| DeWA | Delaware. Wilmington. Delaware Art Museum. |
| DeWI | Delaware. Wilmington. Wilmington Institute Library. |
| DeWint | Delaware. Winterthur. Winterthur Library. |

| | |
|---|---|
| FSpSC | Florida. St. Petersburg. The Science Center Library. |
| FTS | Florida. Tampa. University of South Florida. |
| FTaSU | Florida. Tallahassee. Florida State University. |
| FU | Florida. Gainesville. University of Florida. |
| GEU-S | Georgia. Atlanta. Emory University. |
| GS | Georgia. Savannah. Chatham-Effingham-Liberty Regional Library. |
| GU | Georgia. Athens. University of Georgia. |
| HH | Hawaii. Honolulu. Hawaii State Library. |
| IC | Illinois. Chicago. Chicago Public Library. |
| ICN | Illinois. Chicago. Newberry Library. |
| ICarbS | Illinois. Carbondale. Southern Illinois University at Carbondale. |
| IDeKN | Illinois. De Kalb. Northern Illinois University. |
| IEN | Illinois. Evanston. Northwestern University. |
| INS | Illinois. Normal. Illinois State University. |
| IQ | Illinois. Quincy. Quincy Public Library. |
| IRoC | Illinois. Rockford. Rockford College. |
| IU-Ed | Illinois. Urbana. University of Illinois. Education and Social Science Library. |
| IU-LS | Illinois. Urbana. University of Illinois. School of Library and Information Science. |
| IWW | Illinois. Wheaton. Wheaton College. |
| IaU | Iowa. Iowa City. University of Iowa. |
| IaWbH | Iowa. West Branch. Herbert Hoover Presidential Library. |
| IdU | Idaho. Moscow. University of Idaho. |
| InI | Indiana. Indianapolis. Indianapolis-Marion County Public Library. |
| InMuB | Indiana. Muncie. Ball State University. |
| InNd | Indiana. Notre Dame. University of Notre Dame. |
| InTI | Indiana. Terre Haute. Indiana State University. |
| InU-Li | Indiana. Bloomington. Indiana University. Lilly Library. |
| KEmU | Kansas. Emporia. Emporia State University. |
| KHi | Kansas. Topeka. Kansas State Historical Society. |
| KU | Kansas. Lawrence. University of Kansas. |
| KWPu | Kansas. Winfield. Winfield Public Library. |
| KWS | Kansas. Winfield. Southwestern College. |
| KWi | Kansas. Wichita. Wichita Public Library. |
| KyBgW | Kentucky. Bowling Green. Western Kentucky University. |
| KyLoU | Kentucky. Louisville. University of Louisville. |
| KyU | Kentucky. Lexington. University of Kentucky. |
| L | Louisiana. Baton Rouge. State Library of Louisiana. |
| LN | Louisiana. New Orleans. New Orleans Public Library. |

| | |
|---|---|
| MAA | Massachusetts. Amherst. Amherst College. |
| MAJ | Massachusetts. Amherst. The Jones Library, Inc. |
| MB | Massachusetts. Boston. Boston Public Library. |
| MBAt | Massachusetts. Boston. Boston Athenaeum. |
| MBChM | Massachusetts. Boston. The Children's Museum. |
| MBCn | Massachusetts. Boston. The Congregational Library. |
| MBSi | Massachusetts. Boston. Simmons College. |
| MBU | Massachusetts. Boston. Boston University. |
| MBWS | Massachusetts. Boston. Wheelock College. |
| MBrH | Massachusetts. Brookline. Hebrew College. |
| MCo | Massachusetts. Concord. Concord Free Public Library. |
| MCoA | Massachusetts. Concord. Orchard House/Home of the Alcotts. |
| MCot | Massachusetts. Cotuit. Cotuit Library Association. |
| MDeeP | Massachusetts. Deerfield. The Memorial Libraries. |
| MFiT | Massachusetts. Fitchburg. Fitchburg State College. |
| MH-Ed | Massachusetts. Cambridge. Harvard Graduate School of Education. |
| MHi | Massachusetts. Boston. Massachusetts Historical Society. |
| MNS | Massachusetts. Northampton. Smith College. |
| MSaA | Massachusetts. Salem. Salem Athenaeum. |
| MSaP | Massachusetts. Salem. Peabody Essex Museum. |
| MSanB | Massachusetts. Sandwich. Thornton W. Burgess Society. |
| MSanP | Massachusetts. Sandwich. Sandwich Public Library. |
| MStuO | Massachusetts. Sturbridge. Old Sturbridge Village. |
| MWA | Massachusetts. Worcester. American Antiquarian Society. |
| MWW | Massachusetts. Worcester. Worcester State College. |
| MWalB | Massachusetts. Waltham. Brandeis University. |
| MWelC | Massachusetts. Wellesley. Wellesley College. |
| MWelF | Massachusetts. Wellesley. Wellesley Free Library. |
| MWiW | Massachusetts. Williamstown. Williams College. |
| MdBE | Maryland. Baltimore. Enoch Pratt Free Library. |
| MeB | Maine. Brunswick. Bowdoin College. |
| MeGar | Maine. Gardiner. Gardiner Public Library. |
| MeP | Maine. Portland. Portland Public Library. |
| MePW | Maine. Portland. Westbrook College. |
| MeU | Maine. Orono. University of Maine. |
| MeWC | Maine. Waterville. Colby College. |
| MiD | Michigan. Detroit. Detroit Public Library. |
| MiDW | Michigan. Detroit. Wayne State University. |
| MiDbH | Michigan. Dearborn. Henry Ford Museum & Greenfield Village. |

| | |
|---|---|
| MiEM | Michigan. East Lansing. Michigan State University. |
| MiGrA | Michigan. Grand Rapids. Aquinas College. |
| MiKW | Michigan. Kalamazoo. Western Michigan University. |
| MiMtpT | Michigan. Mount Pleasant. Central Michigan University. |
| MiU | Michigan. Ann Arbor. University of Michigan. |
| MnM | Minnesota. Minneapolis. Minneapolis Public Library. |
| MnSP | Minnesota. St. Paul. St. Paul Public Library. |
| MnSSC | Minnesota. St. Paul. College of St. Catherine. |
| MnU | Minnesota. Minneapolis. University of Minnesota. |
| MoHI | Missouri. Columbia. The State Historical Society of Missouri. |
| MoHM | Missouri. Hannibal. Mark Twain Museum. |
| MoIRC | Missouri. Independence. Reorganized Church of Jesus Christ of Latter Day Saints. |
| MoK | Missouri. Kansas City. Kansas City Public Library. |
| MoS | Missouri. St. Louis. St. Louis Public Library. |
| MoSFi | Missouri. St. Louis. Eugene Field House & Toy Museum. |
| MoSHi | Missouri. St. Louis. Missouri Historical Society Library & Archives. |
| MoSW | Missouri. St. Louis. Washington University. |
| MoStoM | Missouri. Stoutsville. Mark Twain Birthplace Museum. |
| MoWarbT | Missouri. Warrensburg. Central Missouri State University. |
| MsHaU | Mississippi. Hattiesburg. University of Southern Mississippi. |
| NAlU | New York. Albany. University at Albany, State University of New York. |
| NBPu | New York. Brooklyn. Brooklyn Public Library. |
| NBuBE | New York. Buffalo. Buffalo and Erie County Public Library. |
| NBuC | New York. Buffalo. State University College at Buffalo. |
| NCooHi | New York. Cooperstown. New York State Historical Association. |
| NEaHi | New York. Eastchester. Eastchester Historical Society. |
| NGuP | New York. Greenvale. Long Island University. C. W. Post Campus. |
| NHas | New York. Hastings-on-Hudson. Hastings-on-Hudson Public Library. |
| NHem | New York. Hempstead. Hempstead Public Library. |
| NHemH | New York. Hempstead. Hofstra University. |
| NHi | New York. New York. New York Historical Society. |
| NHyF | New York. Hyde Park. Franklin D. Roosevelt Library. |
| NIC | New York. Ithaca. Cornell University. |
| NJQ | New York. Jamaica. Queens Borough Public Library. |
| NMalo | New York. Malone. Franklin County Historical and Museum Society. |
| NN-BrC | New York. New York. Chatham Square Branch. New York Public Library. |
| NN-BrCo | New York. New York. New York Public Library. Countee Cullen Regional Branch. |

NN-BrH      New York. Bronx. Hunt's Point Regional Branch. New York Public Library.

NN-BrR      New York. New York. New York Public Library. Riverside Branch.

NN-Don      New York. New York. New York Public Library. Donnell Library Center.

NN-Rb       New York. New York. New York Public Library. Rare Books and Manuscript Division.

NN-Sc       New York. New York. New York Public Library. Schomburg Center for Research in Black Culture.

NNC         New York. New York. Columbia University.

NNC-T       New York. New York. Teachers College. Columbia University.

NNCbc       New York. New York. Children's Book Council.

NNFI        New York. New York. French Institute/Alliance Française.

NNMMA-U     New York. New York. Metropolitan Museum of Art. Uris Library.

NNMus       New York. New York. Museum of the City of New York.

NNPM        New York. New York. The Pierpont Morgan Library.

NNStJ       New York. Jamaica. St. John's University.

NNU-F       New York. New York. New York University. Fales Library.

NPV         New York. Poughkeepsie. Vassar College.

NRU         New York. Rochester. University of Rochester.

NSyU        New York. Syracuse. Syracuse University.

NWat        New York. Watkins Glen. American Life Foundation and Study Institute.

NWe         New York. Westbury. Westbury Memorial Public Library.

NbSeT       Nebraska. Seward. Concordia College.

NbU         Nebraska. Lincoln. University of Nebraska-Lincoln.

NcCU        North Carolina. Charlotte. University of North Carolina at Charlotte.

NcD         North Carolina. Durham. Duke University.

NcGU        North Carolina. Greensboro. University of North Carolina at Greensboro.

NcU         North Carolina. Chapel Hill. University of North Carolina at Chapel Hill.

NhC         New Hampshire. Concord. New Hampshire State Library.

NhD         New Hampshire. Hanover. Dartmouth College.

NhU         New Hampshire. Durham. University of New Hampshire.

NjFoP       New Jersey. Fort Lee. Free Public Library of the Borough of Fort Lee.

NjMF        New Jersey. Madison. Farleigh Dickinson University.

NjN         New Jersey. Newark. Newark Public Library.

NjP         New Jersey. Princeton. Princeton University.

NjP-C       New Jersey. Princeton. Princeton University. Cotsen Children's Library.

NjR         New Jersey. New Brunswick. Rutgers University.

| | |
|---|---|
| NjR-Z | New Jersey. New Brunswick. Rutgers University. Zimmerli Art Museum. |
| NjSoCo | New Jersey. Somerville. Somerset Public Library. |
| NmAl | New Mexico. Alamogordo. Alamogordo Public Library. |
| NmU | New Mexico. Albuquerque. University of New Mexico. |
| O | Ohio. Columbus. Ohioana Library. |
| OAU | Ohio. Athens. Ohio University. |
| OBgU | Ohio. Bowling Green. Bowling Green State University. |
| OBlC-M | Ohio. Bluffton. Bluffton College. |
| OC | Ohio. Cincinnati. Public Library of Cincinnati and Hamilton County. |
| OCH | Ohio. Cincinnati. Hebrew Union College/Jewish Institution of Religion. |
| OCX | Ohio. Cincinnati. Xavier University. |
| OCl | Ohio. Cleveland. Cleveland Public Library. |
| OCl-FL | Ohio. Cleveland. Cleveland Public Library. Foreign Literature Department. |
| OCl-RB | Ohio. Cleveland. Cleveland Public Library. Rare Books. |
| ODaWU | Ohio. Dayton. Wright State University. |
| OFH | Ohio. Fremont. Rutherford B. Hayes Presidential Center Library. |
| OFiC | Ohio. Findlay. University of Findlay. |
| OHi | Ohio. Columbus. Ohio Historical Society. |
| OHirC | Ohio. Hiram. Hiram College. |
| OKentU | Ohio. Kent. Kent State University. |
| OOxM | Ohio. Oxford. Miami University. |
| OS | Ohio. Springfield. Warder Literacy Center. |
| OSiA | Ohio. Sidney. Amos Memorial Public Library. |
| OU | Ohio. Columbus. Ohio State University. |
| Ok | Oklahoma. Oklahoma City. Oklahoma Department of Libraries. |
| OkAlvN | Oklahoma. Alva. Northwestern Oklahoma State University. |
| OkOk | Oklahoma. Oklahoma City. Metropolitan Library System in Oklahoma County. |
| OkS | Oklahoma. Stillwater. Oklahoma State University. |
| OkT | Oklahoma. Tulsa. Tulsa City-County Library. |
| OkU | Oklahoma. Norman. University of Oklahoma. |
| OrENC | Oregon. Eugene. Northwest Christian College. |
| OrHi | Oregon. Portland. Oregon Historical Society. |
| OrP | Oregon. Portland. Library Association of Portland. |
| OrPS | Oregon. Portland. Portland State University. |
| OrU | Oregon. Eugene. University of Oregon. |
| PBal | Pennsylvania. Bala-Cynwyd. Bala-Cynwyd Library. |
| PHi | Pennsylvania. Philadelphia. Historical Society of Pennsylvania. |
| PMCHi | Pennsylvania. Meadville. Crawford County Historical Society. |

| | |
|---|---|
| PNo | Pennsylvania. Norristown. Montgomery County-Norristown Public Library. |
| PP | Pennsylvania. Philadelphia. Free Library of Philadelphia. |
| PP-RB | Pennsylvania. Philadelphia. Free Library of Philadephia. Rare Book Department. |
| PPD | Pennsylvania. Philadelphia. Drexel University. |
| PPL | Pennsylvania. Philadelphia. Library Company of Philadelphia. |
| PPRF | Pennsylvania. Philadelphia. Rosenbach Museum and Library. |
| PPT | Pennsylvania. Philadelphia. Temple University. |
| PPi | Pennsylvania. Pittsburgh. Carnegie Library of Pittsburgh. |
| PPiC | Pennsylvania. Pittsburgh. Carnegie-Mellon University. |
| PPiU | Pennsylvania. Pittsburgh. University of Pittsburgh. |
| PPiU-LS | Pennsylvania. Pittsburgh. University of Pittsburgh. School of Library and Information Science. |
| PSC | Pennsylvania. Swarthmore. Swarthmore College. |
| PSt | Pennsylvania. University Park. Pennsylvania State University. |
| RP | Rhode Island. Providence. Providence Public Library. |
| RPA | Rhode Island. Providence. Providence Anthenaeum Library. |
| RPB-JH | Rhode Island. Providence. Brown University. John Hay Library. |
| RWe | Rhode Island. Westerly. Westerly Public Library. |
| ScCleU | South Carolina. Clemson. Clemson University. |
| ScCoC | South Carolina. Columbia. Columbia College. |
| ScFlM | South Carolina. Florence. Francis Marion University. |
| ScRhW | South Carolina. Rock Hill. Winthrop University. |
| ScSpW | South Carolina. Spartanburg. Wofford College. |
| ScU | South Carolina. Columbia. University of South Carolina. |
| SdAbN | South Dakota. Aberdeen. Northern State University. |
| TMM | Tennessee. Memphis. Memphis State University. |
| TRuT | Tennessee. Rugby. Thomas Hughes Free Public Library. |
| TxDN | Texas. Denton. University of North Texas. |
| TxDW | Texas. Denton. Texas Women's University. |
| TxDa | Texas. Dallas. Dallas Public Library. |
| TxE | Texas. El Paso. El Paso Public Library. |
| TxF | Texas. Fort Worth. Fort Worth Public Library. |
| TxH | Texas. Houston. Houston Public Library. |
| TxU | Texas. Austin. University of Texas. |
| TxU-Hu | Texas. Austin. University of Texas at Austin. Harry Ransom Humanities Research Center. |
| TxWB | Texas. Waco. Baylor University. |
| ULA | Utah. Logan. Utah State University. |

| | |
|---|---|
| UPB | Utah. Provo. Brigham Young University. |
| ViR | Virginia. Richmond. Richmond Public Library. |
| ViU | Virginia. Charlottesville. University of Virginia. |
| WM | Wisconsin. Milwaukee. Milwaukee Public Library. |
| WMUW | Wisconsin. Milwaukee. University of Wisconsin at Milwaukee. |
| WU | Wisconsin. Madison. University of Wisconsin-Madison. |
| WU-CC | Wisconsin. Madison. University of Wisconsin-Madison. Cooperative Children's Book Center. |
| Wa | Washington. Olympia. Washington State Library. |
| WaChenE | Washington. Cheney. Eastern Washington University. |
| WaElC | Washington. Ellensburg. Central Washington University. |
| WaS | Washington. Seattle. Seattle Public Library. |
| WaSHi | Washington. Seattle. Historical Society of Seattle & King County. |
| WaSPC | Washington. Seattle. Seattle Pacific University. |
| WaSp | Washington. Spokane. Spokane Public Library. |
| WaT | Washington. Tacoma. Tacoma Public Library. |
| WaU | Washington. Seattle. University of Washington. |
| WaU-CM | Washington. Seattle. University of Washington. Curriculum Materials. |
| WvED | West Virginia. Elkins. Davis and Elkins College. |
| WyShF | Wyoming. Sheridan. Sheridan County Fulmer Public Library. |

# Directory of United States Collections

## Alabama

### BIRMINGHAM

Birmingham Public Library (AB)
2100 Park Pl.
Birmingham, AL 35203
phone: 205-226-3665
contact: Grace Reid, Librarian
catalog status: OCLC

*The Grace Hardie Collection of Children's Literature*

A collection of 700 volumes, most published before the turn of the century, is divided among books of instruction and moral tales, books of adventure and travel, books about the natural world, and the classics of children's literature. Some of the most notable works in the collection are first editions of the classics, numerous examples of illustrated works, and turn-of-the-century series books. Included are several hornbooks, a complete run of St. Nicholas, and comic books. (Subjects: Bible and Books of Religious Instruction; Historical; Series Books)

## Alaska

### ANCHORAGE

Z. J. Loussac Public Library (AkA)
Anchorage Municipal Libraries
3600 Denali St.
Anchorage, AK 99503
phone: 907-261-2841
fax: 907-562-1244
contact: Chrystal Carr Jeter, Coordinator of Youth Services
catalog status: Washington Library Network (WLN); GEAC

*Loussac Children's Literature Collection*

This circulating resource contains 4,500 volumes of children's literature history, author and illustrator information, award-winning titles, and books about children's librarianship and programming. Curriculum aids and display ideas are included in this grant-funded collection. (Subjects: Award Books; Children's Literature, Study of; Historical—20th Century; Textbooks)

**FAIRBANKS**

**Fairbanks North Star Borough Public Library (AkFSD)**
1215 Cowles St.
Fairbanks, AK 99701
phone: 907-459-1020
fax: 907-459-1024
contact: Robyn H. Smith, Youth Services Librarian
catalog status: Washington Library Network (WLN); local online catalog

*Arthur Rackham Collection*
Consisting of ca. 100 titles illustrated by Arthur Rackham, this collection is not yet cataloged and is available for in-house use only. (Subject: Rackham, Arthur)

*Juvenile Alaskana Collection*
A collection of about 300 twentieth-century monographs, primarily in English, that are about or set in Alaska. There are some bilingual titles in English and Alaska native languages. (Subject: Alaska)

# Arizona

**TEMPE**

**Arizona State University (AzTeS)**
Special Collections
Box 871006
Tempe, AZ 85287-1006
phone: 602-965-6519
fax: 602-965-9269
contact: Marilyn Wurzburger, Department Head
catalog status: OCLC, local online catalog

*Child Drama Collection*
An extensive collection of 800-plus books about theater for youth is complemented by 200 linear feet of original manuscripts representing fifteen playwrights. Also included are correspondence, periodicals, and production materials for students pre-

school through high school. (Subjects: Drama; Manuscript/Illustration Material)

*Contemporary Authors Manuscripts Collection*
Several Arizona authors are represented in this collection containing 65 linear feet of manuscripts, typescripts, galleys, notes, journals, scrapbooks, reviews, photographs, and correspondence. (Subjects: Arizona—Authors and Illustrators; Cosner, Shaaron; Leonard, Phyllis; Manuscript/Illustration Material; Place, Marian T.; Swarthout, Glendon and Kathryn)

*Historical*
A collection of 1,000-plus volumes published from 1708 to 1900, containing works by Walter Crane, Kate Greenaway, L. Leslie Brooke, and Arthur Rackham. Also included is a small sampling of early textbooks. (Subjects: Historical; Textbooks)

*Lyman Frank Baum and Oz Memorabilia*
This collection consists of 40 volumes authored by Baum as well as *The Baum Bugle* (1959–) and *Oziana* (1971–86). The Nicholas Salerno Collection of Oz Memorabilia includes seventeen boxes of figurines, music boxes, stuffed toys, dolls, paper advertising products, ornaments, and clothing based on the Oz books. (Subject: Baum, Lyman Frank)

*Science Fiction*
More than 800 volumes by twentieth-century science fiction authors Robert Heinlein, Isaac Asimov, Arthur C. Clarke, Frank Herbert, Murray Leinster, Andre Norton, and A. E. Vogt are held, as well as extensive runs of several science fiction periodical titles. (Subjects: Periodicals; Science Fiction)

## TUCSON

**Tucson-Pima Library (AzT)**
101 North Stone
Tucson, AZ 85701
phone: 602-791-4393
fax: 602-791-5249
contact: Roberta Barg, Senior Librarian
catalog status: OCLC, CLSI

*Elizabeth B. Steinheimer Collection of Children's Materials on the Southwest*
Established as a memorial to Elizabeth B. Steinheimer, this collection offers a generation-spanning spectrum of materials that illustrate and interpret the Southwest and its peoples to children. The collection holds 2,000 volumes dating from 1890 to the present, and twelve illustrations by Grace Moon. Included are fiction and nonfiction, print and nonprint materials. This collection provides a picture of Southwest history, geography, and ethnology, focused through the unique prism of children's literature. (Subjects: Manuscript/Illustration Material; Moon, Grace; Southwestern United States)

**University of Arizona (AzU)**
University Library
Tucson, AZ 85721
phone: 602-621-6441
contact: Roger Myers
Internet: sabio.arizona.edu
catalog status: OCLC; Sabio

*Library*
Holdings include 400 titles by eighteenth- and nineteenth-century American and English authors with the earliest imprint being 1727. Books with Arizona as a setting, including Hopi, Navajo, Apache, Tohono O'Odham, and other cultural settings, are held, as well as some bilingual books. A special feature is the papers of Ann Nolan Clark. (Subjects: Arizona; Clark, Ann Nolan; Historical; Manuscript/Illustration Material; Native Americans; Textbooks)

# Arkansas

## CONWAY

**University of Central Arkansas (ArCCA)**
Torreyson Library
201 Donaghey Ave.
Conway, AR 72035-0001
phone: 501-450-5249
fax: 501-450-5208
contact: Carol Powers, Assistant Librarian
catalog status: OCLC, local online catalog

*Children's Literature Collection*
This collection of 18,000 current and historical juvenile and young adult titles is used to promote adults' acquaintance with the selection, utilization, history, and evaluation of children's books. Items in the collection consist mainly of monographs in English, dating from 1833 to the present. (Subjects: Award Books; Historical)

## FAYETTEVILLE

**University of Arkansas (ArU)\*\***
Mullins Library
Fayetteville, AR 72701-1201
phone: 501-575-6702
fax: 501-575-5558

*Gerald J. McIntosh Dime Novel Collection*
The McIntosh Collection holds 1,630 items, including magazines, books, pamphlets, notes, and other materials relating to the history and collection of the American dime novel. Materials are arranged in five series and include complete runs of *Tip Top Weekly* and *New Tip Top Weekly*. (Subjects: Dime Novels; Periodicals)

## LITTLE ROCK

**Central Arkansas Library System (ArL)**
700 Louisiana St.
Little Rock, AR 72201
phone: 501-370-5955
fax: 501-375-7451
contact: Bettye Kerns, Youth Services
catalog status: OCLC

### *Charlie May Simon Collection*
Collection consists of 23 titles written by Arkansas author, Charlie May Simon, from 1934 to 1969. (Subject: Simon, Charlie May)

## STATE UNIVERSITY

**Arkansas State University (ArStC)**
Dean B. Ellis Library
P. O. Box 2040
State University, AR 72467
phone: 501-972-3077
fax: 501-972-5706
contact: Willis Brenner, Documents
 Librarian
e-mail: wbrenner@quapaw.astate.edu
Internet: telnet apache.astate.edu
 (972-3879 if using modem)
catalog status: OCLC, local online
 catalog

### *Lois Lenski Collection*
Included in the 345-volume Lois Lenski Collection are books written by her, books about her, and books from her personal library. Also held are original illustrations, manuscripts, proofs, correspondence, photographs, records, tapes, and films. (Subjects: Lenski, Lois; Manuscript/Illustration Material)

# California

## ANAHEIM

**Anaheim Public Library (CAna)**\*\*
500 W. Broadway
Anaheim, CA 92805-3699
phone: 714-254-1880
fax: 714-254-1731

### *Walt Disney Collection*
This in-depth collection of materials about Walt Disney and his family, Disneyland, Walt Disney Productions, and Walt Disney World includes photographs, news releases, books, clippings, music, recordings, archival records, and synopses of productions from 1953. Also included are numerous Disney periodical titles. (Subjects: Disney, Walt; Periodicals)

## BERKELEY

**Berkeley Public Library (CB)**\*\*
2090 Kittredge St.
Berkeley, CA 94704
phone: 510-644-6095
fax: 510-845-7598

### *Library*
Holdings include 1,100-plus volumes of folklore, mythology, hero legends, and literature based on folklore and legends. In addition, a 700-volume historical/model collection includes very old series; books noted for illustration, text, and bookmaking; and recent publications that display racist or sexist tendencies. (Subjects: Folk and Fairy Tales; Historical)

**University of California at Berkeley
 (CU-EDUC)**
Education-Psychology Library
2600 Tolman Hall
Berkeley, CA 94720
phone: 510-642-4208

fax: 510-642-8224
contact: Sonya Kaufman, Head,
    Reference Services
e-mail: skaufman@library.berkeley.edu
Internet: melvyl.ucop.edu
catalog status: GLADIS, MELVYL

### Hans Christian Andersen Awards 1992

More than 350 books and accompanying documentation (including bio-bibliographical dossiers, illustrations, photographs, and tapes) from the nominated authors and illustrators for the 1992 Hans Christian Andersen Award. Time span of published books covers the last half of the twentieth century, since the award is given for the author's and illustrator's entire body of published work. (Subject: Award Books)

### Japanese Children's Books

This collection consists of 200 titles, primarily from 1970 to 1990, for grades K–3. All titles are in Japanese, including works of contemporary Japanese authors and illustrators, as well as retellings of traditional tales and legends. Some translations into Japanese of classic or well-known American and English titles are included. (Subject: Japanese Language)

## BURBANK

**Walt Disney Archives (CBbWDA)**
500 S. Buena Vista St.
Burbank, CA 91521-1200
phone: 818-560-5424
contact: David R. Smith, Director
catalog status: cards and lists in local
    catalog

### Walt Disney Archives

This archive holds 8,000 volumes of Disney books and comics, spanning from 1930 to the present. Forty languages are represented in the collection, with many being translations of the English titles, while others are created in the foreign

countries. In addition, they hold 435 linear feet of manuscripts and illustrations. Parts of the collection are restricted, and research is by appointment only. (Subjects: Disney, Walt; Manuscript/Illustration Material)

## CLAREMONT

**The Claremont Graduate School**
    **(CCCla)**
131 E. 10th St.
Claremont, CA 91711-6188
phone: 909-621-8555, ext 3670
fax: 909-621-8390
contact: Carolyn Angus, Associate
    Director

### George G. Stone Center
### for Children's Books

This collection contains 30,000 volumes of nineteenth- and twentieth-century children's books and reference works about children's literature. The center is reserved for schoolchildren and their teachers in the morning, while it is open to the public in the afternoon, providing a setting in which young people, parents, teachers, and scholars can utilize the quality literature. The center sponsors the annual Spring Claremont Reading Conference where the Recognition of Merit, presented since 1965, is given. (Subjects: Award Books; Children's Literature, Study of; Historical; Periodicals)

*Publications:* "The Unicorn Book List" (an annotated guide to the best books published each year); "Gifts to Open Again and Again" (an annotated listing of 100-plus classic and contemporary books selected by the center's staff as the best in children's literature; published annually during the holiday season).

Scripps College (CCSc)
Ella Strong Denison Library
Claremont, CA 91711
phone: 909-621-8973
fax: 909-621-8323
contact: Judy Harvey Sahak, Librarian

### Juvenilia

This historical collection contains children's literature dating back to 1554. Emphasis is on moralistic and didactic literature of the 1790s–1840s, fables, tracts, alphabet books, schoolbooks, readers, chapbooks, hornbooks, verses, and riddles. In addition, the collection contains manuscript and/or illustrative materials for several authors and illustrators. (Subjects: Armour, Richard; Fables; Gaze, Harold; Gentry, Helen; Hearn, Lafcadio; Herford, Oliver; Historical; Manuscript/Illustration Material; Robinson, W. W. and Irena Bowen Robinson)

### William S. Ament Collection

One hundred seventy-five volumes by and about Herman Melville comprise this collection. (Subject: Melville, Herman)

## FRESNO

Fresno County Public Library (CF)
2420 Mariposa St.
Fresno, CA 93721
phone: 209-488-3438
fax: 209-488-1971
contact: Karen Bosch Cobb, Associate
County Librarian
catalog status: RLIN, local online

### Doris Gates Collection

Doris Gates (1901–87), recipient of the Newbery Medal for *Blue Willow*, was a children's librarian in Fresno County from 1930 to 1940. The children's room in the central library is named in her honor and includes autographed copies of her eighteen children's works. (Subject: Gates, Doris)

### Nell Strother Mother Goose & Nursery Rhyme Collection

The collection was begun with Nell Strother's donation of the Mother Goose books she had collected. New books are added as they are published, as are older titles when funds are available. The collection currently numbers 168 volumes dating from 1899–1985. A bibliography is available for purchase. (Subject: Mother Goose)

Leo Politi Branch Library (CFlP)
5771 North First
Fresno, CA 93710-6269
phone: 209-431-6450
contact: Jeanne Johnson, Metro Area
Supervisor
catalog status: RLIN

### Leo Politi Collection

The Leo Politi Branch Library has attempted to collect all titles written and/or illustrated by Leo Politi; currently they hold 50 titles. Also held are copies of magazines in which his work appears. Posters and original illustrations are on display. (Subjects: Manuscript/Illustration Material; Politi, Leo)

## FULLERTON

California State University (CFlS)
Fullerton Library
P. O. Box 4150
Fullerton, CA 92634
phone: 714-773-3444 or, -3445
fax: 714-773-2439
contact: Sharon K. Perry, University
Archivist & Special Collections
Librarian
e-mail: sperry@fullerton.edu
catalog status: OCLC; Innovative
Interfaces

*American Comic Books*

A collection of about 4,000 American comic books, dating from 1938 to the present. (Subject: Comic Books)

*American Trade Bindings Collection*

This collection contains 5,000 books with cloth bindings, beautifully illustrated, or decorated with artwork or lettering in colors. The trade bindings are principally American, but there is a sampling from European publishers. Published from the late nineteenth to the early twentieth century, subject areas are popular fiction and nonfiction of the day, including travel, science, and series of interest to children and youth. (Subjects: Bindings; Historical)

*Big Little Books*

Holdings include 856 Big Little books published from the 1920s to the 1970s, many of which are based on film, comic, theater, television, and other popular characters. (Subject: Big Little Books)

**GLEN ELLEN**

**Jack London State Historic Park (CGlen)\*\***
**Betty Hageman Memorial Library**
2400 London Ranch Rd.
Glen Ellen, CA 95442
phone: 707-938-5216

*Research Center*

The Hageman Memorial Library holds 100 Jack London first editions. Currently, this collection is not open to the public. (Subject: London, Jack)

**LONG BEACH**

**Long Beach Public Library (CLob)\*\***
101 Pacific Ave.
Long Beach, CA 90822-1097

phone: 310-590-6291
fax: 310-590-6956

*Library*

Holdings include 350 volumes in Japanese, many of which are quite old, as well as recent gifts from Long Beach's sister city of Yokkaichi. (Subject: Japanese Language)

**LOS ANGELES**

**Los Angeles Public Library (CL)**
630 W. Fifth St.
Los Angeles, CA 90071
phone: 213-228-7260
fax: 213-228-7269
contact: Janine Goodale, Subject
  Department Manager
catalog status: Cataloged, CARL

*California Authors and Illustrators*

Included are some 2,000 titles, dating from 1850, by California authors and illustrators. (Subject: California—Authors and Illustrators)

*California Collection*

Approximately 2,500 titles, both fiction and nonfiction, with California settings, are indexed by author, location, and time period. FOCAL (Friends of Children and Literature), the support group for the Children's Literature Department, has established the FOCAL Award for "excellence in a work which enriches a child's appreciation for and understanding of California" in order to recognize works of merit and encourage authors and publishers to devote more attention to California as a theme. (Subjects: Award Books; California)

## Folk and Fairy Tales

This widely used collection contains some 6,000 volumes, primarily English-language publications for children, including individual titles as well as collections. All contemporary publications are purchased and have been retained since the late nineteenth century. Also acquired are support items for researchers, such as bibliographies, books of critical analysis and interpretive essays, and dictionaries. Critical annotations, prepared by the staff, are placed in each book, describing the authenticity of the retelling and its place in the collection. A small but important collection of recordings and periodicals augments the books. (Subjects: Folk and Fairy Tales)

## Gladys English Collection of Original Art from Children's Books

Established in 1956 by the California Library Association in memory of Gladys English, founder of the Children's Services Chapter of CLA and former LAPL Coordinator of Children's Services, the collection includes more than 190 pieces of original art for children's books dating from 1924 to 1958, with additional pieces from the 1980s. Included are works by Conrad Buff, Roger Duvoisin, Ruth Robbins, Kay Nielson, and Robert Lawson. (Subject: Manuscript/Illustration Material)

## International Doll Collection

This collection comprises 450 dolls representative of more than 40 countries. A descriptive scrapbook, with photos of each doll, is arranged according to the country of origin. China, Japan, and South America are most heavily represented. Although appealing for use in display, the dolls also have reference value for use in costume history, as examples of toys for children in other countries, and as an adjunct to the study of children's literature. (Subject: Dolls)

## International Language Picture Book Collection

Consisting of some 5,000 titles from more than 50 countries, this collection is especially strong in examples of the beautiful artwork in illustrated picture books, folklore, songbooks, and poetry covering the years 1890–1940. Classics of children's literature are collected in their language of origin; i.e., *Pinocchio* in Italian, *Heidi* in German, and Danish editions of Hans Christian Andersen's tales. (Subject: Foreign Languages)

## Leo Politi Collection

This collection contains all books written or illustrated by Leo Politi, including many autographed with hand-painted drawings. There are also twenty-seven original paintings from his books as well as eleven illustrations in the Gladys English Collection. (Subjects: Manuscript/Illustration Material; Politi, Leo)

## Mother Goose Collection

More than 1,000 volumes are currently in this growing collection of Mother Goose titles. Most are twentieth-century American and British imprints, but several nineteenth-century editions are included, with the earliest being 1813. Included are volumes illustrated by prominent artists, adult parodies and adaptations, songbooks, recordings and cassettes, and ephemeral items such as coloring books, pop-ups, and miniature versions. (Subject: Mother Goose)

## Periodicals

More than 350 periodical titles published from the 1790s to the present. Published primarily in England and the United States, most titles have extensive or complete runs. (Subject: Periodicals)

University of California at Los Angeles
(CLU-S/C)
**Special Collections, UCLA Research
Library**
405 Hilgard Ave.
Los Angeles, CA 90024
phone: 310-825-4879
fax: 310-206-1864
contact: James Davis, Rare Books
Librarian
catalog status: OCLC, ORION

*Children's Book Collection*

The Children's Book Collection has been
established through the acquisition of several private collections, notably those of
Elvah Karshner, Bernard M. Meeks, Olive
Percival, May and George Shiers, and
d'Alte Welch. The strength of this collection resides chiefly in English and American publications before 1840 and includes
titles issued by the Newbery family, John
Harris, Benjamin Tabart, and Kendrew of
York. Authors represented in depth include Maria Edgeworth, the Taylors of
Ongar, M. Pelham, and Mmes. Lovechild,
Trimmer, and Sherwood. The English-
language materials are supported by foreign editions, particularly Mme. d'Aul-
noy's fairy tales. Early games, pop-up, and
other movable books form a major seg-
ment of the collection, which includes one
of the most extensive group of harlequinades extant. The collection also includes
some primary and secondary American
textbooks, runs of Newbery and Caldecott Medal winners, and Russian children's books issued between the two world
wars. The department's large collection of
chapbooks complements the Children's
Book Collection. (Subjects: Award Books;
Chapbooks; Edgeworth, Maria; Evans,
Edmund; Harris, John; Historical; Holling,
Holling Clancy and Lucille; Manuscript/
Illustration Material; Newbery, John; Russian Language; Seuss, Dr.; Sherwood,
Mary Martha Butt; Textbooks; Toy and
Movable Books)

*Publication:* Wilbur Jordan Smith. *UC-
LA's Treasure Trove of Rare Children's
Books.* Los Angeles: University of Califor-
nia Library, 1976.

University of California at Los Angeles
(CLU-C)
**William Andrews Clark Memorial
Library**
2520 Cimarron St.
Los Angeles, CA 90018
phone: 213-731-8529
fax: 213-731-8617
contact: John Bidwell, Acting Librarian
catalog status: OCLC, ORION

*Clark Library*

The Clark Library specializes in seven-
teenth- and eighteenth-century British history and literature and modern fine printing. Among its 85,000 volumes are a
significant number of titles by Charles
Dickens and Robert Louis Stevenson, as
well as periodicals. (Subjects: Dickens,
Charles; Periodicals; Stevenson, Robert
Louis)

University of Southern California
(CLSU)**
**Edward L. Doheny Library**
University Park
Los Angeles, CA 90089-0182
phone: 213-740-2928
fax: 213-747-4176

*Special Collections*

Holdings include manuscripts, typescripts,
galley proofs, and correspondence for Leonard Wibberley. (Subjects: Manuscript/
Illustration Material; Wibberley, Leonard)

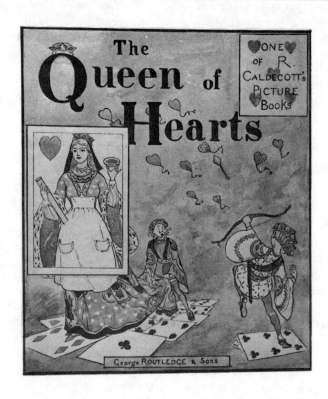

*The Queen of Hearts* by Randolph Caldecott; London:
Routledge [1881].

## NORTHRIDGE

**California State University, Northridge
(CNoS)**
**University Library**
1811 Nordhoff St.
Northridge, CA 91330-8326
phone: 818-885-2832
fax: 818-885-2676
contact: Tony Gardner, Curator Special
  Collections/Archives
e-mail: tgardner@vax.csun.edu
Internet: geac.csun.edu
catalog status: OCLC, GEAC Hermes

### Chase Craig Comic Book Collection

The personal collection of comic-strip writer, artist, and editor Chase Craig was donated to the library in 1984. Approximately 720 comic books bound into sixty volumes dating from 1937 to 1960 were issued by Dell Publishing Company. Included are *Famous Funnies* and Eastern Color publications. There are premiums from cereal boxes, one shots, large feature comics, four-color comics, and bimonthlies and quarterlies. Many Walt Disney, Looney Tunes, and Tom and Jerry characters are included, along with some adventure characters such as Tarzan, Roy Rogers, and Buck Rogers. Included as part of the collection is the comic strip "Foxy Grandpa," ca. 1900, by Charles Edward Schultze. A complete inventory is available upon request. (Subject: Comic Books; Craig, Chase)

*Rare Children's Books*

Holdings include some 250 English-language children's books, published in the nineteenth and twentieth centuries. (Subject: Historical)

## OAKLAND

**Oakland Public Library (COPL)\*\***
125 14th St.
Oakland, CA 94612
phone: 510-238-3281
fax: 510-238-2232

*Library*

Holdings include 375 volumes by and about Jack London, with some in French, Spanish, and Italian. Complete runs of *Jack London Newsletter* and *What's New about Jack London* are also held. (Subjects: London, Jack; Periodicals)

## PASADENA

**City of Pasadena (CP)\*\***
Dept. of Information Services Library
285 East Walnut St.
Pasadena, CA 91101
phone: 818-405-4041
fax: 818-449-2165

*Library*

Among the holdings of the Pasadena Library are 1,400 books, dating primarily from 1900 to 1950, 400 of which are folk and fairy tales. Also held are books and original artwork of Conrad and Mary Buff, Holling Clancy Holling, Grace and Carl Moon, and Leo Politi. (Subjects: Buff, Conrad and Mary; Folk and Fairy Tales; Historical—20th Century; Holling, Holling Clancy; Manuscript/Illustration Material; Moon, Grace and Carl; Politi, Leo)

## POMONA

**Pomona Public Library (CPom)**
625 S. Garey Ave.
Pomona, CA 91766
phone: 909-620-2017
fax: 909-623-0850
contact: Marguerite Raybould,
    Supervisor of Youth Services
catalog status: Cataloged

*Laura Ingalls Wilder Collection*

Contains fifty-one volumes, of which thirty are in translation, including a complete set of signed first edition books illustrated by Helen Sewell and Mildred Boyle, as well as a set of the books illustrated by Garth Williams. Also held are manuscripts for *Little Town on the Prairie* and *By the Shores of Silver Lake*, correspondence, photographs, dolls, and the original illustration for the Laura Ingalls Wilder Medal. (Subjects: Manuscript/Illustration Material; Wilder, Laura Ingalls)

## RIVERSIDE

**Riverside City Library (CRiv)**
3581 7th St.
Riverside, CA 92502
phone: 909-782-5369
fax: 909-788-1528
contact: Nora Jane Natke, Youth
    Services Coordinator
catalog status: Cataloged

*Dorothy Daniels Memorial Collection*

Approximately 1,400 volumes, dating from 1801, represent the progress and change in children's literature. A strength of the collection is examples of children's book illustrators from 1900 to 1950. Periodicals, hornbooks, Patricia Beatty titles, and a complete collection of Children's Book Week Posters from 1941 round out the collection. (Subjects: Children's Book Week Posters; Historical; Illustration of Children's Books)

*Publication: Dorothy Daniels Memorial Children's Book Collection: Selected Catalog.* Riverside, Calif.: Riverside Public Library, 1981.

## ST. HELENA

**The Silverado Museum (CSahS)**
P.O. Box 409
St. Helena, CA 94574-0409
phone: 707-963-3757
contact: Beth Atherton, Curator

*Silverado Museum*

This museum, devoted to the life and works of Robert Louis Stevenson, contains one of the world's largest collections of 8,000 items, including books, his lead soldiers, toys, and photographs. (Subjects: Stevenson, Robert Louis; Toys)

*Publication: The Silverado Museum: A Museum Devoted to the Life and Works of Robert Louis Stevenson.* [St. Helena, Calif.: Silverado Museum, n.d.]

## SAN DIEGO

**San Diego Public Library (CSd)**
820 E St.
San Diego, CA 92101
phone: 619-236-5838
fax: 619-236-5811
contact: Jean Stewart, Children's Room
   Supervisor

*Children's Room*

Within the holdings of the Children's Room are several distinct subject collections. The reference collection contains 100 books of San Diego County children's authors and illustrators and 180 volumes of California history with an emphasis on San Diego County. Author/illustrator Dr. Seuss is represented with seventy volumes and three notebooks of biographical information. Also included is a collection of Newbery and Caldecott winners. (Subjects: Award Books; California; California—Authors and Illustrators; Seuss, Dr.)

*Dime Novels*

This collection, housed in the Wangenheim Room, consists of 779 volumes of serialized dime novels covering the period from 1890 to 1928. Series include *All Around Weekly, Fame and Fortune, Pluck and Luck, Tip Top Weekly, Wide Awake,* and *Work and Win.* (Subject: Dime Novels)

## SAN FRANCISCO

**San Francisco Academy of Comic Art
   (CSfACA)**
2850 Ulloa St.
San Francisco, CA 94116
phone: 415-681-1737
fax: 415-553-8605
contact: Bill Blackbeard, Director
catalog status: RLIN

*Library*

The academy is the world's only cross-referential collection of popular narrative art containing crime stories, science fiction, fantasy, western and adventure fiction, motion pictures (on tape), ballads and poetry, songs (tape and books), comic strips and books, dime novels and penny dreadfuls, story papers, pulp magazines, popular fiction magazines, and newspapers, as well as reference works, historical studies, and biographies relating to all of the foregoing. Many pieces of original art and manuscripts relating to the same subject areas are also held. A great number of their volumes are children's books, although they are not separately distinguished as such. The entire collection consists of more than 30,000 volumes spanning from 1650 to the present. They hold nearly 800 periodical titles consisting of nearly 20,000 issues. (Subjects: Comic Books; Dime Novels; Historical; Manuscript/Illustration Material; Periodicals; Popular Culture Materials; Toys)

**San Francisco Public Library (CSf)**
**Special Collections**
Civic Center
San Francisco, CA 94102
phone: 415-557-4565
fax: 415-557-4205
contact: Andrea Grimes, Special
   Collections Librarian

*George M. Fox Collection of Early*
*Children's Books*

The Fox Collection contains 2,100 American and British imprints from the eighteenth and nineteenth centuries. The collection is particularly strong in early books
embellished with colored illustrations and
wood engravings. They hold prints of the
original woodblocks from the archives of
the McLoughlin Brothers as well as a small
number of McLoughlin woodblocks. Also
held are 600 volumes of fiction, nonfiction, readers, and picture books which
deal with the experience of Black, Native
American, Jewish, Asian/Pacific, and His-
panic peoples in the American culture.
(Subjects: Historical; Illustration of Children's Books; McLoughlin Brothers; Multiculturalism; Woodblocks)

**San Francisco State University (CSfSt)**
**J. Paul Leonard Library**
1630 Holloway Ave.
San Francisco, CA 94132
phone: 415-338-1856
fax: 415-338-1504
contact: Meredith Eliassen, Susan
   Quinlan, Helene Whitson
catalog status: OCLC, GEAC

*Marguerite Archer Collection of Historic*
*Children's Books*

The Archer Collection contains some
5,000 books and periodicals dating from
1790 to the present. Originally based upon
items listed in Blanck's *Peter Parley to Pen-*
*rod*, the collection features works by important historical and contemporary chil-

dren's authors and illustrators, multicultural works, works by California and San
Francisco Bay Area authors and illustrators, moral education, Sunday school literature, fairy tales, folklore, toy and movable books, periodicals, and ephemeral
materials including advertising, educational games, and cards. Supporting the
collection are the professional papers of
Marguerite Archer and Wilhelmina Harper,
information files, and a young person's collection in the main library. (Subjects:
American Sunday School Union; Archer,
Marguerite; Harper, Wilhelmina; Historical; Manuscript/Illustration Material; Miniature Books; Periodicals; Textbooks; Toy
and Movable Books)

## SAN JOSE

**San Jose Public Library (CSj)\*\***
180 West San Carlos St.
San Jose, CA 95113-2096
phone: 408-277-4822
fax: 408-277-3187

*Library*

A collection of 8,000 volumes showing the
development of children's literature and illustration with emphasis on 1880–1930
imprints. Popular series writers are represented, with minor specialties in Sunday
school tracts and Art Nouveau illustrators. (Subjects: Historical; Series Books)

## SAN MARCOS

**California State University, San Marcos**
   **(CSmar)**
San Marcos, CA 92096-0001
phone: 619-752-4070
fax: 619-752-4073
contact: Dr. Isabel Schon, Director
catalog status: OCLC, local online
   catalog

*Center for the Study of Books in Spanish for Children and Adolescents*

The center is an interdisciplinary university unit, serving the university community and the public and housing 11,000 books. The center endeavors to collect all books in Spanish for children and adolescents, as well as books in English about Hispanics and Latinos, published worldwide since 1989. Supplementary holdings include theoretical works on the study and use of books in Spanish, professional journals, clippings, and publisher and vendor catalogs. The center serves as a resource to librarians, teachers, parents, and other adults; provides information about the publishing industry; and encourages and supports research on books in Spanish. (Subjects: Multiculturalism; Spanish Language)

*Publications:* Annotated bibliographies of books in Spanish and books in English about Hispanics/Latinos for children and adolescents are prepared periodically.

## SAN MARINO

**The Huntington Library (CSmH-A)**
1151 Oxford Rd.
San Marino, CA 91108
phone: 818-405-2203
fax: 818-405-0225
contact: Sara S. Hodson, Curator of
    Literary Manuscripts

*Special Collections*

The Manuscripts Division of the Huntington has a wide selection of materials relating to children's literature. Manuscripts, correspondence, and photographs pertaining to some fifty British and American children's authors and illustrators are among their holdings. The Rare Book Collection has early American and English primers, English and American illustrated children's books, Monsignor Francis Weber Miniature Book Collection, and works by Lewis Carroll. (Subjects: Too numerous to list)

## STANFORD

**Stanford University (CSt)\*\***
**Cecil H. Green Library**
Stanford, CA 94305-6004
phone: 415-723-9108
fax: 415-725-6874

*Mary Schofield Collection of Children's Literature*

The Schofield Collection consists of 10,148 items ranging from rarities of the late eighteenth century through the twentieth century. Emphasis is on English and American authors with strengths in French, German, and Russian. Extensive materials on L. Frank Baum, Beatrix Potter, Tasha Tudor, and others. (Subjects: Baum, Lyman Frank; Historical; Potter, Beatrix; Tudor, Tasha)

## STOCKTON

**University of the Pacific (CStoC)**
**Holt Atherton Special Collections**
**University Library**
Stockton, CA 95211
phone: 209-946-2404
fax: 209-946-2810
contact: Don Walker, University
    Archivist
catalog status: OCLC, local online
    catalog

*Howard Pease Papers*

The Holt Atherton Special Collections focus on the Trans-Mississippi West and are strongest in nineteenth- and twentieth-century materials. Included in these special collections are the papers of children's author Howard Pease containing sixty-five books and manuscripts. (Subjects: Manuscript/Illustration Material; Pease, Howard)

# Colorado

## BOULDER

**University of Colorado at Boulder (CoU)**
**Norlin Library**
Campus Box 184
Boulder, CO 80309-0184
phone: 303-492-6144
fax: 303-492-1881
contact: Susie R. Bock, Special
   Collections Cataloging Supervisor
Susan Tach Dean, Head Special
   Collections (for Bloch and Epsteen
   Collections)
Internet: pac.carl.org
catalog status: OCLC, local online
   catalog

### *Donald Beaty Bloch Collection*

The Bloch Collection contains 2,000 nineteenth- and early twentieth-century children's literature titles published primarily in America and England. The collection has a large number of tracts, folk and fairy tales, and Jacob Abbott's Rollo books. This collection is not cataloged, but does have a preliminary accession list. (Subjects: Abbott, Jacob; Folk and Fairy Tales; Historical)

### *Emily Epsteen Collection*

The Epsteen Collection contains nearly 3,000 nineteenth- and early twentieth-century children's literature titles published primarily in America and England. The collection has a large number of textbooks and folk and fairy tales. (Subjects: Folk and Fairy Tales; Historical; Textbooks)

### *Virginia Westerberg Juvenile Literature Collection*

The Westerberg Collection contains 6,000 volumes of twentieth-century children's literature, primarily English-language, but with some foreign-language materials. Also included are works about authors and children's literature. The collection is strong in Colorado authors, award books, ethnic works, and genre studies. (Subjects: Award Books; Children's Literature, Study of; Colorado—Authors and Illustrators; Historical—20th Century; Spanish Language)

## DENVER

**Denver Botanic Gardens (CoDDB)**
**Helen Fowler Library**
909 York St.
Denver, CO 80206-3799
phone: 303-370-8014
fax: 303-370-8196
contact: Solange G. Gignac, Librarian
catalog status: OCLC

### *Children's Collection*

The Children's Collection of more than 1,000 volumes supports the children's programming at the Denver Botanic Gardens, geared toward preschool through middle school students. Botany and horticulture are stressed, although books on natural history, ecology, entomology, and forestry are included, as well as activities using plant materials. (Subjects: Botany; Horticulture; Science)

**Denver Public Library (CoD)\*\***
**Special Collections**
1357 Broadway
Denver, CO 80203-2165
phone: 303-640-8800
fax: 303-595-3034

### *Library*

One thousand five hundred English-language titles from the eighteenth century to the present include a nearly complete collection of McGuffey readers and spellers, as well as complete runs of *St. Nicholas* and the *Youth's Companion*. Also held is an extensive Eugene Field collection consisting of 300 volumes from 1840, 350 manuscripts, personal correspondence, and photographs dating from 1870. (Subjects: Field, Eugene; Historical; Manuscript/Illustration Material; Textbooks)

# Connecticut

## HARTFORD

**Connecticut Historical Society (CtHi)**
1 Elizabeth St.
Hartford, CT 06105
phone: 203-236-5621
contact: Gary E. Wait, Head Catalogue
 Librarian
catalog status: OCLC

### Albert Carlos Bates Collection

The Bates Collection numbers 2,500 American children's books printed up to about 1830, with scattered holdings to 1865. (Subject: Historical)

### Caroline M. Hewins Collection

The Hewins Collection contains 3,500 American children's books and periodicals, as well as American gift books and annuals, published 1820–1920. (Subjects: Annuals and Gift Books; Historical; Periodicals)

### Connecticut Imprints Collection

Includes some 500 children's books printed in Connecticut from 1750 to date, with particular strength in the publications of the Babcocks of New Haven. (Subjects: Babcock, John and Sidney; Connecticut Imprints)

### Connecticut Printers Archive

One thousand two hundred American children's books printed by the Connecticut Printers, Inc., between 1955 and 1969. Includes some working copies and mockups. (Subjects: Connecticut Imprints; Connecticut Printers, Inc.; Historical—20th Century)

### Juveniles Collection

This newly formed collection was begun in 1992 by absorbing children's titles from throughout the existing holdings of the society, as well as the addition of newly acquired juveniles. With an emphasis on American imprints and authors, Connecti-cut illustrators and engravers are identified and indexed. (Subject: Historical)

**Hartford Public Library (CtH)\*\***
500 Main St.
Hartford, CT 06103-3075
phone: 203-293-6000

### Library

Included are 800 volumes in a collection based on the personal library of Caroline Hewins, with representative illustrated first editions and foreign picture books of the 1910s and 1920s. An additional 200 historical and rare items from the nineteenth century are held, as well as fifty original illustrations by well-known artists. The Bulkeley Collection contains 518 volumes for which Kellogg & Bulkeley, now Connecticut Printers, Inc., did the color printing of illustrations from 1931 to 1964. (Subjects: Connecticut Imprints; Foreign Languages; Historical; Kellogg & Bulkeley; Manuscript/Illustration Material)

**Stowe-Day Library (CtHSD)**
77 Forest St.
Hartford, CT 06105
phone: 203-728-5507
fax: 203-522-9259
contact: Diana Royce, Librarian
catalog status: OCLC, online catalog

### Library

The collection includes some 300 general juvenile hardcover works in English from 1800 to 1900, though principally 1870–1896. Of particular emphasis are the juvenile titles by Harriet Beecher Stowe and children's adaptations, both in English and in translation, of Stowe's *Uncle Tom's Cabin*. (Subjects: Historical; Stowe, Harriet Beecher)

**Trinity College (CtHT)**
**Watkinson Library**
Hartford, CT 06106
phone: 203-297-2268

fax: 203-297-2251
contact: Alesandra M. Schmidt,
  Assistant Curator for Reference and
  Manuscripts
Internet: CTW.wesleyan.edu
catalog status: OCLC, online catalog

### Barnard Collection

This collection comprises some 7,000 volumes of school textbooks, primarily American, from the eighteenth century to around 1880. Also included are a number of New England primers and some non-textbook materials, such as Peter Parley titles. (Subject: Textbooks)

### Library

Holdings include about 1,500 volumes of children's books from the eighteenth through the twentieth centuries, primarily American and English. They include nineteenth-century story and picture books, prominent authors and illustrators, as well as a representative collection of twentieth-century authors. In addition, there are significant holdings in children's song and hymn books, mainly American, nineteenth-century periodicals, and ephemera. (Subjects: Historical; Hymn Books; Periodicals)

## NEW BRITAIN

**Central Connecticut State University
  (CtNbT)\*\***
**Elihu Buritt Library**
Wells St.
New Britain, CT 06050
phone: 203-827-7530
fax: 203-827-7961

### Library

One thousand seven hundred volumes from the nineteenth and twentieth centuries include complete runs of several periodical titles. Also held are 329 volumes from 1758 to 1890 in Dutch, including the periodicals. (Subjects: Dutch Language; Historical; Periodicals)

## NEW HAVEN

**New Haven Colony Historical Society
  (CtNhHi)**
**Whitney Library**
114 Whitney Ave.
New Haven, CT 06510
phone: 203-562-4183
contact: James W. Campbell, Librarian
  and Curator of Manuscripts

### Children's Books Collection, 1777–1875

This collection of 200 items brings together most of the children's literature and schoolbooks in the New Haven Colony Historical Society Library. Included are books printed in New Haven and those published elsewhere that belonged to New Haven children. Publishers represented include S. Babcock and Sidney's Press, A. H. Maltby, Durrie and Peck, and Read and Morse. (Subjects: Babcock, John and Sidney; Connecticut Imprints; Historical)

**Southern Connecticut State University
  (CtNhN)**
**Hilton C. Buley Library**
501 Crescent St.
New Haven, CT 06515
phone: 203-397-4511
fax: 203-397-4061
contact: John R. Hill, CSB Cataloger &
  Library Systems Coordinator
e-mail: scsu: Hill
catalog status: OCLC

### Carolyn Sherwin Bailey Collection

A collection of some 2,400 books, primarily American, published from 1800 to 1930. Representative works of popular authors such as Oliver Optic, Sophie May, Edward Stratemeyer, Jacob Abbott, Horatio Alger, and Carolyn Sherwin Bailey are included. (Subjects: Bailey, Carolyn Sherwin; Historical)

*Publication: The Carolyn Sherwin Bailey Historical Collection of Children's Books: A Catalogue*, compiled and edited by Dorothy R. Davis. New Haven, Conn.: Southern Connecticut State College, 1966.

**Yale University (CtY-BR)**
**Beinecke Rare Book and Manuscript**
  **Library**
P.O. Box 208240
New Haven, CT 06520-8240
phone: 203-432-2977
fax: 203-432-4047
contact: Vincent Giroud, Curator of
  Modern Books and Manuscripts;
  Patricia Willis, Curator, Yale
  Collection of American Literature
  (Newell Papers)
Internet:
  URL=gopher://yaleinfo.yale.edu:7000/
  11/Manuscripts/Beinmss/Newell
catalog status: RLIN, local online
  catalog

*Betsy Beinecke Shirley Collection of American Children's Literature*
This collection consists of approximately 2,000 volumes of children's literature from 1690 to the present day. In addition to monographs, holdings also include manuscripts, illustrations, and correspondence. (Subject: Historical)

*Publication: Read Me a Story—Show Me a Book: American Children's Literature 1690–1988.* From the Collection of Betsy Beinecke Shirley. An Exhibition at the Beinecke Rare Book and Manuscript Library, Yale University, October–December 1991. New Haven, Conn.: Yale University, 1991.

*Cary Collection of Playing Cards*
Included are 2,600 packs, 460 sheets, and 150 woodblocks representing playing card production in the last 500 years. In the holdings are packs from all over the world and 200 books about playing cards. (Subject: Games and Pastimes)

*Peter Newell Family Papers*
The Newell Papers contain correspondence, photographs, personal papers, manuscripts, drawings, paintings, graphic arts, sculpture, and toys by illustrator Peter Newell and his family, including his son-in-law, illustrator Alfred Z. Baker. The collection contains more than 3,000 sketches, preparatory drawings, and finished illustrations for Newell's book and magazine work, as well as printed proofs, tearsheets, and copies of his published work. (Subjects: Manuscript/Illustration Material; Newell, Peter)

*Special Collections*
Holdings include extensive collections of books, manuscripts, notebooks, diaries, illustrations, photographs, clippings, and correspondence for noted American and British authors and illustrators, including James M. Barrie, L. Frank Baum, Walter Crane, Charles Dickens, John Ruskin, Robert Louis Stevenson, and Mark Twain. In addition, they hold 350 English chapbooks from the eighteenth and nineteenth centuries, 300 editions of *Robinson Crusoe*, fifteen hornbooks, and 350 books from the press of John and Sidney Babcock. (Subjects: Babcock, John and Sidney; Barrie, James Matthew; Baum, Lyman Frank; Chapbooks; Crane, Walter; Defoe, Daniel; Dickens, Charles; Historical; Hornbooks and Battledores; MacDonald, George; Manuscript/Illustration Material; Ruskin, John; Stevenson, Robert Louis; Twain, Mark)

## NEW LONDON

**Connecticut College (CtNIC)**
**Charles E. Shain Library**
270 Mohegan Ave.
New London, CT 06320-4196
phone: 203-439-2654
fax: 203-442-0761
contact: Brian Rogers, Special
  Collections Librarian
e-mail: bdrog@mvax.cc.conncoll.edu

Internet: 129.133.21.140
catalog status: OCLC, online catalog

### Helen O. Gildersleeve Collection

The Gildersleeve Collection consists of 3,000 volumes of American and English children's books, published from the eighteenth to the twentieth century. The collection is strongest in works by Walter Crane, Kate Greenaway, Arthur Rackham, Lewis Carroll, Robert Lawson, Howard Pyle, L. Frank Baum, and Maud and Miska Petersham. Helen Gildersleeve's original gift comprises the largest part of the collection, augmented by books from the estate of Margaret Sherwood Libby and an ongoing program of selective purchases building upon existing strengths. (Subjects: Historical; Illustration of Children's Books)

### STORRS

**University of Connecticut (CtU)**
**Homer Babbidge Library**
**Special Collections Dept. / U-5SC**
369 Fairfield Rd.
Storrs, CT 06269-1005
phone: 203-486-2524
fax: 203-486-0584
contact: Ellen E. Embardo, Curator
e-mail: hbladm64@uconnvm
Internet: spirit.lib.uconn.edu
catalog status: OCLC, HOMER online catalog

### Northeastern Children's Literature Collections

Holdings comprise nearly 14,000 children's books spanning 200 years and a growing archive of original art and creative materials from today's authors and illustrators. With a focus on the late nineteenth and twentieth centuries, the collections provide an overview of books written and illustrated for children of the United States, and the European influences on American illustrated works. Manu-

script collections and original art form the basis of a repository of original materials documenting the life and work of children's writers and illustrators of the Northeastern United States. (Subjects: Too numerous to list)

# Delaware

### NEWARK

**University of Delaware (DeU)**
**Education Resource Center**
012 Willard Hall Education Building
Newark, DE 19716-2940
phone: 302-831-2335
fax: 302-831-3569
contact: Beth Anderson, Director
e-mail: edubeth@strauss.udel.edu
Internet: delcat.udel.edu
catalog status: DELCAT

### Special Collections

Included in the Special Collections holdings are 16 pieces of correspondence of Howard Pyle and 1.33 linear feet of manuscripts, correspondence, and photographs of Katharine Pyle. (Subjects: Manuscript/Illustration Material; Pyle, Howard; Pyle, Katharine)

### UNICEF Collection at the University of Delaware

The collection of 6,000 books for and about children from around the world, with the emphasis being English-language juvenile works, depicts the life of children and adolescents in developing countries. Housed since 1988 at the University of Delaware College of Education, the books were originally collected by the U.S. Committee for UNICEF as part of their Information Center on Children's Culture in New York. Dating back to 1955, the majority of the titles were published between 1970 and 1985 by American trade publishers. Emphasis is on picture book versions of folktales, collections for interme-

*Marigold Garden* by Kate Greenaway; London: Routledge [1885].

diate through adult readers, and scholarly anthologies. Subjects represented are cookbooks, travel, holidays and social customs. (Subjects: Folk and Fairy Tales; Historical—20th Century; Multiculturalism)

## WILMINGTON

**Delaware Art Museum (DeWA)**✼✼
**Helen Farr Sloan Library**
2301 Kentmere Parkway
Wilmington, DE 19806-2096
phone: 302-571-9590

### *Library*

Library holdings include 600 volumes and an extensive collection of illustrations, scrapbooks, correspondence, clippings, etc., relating to Howard Pyle and his students, Frank Schoonover, Katharine Pyle, and N. C. Wyeth, covering the years 1880–1940. Also included are ten periodical titles from 1876 to 1916. (Subjects: Manuscript/ Illustration Material; Pyle, Howard; Pyle, Katharine; Schoonover, Frank; Wyeth, N. C.)

**Wilmington Institute Library (DeWI)**✼✼
10th and Market Sts.
Wilmington, DE 19801
phone: 302-571-7401
fax: 302-654-9132

### *Author's Room Collection*

Included are 280 illustrations, 110 volumes in which the illustrations appeared, and fifteen binders of correspondence with the authors and illustrators. Emphasis is on recipients of the Caldecott Medal. (Subjects: Award Books; Illustration of Children's Books; Manuscript/Illustration Material)

## WINTERTHUR

**Winterthur Library (DeWint)**
Route 52
Winterthur, DE 19735
phone: 302-888-4699
fax: 302-888-4870
contact: Richard McKinstry, Librarian
catalog status: RLIN

### Maxine Waldron Collection of Children's Books and Paper Toys

In addition to 500 books, this collection consists of a wide variety of paper toys from the seventeenth through the twentieth centuries, including: paper dolls and costumes; miniature soldiers; valentines and Christmas cards; movable and pop-up books; peep shows, panoramas, and toy theaters, complete with characters and scenes; magic lanterns and their slides; board and card games; pattern books for weaving, sewing, paper folding, and paper cutting; and note cards and postcards illustrating dolls and toys of the eighteenth and nineteenth centuries from various other countries. The greater portion of the material is American or English in origin, although there is a fair representation of paper toys from Germany and France. This collection provides examples of the evolution of printing processes, particularly chromolithography and the development of better quality papers, inks, and presses. In addition, Mrs. Waldron's personal memorabilia constitutes part of the collection. (Subjects: Games and Pastimes; Greeting Cards; Historical; Illustration of Children's Books; McLoughlin Brothers; Toy and Movable Books; Toys)

*Publication:* Margaret N. Coughlan. "The Maxine Waldron Collection of Children's Books and Paper Toys," in *Research about Nineteenth-Century Children and Books: Portrait Studies*. Urbana-Champaign: University of Illinois Graduate School of Library Science, 1980.

# District of Columbia

**WASHINGTON, D.C.**

**District of Columbia Public Library (DWP)**
901 G St., N.W.
Washington, DC 20001
phone: 202-727-1151
fax: 202-727-1129
contact: Maria Salvadore, Coordinator, Children's Service
catalog status: Cataloged

### Illustrators Collection

The Illustrators Collection consists of some 13,000 children's books, published from 1800 to the present, assembled to provide examples of pictorial works. This is a non-circulating reference collection utilized by authors and illustrators, children's literature students, book collectors, and the media, and for answering reference questions from the general public. (Subjects: Historical; Illustration of Children's Books)

**Georgetown University (DGU)**
**Special Collections Division**
37th & O Sts. NW
Washington, DC 20057
phone: 202-687-7444
fax: 202-687-7501
contact: George M. Barringer, Special Collections Librarian
catalog status: OCLC, online catalog

### Frank Kurt Cylke Collection of Arthur Ransome

This collection includes a nearly complete run of first editions of Arthur Ransome's works, including variants and many reprints. A limited amount of manuscript materials, films, tapes, etc., accompany the 200 printed volumes dating from the early 1900s. The collection was a gift of Frank Kurt Cylke. (Subject: Ransome, Arthur)

### Lynd Ward-May McNeer Papers

The Ward-McNeer Papers document the entire artistic careers of the American printmaker and illustrator Lynd Ward and his wife, author May McNeer Ward. The papers chronicle Ward's career from his student days at Columbia through the period of his "wood-cut novels," to his establishment as one of the premier book illustrators in this country. They also provide insight into political and labor activities among American artists in the 1930s and 1940s and include the extant records of the Equinox Cooperative Press, founded by Ward and a few associates in 1932. The papers have been microfilmed by Archives of American Art. In addition, the Lynd Ward Collection, donated by Nanda Ward and Robin Ward Savage, includes more than 1,000 paintings, drawings, sketches, and prints, many never published. The artist's entire career is well represented, as is the range of media in which he worked. (Subjects: Equinox Cooperative Press; Manuscript/Illustration Material; McNeer, May Yonge; Ward, Lynd)

**Library of Congress (DLC)**
101 Independence Ave. at First St. SE
Washington, DC 20540
phone: 202-707-5000
fax: 202-707-5844
contact: Sybille Jagusch, Head
Internet: telnet locis.loc.gov or
    140.147.254.3
catalog status: OCLC, RLIN

*Children's Literature Center*
Founded in 1963 as an information center within the Library of Congress, the Children's Literature Center received the mandate to serve those organizations and individuals who study, produce, collect, interpret, and disseminate children's books, films, television programs, or other forms of materials destined for children's information and recreational use, usually outside of the classroom. The center does not serve children directly. The center assists users in gaining access to all children's materials dispersed throughout the Library. The Library holds some 180,000 children's books and related items, such as boxed and board games, sound recordings, maps, and illustrations. The books and all other materials can be retrieved by accessing the Library's databases. The cen-

ter's small public reading room holds a ready reference collection of secondary literature. In addition to answering requests for information, the center publishes information about children's books. A list of the center's publications is available on request, and some of the titles are listed below. (Subjects: Too numerous to list)

*Publications: Books for Children* (annual list). Washington, D.C.: Library of Congress, 1985– . *Children's Literature: A Guide to Reference Sources*, edited by Virginia Haviland. 3 vols. Washington, D.C.: Library of Congress, 1966, 1972, 1977. *Yankee Doodle's Literary Sampler of Prose, Poetry and Pictures*, selected from the Rare Book Collections of the Library of Congress and introduced by Virginia Haviland and Margaret N. Coughlan. New York: Crowell, 1974.

# Florida

## GAINESVILLE

**University of Florida (FU)**
208 Smathers Library East
Gainesville, FL 32611
phone: 904-392-0369
fax: 904-392-4788
contact: Rita Smith, Coordinator,
    Academic Support Services
e-mail: ritsmit@nervm.nerdc.ufl.edu
catalog status: OCLC, RLIN; NOTIS

*Baldwin Library of Historical Children's Literature*
The Baldwin Library contains some 85,000 children's books in English, published between 1775 and the present. Emphasis is on the entire spectrum of books known to have been read by children. Included are examples of picture books, moral tales, adolescent fiction, adventure stories, poetry, pop-up books, geographies, and biographies. Of particular interest are the more than 6,000 tracts and books representing eighty-three religious

publishers of the nineteenth century. More than 800 titles published in North America before 1820 are included, as are early chapbooks, Victorian alphabets, and extensive runs of nineteenth century children's magazines and annuals. The collection was assembled by Ruth Baldwin, who donated it to the University of Florida in 1977. Only about 5,000 of the titles are retrievable through NOTIS, but a card catalog in the collection provides information on the greater part of the collection. (Subjects: Too numerous to list)

*Publication: Index to the Baldwin Library of Books in English before 1900, Primarily for Children.* 3 volumes. Boston: G. K. Hall, 1981.

## ST. PETERSBURG

**The Science Center Library (FSpSC)****
7701-22nd Ave. North
St. Petersburg, FL 33710
phone: 813-342-8691

*Library*

Fifteen thousand volumes provide information in various fields of science for grades 4–12, as well as material for advanced research. (Subject: Science)

## TALLAHASSEE

**Florida State University (FTaSU)**
**Robert Manning Strozier Library**
**Special Collections**
Tallahassee, FL 32306-2047
phone: 904-644-3271
fax: 904-644-5016
contact: Gay Dixon, Special Collections
  Department Head

*John M. Shaw Collection*

More than 25,000 volumes, including 300 hymnals and nearly 500 annuals and gift books. Strong in major illustrated editions of poetry, in works of criticism, biography, and reference. In addition, there are complete runs of several periodicals and a significant collection of manuscripts. (Subjects: Annuals and Gift Books; Historical; Hymn Books; Illustration of Children's Books; Manuscript/Illustration Material; Periodicals; Poetry)

*Publication: Childhood in Poetry: A Catalogue . . . of the Books of English and American Poets Comprising the Shaw Childhood in Poetry Collection in the Library of the Florida State University*, by John Mackay Shaw. Detroit: Gale Research, 1967, 1972, 1976, 1980.

*Lois Lenski Collection*

Approximately 250 books written and/or illustrated by Lenski supplemented by 1,011 manuscripts, galley proofs, correspondence, illustrations, scrapbooks, taped interviews, and memorabilia. (Subjects: Lenski, Lois; Manuscript/ Illustration Material)

*Publication: The Lois Lenski Collection in the Florida State University Library*, compiled by Nancy Bird. Tallahassee: Florida State University, 1966.

## TAMPA

**University of South Florida (FTS)**
**Tampa Campus Library**
**Special Collections Department**
4202 East Fowler Ave.
Tampa, FL 33620
phone: 813-974-2731
fax: 813-974-5153
contact: Thomas J. Kemp, Head of
  Special Collections
e-mail: tomkemp@lib.usf.edu
Internet: luis.nerdc.ufl.edu
catalog status: OCLC, online catalog

*The Everett Collection*

Containing more than 8,000 volumes of twentieth-century American picture books, this collection has extensive holdings of Newbery and Caldecott winners. (Subjects: Award Books; Illustration of Children's Books)

*Henry K. Hudson American Boys' Series Books*

This 4,000-volume collection is currently being microfilmed as part of the Southeastern Library Network's Preservation Microfilming Project. The boys' series books are complemented by collections of 2,500 girls' series titles and 500 anthropomorphic animal series books. (Subject: Series Books)

*Publication: American Boys' Series Books 1900 to 1980* (Bibliographic Series No. 1). Tampa: University of South Florida Library Associates, 1987.

*Historical Children's Literature*

Within the holdings of the Special Collections Department are 40,000 books, serials, and other historical literary works for children, with an additional 300 linear feet of archival materials. Holdings range in date from the eighteenth century to the present, including specimens of children's books from many nations. The focus, however, is on American juvenile literature of the nineteenth and early twentieth centuries. Particular strengths are in the areas of nineteenth-century American popular juvenile literature (10,000 volumes), pre-Civil War American schoolbooks (10,000 volumes), and dime novels (8,000 volumes). British authors are represented by an outstanding collection of 500 volumes written by George Alfred Henty. (Subjects: Abbott, Jacob; Arthur, Timothy Shay; Chapbooks; Dime Novels; Floethe, Louise; Floethe, Richard; Florida; Florida — Authors and Illustrators; Henty, George Alfred; Historical; Manuscript/Illustration Material; Miniature Books; Textbooks; Toy and Movable Books)

# Georgia
## ATHENS

**University of Georgia (GU)\*\***
**University Libraries**
Athens, GA 30602
phone: 706-542-0621
fax: 706-542-6522

*Confederate Imprint Collection*

Includes children's books that were published in the Confederacy during the Civil War. (Subjects: Confederate Imprints; Historical)

*Library*

Included in the holdings are 179 volumes by George A. Henty as well as complete runs of several periodicals. (Subjects: Henty, George Alfred; Periodicals)

*Robert Burch Collection*

The Burch Collection contains 135 folders of manuscripts, typescripts, galleys, proofs, and reviews. (Subjects: Burch, Robert; Manuscript/Illustration Material)

## ATLANTA

**Emory University (GEU-S)**
**Robert W. Woodruff Library**
**Special Collections**
Atlanta, GA 30322
phone: 404-727-6887
fax: 404-727-0053
contact: Beverly B. Allen, Reference
   Archivist
e-mail: libbdb@emuvm1
Internet: emuvm1.cc.emory.edu
   (TN3270 emulation required)
catalog status: RLIN, OCLC, online
   catalog

*Joel Chandler Harris Collection*

The Harris Collection contains more than 300 volumes dating from 1880, including first editions of all forty of Harris's books, later editions, translations, *Uncle Remus's Magazine,* and books about Harris. Fifteen linear feet of original artwork by A. B. Frost, Barry Moser, Frederick Stuart Church, E. Boyd Smith, and others are included, as well as correspondence, manuscript drafts, photographs, clippings, and memorabilia. (Subjects: Frost, A. B.; Harris, Joel Chandler; Manuscript/Illustration Material; Moser, Barry; Smith, E. Boyd)

### Joyce Blackburn Papers and Books

The Blackburn Papers consist of typescripts, manuscripts, research materials, proofs, correspondence, and related materials of author Joyce Blackburn. Typescripts include those for the Suki books and several biographies. Visual materials include photographs, children's artwork in response to the Suki books, and illustrations by Stephanie Clayton. Drafts for WMBI radio broadcasts are also included. (Subjects: Blackburn, Joyce; Manuscript/Illustration Material)

### SAVANNAH

**Chatham-Effingham-Liberty Regional Library (GS)**
2002 Bull St.
Savannah, GA 31499-4301
phone: 912-234-5127
fax: 912-236-7782
contact: Irma Harlan, Library Director

### Hortense Orcutt Collection

This memorial collection was started in 1937 to honor Hortense Orcutt, a well-known Savannahian who made significant contributions to the local development of kindergarten facilities. The purpose of the Orcutt Collection is to make available, primarily to adults, examples of outstanding children's books, with emphasis on those books of interest to younger readers. Included in the collection of more than 500 volumes are works by many well-known illustrators, as well as books about these artists. Alphabet books, story collections, and books on storytelling technique

round out the collection. (Subjects: Children's Literature, Study of; Illustration of Children's Books)

## Hawaii

### HONOLULU

**Hawaii State Library (HH)**
478 S. King St.
Honolulu, HI 96813
phone: 808-586-3510
fax: 808-586-3584
contact: Melode Reinker, Children's
    Librarian
catalog status: partially cataloged in
    Dewey, online catalog

### Edna Allyn Room Memorial Collection

Several different collections are housed in the Edna Allyn Room at the Hawaii State Library. The general collection of some 600 children's books dates from 1855 to 1971, with the primary focus on the pre-1930 titles. The Igoe Collection of Alphabet Books contains 175 volumes of children's alphabet books, 1929 to the present. The Nene Autograph Collection contains autographed copies of the winners of the Nene Award. The Nene Award is an annual children's choice award established in 1964 and chosen by the schoolchildren of Hawaii. (Subjects: Alphabet Books; Award Books; Historical)

## Idaho

### MOSCOW

**University of Idaho (IdU)**
**University Library**
Rayburn St.
Moscow, ID 83844-2350
phone: 208-885-6534
fax: 208-885-6817
contact: Barbara Jordan, Library
    Assistant

*Special Collections*

The University Library at the University of Idaho holds some twenty titles in the Basque language published in the mid-twentieth century. (Subject: Basque Language)

# Illinois

## CARBONDALE

**Southern Illinois University at Carbondale (ICarbS)\*\***
**Morris Library**
Carbondale, IL 62901
phone: 618-453-2522
fax: 618-453-3440

*Special Collections*

Included are 6,000 volumes of trade books, textbooks, and periodicals, mainly American and English, dating from the late eighteenth century through the twentieth century. (Subjects: Historical; Textbooks)

## CHICAGO

**Chicago Public Library (IC)**
**Harold Washington Library Center**
400 S. State St.
Chicago, IL 60605
phone: 312-747-4200
fax: 312-747-4223
contact: Marsha Huddleston, Librarian
catalog status: OCLC, local online
    catalog

*Thomas Hughes Children's Library*

The holdings of the Hughes Children's Library are quite diverse and offer several distinct research collections. A retrospective collection of 10,000 volumes published from 1900 to 1950 was formed as a last-copy depository for the Chicago Public Library system. This collection will soon be augmented with 40,000 volumes transferred from the former Illinois State

Library's juvenile collection with imprints predominantly from 1930 to 1970. The Newbery/Caldecott Reference Collection contains some 300 volumes of award-winning titles, many of which are autographed. Holdings also include 85 storybooks, songbooks, and books based on the films of Walt Disney, once a resident of Chicago. A collection of 135 Mother Goose titles published since 1900 is also included. The library's holdings also include the microfiche edition of the Opie Collection and the microfilm for *Nineteenth Century Children's Periodicals*. (Subjects: Award Books; Disney, Walt; Folk and Fairy Tales; Historical—20th Century; Mother Goose)

**Newberry Library (ICN)**
60 West Walton St.
Chicago, IL 60610
phone: 312-943-9090
contact: Reference Department
catalog status: OCLC

*Newberry Library*

While the Newberry Library has never had a children's department or bought with child readers in mind, the library does own a strong historical collection of children's books. Holdings in this area concern specific subjects or genres which were used by publishers for children, but which also extend well beyond the field of children's books. Children's books are not housed or classified separately, but can be found in many subject classifications and collections. Current collecting areas include, but are not limited to, general Americana to 1918, general British to 1918, and European to 1820, music and occasional verse for children to 1900 (British and American), alphabet books, handwriting books, geography and other textbooks, specific artists and writers for children, specific publishers, and reference materials and criticism. (Subjects: Too numerous to list)

## DE KALB

**Northern Illinois University (IDeKN)**
**The University Libraries**
Normal Rd.
De Kalb, IL 60115
phone: 815-753-0255
fax: 815-753-9803
contact: Samuel T. Huang, Head of Rare
  Books & Special Collections
catalog status: OCLC, ILLINET

### American Popular Literature Collection

This is a collection of mass-appeal publications issued in America from 1865 to 1920. Currently numbering 2,000 volumes, the collection includes works by Horatio Alger, Oliver Optic, Mark Twain, and many other popular writers. (Subjects: Alger, Horatio; Historical; Optic, Oliver; Series Books; Twain, Mark)

### Johannsen Collection

The Johannsen Collection contains 7,500 dime novels and other popular publications of Beadle and Adams in the late nineteenth century. Special strength in years from 1865 through 1895. Complete runs of several Beadle and Adams' periodicals. (Subjects: Beadle and Adams; Dime Novels)

### Southeast Asia Children's Book Collection

A collection of more than 350 Southeast Asian children's books in English, as well as in Thai, Malay, Tagalog, Vietnamese, and other Southeast Asian languages. Contact May Kyi Win, Head of the Hart Collection, for information. (Subject: Southeast Asian Languages)

### Special Collections

In addition to the collections previously discussed, Rare Books and Special Collections contains several other groupings of literature. Included are more than 200 periodical titles of science fiction, western fiction, and children's magazines published from 1905 to 1955, and about 800 comic books and strips including *Pogo, Wonder Woman,* and Dell Comics Movie Classics. The Edward Ardizzone Collection includes 172 British and American editions of this British author/illustrator. (Subjects: Ardizzone, Edward; Comic Books; Periodicals)

## EVANSTON

**Northwestern University (IEN)**
**University Library**
1935 Sheridan Rd.
Evanston, IL 60208
phone: 708-491-7602
fax: 708-491-8306
contact: Leslie Bjorncrantz, Curriculum
  Librarian
e-mail: 1-bjorncrantz@nwu.edu
Internet: telnet 129.105.54.2 or
  lib.ucc.nwu.edu
catalog status: Cataloged, local online
  catalog

### Curriculum Collection

The nearly 14,000 children's literature titles held in the Curriculum Collection include award-winning and highly recommended children's books, fiction and nonfiction, published primarily in the United States since 1940. Also included are reference books on the study and teaching of children's literature. (Subjects: Award Books; Children's Literature, Study of; Historical—20th Century)

## NORMAL

**Illinois State University (INS)**
**Milner Library**
Normal, IL 61790-8900
phone: 309-438-2871
fax: 309-438-3676
contact: E. Stephen Meckstroth, Head of
  Special Collections
Internet: uicmvsa.aiss.uic.edu
catalog status: OCLC, Illinet

### Circus Collection

The Circus Collection includes some 600 books and sixty dime novels from the eighteenth century to the present. Many foreign editions, particularly French, German, Dutch, and Italian are included, as well as photographs, slides, films, recordings, ephemera, and toys. (Subjects: Circus; Dime Novels; Toys)

*Publication: A Descriptive and Bibliographic Catalog of the Circus and Related Arts Collection at Illinois State University, Normal, Illinois,* by Robert Sokan. Bloomington, Ill.: Scarlet Ibis Pr., 1976.

### Historical Children's Literature

Approximately 2,250 volumes of historical children's books and periodicals dating from the mid-1800s to the turn of the century. Nearly 250 of the volumes are by Jacob Abbott. (Subjects: Abbott, Jacob; Historical)

### Historical Textbooks Collection

This textbook collection contains more than 1,000 volumes in all subject areas including grammars, readers, and books on mathematics published from the late 1700s to 1900. Books are cataloged by subject. (Subject: Textbooks)

### Lois Lenski Collection

The Lenski Collection contains 200 volumes written by or about Lois Lenski. Included are foreign translations of her books, photograph albums, and bookmarks and Christmas cards designed by her, as well as toys that Lenski used as models for her illustrations. The collection also contains correspondence, manuscripts, proofs, original artwork, and scrapbooks dealing with *Corn Farm Boy* and *Houseboat Girl.* (Subjects: Lenski, Lois; Manuscript/Illustration Material; Toys)

### Will Johnson Collection

Donated by area teacher and bookstore owner Will Johnson, this collection includes more than 400 trade books published from 1930 to 1950, many autographed by the author or illustrator.

Included are award winners and representative authors of that period. (Subjects: Award Books; Historical—20th Century)

## QUINCY

**Quincy Public Library (IQ)**
526 Jersey St.
Quincy, IL 62301
phone: 217-223-4498
fax: 217-222-3952
contact: Judy J. Decker, Head of
　Children's Dept.
catalog status: OCLC, Dynix

### Allegra Montgomery Gleeson Collection

The Gleeson Collection contains nearly 200 volumes of historical children's books, primarily in English, with several in German. (Subject: Historical)

## ROCKFORD

**Rockford College (IRoC)***
**Howard Colman Library**
5050 E. State St.
Rockford, IL 61108-2393
phone: 815-226-4035
fax: 815-226-4084

### Library

The Colman Library holds 800 volumes of alphabet books from the late sixteenth through the early twentieth centuries, representing nearly fifteen languages. Included are rag books, coloring books, panoramas, hornbooks, battledores, primers, catechisms, and tracts with examples of children's, adult, and collegiate rhymes. (Subject: Alphabet Books)

## URBANA

**University of Illinois (IU-Ed)**
**Education and Social Science Library**
1408 W. Gregory Dr.
Urbana, IL 61801
phone: 217-333-2305
fax: 217-244-0398
contact: Nancy P. O'Brien, Education
　Subject Specialist

e-mail: nobrien@ux1.cso.uiuc.edu
Internet: illinet.aiss.uiuc.edu
catalog status: OCLC, Illinet

### School Collection of Children's & Young Adult Literature

The School Collection of the Education and Social Science Library consists of 43,000 volumes of children's and young adult literature, both fiction and nonfiction. Included are children's classics, easy readers, picture books, biographies, folk literature, mythology. National award-winning and notable books are collected, as are wordless picture books, alphabet books, and pop-up books. Additionally, the School Collection holds 47,800 textbooks, as well as historical children's literature dating to the early nineteenth century. (Subjects: Alphabet Books; Award Books; Fables; Historical; Textbooks; Toy and Movable Books)

Note: The Library at the University of Illinois at Urbana-Champaign was awarded the Center for Research Libraries' 58,000-volume collection of children's books. In addition, the Center for Children's Books recently relocated to the University of Illinois and now deposits its books in the library.

### University of Illinois (IU-LS)
**Children's Research Center, Room 19**
52 Gerty Dr.
Urbana-Champaign, IL 61820
phone: 217-384-5860
contact: Julie James, Graduate Research Assistant
e-mail: ccb@alexia.lis.uiuc.edu
Internet: illinet.aiss.uiuc.edu
catalog status: OCLC, Illinet

### Center for Children's Books

The Center for Children's Books, associated with the University of Illinois at Urbana-Champaign's Graduate School of Library and Information Science (GSLIS), is a collection of 14,000 trade books written for children and 800 professional and reference books on children's literature. *The Bulletin of the Center for Children's Books* is a forty-five-year-old reviewing journal now published by the GSLIS. Each year the *Bulletin* receives 5,000 children's books for review, selecting some 1,000. The reviewed books are then added to the center's collection, and the others are placed in the library at the University of Illinois. (Subjects: Children's Literature, Study of; Historical—20th Century)

## WHEATON

**Wheaton College (IWW)**
**Marion E. Wade Center**
Wheaton, IL 60187-5593
phone: 708-752-5908
fax: 708-752-5855
contact: Marie Hass, Assistant Archivist
e-mail: mhass@david.wheaton.edu
catalog status: Cataloged on Procite

### The Marion E. Wade Center

The Wade Center holds 12,000 volumes dating from the 1840s and consisting of books, periodicals, dissertations, and theses relating to the works of C. S. Lewis, George MacDonald, Dorothy L. Sayers, Madeleine L'Engle, and J. R. R. Tolkien, among others. In addition, they hold manuscript materials, photographs, correspondence, sound recordings, and oral history interviews for the same authors. They also hold 500 volumes of detective fiction, fantasy, and Arthurian literature. (Subjects: Historical; L'Engle, Madeleine; Lewis, C. S.; MacDonald, George; Manuscript/Illustration Material; Sayers, Dorothy; Tolkien, J. R. R.)

*Publication: George MacDonald: A Bibliographical Catalog and Record,* compiled by Mary Nance Jordan. Wheaton, Ill.: Wheaton College, 1984.

# Indiana

## BLOOMINGTON

**Indiana University (InU-Li)**
The Lilly Library
Bloomington, IN 47405
phone: 812-855-2452
fax: 812-855-3143
contact: Lilly Librarian
e-mail: liblilly indiana.edu
Internet: telnet iuis.ucs.indiana.edu
(login: guest)
catalog status: OCLC for books

*Lilly Library*

The Lilly Library contains 400,000 volumes dating from 1455 to the present. Within those holdings, more than 15,000 books and related materials from the fifteenth to twentieth centuries pertain to children's literature. The Elisabeth Ball Collection of Historical Children's Materials, formed by Elisabeth Ball and her father, George Ball, contains more than 8,000 books. Other collections include the Virginia Warren Collection of Street Cries, the Kenyon Starling George Cruikshank Collection, and the J. K. Lilly, Jr. Collection. Strengths of the library's holdings include ABC books, chapbooks, comic books, miniature books, hornbooks, illustrated books, science fiction, street cries, toy books, *Peter Parley to Penrod* titles, original illustrations, books of instruction, and extensive holdings of early English children's publishers, such as Newbery, Darton, Harris, and Marshall. The papers of the Bobbs-Merrill Company are held as well. (Subjects: Too numerous to list.)

## INDIANAPOLIS

**Indianapolis-Marion County Public Library (InI)**\*\*
P.O. Box 211
40 East St. Clair St.
Indianapolis, IN 46206-0211
phone: 317-269-1700
fax: 317-269-1768

*Special Collections*

Within Special Collections, they hold more than 1,500 volumes from the nineteenth century to the present (with a special emphasis on illustrated volumes), 435 volumes about Indiana and by Indiana authors, and the Harding Memorial Storytelling Collection of 1,170 volumes. (Subjects: Historical; Illustration of Children's Books; Indiana; Indiana—Authors and Illustrators; Storytelling)

## MUNCIE

**Ball State University (InMuB)**\*\*
2000 University Ave.
Muncie, IN 47306-1099
phone: 317-285-5277
fax: 317-285-5351

*Library Science Library*

Holdings include 670 children's books published from 1890 to 1910. (Subject: Historical)

## NOTRE DAME

**University of Notre Dame (InNd)**
Department of Special Collections
102 Hesburgh Library
Notre Dame, IN 46556
phone: 219-631-5636
fax: 219-631-6772
contact: Laura Fuderer, Rare Book
Librarian
e-mail: l4ffcj@irishmvs.edu
Internet: irishmvs.cc.nd.edu
catalog status: OCLC, NOTIS

*Frank Merriwell Collection*

The Merriwell Collection includes 545 titles by Burt L. Standish published in the United States from 1898 to 1930. These include 203 titles of the Merriwell series from 1898 to 1915. (Subjects: Series Books; Standish, Burt L.)

## TERRE HAUTE

**Indiana State University (InTI)**
**Cunningham Memorial Library**
Terre Haute, IN 47809
phone: 812-237-2610
fax: 812-237-2567
contact: David Vancil, Head of Rare
 Books
e-mail: libvanc@cml.indstate.edu
Internet: 139.102.4.10 (TN3270
 emulation required)
catalog status: OCLC, NOTIS

### Cunningham Collection

The philosophy and psychology of American education are the subject matter of the 2,000 volumes contained in the Cunningham Collection. Included are some early textbooks and children's books. (Subjects: Education; Textbooks)

### Floyd Family Collection

The Floyd Family Collection includes 1,500 textbooks by Indiana authors or published/used in Indiana, primarily from 1840 to 1945. (Subject: Textbooks)

### Indiana Collection

Works written by Indiana children's authors are represented in this collection of 4,800 volumes. (Subject: Indiana—Authors and Illustrators)

### Rare Books Collection

Six thousand five hundred volumes dating from 1472 to the present pertaining to printing, culture, literature, discovery, and travel are included. Examples are collected from the inception of printing to the present. Many subcollections exist, including Jesse Stuart and small-press books. Children's books are included in this collection as examples of printing and binding rather than to emphasize children's literature. (Subject: Historical)

### Walker Collection

Nine hundred volumes dating from the eighteenth and nineteenth centuries provide examples of notable American textbooks, particularly those from New England, which form the core of the holdings. (Subjects: New England; Textbooks)

# Iowa

## IOWA CITY

**University of Iowa (IaU)**
**University Libraries**
**Special Collections Department**
Iowa City, IA 52242-1420
phone: 319-335-5921
fax: 319-335-5900
contact: Robert A. McCown, Head,
 Special Collections
e-mail: cadrmcts@uiamus.bitnet
Internet: telnet oasis.uiowa.edu
catalog status: RLIN, local online
 catalog

### Special Collections

The Special Collections Department has both printed and manuscript material relating to children's literature including the Alden Chase and C. M. Hulett collections of 360 dime novels; books and manuscripts by Iowa authors and illustrators; the Bernice E. Leary collection of 1,200 books, primarily nineteenth-century American titles; and the G. Robert Carlsen Collection of Adolescent Literature consisting of more than 400 books. (Subjects: Dime Novels; Eyerly, Jeannette Hyde; Felsen, Henry Gregor; Historical; Holmes, Marjorie; Iowa—Authors and Illustrators; Manuscript/Illustration Material; Sabin, Edwin L.; Veglahn, Nancy; Young Adult Literature)

**WEST BRANCH**

**Herbert Hoover Presidential Library (IaWbH)**
P.O. Box 488
Parkside Dr.
West Branch, IA 52358
phone: 319-643-5301
fax: 319-643-5825
contact: Dwight Miller, Archivist
catalog status: finding aid for collection

*Laura Ingalls Wilder Series*

The Laura Ingalls Wilder material is a series of documents within the papers of Rose Wilder Lane, her daughter. Included are four boxes of correspondence files, book drafts, and final printed copies. Rose Wilder Lane, herself an accomplished author, worked closely with her mother on the various "Little House" books. (Subjects: Lane, Rose Wilder; Manuscript/Illustration Material; Wilder, Laura Ingalls)

# Kansas

**EMPORIA**

**Emporia State University (KEmU)\*\***
**William Allen White Library**
1200 Commercial St.
Emporia, KS 66801
phone: 316-341-5208
fax: 316-341-5997
contact: Mary Bogan

*Elizabeth Yates Collection*

Manuscripts, proofs, illustrations, and related materials for *Amos Fortune, Free Man* and *Prudence Crandell, Woman of Courage*. (Subjects: Manuscript/Illustration Material; Yates, Elizabeth)

*Historical Children's Literature Collection*

Four hundred thirty-six books published in the nineteenth and twentieth centuries. Examples of original artwork by Kurt Weise, Marguerite deAngeli, and Helen Sewell. Complete runs of several periodicals. (Subjects: Historical; Periodicals)

*May Massee Collection*

A collection of 1,291 volumes, 139 of which are from May Massee's personal library. Included are books published by May Massee for Doubleday, Page and Company from 1933 to 1963. Holdings include an extensive collection of manuscripts, artwork, proofs, and correspondence for James Daugherty, C. B. Falls, Don Freeman, Robert McCloskey, and Kate Seredy. (Subjects: Daugherty, James Henry; Falls, C. B.; Freeman, Don; Historical—20th Century; Manuscript/Illustration Material; Massee, May; McCloskey, Robert; Seredy, Kate)

*Publication: The May Massee Collection: Creative Publishing for Children 1923–1963: A Checklist,* edited by George V. Hodowanec. Emporia, Kansas: William Allen White Library, Emporia State University, 1979.

*Ruth Garver Gagliardo Collection*

A collection of 1,804 volumes from Gagliardo's personal library, many inscribed, with the majority published in the nineteenth and twentieth centuries. Includes correspondence between her and authors, editors, and illustrators. (Subjects: Gagliardo, Ruth Garver; Historical; Manuscript/Illustration Material)

*William Allen White Children's Book Award*

This collection contains 590 volumes associated with the William Allen White Award as well as manuscripts, artwork, audio- and videotapes, photographs, information about winning authors and those on the Master Lists, and all recordings related to the award. (Subject: Award Books)

## LAWRENCE

**University of Kansas (KU)\*\***
**Watson Library**
Lawrence, KS 66045-2800
phone: 913-864-3956
fax: 913-864-3855

*Special Collections*

Special Collections include 1.5 linear feet of personal papers, correspondence, clippings, and monographs of Ruth Garver Gagliardo. More than 6,500 British and American titles from the late eighteenth to mid-twentieth centuries are held, as well as full runs of numerous periodical titles. (Subjects: Gagliardo, Ruth Garver; Historical; Manuscript/Illustration Material; Periodicals)

## TOPEKA

**Kansas State Historical Society (KHi)**
**Center for Historical Research**
120 W. Tenth
Topeka, KS 66612-1291
phone: 913-296-4776
fax: 913-296-1005
contact: Leslie A. Cade, Head, Reference
    Section

*Center for Historical Research*

The Library and Archives Division of the Kansas State Historical Society holds some 250 children's literature titles, including books, periodicals, and plays by Kansas authors and/or concerning Kansas topics. (Subjects: Kansas; Kansas—Authors and Illustrators)

## WICHITA

**Wichita Public Library (KWi)\*\***
223 South Main St.
Wichita, KS 67202
phone: 316-262-0611
fax: 316-262-4540

*Ruth Garver Gagliardo-Frances Sullivan Gallery Collection*

This collection contains original illustrations representing the work of several prominent artists of the mid-1900s. Also included are sketchbooks, letters, memorabilia, and manuscripts. (Subjects: d'Aulaire, Edgar Parin and Ingri; deAngeli, Marguerite Lofft; Dennis, Wesley; Hader, Berta and Elmer; Lenski, Lois; Manuscript/Illustration Material; Milhous, Katherine; Newberry, Clare Turlay; Sewell, Helen)

## WINFIELD

**Southwestern College (KWS)\*\***
**Memorial Library**
100 College St.
Winfield, KS 67156-2498
phone: 316-221-4150
fax: 316-221-8382

*Library*

Holdings include autographed volumes and original ink etchings of Lois Lenski. (Subject: Lenski, Lois)

**Winfield Public Library (KWPu)\*\***
605 College
Winfield, KS 67156-3199
phone: 316-221-4470

*Laura Ingalls Wilder Collection*

This collection contains eight autographed books, a scrapbook of newspaper clippings, photographs, and correspondence. (Subject: Wilder, Laura Ingalls)

# Kentucky

## BOWLING GREEN

**Western Kentucky University (KyBgW)**
**Department of Library Special**
  **Collections**
1526 Russellville Rd.
Bowling Green, KY 42101-3576
phone: 502-745-5083
fax: 502-745-4878
contact: Connie Mills, Kentucky Library
  Coordinator; Patricia M. Hodges,
  Manuscripts and Archives Supervisor
catalog status: OCLC

### Library Special Collections

Special Collections holds both monograph
and manuscript materials relating to children's literature, including, 4,000 volumes
of Victorian children's literature, as well as
titles by Kentucky authors Alice Hegan
Rice, Annie Fellows Johnston, Jesse Stuart, Rebecca Caudill, Billy C. Clark,
George Ella Lyon, and others. Manuscript
materials are held for Kentucky authors
Dorothy Grider, Alice Hegan Rice, and
Anne Pence Davis. Also of interest are
childhood diaries written by Kentuckians
Clara Louise Robertson and Josephine
Calvert. (Subjects: Davis, Anne Pence;
Grider, Dorothy; Historical; Kentucky—
Authors and Illustrators; Manuscript/Illus-
tration Material; Rice, Alice Hegan)

## LEXINGTON

**University of Kentucky (KyU)**
**Margaret I. King Library**
**Special Collections**
Lexington, KY 40506-0039
L. Terry Warth, Special Collections
phone: 606-257-3801
fax: 606-257-8379

### Rebecca Caudill Papers

Included in the Caudill papers are thirteen
boxes of manuscript materials, printers copies, and twelve tapes. (Subjects: Caudill,
Rebecca; Manuscript/Illustration Material)

## LOUISVILLE

**University of Louisville (KyLoU)**
**Ekstrom Library**
**Special Collections Dept.**
Louisville, KY 40292
phone: 502-852-8729, 502-852-6752
fax: 502-852-8753, 502-852-7394
contact: George T. McWhorter, Donor
  and Curator; Delinda Stephens Buie,
  Curator
e-mail: dsbuie01@ulkyvm.louisvil6.edu
Internet: ulkyvm.louisville.edu
catalog status: OCLC; local online

### Arthur Rackham Memorial Collection

A complete collection of all published
works of Arthur Rackham. Nearly 300
volumes include signed and limited editions in English, French, German, and
Dutch; 200 periodicals; original paintings
and drawings; correspondence; biography;
and bibliography. (Subjects: Manuscript/
Illustration Material; Rackham, Arthur)

**Publication:** *Arthur Rackham Memo-*
*rial Collection: A Checklist of Titles Ar-*
*ranged Alphabetically,* by George T.
McWhorter, 1972.

### Edgar Rice Burroughs Memorial Collection

Collection containing 60,000 items in
thirty-four languages covers every aspect
of the life and literary legacy of Edgar Rice
Burroughs. Includes all jacketed first editions, pre-publication review copies, reprints, pulps, comics, newspaper serials,
Tarzan Sunday and daily strips, fanzines,
children's adaptations and abridgements,
spin-offs, movies, film stills and photographs, scrapbooks, posters, original art,
radio shows and scripts, toys and games,
correspondence, and memorabilia. This
collection is the international headquarters of "The Burroughs Bibliophiles" and
publishes *The Burroughs Bulletin,* a quarterly magazine. (Subjects: Burroughs,
Edgar Rice; Comic Books)

*Publication: Edgar Rice Burroughs Memorial Collection: A Catalog,* by George T. McWhorter; House of Greystoke, 1991.

### Rare Books and Special Collections

The Rare Book Collection includes children's books within the general collection of 30,000 volumes published from 1800 to the present, but primarily nineteenth century. Author L. Frank Baum is represented by 150 volumes; 200 volumes by George A. Henty; and the rare children's books written by Graham Greene. Also included are runs of several children's periodicals. (Subjects: Baum, Lyman Frank; Henty, George Alfred; Historical; Periodicals)

# Louisiana

### BATON ROUGE

**State Library of Louisiana (L)**
P.O. Box 131
Baton Rouge, LA 70821
phone: 504-342-4951
fax: 504-342-3547
contact: Dorothy White, Public Library
   Consultant, Children's Coordinator
catalog status: OCLC, online catalog

### Louisiana Collection

Several hundred children's books written by Louisiana authors or books about Louisiana are a part of the Louisiana Collection. (Subjects: Louisiana; Louisiana—Authors and Illustrators)

### NEW ORLEANS

**New Orleans Public Library (LN)**
**Central (Main) Library**
219 Loyola Ave.
New Orleans, LA 70140
phone: 504-596-2588
fax: 504-596-2609
contact: Children's Room Librarian,
   Central Library
catalog status: OCLC, Dynix

### Juvenile Historical Reference Collection

This special collection of historically important or interesting children's books has 150 volumes dating from 1787 to 1969, although the bulk of the items were published in the nineteenth century. Included are McGuffey readers and primers. (Subjects: Historical; Textbooks)

# Maine

### BRUNSWICK

**Bowdoin College (MeB)**
**Bowdoin College Library**
**Special Collections**
Brunswick, ME 04011
phone: 207-725-3288
fax: 207-725-3083
contact: Dianne M. Gutscher, Curator of
   Special Collections
e-mail: dgutsche@bowdoin.edu
catalog status: monographs are
   cataloged, manuscripts have finding
   aids

### Special Collections

Special Collections at Bowdoin College Library hold both monographs and manuscript materials for a number of children's literature authors, including Charles Asbury Stephens, a writer for *The Youth's Companion;* Kate Douglas Wiggin; Henry Beston and his wife, Elizabeth Coatsworth; and Elijah Kellogg. In addition, the Abbott Memorial Collection contains both printed and manuscript materials relating to Jacob Abbott and other members of his family. There are twenty-six linear feet of correspondence, diaries, journals, literary manuscripts, sermons, addresses, and the Lyman Abbott Autograph Collection. (Subjects: Abbott, Jacob; Beston, Henry; Coatsworth, Elizabeth; Historical; Kellogg, Elijah; Manuscript/Illustration Material; Stephens, Charles Asbury; Wiggin, Kate Douglas)

## GARDINER

**Gardiner Public Library (MeGar)**
152 Water St.
Gardiner, ME 04345
phone: 207-582-3312
contact: Glenna Nowell, Director;
    Danny D. Smith, Chair Special
    Collections
catalog status: published inventory of
    collection

*Yellow House Papers: The Laura E.
Richards Collection*

The Yellow House Papers represent the literary legacy of famed children's author Laura E. Richards. Although the collection concerns itself with nine generations of her family from the 1760s to the 1980s, including many unique items pertaining to her mother, Julia Ward Howe of *Battle Hymn* fame, the focus of the collection is on Laura E. Richards. Approximately 100 volumes of her published books are augmented by seventy linear feet of manuscript materials, including the original manuscript of *Captain January*. The collection is owned by the Gardiner Library Association and is deposited on indefinite loan at Colby College in Waterville, Maine, with the exception of the bound scrapbooks, "Home Logs," and the published books. Approximately five linear feet of photoduplicated materials are available at the Gardiner Library for the convenience of local researchers. (Subjects: Manuscript/Illustration Material; Richards, Laura E.)

*Publication: The Yellow House Papers: The Laura E. Richards Collection, An Inventory and Historical Analysis,* by Danny D. Smith. Gardiner, Maine: Gardiner Library Association, 1991.

## ORONO

**University of Maine (MeU)**
**Raymond H. Fogler Library**
**Special Collections Department**
5729 Fogler Library
Orono, ME 04469-5729
phone: 207-581-1688
fax: 207-581-1653
contact: Muriel A. Sanford, Head,
    Special Collections Department
Internet: ursus.maine.maine.edu
catalog status: OCLC, RLIN, local
    online catalog

*Special Collections*

Within Special Collections are nearly 2,000 books by Maine authors and illustrators, books published in Maine, and books with Maine as the subject. These works have imprint dates from 1900 to the present. (Subjects: Maine; Maine—Authors and Illustrators)

## PORTLAND

**Portland Public Library (MeP)**
Five Monument Square
Portland, ME 04101
phone: 207-871-1700
contact: Thomas L. Gaffney, Special
    Collections Librarian
catalog status: Cataloged

*Children's Antique Collection*

This collection of historical children's literature contains 600 items, primarily published in the nineteenth century. (Subject: Historical)

**Westbrook College (MePW)**
**Abplanalp Library**
Stevens Ave.
Portland, ME 04103
phone: 207-797-7261, ext. 329
fax: 207-797-5779
contact: Mary Anne Wallace, Special
    Collections Librarian
catalog status: OCLC

*Maine Women Writers Collection*

The Maine Women Writers Collection is a special collection of published and non-published literary, cultural, and social history sources by and about women authors, either born or residing in Maine. These sources document and illustrate the times, circumstances, and experiences of some 500 women, revealing their public actions and private thoughts. Founded in 1959, the collection contains books, correspondence, photographs, diaries, manuscripts, typescripts, artifacts, and audiocassettes. Children's authors Sophie May, Elizabeth Coatsworth, and Kate Douglas Wiggin are included. (Subjects: Clarke, Rebecca Sophia; Coatsworth, Elizabeth; Historical; Maine—Authors and Illustrators; Manuscript/Illustration Material; Wiggin, Kate Douglas)

## WATERVILLE

**Colby College (MeWC)**
**Miller Library**
Mayflower Hill Dr.
Waterville, ME 04901
phone: 207-872-3284
fax: 207-872-3555
contact: Patience-Anne W. Lenk, Acting
   Head, Special Collections
Internet: telnet Library@colby.edu (login:
   Library)
catalog status: OCLC

*Special Collections*

The children's literature collection of 1,500 volumes is largely nineteenth- and early twentieth-century American (specifically New England) materials which have accumulated over the past 175 years. Outstanding holdings include more than 700 volumes written by Jacob Abbott and John S. C. Abbott. Other authors include Laura Richards, Kate Douglas Wiggin, Elizabeth Coatsworth, Elijah Kellogg, Sophie May, G. W. Hinckley, Alvin Schwartz, and Dahlov Ipcar. Periodical titles include nearly complete runs of *St. Nicholas* and

*Tip Top Weekly.* (Subjects: Abbott, Jacob; Folk and Fairy Tales; Historical; New England; Periodicals; Richards, Laura E.; Twain, Mark; Wiggin, Kate Douglas)

# Maryland

## BALTIMORE

**Enoch Pratt Free Library (MdBE)**\**
400 Cathedral St.
Baltimore, MD 21201-4484
phone: 410-396-5430
fax: 410-396-6856

*Library*

Included are 840 uncataloged books representing nineteenth- and early twentieth-century writers, and an additional 1,600 cataloged books from the late nineteenth century to the present. Five hundred titles in the Holme Collection and an additional 114 titles in the George Peabody Collection focus on illustration of children's books. (Subjects: Historical; Illustration of Children's Books)

# Massachusetts

## AMHERST

**Amherst College (MAA)**
**Library**
**Special Collections**
Amherst, MA 01002-5000
phone: 413-542-2299
fax: 413-542-2662
contact: John Lancaster, Curator of
   Special Collections
e-mail: jlancaster@amherst.edu
catalog status: OCLC, local online
   catalog

*S. G. Goodrich (Peter Parley) Collection*

Based on the Harmon S. Boyd (manuscripts) and Morris Cohen (printed books)

collections, the Goodrich Collection covers his entire authorial and publishing life, as well as the imitations and piracies of others issued under the name "Peter Parley." The collection consists of 700 volumes published between 1814 and 1900, forty manuscripts and associated items, and advertising ephemera relating to Goodrich or Parley publications. (Subjects: Manuscript/Illustration Material; Parley, Peter)

**The Jones Library, Inc. (MAJ)**
43 Amity St.
Amherst, MA 01002
phone: 413-256-4090
fax: 413-256-4096
contact: Daniel Lombardo, Curator of
    Special Collections

### Clifton Johnson Collection

Clifton Johnson, a resident of Hadley, Masachusetts, was well-known for his research and writings on children and education. Between 1890 and 1938, he authored, edited, or illustrated over 100 books and hundreds of articles. By the end of his life, he had amassed an important collection of juvenile literature and schoolbooks. These books are the core of the Clifton Johnson Collection, donated to the library in 1939. The collection consists of 1,200 volumes from the seventeenth and eighteenth centuries, mostly American imprints. The collection is particularly strong in readers and spellers. (Subjects: Historical; Textbooks)

## BOSTON

**Boston Athenaeum (MBAt)**
10 1/2 Beacon St.
Boston, MA 02108-3777
phone: 617-227-0270
fax: 617-227-5266
contact: Stephen Z. Nonack, Head of
    Reference
catalog status: OCLC

### Children's Collection

The Children's Collection is a historical English-language collection of more than 4,000 volumes dating from about 1790. Strengths include early chapbooks and ABC books, rare and unusual picture books, and first editions of prominent illustrators. The Athenaeum continues to collect both contemporary picture books and illustrated books from the Victorian and Edwardian periods. The collection contains many nineteenth-century periodicals for children, including complete runs of a number of periodical titles. Also included are the books, journals, and two unpublished manuscripts of Isabel Anderson. (Subjects: Alphabet Books; Anderson, Isabel; Chapbooks; Historical; Illustration of Children's Books; Manuscript/Illustration Material; Periodicals)

*Publication: Once upon a Time: An Exhibition of Illustrated Children's Books and Children's Book Illustrations from the Collections of the Boston Athenaeum and Two Friends of the Library.* September 12 to November 3, 1990. Boston: Boston Athenaeum.

**Boston Public Library (MB)**
**Research Library Office**
Copley Square
Boston, MA 02116
phone: 617-536-5400, ext. 238
fax: 617-536-7758
contact: Mary Beth Dunhouse,
    Coordinator of Resources and
    Processing
e-mail: mbdunhouse@bpl.org
catalog status: OCLC, local online
    catalog

*Alice M. Jordan Collection*

The goal of the Jordan Collection is to provide, for research, a comprehensive worldwide selection of children's literature. The types of books collected include picture books, fairy tales, folklore, poetry, drama, toy and movable specimens, as well as fiction and nonfiction from the infant to young adult level. The collection of 160,000 volumes includes not only well-regarded, award-winning literature, but also "grocery store/street vendor" type books to provide an accurate reflection of the diversity of children's reading habits. Since the mid-1970s, one copy of each juvenile title added to the circulating collection has been placed in the Jordan Collection to augment the historical English-language material dating from 1870. Foreign juvenile imprints, representing 100 countries and fifty languages, became an important component of the collection's holdings with the launching of the Children's Books International Symposia in 1974. The New England Round Table of Children's Librarians Archives is included. (Subjects: Folk and Fairy Tales; Foreign Language; Historical; New England Round Table of Children's Librarians)

*Publication: A Goodly Heritage: Children's Literature in New England 1850–1950.* An exhibition from the Alice M. Jordan Collection . . . . Boston: Boston Public Library, 1989.

**Boston University (MBU)**
**Mugar Memorial Library**
**Department of Special Collections**
771 Commonwealth Ave.
Boston, MA 02215
phone: 617-353-3696
fax: 617-353-2838
contact: Dr. Howard B. Gotlieb,
   Director of Special Collections
catalog status: OCLC for books,
   manuscripts in card catalog

*Twentieth Century Archives*

Special Collections contains monographic and manuscript materials for a number of authors and illustrators of children's literature. The collection contains published books, variant editions, and foreign translations, as well as manuscripts, typescripts, galley proofs, notes, journals, diaries, scrapbooks, reviews, cuttings, photographs, and personal and professional correspondence. (Subjects: Anglund, Joan Walsh; Asimov, Isaac; Bond, Michael; Bothwell, Jean; Burnett, Frances Hodgson; Godden, Rumer; Goodwin, Harold L.; Hirshberg, Albert; Manuscript/Illustration Material; McCormick, Wilfred; North, Sterling; Tunis, John R.; Williams, Jay; Wise, William; Yates, Elizabeth)

**The Children's Museum (MBChM)**
300 Congress St.
Boston, MA 02210-1034
phone: 617-426-6500, ext 230
fax: 617-426-1944
contact: A. Kacker, Librarian
e-mail: Kacker@TCM.org
catalog status: OCLC

*Resource Center*

The Resource Center maintains a collection of 10,000 volumes that supports museum exhibits, the interests of museum staff, and curriculum resources for educators, primarily in the area of multicultural education. Strengths lie in multicultural works and the natural and physical sciences. (Subjects: Historical—20th Century; Multiculturalism; Science)

**The Congregational Library (MBCn)**
14 Beacon St.
Boston, MA 02108
phone: 617-523-0470
fax: 617-523-0491
contact: Dr. Harold F. Worthley,
   Librarian
catalog status: Cataloged

*Library*

This is the library of deposit for the publications of the Massachusetts Sabbath School Society, 1840–1890; the Congregational Publishing Society, 1875–1900; and Pilgrim Press, 1900–1960. Also included are publications of the American Tract Society, 1820–1860; American Sunday School Union, 1830–1850; and Congregational Sunday School curricula, 1880–1960, which was succeeded by the United Church of Christ curricula. (Subjects: American Sunday School Union; American Tract Society; Bibles and Books of Religious Instruction; Congregational Publishing Society; Congregational Sunday School Curricula; Massachusetts Sabbath School Society; Pilgrim Press)

**Massachusetts Historical Society (MHi)**
1154 Boylston St.
Boston, MA 02215
phone: 617-536-1608
fax: 617-859-0074
contact: Mary E. Cogswell, Associate
    Librarian
catalog status: OCLC

*Children's Literature*

This collection of some 600 volumes ranges from the eighteenth to the twentieth centuries. The bulk of the collection is American, although there are some early English titles. Most of the twentieth-century titles are devoted to American history. This is not a systematic collection, but New England and Massachusetts imprints are most heavily represented. (Subjects: Historical; Massachusetts Imprints; New England)

*Horace Mann Papers*

The personal papers of educational reformer Horace Mann encompass twenty-four boxes and ten volumes. The papers contain information about the selection of children's books and schoolbooks for Mas-

sachusetts schools and school libraries from the 1830s to the 1850s. Also included are the papers of kindergarten reformers Mary Tyler Peabody Mann and Elizabeth Palmer Peabody. (Subjects: Education; Mann, Horace; Manuscript/Illustration Material)

*School Books*

This collection holds 500 pre-1820 titles and 1,250 post-1820 schoolbooks used, for the most part, in early American academies and public schools. Foreign languages, classical languages, geography, and mathematics form a significant part of the collection. While most imprints are American, there are a number of early English books. (Subject: Textbooks)

**Simmons College (MBSi)**
**Simmons College Libraries**
**Archives Dept.**
300 The Fenway
Boston, MA 02115
phone: 617-521-2440
fax: 617-521-3199
contact: Megan Sniffin-Marinoff,
    Archivist
e-mail: msniffin@vmsvax.simmons.edu
Internet: library.simmons.edu
catalog status: OCLC, Innopac

*Horn Book Magazine Archives*

The Horn Book records document the history of the *Horn Book* magazine from its founding in 1924; the Horn Book, Inc., since 1936; and The Bookshop for Boys and Girls, the precursor to and first publisher of the *Horn Book* magazine from 1916 to 1936. The collection also documents the growth of the field of children's literature from the early to mid-twentieth century, primarily through correspondence with authors, illustrators, editors, publishers, educators, and librarians. The Horn Book records constitute 23.5 linear feet and contain office files, editorial correspondence, lists, illustrations, speeches, manuscripts and proofs, financial records, clippings, minutes, publications, scrapbooks, photographs, and printed materials. The editors' records document the tenure of Bertha Mahoney Miller, Jennie D. Lindquist, and Ruth Hill Viguers. (Subjects: Children's Literature, Study of; Historical—20th Century; *Horn Book* Magazine; Illustration of Children's Books)

## *Knapp Collection*

The Knapp Collection contains 1,200 volumes of English and American children's literature published mostly before World War I, with a concentration in late nineteenth-century American titles. There is a complete run of *St. Nicholas* and scattered holdings of other nineteenth-century periodicals. Girls' series books, religious instruction books, and a sampling of textbooks are included. (Subjects: Historical; Series Books)

## Wheelock College (MBWS)
**Wheelock College Library**
132 The Riverway
Boston, MA 02215
phone: 617-734-5200, ext. 225
fax: 617-566-7369
contact: Sue Kaler, Reference Services
    Librarian/Assistant Director
Internet: telnet FLO.ORG (username:
    WHE _PAC; Exit: CNTL-Z)
catalog status: OCLC, local online
    catalog

## *Ingraham Collection*

The collection of 500 British and American volumes dates primarily from the nineteenth century, but spans the mid-eighteenth through twentieth centuries. Included are a battledore, chapbooks, miniatures, periodicals, primers, and other early textbooks, as well as works by well-

known authors and illustrators. (Subjects: Chapbooks; Historical; Miniature Books; Textbooks)

## BROOKLINE

**Hebrew College (MBrH)**
43 Hawes St.
Brookline, MA 02146
phone: 617-232-8710
fax: 617-734-9769
contact: Dr. Maurice Tuchman, Director
    of Library Services
e-mail: bm.hct@rlg.bitnet
catalog status: RLIN

## *Helen H. Sarna Hebrew Children's Literature*

This collection of 5,000 volumes and phonograph recordings consists of children's literature on Jewish themes and a section of children's literature in Hebrew translation. While the bulk of the collection is in Hebrew and English, there are also volumes in German and Yiddish. Included are picture books, stories, fairy tales, and nonfiction on all aspects of Judaica from the Bible, archaeology, and history to quiz books and science. The collection contains early and mid-nineteenth-century volumes such as the works of David Zamosc, the first Hebrew author to devote himself to children's literature, and the publications of E. I. Schapira, the founder of the first Jewish publishing house for children's literature. The major twentieth-century Israeli children's authors are included—among them, Nahum Gutmann, Devorah Omer, Uriel Ofek and Puzo—as well as many American-Jewish authors. Of note are the rare late nineteenth-century children's magazine *Sabbath Visitor* and early twentieth-century Zionist magazines. (Subjects: Hebraic Language; Historical; Judaica; Periodicals; Recordings)

## CAMBRIDGE

**Harvard Graduate School of Education (MH-Ed)**
Monroe C. Gutman Library
Appian Way
Cambridge, MA 02138
phone: 617-496-3108
fax: 617-495-0540
contact: Marylene Altieri, Special
   Collections Librarian/Archivist
Internet: hollis.harvard.edu
catalog status: OCLC, HOLLIS

*Historical Textbook Collection*
This collection contains 35,000 volumes, published between 1800 and 1950, that were used in elementary and secondary schools. Subjects range from mathematics and science to home economics and penmanship. The collection is particularly strong in the areas of reading, geography, and history. Multiple editions of many titles are held. (Subject: Textbooks)

## CONCORD

**Concord Free Public Library (MCo)**
129 Main St.
Concord, MA 01742
phone: 508-371-6240
fax: 508-371-6244
contact: Marcia E. Moss, Curator

*Children's Collection*
The Children's Collection contains books written and illustrated by Concord residents, as well as books formerly owned by these Concord authors and artists. In the group are titles by Louisa May Alcott, Walter Edmonds, Nancy Bond, Betty Cavanna, and Margaret Sidney. Manuscripts, photographs, and memorabilia complement the published book collection. (Subjects: Manuscript/Illustration Material; Massachusetts—Authors and Illustrators)

   **Publication:** *A History of the Concord Free Public Library: Being an Account of the First Hundred Years of That Institution Narrated in Three Segments* by Allen French, T. Morris Longstreth, and David B. Little. Concord, Mass.: Members of the Library Corporation, 1973.

**Orchard House/Home of the Alcotts (MCoA)**
399 Lexington Rd.
Concord, MA 01742
phone: 508-369-4118
contact: Stephanie N. Upton, Director

*Louisa May Alcott Memorial Association*
Housed at the home of the Alcotts are about 150 volumes of the library of Amos Bronson Alcott and Louisa May Alcott, as well as some thirty-five periodicals. Also held are personal letters, notebooks, sketchbooks, playbills, and memorabilia. (Subjects: Alcott, Louisa May; Manuscript/Illustration Material; Periodicals)

## COTUIT

**Cotuit Library Association (MCot)**
P.O. Box 648
Main St.
Cotuit, MA 02635
phone: 508-428-8141
fax: 508-428-4636
contact: Kathleen Pratt, Cataloguer
catalog status: Cataloged

*Children's Retrospective Collection*
The collection of nearly 2,000 volumes, published from 1770 to 1950, provides a good sampling of children's literature and school texts, particularly for 1840–1930. The standard authors are represented, along with tracts, textbooks from the mid-1800s, and boys' series books. Also included are some 150 volumes written by Peter Parley. (Subjects: Historical; Parley, Peter; Series Books; Textbooks)

## DEERFIELD

**The Memorial Libraries (MDeeP)**
P.O. Box 53
Memorial St.
Deerfield, MA 01342
phone: 413-774-5581
fax: 413-773-7415
contact: David R. Proper, Librarian
catalog status: Cataloged

### Pocumtuck Valley Memorial Association Library

Although this library does not have a children's collection as such, they do have monographs and manuscript materials representative of the field. The general stacks include numerous volumes published from the eighteenth to the twentieth centuries, including chapbooks and textbooks. Of particular interest are the published works of two local writers, Mary Prudence Wells Smith and Elizabeth Williams Champney. (Subjects: Champney, Elizabeth W.; Historical; Smith, Mary Prudence Wells; Textbooks)

## FITCHBURG

**Fitchburg State College (MFiT)\*\***
160 Pearl St.
Fitchburg, MA 01420
phone: 508-345-2151, ext 3195
fax: 508-345-4270

### Robert Cormier Collection

Original drafts of books and short stories, typed manuscripts and galley proofs, several unpublished manuscripts, taped speeches, correspondence, and newspaper columns of author Robert Cormier. (Subjects: Cormier, Robert; Manuscript/Illustration Material)

## NORTHAMPTON

**Smith College (MNS)**
**William Allan Neilson Library**
**Mortimer Rare Book Room**
Northampton, MA 01063
phone: 413-585-2907
fax: 413-585-2904
contact: Karen V. Kukil, Acting
  Curator
catalog status: Cataloged

### Children's Book Collection

Approximately 1,000 volumes, seventeenth to twentieth centuries, which include primers, chapbooks, alphabet books, school books, catechisms, Bibles and hieroglyphic Bibles, toy books, and picture books in first editions. Publishers John Newbery, Isaiah Thomas, and M. J. Godwin are represented. Several manuscript collections augment the books. (Subject: Historical)

## SALEM

**Peabody Essex Museum (MSaP)**
**James Duncan Phillips Library**
East India Square
Salem, MA 01970
phone: 508-745-1876
fax: 508-744-0036
contact: William T. La Moy,
  Director
catalog status: Cataloged

### Library

The juvenile holdings of the Peabody Essex Museum include more than 5,000 titles, from the eighteenth century to 1920, with the majority before 1875. Of particular interest are thirty nineteenth-century periodical titles. (Subjects: Historical; Periodicals)

**Salem Athenaeum (MSaA)**
337 Essex St.
Salem, MA 01970
contact: Cynthia Wiggin, Librarian
phone: 508-744-2540
catalog status: Cataloged

*Library*
Juvenile holdings of the Salem Athenaeum consist of 326 volumes from the eighteenth through the twentieth centuries, including miniature books, first editions, series books, and folk and fairy tales. A number of nineteenth-century periodicals include complete runs of *Wide Awake* and *St. Nicholas.* (Subjects: Historical; Periodicals)

## SANDWICH

**Sandwich Public Library (MSanP)**
142 Main St.
Sandwich, MA 02563
phone: 508-888-0625
fax: 508-833-1076
contact: Lauren L. Robinson, Children's
   Librarian

*Children from Many Lands Illustrate Grimm's Fairy Tales*
The collection consists of fifteen framed original paintings illustrating various Grimm fairy tales done by children from Belgium, Denmark, Finland, Israel, Italy, Korea, Mexico, Portugal, and the United States. The art was done in 1966 and submitted to the Follett Publishing Company as part of a contest. The art was part of a circulating collection and is now permanently displayed in the Children's Room of the library. (Subjects: Folk and Fairy Tales; Manuscript/Illustration Material)

**Thornton W. Burgess Society (MSanB)**
6 Discovery Hill Rd.
Sandwich, MA 02537
phone: 508-888-6870
contact: Gwen Brown, Curator
catalog status: Indexed

*Thornton Waldo Burgess Collection*
This is the largest known collection of the works of Thornton Waldo Burgess, children's author, naturalist, and environmental pioneer. Total holdings of 1,700 volumes include first editions of all of his works, as well as comprehensive holdings of all reprint editions. Also included are some 350 original illustrations by Harrison Cady and thirty by Phoebe Erickson that were used in Burgess's books. (Subjects: Burgess, Thornton Waldo; Cady, Harrison; Erickson, Phoebe; Manuscript/Illustration Material)

## STURBRIDGE

**Old Sturbridge Village (MStuO)**
**The Research Library**
One Old Sturbridge Village Rd.
Sturbridge, MA 01566-1198
phone: 508-347-3362
fax: 508-347-5375
contact: Joan Allen, Assistant Librarian
e-mail: bm.osc@rlg.stanford.edu
catalog status: RLIN, OCLC

*Research Library*
Holdings of the Research Library support the museum's mission to bring to life the first fifty years of the American Republic. The history and material culture of rural New England from 1790 to 1840 are the focus of the museum's collections. Juvenile holdings include 350 volumes of English and American imprints, including primers, elementary and secondary school textbooks, rewards of merit and manuscript exercise books. (Subjects: Copy Books; Historical; New England; Textbooks)

## WALTHAM

**Brandeis University (MWalB)**
University Library
Waltham, MA 02254-9110
phone: 617-736-4685
fax: 617-736-4675
contact: Charles Cutter, Head Judaica
and Special Collections Department

### Dime Novel Collection

The collection includes 4,000 volumes of
dime novels. In addition, the collection includes complete runs of several related periodicals. Although not cataloged on
OCLC, a finding aid is available. (Subject:
Dime Novels)

## WELLESLEY

**Wellesley College (MWelC)**
Margaret Clapp Library
Special Collections
106 Central St.
Wellesley, MA 02181
phone: 617-283-2129
fax: 617-283-3640
contact: Ruth R. Rogers, Special
Collections Librarian
Internet: luna.wellesley.edu (login:
library)
catalog status: OCLC, local online
catalog

### Juvenile Collection

The Juvenile Collection, almost all acquired by gift, has grown over the years to
nearly 800 volumes. Although it contains
some eighteenth-century works, it is primarily nineteenth- and early twentieth-
century material. Primers, songbooks,
folktales, and fairy tales provide a rela-
tively new field of interest for students of
literature, education, psychology, or book
illustration. Well represented are the works
of many prominent illustrators, both British and American. The Juvenile Collection is partially cataloged and accessioned.
(Subject: Historical)

**Wellesley Free Library (MWelF)**
530 Washington St.
Wellesley, MA 02181
phone: 617-235-1610
contact: Anne Sheehan, Children's
Librarian
catalog status: OCLC, DRA

### Ruth Hill Viguers Collection

The Viguers Collection consists of 1,680
volumes of historical children's literature.
(Subject: Historical)

## WILLIAMSTOWN

**Williams College (MWiW)**
Chapin Library
Stetson Hall
P.O. Box 426
Williamstown, MA 01267
phone: 413-597-2462
fax: 413-597-2929
contact: Robert L. Volz, Custodian
e-mail: robert.l.volz@williams.edu
Internet: library.williams.edu
catalog status: OCLC, local online
catalog

### Children's Books Collection

This collection includes 400 volumes dating from 1678 to 1989. Also included are
thirty-five linear feet of original manuscript holdings. (Subjects: Historical;
Manuscript/Illustration Material)

## WORCESTER

**American Antiquarian Society (MWA)**
185 Salisbury St.
Worcester, MA 01609
phone: 508-755-5221
fax: 508-754-9069
contact: Laura Wasowicz, Senior
Cataloguer, American Children's
Books
catalog status: RLIN, MaRK

*American Juvenile Literature Collection*

The American Juvenile Literature Collection contains comprehensive holdings of American books and periodicals published between 1700 and 1899. In addition, the AAS Manuscripts Collection holds the papers of relevant authors and publishers. The children's books total some 17,000 volumes, including fiction and pedagogical titles; significant holdings of Jacob Abbott (373 titles), Samuel Goodrich (296 titles), and William Taylor Adams (124 titles), as well as 1,500 titles issued by the McLoughlin Brothers publishing firm. Periodical holdings extend from about 1789 to 1915, with a total of some 357 titles, including the first American children's periodical, *The Children's Magazine* (1789). Amateur periodical holdings extend from 1805 to post-1900. The collection consists of about 5,500 titles from every state except Alaska and Hawaii. Manuscript holdings include the papers of author Goold Brown, as well as publishers Morris Cotton; Dodd, Mead and Company; and Lee and Shepard. (Subjects: Abbott, Jacob; Amateur Periodicals; Brown, Goold; Cotton, Morris; Dodd, Mead and Company; Historical; Lee and Shepard; Manuscript/Illustration Material; McLoughlin Brothers; Optic, Oliver; Parley, Peter; Periodicals)

*Publication: Under Its Generous Dome: The Collections and Programs of the American Antiquarian Society,* 2nd ed., revised. Worcester, Mass.: American Antiquarian Society, 1992.

**Worcester State College (MWW)**
486 Chandler St.
Worcester, MA 01602
phone: 508-793-8000, ext. 8531
contact: Bruce Plummer
catalog status: OCLC

*Children's Library*

The Children's Library at Worcester State College contains 11,000 volumes of children's literature published since 1950. (Subject: Historical—20th Century)

# Michigan

## ANN ARBOR

**University of Michigan (MiU)\*\***
**Information & Library Studies**
300 Hatcher North
Ann Arbor, MI 48109-1205
phone: 313-764-9356
fax: 313-763-5080

*Library*

Included in their collection are 900 volumes published before 1900. (Subject: Historical)

## DEARBORN

**Henry Ford Museum & Greenfield**
**Village (MiDbH)**
20900 Oakwood Blvd.
P.O. Box 1970
Dearborn, MI 48124-1970
phone: 313-271-1620
contact: Carolynn Martin Miller, Access
System Administrator
catalog status: Cataloged

*Titus Geesey Collection*

Included are examples of nineteenth-century American children's books, including a good collection of McGuffey readers, several dozen New England primers, and some Websteriana. (Subjects: Historical; Textbooks)

## DETROIT

**Detroit Public Library (MiD)**
**Rare Book Collection**
5201 Woodward Ave.
Detroit, MI 48202
phone: 313-833-1492
fax: 313-832-0877
contact: Cally Kypros, Chief of
   Children's Dept.
e-mail: c.kypros@cms.cc.wayne.edu
Internet: telnet hermes.merit.edu (at
   Host type: WSUNET, at menu type:
   LUIS)
catalog status: Cataloged; LUIS

*Elsie Gordon Memorial Collection*

Consists of sixty-three volumes of *Alice's Adventures in Wonderland* from 1895 to 1993. Some translations. (Subject: Carroll, Lewis)

*Kate Greenaway Collection*

In 1959, John Newberry, library benefactor and friend, purchased a collection of Kate Greenaway materials including manuscripts, letters, original drawings and watercolors, first editions, greeting cards, and memorabilia. This initial gift was augmented by the purchase of the estate of Robert Patridge. (Subjects: Greenaway, Kate; Manuscript/Illustration Material)

   *Publication: Kate Greenaway: A Catalogue of the Kate Greenaway Collection,* Rare Book Room, Detroit Public Library, compiled by Susan Thompson. Detroit: Wayne State University Pr., 1977.

*Rare Books Collection*

The juvenile holdings are extensive and varied. A collection of historical volumes published prior to 1837 are complemented by 1,000 titles in more than twenty languages. Also included are 600 volumes of folk and fairy tales, 135 volumes of Mother Goose rhymes published from 1878 to the present, and twenty-three his-

torical editions of *Robinson Crusoe.* They hold manuscript and illustration materials for a number of authors and illustrators. Also held are 350 items of Walter Crane, including correspondence, illustrations, first editions, wallpaper designs, and ceramic tiles. (Subjects: Bemelmans, Ludwig; Boyle, Mildred; Crane, Walter; de Angeli, Marguerite Loftt; Defoe, Daniel; Folk and Fairy Tales; Foreign Languages; Gag, Wanda; Historical; Lenski, Lois; Manuscript/Illustration Material; Mother Goose; Ness, Evaline; Rhead, Louis; Sewell, Helen; Smith, Jessie Willcox; Wilder, Laura Ingalls)

**Wayne State University (MiDW)**
**Purdy/Kresge Library**
Detroit, MI 48202
phone: 313-577-6425 or 313-577-6446
fax: 313-577-4172
contact: Karen Bacsanyi, Children's
   Literature Bibliographer
e-mail: kbacsany@cms.cc.wayne.edu
Internet: telnet hermes.merit.edu (at
   Host type: WSUNET, at menu type:
   LUIS)
catalog status: OCLC, local online
   catalog

*Eloise Ramsey Collection of Literature for Young People*

The Ramsey Collection consists of 14,000 volumes dating from 1601 to the present, concentrating on American and British imprints. Included are ABC books, tracts of the American Sunday School Union, Isaac Watts and Lewis Carroll. Also, extensive resources relating to the study of children's literature and award-winning books are included. Manuscripts and related materials of Eve Titus. (Subjects: Alphabet Books; American Sunday School Union; Award Books; Carroll, Lewis; Children's Literature, Study of; Foreign Languages; Historical; Titus, Eve)

*Publication: The Eloise Ramsey Collection of Literature for Young People,* compiled by Joan Cusenza. Detroit: Wayne State University, 1967.

### Millicent A. Wills Collection of Urban/Ethnic Materials for Young People

Started at the request of the Children's Literature Department in the College of Education, this collection was designed to procure books that illustrated life in urban centers. In 1990 the collection was dedicated to the memory of M. A. Wills, who left a bequest to Wayne State University. Monies from the bequest are used to expand the collection to include materials by and about people of all ethnic groups. Currently, the 1,500 books in the collection range in age and reading level from kindergarten through high school. (Subject: Multiculturalism)

## EAST LANSING

**Michigan State University (MiEM)****
**University Libraries**
East Lansing, MI 48824-1048
phone: 517-353-8700
fax: 517-336-3532

### Juvenile Series Collection

This collection includes 25,000 items within four principal categories. Held are an extensive collection of big little books, comic art, reprints and anthologies, and 10,500 dime novels. (Subjects: Big Little Books; Comic Books; Dime Novels)

## GRAND RAPIDS

**Aquinas College (MiGrA)**
**Woodhouse Library**
1607 Robinson Rd. SE
Grand Rapids, MI 49506
phone: 616-459-8281
fax: 616-732-4534

contact: Sister Rose Marie Martin
catalog status: OCLC, Innovative
    Interfaces

### Mother Goose Collection

This collection consists of fifty-five editions of Mother Goose rhymes in a variety of languages. (Subject: Mother Goose)

## KALAMAZOO

**Western Michigan University (MiKW)**
**Dwight B. Waldo Library**
Kalamazoo, MI 49008
phone: 616-387-5221
contact: Professor Beatrice H. Beech
catalog status: OCLC

### Historical Children's Collection

Contains 1,000 volumes published during the nineteenth and twentieth centuries, including popular American authors, autographed copies of award-winning books, and works illustrated by the prominent artists of the day. Collection also holds original woodblocks engraved by Edmund Evans from designs by Randolph Caldecott. (Subjects: Caldecott, Randolph; Evans, Edmund; Historical; Illustration of Children's Books; Woodblocks)

### Le Fevre Miniature Book Collection

This collection contains 315 examples of miniature book printing dating from 1780 to the present. (Subject: Miniature Books)

## MOUNT PLEASANT

**Central Michigan University (MiMtpT)**
**Clarke Historical Library**
Mount Pleasant, MI 48859
phone: 517-774-3352
fax: 517-774-4499

contact: Evelyn Leasher, Public Services
Librarian
catalog status: Cataloged

### Lucile Clarke Memorial Children's Library

This collection was donated to the Clarke
Historical Library by Dr. Norman Clarke,
Sr., in 1971. Numbering over 8,000 items,
mainly monographs, the collection also includes manuscripts, graphics, and realia.
Published materials date from 1648 to the
present, with emphasis on nineteenth-
century English and American children's
literature. Special areas of note are first
editions of some 85 percent of the items
listed in Blanck's *Peter Parley to Penrod*,
over 500 items written by or about Horatio Alger, and the Ruth Adomeit Action
Book Collection. (Subjects: Abbott, Jacob; Alger, Horatio; Baum, Lyman Frank;
Bibles and Books of Religious Instruction;
Chapbooks; DeJong, Meindert; Fox,
Frances; Historical; Hollands, Hulda
Theodate; Manuscript/Illustration Material; Michigan; Michigan—Authors and Illustrators; Miniature Books; Smith, Allen
Field; Textbooks; Toy and Movable Books;
Twain, Mark)

# Minnesota

## MINNEAPOLIS

**Minneapolis Public Library (MnM)**
300 Nicollet Mall
Minneapolis, MN 55401-1992
phone: 612-372-6532
fax: 612-372-6623
contact: Kathleen Johnson, Head
Children's Services Dept.
catalog status: OCLC, local online
catalog

### Children's Folklore Collection

The Folklore Collection contains 3,000
volumes, primarily twentieth century, of
folk and fairy tales, myths and legends,
songs, games, superstitions, and nursery
rhymes. Includes reference and bibliographic aids, history of folklore, illustrations and text variants, and biographical
material on folklorists and collectors. (Subjects: Folk and Fairy Tales; Games and
Pastimes)

### Children's Foreign Language Collection

Included are more than 1,800 volumes of
children's literature in more than forty-
four European, Middle and Far Eastern,
African, and Native American languages
published in the twentieth century. The
majority are in the original language of
publication. (Subject: Foreign Languages)

### Children's Historical Collection

This collection consists of 4,400 volumes,
eighteenth century to the present, primarily representing the history and development of children's literature. Also included
are extensive Minnesota-related holdings,
textbooks, comics, novelty and toy books,
posters, dolls, several periodical titles, and
several original illustrations. (Subjects:
Brink, Carol Ryrie; Brock, Emma Lillian;
Historical; Manuscript/Illustration Material; Minnesota; Minnesota—Authors and
Illustrators; Periodicals; Puppetry; Toys)

**University of Minnesota (MnU)**
**109 Walter Library**
117 Pleasant St. SE
Minneapolis, MN 55455
phone: 612-624-4576
fax: 612-625-5525
contact: Dr. Karen Nelson Hoyle,
Curator and Professor
e-mail: k-hoyl@vm1.spcs.umn.edu
Internet: pubinfo.ais.umn.edu (or
128.101.109.1) for full screen
TN3270 telnet

catalog status: OCLC and RLIN;
LUMINA

### Beulah Counts Rudolph Collection

An assistant professor of English at State
University of Oswego, New York, Beulah
Counts Rudolph began collecting figurines
and other materials related to children's
literature while a graduate student and
collected over a twenty-five-year period.
The collection came to the university in
1974 as a gift of her family and consists
of over 500 figurines, sixty-eight wall
hangings, and 775 bookmarks. All of the
items represent characters or scenes from
children's literature. A portion of the collection is always on display in the Arthur
Upton Room in Walter Library. (Subject:
Figurines)

### Denis R. Rogers/Edward S. Ellis Collection

This extensive collection of the work of
Edward S. Ellis came to the university in
1986 and was collected by Denis R. Rogers, a British scholar of Ellis's work. It is
the largest single collection of works by Ellis in existence. Included are scarce dime
novels, examples of his nonfiction, and
multiple editions of his boys' success and
adventure stories. (Subjects: Dime Novels; Ellis, Edward S.; Periodicals)

### Hess Collection

George H. Hess, Jr., began to collect dime
novels in 1928, partly motivated by the
hope of finding copies he had owned as a
boy. Though he never found one with his
signature, he did accumulate a collection
of about 80,000 items, including many
outside his original collecting scope. The
collection came to the university after Mr.
Hess's death in 1954 and included over
50,000 American dime novels and other
popular literature items, as well as 17,000
British dime novels and periodicals, and
several hundred Victorian boys' books issued in parts. His collection also included
over 5,000 boys' and girls' series books,
which now number about 9,000. (Subjects: Big Little Books; Comic Books; Dime
Novels; Periodicals; Pulps; Series Books;
Story Papers)

*Publications:* The Hess Collection,
compiled by George H. Hess, Jr. University of Minnesota Libraries. "The Hess
Collection: Past, Present and Future," by
Deidre Johnson. *Dime Novel Round-Up*
60 (April 1991).

### Kerlan Collection

This collection was begun in the 1940s by
University of Minnesota alumnus, Irvin
Kerlan, and came to the University Libraries in Minneapolis in 1949. The collection
includes more than 60,000 children's
books, dating from the 1700s to the
present, and representing 68 languages;
manuscript materials for over 3,900 titles;
illustration materials for more than 4,090
titles; and 226 periodical titles. There are
many other resources for the study of children's literature: over 1,200 reference
titles, 3,090 vertical subject file entries,
over 1,800 publishers' catalogs representing 135 publishers, and other unique materials, including audiovisual materials,
figurines, photographs, posters, and toys.
(Subjects: Too numerous to list)

*Publication:* The Kerlan Collection
Manuscripts and Illustrations for Children's Books: A Checklist, compiled by
Karen Nelson Hoyle. Minneapolis: University of Minnesota Libraries, 1985.

### Paul Bunyan Collection

This unique collection of books, manuscripts, pamphlets, photographs, and other
memorabilia connected with northwoods
logging folklore was begun in the late
1940s at the University of Minnesota with
the acquisition of the papers of W. W.
Charters. Further acquistions included the
collection of Dorothy Moulding Brown
and the papers of William Laughead and
James Stevens. Included are 145 volumes

and nine linear feet of manuscripts. (Subject: Paul Bunyan)

## ST. PAUL

College of St. Catherine (MnSSC)
Saint Catherine Library
2004 Randolph Ave.
St. Paul, MN 55105
phone: 612-690-6553
fax: 612-690-8636
contact: Sister Margery Smith, CSJ
Internet: Host.clic.edu
catalog status: OCLC

### Ruth Sawyer Collection

The 2,550 volumes in the Ruth Sawyer Collection include all of her own books, except for one title, some foreign translations, 220 personal letters from her and her family, her three medals, and a scrapbook. Also included are original drawings and manuscripts from some of her books, as well as a collection of letters from Anne Carroll Moore. (Subjects: Manuscript/Illustration Material; Sawyer, Ruth)

St. Paul Public Library (MnSP)**
90 West Fourth St.
St. Paul, MN 55102-1668
phone: 612-292-6311
fax: 612-292-6660

### Library

Included in their holdings are over 800 volumes of children's classics; 1,000 foreign-language titles with strengths in Spanish, French, and German; and 200 titles by Minnesota authors. (Subjects: Foreign Languages; Historical; Minnesota—Authors and Illustrators)

# Mississippi

## HATTIESBURG

University of Southern Mississippi
  (MsHaU)
University Libraries
McCain Library & Archives
Box 5148
Hattiesburg, MS 39406
phone: 601-266-4349
fax: 601-266-4409
contact: Dee Jones, Curator
e-mail: dee_jones@bull.cc.usm.edu
Internet: library.lib.usm.edu or telnet
  131.95.89.2
catalog status: OCLC, GEAC

### de Grummond Children's Literature Research Collection

Begun in 1966, this comprehensive research collection consists of 52,000 published volumes dating from 1530 to the present, as well as original manuscript and illustrative materials for more than 1,200 authors and illustrators. The book collection comprises all types of literature, including alphabet books, chapbooks, boys' and girls' series books, folk and fairy tales, nursery rhymes, fables, illustrated classics, children's magazines, reference works, and textbooks. Manuscript materials focus primarily on United States authors and illustrators, although Britons are included. Featured are the books and original illustrations of Kate Greenaway and the extensive archive of Ezra Jack Keats's work. A vertical file containing information on 1,600 authors, illustrators, and related subjects supplements the reference collection. (Subjects: Too numerous to list)

*Publications: The Image of the Child: An Exhibition Catalogue,* compiled by Dee Jones. Hattiesburg: University of Southern Mississippi, 1991. *Kate Greenaway: An Exhibition Catalogue,* compiled by Dee Jones. Tokyo: Book Globe Co., 1993.

April 20, 1966

Dear Mrs. de Grummond,

Your very kind letter of March 30 finally reached me — via Houghton Mifflin. Shame on the postmaster in New York who first returned it to you as undeliverable — he did have my new address.

In a separate mailing tube I am sending you an autographed proof sheet of "C.G. goes to the Hospital" and a Star chart; and enclosed goes an autobiographical folder, a set of miniature book jackets, a photo of author plus monkey (it isn't George but a borrowed little chimpanzee girl), a fan-mail-answering card, and our last year's and this year's New Year's card — and also a small rough sketch of George about to swallow a piece of the jig-saw puzzle.

I hope you can use the material, & we both wish you the very best for your new career —

Yours sincerely,

Letter from H. A. Rey to Lena de Grummond April 20, 1966. Bottom left shows Curious George carrying his rolled-up artwork to Hattiesburg for inclusion in de Grummond's new collection of children's literature.

# Missouri

## COLUMBIA

**The State Historical Society of Missouri (MoHI)**
1020 Lowry
(housed in Elmer Ellis Library,
  University of Missouri-Columbia)
Columbia, MO 65201
phone: 314-882-7083
fax: 314-884-4950
contact: Elizabeth Bailey, Reference
  Specialist
catalog status: Cataloged

### Alice Irene Fitzgerald Collection of Missouri's Literary Heritage for Children and Youth

This collection was created in 1981 from the gift of the majority of books annotated in Dr. Fitzgerald's bibliography, *Missouri's Literary Heritage for Children and Youth*. Fitzgerald, a distinguished Missouri educator and authority on children's literature, has expanded the collection with other Missouri books. Donations of books from publishers, authors, libraries, and schools also have been added. This noncirculating collection includes over 1,000 volumes of fiction, nonfiction, and poetry dating from the nineteenth century to the present for readers under the age of fourteen by Missouri authors, and literature written by non-Missourians on subjects relating to the state. Vertical files have been created containing information on Missouri authors as well. (Subjects: Missouri; Missouri—Authors and Illustrators)

*Publication: Missouri's Literary Heritage for Children and Youth: An Annotated Bibliography of Books about Missouri,* by Alice Irene Fitzgerald. Columbia and London: University of Missouri Pr., 1981.

## HANNIBAL

**Mark Twain Museum (MoHM)**
**Library**
208 Hill St.
Hannibal, MO 63401
phone: 314-221-9010
contact: Henry Sweets, Director
catalog status: Cataloged

### Mark Twain Museum Library

This library contains 1,200 works by or about Mark Twain. This extensive collection includes numerous editions, both domestic and foreign, of Twain's works, as well as original manuscripts. (Subjects: Manuscript/Illustration Material; Twain, Mark)

## INDEPENDENCE

**Reorganized Church of Jesus Christ of Latter Day Saints (MoIRC)\*\***
1001 W. Walnut
P.O. Box 1059
Independence, MO 64051
phone: 816-833-1000
fax: 816-521-3095

### Library

The collection includes about seventy volumes on the history of the church and religious instruction, and several periodical titles. (Subject: Bibles and Books of Religious Instruction)

## KANSAS CITY

**Kansas City Public Library (MoK)**
311 E. 12th St.
Kansas City, MO 64106
phone: 816-221-2685
fax: 816-842-6839
contact: Elizabeth Breting, Coordinator
  of Youth Services
catalog status: OCLC, local online
  catalog

### Historical Children's Literature Collection

A carefully selected collection of 7,200 children's titles published from 1800 to the present, including a miscellany of concept books, picture books, fiction, nonfiction, reference works, and bibliographic tools. (Subject: Historical)

## ST. LOUIS

### Eugene Field House & Toy Museum (MoSFi)
634 South Broadway
St. Louis, MO 63102
phone: 314-421-4689
contact: Frances Kerber Walrond, Director

### Eugene Field House

The Eugene Field House holds 200 volumes of works by Eugene Field, dating from 1800 to the 1970s, in addition to correspondence, royalty reports, photographs, and other memorabilia. The library was not open to the public at the time of publication. (Subjects: Field, Eugene; Manuscript/Illustration Material)

### Missouri Historical Society Library & Archives (MoSHi)
P.O. Box 11940
St. Louis, MO 63112-0040
phone: 314-746-4500
catalog status: Cataloged

### Library & Archives

Within the holdings of the Missouri Historical Society, there are books and manuscript materials created by Missouri children's author, Eugene Field. Holdings include forty-six volumes of published works, papers from 1855 to 1940, proof sheets, correspondence, clippings, and notes. (Subject: Field, Eugene; Manuscript/Illustration Material)

### St. Louis Public Library (MoS)
Rare Books Department
1301 Olive St.
St. Louis, MO 63103
phone: 314-539-0380
fax: 314-241-3840
contact: Patty Carleton, Manager, Central Youth Services; Jean Gosebrink, Rare Books Librarian
catalog status: OCLC, online catalog

### Historical

Within the Rare Books Department of the St. Louis Public Library there is a large and diverse collection of historical children's literature consisting of 6,000 volumes dating from 1800. This is a representative collection with nursery rhymes, alphabet books, and works by popular writers and illustrators of the nineteenth and twentieth centuries. In addition, they hold a folklore and fairy tale collection of 2,500 volumes, 100 chapbooks (most in their original wrappers), 550 volumes of storytelling books, and an extensive selection of works on the history and criticism of children's literature. (Subjects: Chapbooks; Children's Literature, Study of; Folk and Fairy Tales; Historical; Mother Goose; Storytelling; Twain, Mark)

### Washington University (MoSW)
Olin Library
One Brookings Dr.
P.O. Box 1061
St. Louis, MO 63130
phone: 314-935-5495
fax: 314-935-4045
contact: Holly Hall, Head, Special Collections
e-mail: spec@wulibs.wustl.edu
catalog status: Cataloged

### Henrietta Maizner Hochschild Collection

A collection of 2,000 children's books, mainly American, published from 1880 to the present. All genres are represented. (Subject: Historical)

*Special Collections*

Included are holdings of published books, manuscripts, correspondence, clippings, and related materials for children's authors Eugene Field and William Jay Smith. (Subjects: Field, Eugene; Manuscript/Illustration Material; Smith, William Jay)

## STOUTSVILLE

**Mark Twain Birthplace Museum (MoStoM)**\*\*
**Research Library**
P.O. Box 54
Stoutsville, MO 65283-9722
phone: 314-565-3449

*Library*

This collection contains 275 books and manuscripts pertaining to Mark Twain from 1869 to 1980. Foreign-language editions include French, Spanish, Russian, and German. Artifacts of the author's life from 1835 to 1910 are included. (Subjects: Manuscript/Illustration Material; Twain, Mark)

## WARRENSBURG

**Central Missouri State University (MoWarbT)**
**Ward Edwards Library**
Warrensburg, MO 64093
phone: 816-543-8850
fax: 816-543-8001
contact: Ophelia Gilbert, Curator
e-mail: ogilbert@cmsuvmb.cmsu.edu
catalog status: OCLC, local online catalog

*Ophelia Gilbert Room*

The Ophelia Gilbert Room, established by authorization of the Board of Regents in 1986, contains 12,000 volumes by established children's authors, dating from 1799 to the present. Areas of collection emphasis are: Missouri authors and illustrators, adolescent novels, Mother Goose, alphabet and counting books, toy and movable books, foreign-language and Victorian series books, as well as the complete works of authors and illustrators who have contributed manuscripts and/or illustrations to the collection. In addition, the collection is also the depository for a complete collection of books from Missouri's Mark Twain Reading Award, housing 465 titles, 288 of which are first editions, and 133 autographed. The collection also houses several thousand first editions and autographed books, as well as correspondence, photographs, and original interviews from 200 contemporary writers. (Subjects: Too numerous to list)

# Nebraska

## LINCOLN

**University of Nebraska-Lincoln (NbU)**\*\*
**Don L. Love Memorial Library**
Lincoln, NE 68588-0410
phone: 402-472-2526
fax: 402-472-5131

*Special Collections*

The Special Collections Department holds a variety of published books, original manuscripts, proofs, correspondence, and research materials for Mari Sandoz and Harold William Felton. In addition, there are 450 elementary textbooks from 1820 to 1960. (Subjects: Felton, Harold William; Manuscript/Illustration Material; Sandoz, Mari; Textbooks)

## SEWARD

**Concordia College (NbSeT)**\*\*
**Link Library**
800 N. Columbia Ave.
Seward, NE 68434-1595
phone: 402-643-7258
fax: 402-643-4218

*Renata Koschman Memorial Children's Collection*

This special collection includes 12,500 volumes of children's literature. (Subject: Historical)

# New Hampshire

## CONCORD

**New Hampshire State Library (NhC)**
20 Park St.
Concord, NH 03301
phone: 603-271-2864
fax: 603-271-2205
contact: Judith A. Kimball, Supervisor, Library Development Services
catalog status: Cataloged

*Children's Historical Collection*

The New Hampshire State Library's Children's Historical Collection is an eclectic collection of 5,600 volumes spanning the nineteenth and twentieth centuries. Its treasures are not in rare books, but rather in the ordinary books that children read at home and from the developing nineteenth-century network of small public libraries in the state. The "best" books are included, as are the series, the Sunday school tracts, the nonfiction, and, yes, the "trash." The emphasis is on books by New Hampshire authors and illustrators and those books about New Hampshire. Many of these are out of print and available from no other source. Of special note are complete collections of the works of Elizabeth Yates and Tasha Tudor, as well as Newbery- and Caldecott-winning titles. (Subjects: Abbott, Jacob; Award Books; Bibles and Books of Religious Instruction; Historical; New Hampshire; New Hampshire—Authors and Illustrators; Series Books; Tudor, Tasha; Yates, Elizabeth)

## DURHAM

**University of New Hampshire (NhU)**\*\*
Special Collections
University Library
Durham, NH 03824-3592
phone: 603-862-1540
fax: 603-862-2637

*Historical Juvenile Collection*

Contains 1,200 volumes, mainly nineteenth-century imprints, that are significant in the history and development of children's literature. Also included is a growing collection of books by New Hampshire–related authors and illustrators. (Subjects: Historical; New Hampshire—Authors and Illustrators)

## HANOVER

**Dartmouth College (NhD)**\*\*
Library
Hanover, NH 03755
phone: 603-646-2236
fax: 603-646-3702

*Illustrated Books Collection*

Many juvenile titles are among the 1,400 volumes representing all periods of illustration. (Subject: Illustration of Children's Books)

*Library*

Included are 900 volumes representing the work of a number of boys' series authors of the late nineteenth and early twentieth centuries, as well as 275 chapbooks. (Subjects: Alger, Horatio; Barbour, Ralph Henry; Castlemon, Harry; Chapbooks; Ellis, Edward; Optic, Oliver; Series Books; Snell, Roy Judson)

*1926 Memorial Collection*

Two thousand four hundred volumes showing examples of illustrated books published throughout the New England states during Dartmouth's first century, 1769–1869. (Subjects: Illustration of Children's Books; New England)

# New Jersey

## FORT LEE

Free Public Library of the Borough of
 Fort Lee (NjFoP)**
320 Main St.
Fort Lee, NJ 07024
phone: 201-592-3614
fax: 201-585-0375

### Library

One thousand five hundred volumes of
children's books in Japanese, including
picture books, fiction, nonfiction, and reference books. (Subject: Japanese Language)

## MADISON

Fairleigh Dickinson University (NjMF)
Friendship Library
285 Madison Ave.
Madison, NJ 07940
contact: James Fraser, Director
phone: 201-593-8515
fax: 201-593-8525
e-mail: fraser@fdumad.fdu.edu
Internet: fdumad.edu.edu (login:
 TRICAT)
catalog status: OCLC

### Harry A. Chesler Collection

The Chesler Collection contains approximately eighty items of artwork created by
Winsor McCay. (Subjects: Manuscript/Il-
lustration Material; McCay, Winsor)

## NEW BRUNSWICK

Rutgers University (NjR)
Archibald S. Alexander Library
New Brunswick, NJ 08903
phone: 908-932-7006
contact: Ronald L. Becker, Head, Special
 Collections
catalog status: RLIN

### Harry Bischoff Weiss Collection of British and American Chapbooks

Part of the chapbook collection consists of
children's titles, folktales, and fairy tales
normally associated with children's literature. With holdings of some 300 titles,
written in English and published between
1800 and 1850, the chapbooks contain
many crude examples of popular illustration rendered in woodcut, copperplate engraving, and wood engraving. (Subject:
Chapbooks)

### Rutgers University Collection of Children's Literature

An artificial collection consisting of the literary papers (corrected typescripts, galley
and page proofs, correspondence, and
other papers) of contemporary children's
authors, many of whom are residents of
New Jersey. Related artwork is held by the
Zimmerli Museum (see entry). (Subjects:
Brancato, Robin; Chen, Tony; Cohen, Barbara; Duvoisin, Roger A.; Gauch, Patricia; Girion, Barbara; Gorog, Judith; Kettel-
camp, Larry; Lipsyte, Robert; Loeper, John
J.; Manuscript/Illustration Material; Masterman-Smith, Virginia; New Jersey—Authors and Illustrators; St. George, Judith;
St. Tamara; Shuttlesworth, Dorothy;
Smith, Datus Clifford; Snyder, Carol; and
Viorst, Judith)

### Textbook Collection

Rutgers 550-volume Textbook Collection
consists primarily of American imprints,
1750–1900, but does include English,
French, Scottish, German, and Irish titles,
ca. 1700–1900. Popular authors such as
Webster, Morse, Murray, Bingham, Pick-
ett, Cobb, Lincoln, Hale, Brown, Dil-
worth, and Adams are included. (Subject:
Textbooks)

**Rutgers University (NjR-Z)**
**Zimmerli Art Museum**
George & Hamilton Sts.
New Brunswick, NJ 08903
phone: 908-932-7237
fax: 908-932-8201
contact: Trudy Hansen, Curator of
   Prints and Drawings
catalog status: Inventory lists

*Rutgers Collection of Children's
Literature*

The Rutgers Collection of Children's Literature was founded in 1979 with support from the New Jersey Council on the Arts. Its purpose is to serve as a repository for the original manuscripts and illustrations of contemporary children's books. The Zimmerli Art Museum houses all visual aspects of the artistic creation of a children's book, such as preliminary drawings, dummies, paste-ups, page layouts, color separations and overlays, as well as the finished full-color illustrations and completed books. Since 1979, the collection has grown to contain more than 3,000 items. Original manuscripts and archival materials are collected and preserved by the Special Collections Department at the Archibald S. Alexander Library (see entry). (Subjects: Too numerous to list)

## NEWARK

**Newark Public Library (NjN)***
**Business Information Center**
34 Commerce St.
Newark, NJ 07102
phone: 201-733-7779
fax: 201-733-5750

*Wilbur Macey Stone Collection*

This collection consists of 900 volumes of stories read by children in America from the eighteenth century to the present. (Subject: Historical)

## PRINCETON

**Princeton University (NjP)**
**University Library**
Princeton, NJ 08544-2089
phone: 908-258-3197
contact: Dale Roylance, Curator

*Graphic Arts Collection*

The collection attempts to gather together outstanding examples of pictorial illustration for children in books of all countries, including China, Japan, and the smaller countries of Europe. The collection numbers more than 100 volumes published from the sixteenth to the twentieth centuries. Outstanding examples of early American children's books can be found in the library's Hamilton Collection of American Illustrated Books from 1670 to 1870. (Subjects: Foreign Languages; Illustration of Children's Books)

## PRINCETON

**Princeton University (NjP-C)**
**Harvey S. Firestone Memorial Library**
One Washington Rd.
Princeton, NJ 08544
phone: 609-258-3184
fax: 609-258-4105
contact: Curator, Cotsen Children's
   Library

*Cotsen Children's Library*

To open for public use in mid-1996. The Cotsen Children's Library is a gathering of several collections and is intended by the donor, Lloyd E. Cotsen, to be a "living library . . . with a capacity for interaction with primary and secondary schoolchildren as a key part of its mission." Mr. Cotsen "expects it to entertain and stimulate children to enter the world of books and reading. The broader mission of the library is the study of childhood, using these materials from many countries and different eras to describe the education, socialization, and development of children in different cultures." The Cotsen Children's Library is administered as part of the Department of Rare Books and Special Collections, since so much of the collection is historical in focus.

As of February 1995, the Cotsen Children's Library consisted of the core collection of over 21,000 printed books, works of art, and manuscripts dating from the sixteenth to the twentieth centuries in a variety of languages. This collection includes major types of children's literature such as alphabet books, chapbooks, folk and fairy tales, and illustrated classics, with the main focus being on illustration. One of the major strengths is the gathering of the publications of John Newbery, including the only known copy of his first publication for children.

Complementing the Cotsen Children's Library are the Skelt and Webb Archive, consisting of over 135 boxes related to the nineteenth-century English publishers of juvenile drama (toy theaters) and the Tillson Collection of over 250 boxes of materials relating to the teaching of music to children from the Renaissance to the early twentieth century. (Subjects: Chapbooks; Chinese Language; French Language; German Language; Greek Language; Hebraic Language; Historical; Illustration of Children's Books; Japanese Language; Manuscript Illustration Material; Newbery, John (publisher); Russian Language; Spanish Language)

## SOMERVILLE

**Somerset Public Library (NjSoCo)\*\***
35 West End Ave.
Somerville, NJ 08876
phone: 908-725-1336
fax: 908-231-0608

### *Library*

Two hundred eighty-five volumes representing all parts of the state and various ethnic groups, from the Revolutionary War to the present, with the earliest publication in 1896. (Subject: New Jersey)

# New Mexico

## ALAMOGORDO

**Alamogordo Public Library (NmAl)\*\***
920 Oregon Ave.
Alamogordo, NM 88310
phone: 505-439-4140

### *Lillian Maddox Mother Goose Collection*

This collection contains ninety volumes of Mother Goose editions. (Subject: Mother Goose)

## ALBUQUERQUE

**University of New Mexico (NmU)\*\***
**General Library**
Albuquerque, NM 87131
phone: 505-277-4241
fax: 505-277-6019

### *Anita Osuna Carr Bicultural Bilingual Collection*

This multicultural collection includes 1,000 print and 100 nonprint materials in Spanish, Spanish-English, and Native American language-English. (Subjects: Multiculturalism; Native American Language; Spanish Language)

# New York

## ALBANY

**University at Albany, State University of New York (NAlU)**
**University Libraries**
**Dept. of Special Collections & Archives**
1400 Washington Ave.
Albany, NY 12222
phone: 518-442-3544
fax: 518-442-3567

contact: Dorothy Christiansen, Head,
Special Collections and Archives;
Mary Osielski, Special Collections
Librarian
e-mail: dc079@uacsc1.albany.edu or
mo374@uacsc1.albany.edu
Internet: telnet 128.204.11.3
catalog status: OCLC, RLIN, local
online catalog

### Clement Moore Collection

This collection contains some 200 volumes of twentieth-century English-
language editions of "A Visit from St.
Nicholas," with some facsimiles of earlier
publications showing numerous formats
and types of illustrations. Included are periodicals, clippings, posters, greeting cards,
phonorecords, and toys. (Subject: Moore,
Clement Clarke)

### Marcia Joan Brown Papers

The papers of Marcia Brown contain
twenty-seven linear feet of manuscripts,
rough sketches, dummies, revisions, correspondence, speeches, and published
books from 1947 to 1993. Also included
are the papers of Helen A. Masten which
consist mainly of correspondence with
those interested in children's literature.
(Subjects: Brown, Marcia; Manuscript/
Illustration Material; Masten, Helen A.)

### Maud and Miska Petersham Papers

Included in this collection are manuscripts
and a dummy created by this husband-
wife team from New York State. (Subjects: Manuscript/Illustration Material; Petersham, Maud and Miska)

### Miriam Snow Mathes Historical Children's Literature Collection

Includes 7,000 English and American children's books of the nineteenth and early
twentieth centuries. Special emphasis is
placed on representative and forgotten
works published in the U.S. from 1875 to
1950, including series, gender-specific stories, historical fiction, fantasy, minorities,
animal stories, technology, travel and
people-of-other-lands stories, adaptations
and retellings, anthologies, and miscella-
nies. (Subjects: Historical; Multiculturalism; New York; Series Books; Travel and
Geography)

## BRONX

**Hunt's Point Regional Branch (NN-BrH)\*\***
**New York Public Library**
877 Southern Blvd.
Bronx, NY 10459
phone: 718-617-0338
fax: 718-893-3491

### Library

Included in their holdings are 750 Spanish-
language titles published from 1950 to the
present. (Subject: Spanish Language)

*Publication: Libros en Espanol: An An-
notated List of Children's Books in Spanish.* The New York Public Library, 1978.

## BROOKLYN

**Brooklyn Public Library (NBPu)**
**Central Children's Room**
Grand Army Plaza
Brooklyn, NY 11238
phone: 718-780-7717
fax: 718-230-0417
contact: Kathryn White, Division Chief
catalog status: OCLC

### Central Children's Room

The Central Children's Room of the
Brooklyn Public Library contains a diverse
selection of materials to support the study
of historical and contemporary children's
literature. Included are more than 3,000
volumes dating from 1741 to 1920, 1,000
volumes of folk and fairy tales from the
late nineteenth century to the present, a selective collection of over 200 miniature
books, eighty periodical titles representing professional literature and children's

magazines, a collection of books written and/or illustrated by those born or residing in Brooklyn, and a growing collection of 2,000 reference works on the history and criticism of children's literature. In addition, the library holds Ezra Jack Keats's personal working file of source material for his writing and illustration. (Subjects: Children's Literature, Study of; Folk and Fairy Tales; Historical; Keats, Ezra Jack; Miniature Books; New York—Authors and Illustrators; Periodicals)

## BROOKVILLE

**Long Island University (NGuP)**
**C. W. Post Campus**
**B. Davis Schwartz Memorial Library**
Northern Blvd.
Greenvale, NY 11548
phone: 516-299-2880
fax: 516-299-4169
contact: Conrad Schoeffling, Special
   Collections Librarian
e-mail: vax86:schoeff
Internet: ajc@vax86.liunet.edu
catalog status: OCLC, local online
   catalog

### American Juvenile Collection

This research collection contains 4,000 volumes of fiction and folklore published in America between 1910 and 1960, the vast majority of which are first editions. In addition, the collection contains original artwork by Valenti Angelo, Paul Brown, Leonard Weisgard, and others. This collection has an active duplicate trading list. (Angelo, Valenti; Brown, Paul; Folk and Fairy Tales; Historical—20th Century; Manuscript/Illustration Material; Weisgard, Leonard Joseph)

*Publications: The American Juvenile Collection: A Research Collection of Fiction & Folklore in Children's Books, 1910–1960,* by Diana L. Spirt, published by American Publishers, 1991. *An Ex-*

*hibit of the American Juvenile Collection.* Hutchins Gallery, November 1981.

### Christine B. Gilbert Historical Collection of Children's Literature

This collection, primarily used for teaching examples, contains 1,500 titles, chiefly from Western Europe and America, published in the eighteenth and nineteenth centuries, to 1909. Also included are periodicals, rare books, and examples of illustrated works by Kate Greenaway, Arthur Rackham, and others. (Subjects: Folk and Fairy Tales; Historical)

## BUFFALO

**Buffalo and Erie County Public Library**
   **(NBuBE)**
Lafayette Square
Buffalo, NY 14203-1887
phone: 716-858-8900
fax: 716-858-6211
contact: William H. Loos, Curator, Rare
   Book Room; Peggy Skotnicki,
   Children's Department Head
   Librarian

### Rare Book Room

The library's Rare Book Room is primarily devoted to adult materials, although the literary collections do have first and fine editions of many of the great authors and illustrators of nineteenth-century British and American children's literature. Of particular interest are more than 500 ABC books dating from 1790 to the present, nearly 500 books and other items relating to Mark Twain, hieroglyphic Bibles, 150 miniature books, and 250 books and other items relating to Rip Van Winkle. The Children's Department holds a significant collection of Hans Christian Andersen publications. (Subjects: Alphabet Books; Andersen, Hans Christian; Bibles and Books of Religious Instruction; Eichenberg, Fritz; Historical; Irving, Washington; Miniature Books; Twain, Mark)

*Publication: Huckleberry Finn: A Descriptive Bibliography of the Huckleberry Finn Collection at the Buffalo Public Library,* compiled by Lucille Adams. Buffalo: Buffalo Public Library, 1950.

**State University of New York College at Buffalo (NBuC)\*\***
E. H. Butler Library
1300 Elmwood Ave.
Buffalo, NY 14222
phone: 716-878-6304
fax: 716-878-3134
contact: Sister Martin Joseph Jones, Archives/Special Collections

*Lois Lenski Collection*
The Lois Lenski Collection contains 241 autographed first editions of her works, published from 1927–1974, as well as manuscripts, dummies, 123 original illustrations, photographs, and personal correspondence for *Project Boy.* (Subjects: Lenski, Lois; Manuscript/Illustration Material)

**COOPERSTOWN**

**New York State Historical Association (NCooHi)**
P.O. Box 800
Lake Rd.
Cooperstown, NY 13326
phone: 607-547-2509
contact: Special Collections Librarian

*Special Collections*
Children's literature holdings of the New York State Historical Association are numerous and varied. Included are 500 nineteenth-century American chapbooks; fifty miniature books; 100 volumes of dime novels and a few manuscripts relating to Erastus Beadle, the father of the dime novel; nineteenth-century upstate New York imprints and Cooperstown imprints published by Phinney; and nineteenth-century periodical titles. (Subjects: Beadle and Adams; Chapbooks; Dime Novels; Historical; Miniature Books; New York Imprints; Periodicals)

**EASTCHESTER**

**Eastchester Historical Society (NEaHi)**
Box 37
Eastchester, NY 10709
phone: 914-793-1900
contact: Michael De Stefano, President
catalog status: Cataloged

*Juvenile Books of the Nineteenth Century*
In connection with their museum, which is an 1835 stone one-room schoolhouse, the Eastchester Historical Society collects juvenile literature and textbooks of the nineteenth century. The collection of 1,500 volumes dating from 1790 to 1900 are used with local elementary schoolchildren and with college groups who visit the museum. (Subjects: Historical; Textbooks)

**HASTINGS-ON-HUDSON**

**Hastings-on-Hudson Public Library (NHas)**
Seven Maple Ave.
Hastings-on-Hudson, NY 10706
contact: Elaine Mittelgluck, Librarian

*Michael Jasper Gioia Collection of Children's Books*
This special collection was created to perpetuate the memory of Michael Jasper Gioia, son of Dana and Mary Gioia, who died suddenly at the age of four months from SIDS. The intent of the memorial is to benefit the children of Hastings-on-Hudson. To this end, a collection of books written and illustrated by authors and illustrators born in Hastings was assembled. Included are James Howe, Judith Seixas, Ed Young, and Charlotte Zolotow, among others. (Subject: New York—Authors and Illustrators)

## HEMPSTEAD

**Hempstead Public Library (NHem)**
115 Nichols Ct.
Hempstead, NY 11550
phone: 516-481-6990
fax: 516-481-6719
contact: Rosalie Zacharias, Head of
Children's Services

### Children's Foreign Language Collection

This collection of over 2,500 volumes includes books in Italian, French, Greek, Chinese, Japanese, Korean, Cambodian, Russian, Punji, Arabic, Polish, Portugese, Spanish, and many others. The works date from 1967 to the present and consist mainly of fiction. (Subject: Foreign Languages)

**Hofstra University (NHemH)**
**University Library - West Campus**
619 Fulton Ave.
Hempstead, NY 11550-4575
phone: 516-463-6409
fax: 516-463-6438
contact: Barbara M. Kelly, Curator
e-mail:libspbmk@vaxc.Hofstra.edu
Internet: vaxa@hofstra.edu (username:
Library)
catalog status: OCLC, RLIN

### Hofstra University Collection of Children's Literature

This collection consists of 1,000 books and anthologies of recreational reading published for children from 1825 to 1940. This collection parallels their Nilda B. Smith Collection, which centers on instructional reading materials, rather than those read for pure enjoyment. (Subject: Historical)

### Nila B. Smith Historical Collection in Reading

This collection contains 2,500 volumes used in reading instruction in America from 1620 to 1950. Included are instructional materials from hornbooks to basal readers, along with workbooks, peripherals, and teacher's manuals. (Subjects: Reading; Textbooks)

## HYDE PARK

**Franklin D. Roosevelt Library (NHyF)**
511 Albany Post Rd.
Hyde Park, NY 12538
phone: 914-229-8114
contact: Sheryl Griffith, Librarian
catalog status: Cataloged

### Nineteenth-Century American Juvenile Literature

The juvenile collection in the Roosevelt Library contains some 500 items dating from the late eighteenth to the early twentieth centuries. Most are American imprints, but some British, French, and German works are included. While all 500 items were collected by President Roosevelt, nearly 100 of the books are from his childhood library. Other items include 268 chapbooks, moral tales of the various tract societies, and rare imprints from New York, Massachusetts, New Hampshire, Connecticut, Maryland, and Rhode Island. (Subjects: Chapbooks; Historical)

## ITHACA

**Cornell University (NIC)**
**Carl A. Kroch Library**
**Division of Rare & Manuscript**
  **Collections**
Ithaca, NY 14853-5302
phone: 607-255-3530
fax: 607-255-9524
contact: Mark Dimunation, Curator of
Rare Books
catalog status: RLIN, NOTIS

### Special Collections

Although the Cornell University Library does not maintain a special collection in children's literature as such, their collections do contain many holdings important to the study of children's literature.

They include a large collection of books and manuscripts of Rudyard Kipling; a large collection of books in variant editions and bindings of George Alfred Henty; the principal collection of E. B. White, including manuscripts, letters, and published books; some early editions of children's books written by Lydia Maria Child; and the papers and illustrations of Newbery recipient Hendrik Willem van Loon. In addition, the Department of Rare Books in Olin Library houses many significant editions published from the eighteenth through the twentieth centuries. (Subjects: Henty, George Alfred; Historical; Kipling, Rudyard; Manuscript/Illustration Material; Van Loon, Hendrik; White, E. B.)

## JAMAICA

**Queens Borough Public Library (NJQ)\*\***
**Central Library**
89-11 Merrick Blvd.
Jamaica, NY 11432
phone: 718-990-0700
fax: 718-658-8342

### Augusta Baker Black Heritage Reference Collection

This collection includes 2,000 titles of nineteenth- and twentieth-century fiction, fairy and folktales, and series books. Also included are 400 African-American titles. (Subjects: Folk and Fairy Tales; Historical; Multiculturalism; Series Books)

**St. John's University (NNStJ)**
8000 Utopia Pkwy.
Jamaica, NY 11439
phone: 718-990-6737
fax: 718-380-0353
contact: Szilvia E. Szmuk, Librarian
catalog status: OCLC, local online catalog

### Children's Historical Collection

The core of this collection was donated by Anne Thaxter Eaton and consists of 250 volumes, primarily representing the nineteenth century. Included are Caldecott picturebooks, McGuffey readers, fables, and fairy tales. Another 300 volumes of twentieth-century illustrated books have recently been added to this collection. In its entirety, the collection represents a good cross-section of the variety and types of educational and recreational storybooks, primers, novels, and periodicals available to children of the past century. (Subjects: Historical; Illustration in Children's Books; Textbooks)

## MALONE

**Franklin County Historical and Museum Society (NMalo)\*\***
Library
51 Milwaukee St.
Malone, NY 12953
phone: 518-483-2750

### Alice Wilder Collection

Contains letters of the James Wilder family from 1872 to 1880. (Subject: Wilder, Laura Ingalls)

### Eliza Jane Wilder Collection

Includes family letters written between 1890 and 1916. (Subject: Wilder, Laura Ingalls)

## NEW YORK

**Chatham Square Regional Branch Library (NN-BrC)**
**New York Public Library**
33 East Broadway
New York, NY 10002
phone: 212-964-6598
fax: 212-385-7850
contact: Virginia Swift, Regional Librarian

## Chinese Heritage Collection

This collection includes reference and circulating materials in Chinese and English on Chinese history, culture, literature, and language. Special attention is given to the Chinese experience in the United States. Included are about 3,000 Chinese-language books for children, with emphasis on picture books, fairy tales, stories, and general nonfiction. (Subject: Chinese Language)

## Children's Book Council (NNCbc)

568 Broadway, Suite 404
New York, NY 10012
phone: 212-966-1990
fax: 212-966-2073
contact: Paula Quint, President

### Library

The collection at the Children's Book Council consists of critical and historical studies, books about authors and illustrators, facsimile editions, books on publishing, publishers' catalogs, and vertical file materials. They also have 200 periodical titles, 7,000 volumes published during the preceding two years, a complete set of Children's Book Week Posters, and winners of several major book awards. (Subjects: Award Books; Children's Book Week Posters; Children's Literature, Study of; Historical—20th Century; Periodicals)

## Columbia University (NNC)
## Rare Book and Manuscript Library
## Butler Library

535 W. 114th St., Sixth Floor
New York, NY 10027
phone: 212-854-2231
fax: 212-222-0331
contact: Rudolph Ellenbogen, Curator of
  Rare Books
e-mail: ellenbog@columbia.edu
Internet: columbianet.cc.columbia.edu
catalog status: RLIN, CLIO

### Arthur Rackham Collection

This collection includes over 400 English and American first editions and printed ephemera, original letters from Rackham and letters relating to him, manuscripts, documents, and notebooks. Of special note are thirty original sketchbooks and more than 500 original drawings, watercolors, and oil paintings. Also included are the proofs of Derek Hudson's *Arthur Rackham: His Life and Work.* (Subjects: Manuscript/Illustration Material; Rackham, Arthur)

*Publications: Arthur Rackham: His Life and Work,* by Derek Hudson. New York: Scribner's, 1960. *Century of Arthur Rackham's Birth, September 19, 1867; An Appreciation of His Genius and a Catalogue of His Original Sketches, Drawings, and Paintings in the Berol Collection,* by Ronald Baughman. New York: Columbia University Libraries, 1967.

### Frances Henne Collection

This collection consists of 3,100 American and English children's books, the largest group being McLoughlin Brothers imprints. Spanning from the late eighteenth century, the collection is well represented by nineteenth-century imprints and twentieth-century titles from popular trade series. These materials are uncataloged and therefore not accessible through RLIN. (Subjects: Children's Literature, Study of; Historical; McLoughlin Brothers; Popular Culture Materials)

### Historical Collection of Children's Literature

Although primarily English-language, other European and Asian languages are represented in this historical grouping. Most of the 10,000 volumes were printed between the eighteenth and twentieth centuries, with some dating from the early 1600s. The collection is composed of representative and rare or unusual items. The Velma V. Varner, Bertha Gunterman, and

Mabel Louise Robinson collections are included under the auspices of this larger collection. Also included are 450 periodical titles dating mainly from the nineteenth century, the majority of which are English-language publications. (Subjects: Bannerman, Helen; Bibles and Books of Religious Instruction; Foreign Languages; Historical; Periodicals)

### L. Frank Baum Collection

This collection of material by and about L. Frank Baum is an adjunct to the collection of first editions of Baum's writings made by Roland O. Baughman over a period of many years. An important part of the collection consists of the correspondence and papers related to the centenary exhibition mounted at the Columbia University Libraries in 1956. Also included are forty-two illustrations by W. W. Denslow. (Subjects: Baum, Lyman Frank; Denslow, William Wallace; Manuscript/Illustration Material)

*Publication: L. Frank Baum: The Wonderful Wizard of Oz; An Exhibition of His Published Writings, in Commemoration of the Centenary of His Birth, May 16, 1956.* Columbia University Libraries, January 16–March 16, 1956. [Arranged and described by Joan Baum and Roland Baughman, Department of Special Collections, Columbia University Libraries, New York, 1956]

### Plimpton Library

The Plimpton Library comprises two collections: (1) 5,000 textbooks in English, French, Latin, and other foreign languages, and (2) 200 European and 750 American imprints of juvenile materials. Of special interest are the ABC books, primers, catechisms, battledores, hornbooks, and textbooks. Imprint dates from the sixteenth century to the early twentieth century. (Subjects: Alphabet Books; Historical; Hornbooks and Battledores; Textbooks)

### Tibor Gergely Papers

Correspondence, manuscripts, drawings, watercolors, sketches, proofs, and printed materials of the Hungarian-born painter and illustrator. Included are some 200 watercolors, fifty-eight pen-and-ink drawings, and nearly 3,000 sketches. (Subjects: Gergely, Tibor; Manuscript/Illustration Material)

### Walter Farley Papers

The Farley Papers contain notes, outlines, drafts, typescripts, editorial correspondence, and reviews of twenty novels from *The Black Stallion*, published in 1941, through *The Great Dane Thor*, published in 1966. (Subjects: Farley, Walter; Manuscript/Illustration Material)

## French Institute/Alliance Française (NNFI)

22 East 60th St.
New York, NY 10022
phone: 212-355-6100
fax: 212-935-4119
contact: Fred J. Gitner, Library Director
catalog status: Cataloged

### Library

Within the holdings of the French Institute are some 1,500 late nineteenth- and early twentieth-century children's books in French. A small collection of children's recordings in French are also included. (Subjects: French Language; Recordings)

## Metropolitan Museum of Art (NNMMA-U)

1000 Fifth Ave.
New York, NY 10028-0198
phone: 212-570-3788
fax: 212-570-3972
contact: Mary Grace Whalen, Associate Museum Librarian
catalog status: RLIN

*Ruth and Harold D. Uris Library and Resource Center*

The library's collection of 800 books, periodicals, and videotapes offers readers of all ages a range of interpretive materials concerning the museum's exhibitions and permanent collections. In addition, curriculum resources specifically for teachers are collected. They include state and local curricula, federal education reports, materials from other New York City museums, and publications that assist teachers to incorporate art and art history into their classroom activities. (Subject: Art; Art Education)

**Museum of the City of New York (NNMus)**
Fifth Avenue at 103rd St.
New York, NY 10029
phone: 212-534-1672
fax: 212-534-5974
contact: Curator of the Toy Collection

*Children's Books Collection*

This collection consists of 1,000 children's books, dating from 1750 to 1970. Also included are ten nineteenth-century periodical titles. Special subjects include the history of New York and Christmas. (Subjects: Christmas; Historical; New York)

**New York Historical Society (NHi)**
170 Central Park West
New York, NY 10024
phone: 212-873-3400
fax: 212-875-1591
catalog status: RLIN

*Children's Literature Collection*

This collection of 2,300 volumes consists largely of eighteenth- and nineteenth-century books, most with U.S. or British imprints, with American works of the nineteenth century being predominant. Holdings also include thirty-nine periodical titles. A feature of the collection are McLoughlin Brothers woodblocks and an extensive collection of published books. (Subjects: Historical; McLoughlin Brothers; Periodicals; Woodblocks)

**New York Public Library (NN-BrCo)**
**Countee Cullen Regional Branch**
104 W. 136th St.
New York, NY 10030
phone: 212-491-2070
fax: 212-491-6541
contact: Heather Caines, Supervising
    Assistant Branch Librarian/Children's
    Specialist
catalog status: Cataloged

*James Weldon Johnson Memorial Collection*

A grouping of nearly 2,000 current children's books about the African-American experience. It is kept on permanent reserve for use in the Countee Cullen Children's Room and reflects the titles listed in the current edition of *The Black Experience in Children's Books*, a publication issued every five years by the New York Public Library. As new editions of *The Black Experience* are published, titles from the previous edition are sent to the Schomburg Center for Research in Black Culture. (Subject: Multiculturalism)

**New York Public Library (NN-Don)**
**Donnell Library Center**
**Central Children's Room**
20 West 53rd St.
New York, NY 10019
phone: 212-621-0636
fax: 212-245-5272
contact: Angeline Moscatt, Supervising
    Librarian
Internet: nypl.gate.nypl.org
catalog status: OCLC, ONLICATS

### Central Children's Room

A comprehensive collection, both current and retrospective, of 55,000 volumes for reference use which reflect the historical development of children's literature. In-depth coverage is given to picture books, juvenile book illustration, folklore, poetry, and fiction. Of special interest to researchers are the bibliographies, information on children's authors and artists, book reviews, and indexes. Special holdings include the five stuffed animals that inspired the writing of *Winnie the Pooh*. International children's book publishing is represented by the more than 9,000 volumes in more than forty languages. The "Old Book Collection" of some 2,000 volumes features early American and English children's books from the eighteenth and nineteenth centuries. Also included are manuscripts and illustrations from some forty children's authors and artists. A listening collection of records and cassettes highlighting storytelling is also available. (Subjects: Too numerous to list)

**New York Public Library (NN-Rb)**
**Rare Books and Manuscript Division**
Fifth Avenue and 42nd St.
New York, NY 10018-2788
phone: 212-930-0805
fax: 212-302-4815
contact: Virginia L. Bartow, Curator of
    Rare Books and the Arents
    Collections

*Publication: Guide to the Research Collections of the New York Public Library*, by Sam P. Williams. Chicago: American Library Assn., 1975.

### Arents Collection

Includes original drawings of nineteenth-century artists such as Kate Greenaway, Randolph Caldecott, and the Cruikshanks. (Subject: Manuscript/Illustration Material)

### C. C. Darton Collection

This collection contains 427 titles from the late eighteenth to the mid-nineteenth centuries. (Subject: Historical)

*Publication: A Checklist of the C. C. Darton Collection of Children's Books*, by C. C. Darton. London: G. Michelmore & Co., ca. 1930.

### Library

Contains 11,000 titles, primarily fiction, from the nineteenth and twentieth centuries. (Subject: Historical)

### Schatski Collection

Contains 700 titles from the seventeenth to nineteenth centuries, primarily German with some French and English volumes. (Subjects: German Language; Historical)

### Spencer Collection

This collection consists of illustrated books from all periods and cultures from about 800 A.D. to the present, including manuscript materials and original illustrations for a number of English and American children's books of the nineteenth and twentieth centuries. (Subjects: Historical; Illustration of Children's Books; Manuscript/Illustration Material)

**New York Public Library (NN-BrR)**
**Riverside Branch**
127 Amsterdam Ave. at 65th St.
New York, NY 10023
phone: 212-870-1634
fax: 212-870-1819
contact: Elizabeth Long, Senior
    Children's Librarian

### Children's Performing Arts Collection

In September 1992, the Children's Collection of the Performing Arts Library at Lincoln Center moved across the street into a new building where they combined with the existing Riverside Branch Library. It is now a general children's room with emphasis on the performing arts. Included are 3,000 books about theater, children's plays, dance, songbooks, history of music and musical instruments, puppetry, circus, magic, and storytelling, with a large collection of fairy tales. Much of the material is geared toward teachers and adults working with children. In addition, there are audiocassettes, LPs, and videocassettes. (Subjects: Folk and Fairy Tales; Performing Arts; Puppetry)

**New York Public Library (NN-Sc)**
**Schomburg Center for Research in Black Culture**
**Manuscripts, Archives and Rare Books Division**
515 Malcolm X Blvd.
New York, NY 10037-1801
phone: 212-491-2224
fax: 212-491-6760
contact: Diana Lachatanere, Curator
catalog status: RLIN

### Library

Although the Schomburg Center does not have a children's collection per se, they do have manuscript collections for author/illustrator John L. Steptoe and librarian/author Regina M. Andrews. Books published from 1890 to the 1930s are also included. (Subjects: Andrews, Regina M.; Manuscript/Illustration Material; Steptoe, John L.)

**New York University (NNU-F)**
**Fales Library**
70 Washington Square South
New York, NY 10012
phone: 212-998-2596
fax: 212-995-4070
contact: Marvin Taylor, Fales Librarian
e-mail: taylorm@elmer1.bobst.nyu.edu
Internet: bobcat@elmer1.bobst.nyu.edu
catalog status: RLIN

### Alfred C. Berol Collection of Lewis Carroll

Collected by Alfred C. Berol, this is one of the largest collections of materials about the life and writings of Lewis Carroll. It compares favorably to the collections at Oxford University and at the British Library. It includes over 650 books, periodicals, manuscripts, autograph letters, photographs, and pieces of ephemera relating to Carroll. It is especially strong in materials relating to *Alice in Wonderland* and the many adaptations and theatrical performances of the work. An unpublished finding aid is available in the library. (Subjects: Carroll, Lewis; Manuscript/Illustration Material)

### Fales Collection

A major collection of British and American novels printed from the middle of the eighteenth century to the present. The collection of 150,000 volumes is not limited to rare editions and is rich in background material and research resources. In English literature all major and minor nineteenth-century authors are comprehensively represented. The collection is especially strong in the works of Charles Dickens, George A. Henty, William Thackery, and Charlotte Yonge, among many others. Many children's authors are scattered among the nineteenth-century holdings. (Subjects: Cruikshank, George; Dickens, Charles; Henty, George Alfred; Historical; Tenniel, John; Yonge, Charlotte Mary)

*Publication: Charles Dickens in the Fales Library*, by J. W. Egerer. New York: New York University Libraries, 1965.

### Levy Dime Novel Collection

The Levy Dime Novel Collection comprises more than 15,000 printed items, including story papers, periodicals, clothbound novels, and a large number of paperback series of American popular fiction from the end of the nineteenth century. An unpublished finding aid is available in the library. (Subject: Dime Novels)

### Nelson Adkins Collection of American Literature

This collection contains 500 volumes of American fiction and is rich in minor works by American authors of the nineteenth and early twentieth centuries. A large number of children's books, including prize books, gift books, etc., are held in the collection. The books are cataloged in the main NYU card catalog. (Subjects: Annuals and Gift Books; Historical)

**The Pierpont Morgan Library (NNPM)**
29 East 36th St.
New York, NY 10016
phone: 212-685-0008
fax: 212-685-4740
contact: Anna Lou Ashby, Associate
   Curator of Printed Books & Bindings
e-mail: bm.pmv@rlg.bitnet (or)
   bm.pmv@rlg.stanford.edu
catalog status: RLIN

### Early Children's Book Collection

Approximately 10,000 early children's books and related works from the third century A.D. to the early twentieth century, principally English, Continental, and American. In addition to works acquired by Pierpont Morgan and his son, J. P. Morgan, Jr., and subsequent curators, the collection includes the 1965 Elisabeth Ball gift of English and French books (the Gumuchian copies); the 1987 Gordon N. Ray bequest of English and French literature and illustrated books, primarily nineteenth and twentieth centuries with children's books and minor fiction read by juveniles; the Arthur A. Houghton Lewis Carroll collection (1987) of printed books, letters, photographs, and objects; and the 1991 gift of 1,400 volumes from the collection of Miss Julia P. Wightman, including boxed library sets, toy books, and pop-up books. Manuscript materials include such masterpieces as Perrault's *Contes de ma Mere l'Oye* (1659), Thackeray's *The Rose and the Ring* (1853–54), and Saint-Exupery's *Little Prince* (ca. 1943); letters from Beatrix Potter to Noel Moore and a sketch of her ideas for a first Peter Rabbit board game; and original illustrations by Charles Bennett, Randolph Caldecott, Richard Doyle, Harry Furniss, Kate Greenaway, Beatrix Potter, and John Tenniel. (Subjects: Bennett, Charles; Caldecott, Randolph; Carroll, Lewis; Doyle, Richard; French Language; Historical; Illustration in Children's Books; Lawson, Robert; Manuscript/Illustration Material; Perrault, Charles; Potter, Beatrix; Toy and Movable Books)

*Publications: In August Company: The Collections of the Pierpont Morgan Library.* New York: The Pierpont Morgan Library, 1993. *Early Children's Books and Their Illustration,* by Gerald Gottlieb. New York: The Pierpont Morgan Library, and Boston: David R. Godine, 1975. *Lewis Carroll and Alice, 1832–1982,* by Morton N. Cohen. [New York]: The Pierpont Morgan Library, 1982. Catalog of an exhibition drawn primarily from the Arthur A. Houghton collection. *Be Merry and Wise: The Early Development of English Children's Books,* by Felix DeMarez Oyens and Brian Alderson (to be published in 1995).

## POUGHKEEPSIE

**Vassar College (NPV)\*\***
Library
P.O. Box 20, Raymond Ave.
Poughkeepsie, NY 12601-6198
phone: 914-437-5760
fax: 914-437-7187

### Special Collections

Within the Special Collections Department are some 8,000 volumes, published in the eighteenth and early nineteenth centuries, including hornbooks and chapbooks. (Subject: Historical)

## ROCHESTER

**University of Rochester (NRU)\*\***
**Rush Rhees Library**
Wilson Blvd.
Rochester, NY 14627
phone: 716-275-4461
fax: 716-273-1032

### Rare Books and Special Collections

Within the special collections are 2,000 volumes, with strength in nineteenth-century American titles, particularly those by publisher Mahlon Day. Holdings include a complete run of *St. Nicholas*. (Subjects: Day, Mahlon; Historical)

## SYRACUSE

**Syracuse University (NSyU)**
**Special Collections Dept.**
600 Bird Library
Syracuse, NY 13244-2010
phone: 315-443-2697
fax: 315-443-9510
contact: Mark F. Weimer, Curator of
    Special Collections
e-mail: Arents1@hawk.syr.edu
Internet: telnet ascnet.syr.edu (summit,
    vt100, summit)
catalog status: RLIN, local online
    catalog

### Special Collections

The Special Collections at Syracuse University has diverse holdings of both monographic and manuscript materials that pertain to children's literature. In addition to a small collection of historical children's books, they have extensive holdings for the American Book Company and the E. P. Dutton Company. Included are the firms' published books, business records, author files, publication listings, production and publicity files, photographs, and illustrations. Six authors and illustrators are represented with manuscript collections, including typescripts, correspon-

dence, illustrations, and sketches, as well as examples of their published books. (Subjects: American Book Company; Artzybasheff, Boris Miklailovich; Baum, Lyman Frank; Bontemps, Arna; Dutton, E. P; Garis, Howard; Hearn, Lafcadio; Historical; Lenski, Lois; Manuscript/Illustration Material; Sandoz, Mari; Textbooks; Twain, Mark)

## WATKINS GLEN

**American Life Foundation and Study**
    **Institute (NWat)\*\***
Old Irelandville
Watkins Glen, NY 14891
phone: 607-535-4737

### Library

The institute's holdings consist of 2,700 books from 1800 to the 1950s, including picture books, comics, and early textbooks. Also in the Ruth S. Freeman Picture Book Collection are more than 1,000 volumes and manuscripts, typescripts, and research notes of Ruth Freeman. (Subjects: Freeman, Ruth; Historical; Illustration in Children's Books)

## WESTBURY

**Westbury Memorial Public Library**
    **(NWe)**
374 School St.
Westbury, NY 11590
phone: 516-333-0176
contact: Ann T. Maria, Children's
    Librarian

### Old English and American Children's Books

Holdings include more than 1,500 volumes of children's literature dating from 1774 to the present. Included are seventy chapbooks, complete runs of several periodical titles, an extensive collection of dolls and games, and original artwork of several prominent illustrators. (Subjects: Chapbooks; Historical; Manuscript/Illustration Material; Toys)

# North Carolina

## CHAPEL HILL

**University of North Carolina at Chapel Hill (NcU)**
**Wilson Library, CB#3936**
**Rare Book Collection**
Chapel Hill, NC 27514-8890
phone: 919-962-1143
fax: 919-962-4452
contact: Libby Chenault, Rare Book Collection Librarian for Public Services
e-mail: chenault@gibbs.oit.unc.edu
catalog status: Cataloged

### Kellam Collection of The Night before Christmas

This collection of 1,000 items printed from 1823 to the present includes various printings of "The Night before Christmas" by Clement Clarke Moore, parodies of the poem, information about the author, and Christmas memorabilia. The collection is frequently exhibited and is available to scholars year-round. (Subjects: Christmas; Moore, Clement Clarke)

## CHARLOTTE

**University of North Carolina at Charlotte (NcCU)**
**Atkins Library**
**Special Collections Unit**
Charlotte, NC 28223
phone: 704-547-2449
fax: 704-547-3050
contact: Robin Brabham, Special Collections Librarian
e-mail: ali00rfb@unccvm.uncc.edu
Internet: TN152.15.100.90
catalog status: OCLC

### Special Collections Unit

Within the Special Collections unit there are 1,000 volumes of children's literature dating from 1780. The books, primarily published in the United States and Great Britain, include fiction, textbooks, periodicals, and boys' series books. Of special interest are antebellum and Civil War–era North Carolina imprints. Also included are manuscript materials of several North Carolina authors, as well as books from collector Wilbur Macy Stone. (Subjects: Award Books; Comic Books; Gillett, Mary; Historical; Hopkins, Lila; Hurmence, Belinda; Manuscript/Illustration Material; North Carolina—Authors and Illustrators; North Carolina Imprints; Series Books; Stone, Wilbur Macey; Textbooks; Tucker, Bruce)

## DURHAM

**Duke University (NcD)**
**Special Collections Library**
Box 90185
Durham, NC 27708
phone: 919-660-5820
fax: 919-684-2855
contact: Linda McCurdy, Assistant Director for Research Services
Internet: ducatalog.lib.duke.edu
catalog status: OCLC, local online catalog

### Juvenile Literature

The Juvenile Literature Collection holdings contain over 500 volumes from the eighteenth through twentieth centuries. Particular strengths are in Edwardian literature for boys and German Nazi literature for children. (Subjects: Historical; Nazi Literature)

## GREENSBORO

**University of North Carolina at Greensboro (NcGU)**
**Walter Clinton Jackson Library**
Greensboro, NC 27412
phone: 910-334-5246
fax: 910-334-5399
contact: Emilie Mills, Special Collections Librarian
Internet: telnet steffi.uncg.edu (username: jaclin)
catalog status: OCLC, DRA (JACLIN+)

*Early Juvenile Books Collection*

In 1968, Lois Lenski presented her collection of 700 early children's books to the library, forming the nucleus of the juvenile book collection. Since the Lenski gift, additional rare titles dating from the 1750s have been added, bringing the total collection to 1,800 titles. Included are examples of American textbooks published before 1850, chapbooks, battledores, hornbooks, New England primers, and miniature books, as well as publications of John Newbery, John Marshall, and Isaiah Thomas. In addition, a collection of more than 350 girls' series books dating from the late 1800s to the 1950s represents 280 different series titles. (Subjects: Historical; Series Books; Textbooks)

*Manuscript Collection
of Children's Books*

This collection includes original holographs, typescripts, illustrations, photographs, correspondence, published books, toys, and artifacts of ten North Carolina authors and illustrators of children's literature. In addition, 230 books and twelve linear feet of manuscript materials—including drawings, watercolors, photographs, research notebooks, bibliographies, and toys of Lois Lenski—are held. (Subjects: Bell, Thelma and Corydon; Burgwyn, Mebane H.; Carroll, Ruth and Latrobe; Forbus, Ina B.; Lenski, Lois; Manuscript/Illustration Material; North

Carolina—Authors and Illustrators; Perry, Octavia Jordan; Rowlett, Margaret; Street, Julia Montgomery; Tippett, James S.; Toys)

# Ohio

## ATHENS

**Ohio University (OAU)\*\***
**Vernon R. Alden Library**
Park Place
Athens, OH 45701-2978
phone: 614-593-2703
fax: 614-593-2959

*Children's Literature Historical Collection*

This collection consists of 1,400 volumes by American and English authors, dating from 1870 to 1930. Included are numerous series books and seventy-eight McGuffey readers. Several nineteenth-century periodical titles are held. (Subjects: Abbott, Jacob; Alger, Horatio; Ewing, Juliana Horatia; Finley, Martha; Henty, George Alfred; Historical; Series Books; Textbooks)

## BLUFFTON

**Bluffton College (OBlC-M)\*\***
**Musselman Library**
Bluffton, OH 45817-1195
phone: 419-358-3272

*Mennonite Historical Library*

This library holds 125 volumes, published from 1930 to the present and relating to the Mennonite and Amish churches, and Church of the Brethren. Periodical titles are included. (Subject: Bibles and Books of Religious Instruction)

## BOWLING GREEN

**Bowling Green State University (OBgU)**
**Jerome Library**
Bowling Green, OH 43403
phone: 419-372-2450
fax: 419-372-7996
contact: Alison M. Scott, Head Librarian
e-mail: ascott@andy.bgsu.edu
Internet: bglink.bgsu.edu
catalog status: OCLC, online catalog

*Popular Culture Library*

The Popular Culture Library was created in 1969 to support the university's innovative program in cultural studies. This repository is dedicated to acquiring and preserving primary research materials on nineteenth- and twentieth-century American popular culture. Of particular interest for children's literature are more than 100 Big Little Books, dime novels, over 42,000 issues of twentieth-century comic books, more than 750 volumes of nineteenth- and twentieth-century boys' and girls' series books, and 250 historic children's books. Holdings also include the Allen and John Saunders collection which is composed of correspondence and reader mail, clippings, photographs, scripts, artwork, proof sheets, and other materials relating to newspaper comic strips dating from 1909 to 1986. (Subjects: Big Little Books; Comic Books; Historical; Manuscript/Illustration Material; Popular Culture Materials; Saunders, Allen and John; Series Books)

**Rare Books and Special Collections**
**Center for Archival Collections**
phone: 419-372-2411
fax: 419-372-0155
contact: Lee N. McLaird, Curator of
   Rare Books
e-mail: lmclair@opie.bgsu.edu

The holdings of the Rare Books and Special Collections Center includes: manuscripts, galley proofs, illustrations, mock-ups, correspondence, speeches, and memorabilia. (Subjects: Manuscript/Illustration Material; Wahl, Jan)

## CINCINNATI

**Hebrew Union College/Jewish**
   **Institution of Religion (OCH)\*\***
**Klau Library**
3101 Clifton Ave.
Cincinnati, OH 45220-2488
phone: 513-221-1875
fax: 513-221-0321

*Library*

Included are a significant number of children's works concerning the Bible, Zionism, Israel, Jewish history, and the Holocaust. Most titles are in Hebrew or English. Also included are a large number of juvenile Jewish periodical titles. (Subjects: Bible and Books of Religious Instruction; Hebraic Language; Judaica; Periodicals)

**Public Library of Cincinnati and**
   **Hamilton County (OC)\*\***
**Library Square**
800 Vine St.
Cincinnati, OH 45202-2071
phone: 513-369-6900
fax: 513-369-6067

*Cincinnati Schoolbook Collection*

Includes textbooks published in Cincinnati during the nineteenth century, including McGuffey readers and Ray's arithmetics. (Subject: Textbooks)

*George Cruikshank Collection*

Included are 206 volumes of Cruikshank's *Fairy Library* and the first issue of Grimms' *German Popular Stories* (and proofs of the plates). Periodical titles are included. (Subject: Cruikshank, George)

*Jean Alva Goldsmith Collection*

The Goldsmith Collection of 3,800 volumes includes battledores, hornbooks, and foreign-language titles. Original illustrations, figurines, and dolls from Robert McCloskey's *One Morning in Maine* are held. (Subjects: Historical; McCloskey, Robert; Toys)

### Peter G. Thomson and Children's Book Collection

This collection contains 100 volumes of chromolithographic-paper-wrapped booklets published in the 1800s. Included are three volumes of original sketches used to illustrate the booklets. (Subjects: Historical; Illustration of Children's Books)

### Rare Books

Included in the Rare Books Department are extensive runs of series books, 245 volumes of Frank and Dick Merriwell, 550 issues of comic books from the 1950s and 1960s, twenty-five volumes of moralistic tales, and poetry from the 1830s. (Subjects: Comic Books; Dime Novels; Series Books)

## Xavier University (OCX)
**Xavier University Library**
3800 Victory Pkwy.
Cincinnati, OH 45207
phone: 513-745-3881
fax: 513-745-1932
contact: Elaine Cheng, ILL Librarian
e-mail: Cheng@xavier.xu.edu
catalog status: Cataloged Innovative Interfaces

### Father Francis J. Finn Collection

This collection consists of 683 items, including books, short stories, sermons, dramas, lectures, diaries, and poems. (Subject: Finn, Francis J.)

## CLEVELAND

**Cleveland Public Library (OCl)**
**Children's Literature Department**
325 Superior Ave., N.E.
Cleveland, OH 44114
phone: 216-623-2834
fax: 216-623-7015
contact: Ruth Hadlow, Head of Children's Literature
e-mail: chliti@library.cpl.org
Internet: library.cpl.org
catalog status: OCLC, CLEVNET

### Children's Literature Department: Special Holdings

Included are 8,000 juvenile fiction titles published from 1900 through 1960, a collection of nineteenth- and early twentieth-century periodicals, and a collection of early editions of, and books about, *Alice in Wonderland*. (Subjects: Carroll, Lewis; Historical—20th Century; Periodicals)

**Cleveland Public Library (OCl-RB)**
**Special Collections Department, Rare Books**
325 Superior Ave., N.E.
Cleveland, OH 44114
phone: 216-623-2818
fax: 216-623-7050
contact: Alice N. Loranth, Head of Fine Arts & Special Collections
e-mail: fine3@library.cpl.org
Internet: library.cpl.org
catalog status: OCLC, CLEVENET

### John G. White Collection of Folklore

The White Collection consists of 761 volumes of the Arabian Nights in fifty-seven languages, 757 volumes of *Robin Hood*, and over 3,000 chapbooks in English, Germanic, Romance, and Slavic languages. (Subjects: Arabian Nights; Chapbooks; Folk and Fairy Tales; Robin Hood)

*Special Collections Department, Rare Books: Children's Literature Collection*

Within the rare book holdings are 1,500 nineteenth- and early twentieth-century children's books, primarily in English. (Subject: Historical)

**Cleveland Public Library (OCl-FL)**
325 Superior Ave., N.E.
Cleveland, OH 44114
phone: 216-623-2895
fax: 216-623-7015
contact: Karen D. Long, Head of
    Foreign Literature
e-mail: forlit4@library.cpl.org
Internet: library.cpl.org
catalog status: OCLC, CLEVENET

*Foreign Literature Department*

Special holdings in children's literature include nearly 9,000 nineteenth- and twentieth-century juvenile titles in thirty-four languages. Also held are audiocassettes of children's books in a variety of languages, including French, German, Greek, Japanese, Russian, Spanish, and Ukrainian. (Subject: Foreign Languages)

**COLUMBUS**

**Ohio Historical Society (OHi)**
1982 Velma Ave.
Columbus, OH 43211-2497
phone: 614-297-2510
fax: 614-297-2546
contact: Stephen Gutgesell, Head,
    Library Services Department
catalog status: OCLC

*Archives/Library Division*

The Ohio Historical Society holdings include 800 volumes of textbooks from the latter half of the nineteenth century, including McGuffey Readers, geography texts, arithmetics, and spellers. (Subject: Textbooks)

**Ohio State University (OU)**
**Edgar Dale Media Center**
260 Ramseyer Hall
29 West Woodruff Ave.
Columbus, OH 43210
phone: 614-292-1177
fax: 614-292-7900
contact: Shirley V. Morrison
catalog status: OCLC, VTLS

*Charlotte Huck Historical Collection*

The collection consists primarily of materials in English from the latter part of the nineteenth century and the first half of the twentieth century. The 800 volumes include biographical and critical studies, as well as materials written and/or illustrated by noteworthy individuals in the field of children's literature. A portion of the collection consists of facsimiles of early books. (Subjects: Children's Literature, Study of; Historical)

*Publication: Two Centuries of Children's Book Illustration: An Exhibit of the Edgar Dale Educational Media and Instructional Materials Laboratory, College of Education, Ohio State University.* Columbus: Ohio State University Libraries, 1992.

**Ohioana Library (O)**
65 South Front St.
Suite 1105
Columbus, OH 43215
phone: 614-466-3831
fax: 614-466-3831 (call)
contact: Barbara Maslekoff, Librarian
catalog status: OCLC

*Works by Ohio Writers and Illustrators*

This collection is limited to works by Ohio authors and illustrators, or about Ohio and Ohioans. Many children's titles are included in the 40,000 volumes held in the library. Also included are original manuscripts and illustrations by prominent Ohio authors and illustrators. (Subjects: Lenski, Lois; Manuscript/Illustration Material; Ohio; Ohio—Authors and Illustrators)

## DAYTON

**Wright State University (ODaWU)**
**Paul Laurence Dunbar Library**
**Special Collections and Archives**
Dayton, OH 45435
phone: 513-873-2092
fax: 513-873-2092
contact: Robert H. Smith, Head, Special
  Collections and Archives
Internet: telnet libnet.wright.edu
catalog status: OCLC, online catalog

### Arthur Rackham Collection

Special Collections and Archives houses a
special collection of children's literature
books. The core of this collection was donated by the late Mary Harbage, a professor at Wright State, and consists of over
100 rare books, illustrated by Arthur
Rackham and published from 1894 to
1974. Also included are four pieces of
original art by Rackham. In addition to
the Rackham materials, the special collections also hold children's magazines and
nearly 500 other children's historical
books. (Subjects: Historical; Manuscript/
Illustration Material; Periodicals; Rackham, Arthur)

  **Publications:** *The Arthur Rackham*
*Collection.* Mary Harbage Children's Literature Room, University Library, Wright
State University, compiled by Nancy Van-
derglas. Dayton: Wright State University,
1987.

## FINDLAY

**University of Findlay (OFiC)**
1000 N. Main St.
Findlay, OH 45840
phone: 419-424-4560
fax: 419-424-4822
contact: Jerry J. Mallett, Director

### Mazza Collection

The Mazza Collection consists of original
artwork by the most distinguished and
honored illustrators of children's books. It
has the distinction of being the only teaching gallery in the world specializing in such
art. The collection was established by Dr.
August C. Mazza and his late wife as part
of the university's centennial celebration in
the fall of 1982. Consisting of more than
300 pieces of original art, the Mazza Collection specializes in the work of contemporary American illustrators, although the
greats of historical British illustration are
represented. A listing of the artwork is
available. (Subjects: Illustration of Children's Books; Manuscript/Illustration Material)

## FREMONT

**Rutherford B. Hayes Presidential Center**
  **Library (OFH)\*\***
Spiegel Grove
1337 Hayes Ave.
Fremont, OH 43420-2796
phone: 419-332-2081

### Library

Included in the holdings of the Hayes Library are books owned by the Hayes children, as well as schoolbooks from the latter part of the nineteenth century. (Subjects:
Historical; Textbooks)

## HIRAM

**Hiram College (OHirC)\*\***
**Teachout-Price Memorial Library**
P.O. Box 98
Hiram, OH 44234-9998
phone: 216-569-5359
fax: 216-569-5491

### Children's Literature Collection

This collection contains 200 volumes dating from 1828. Some periodical titles are
included. (Subjects: Historical; Periodicals)

## KENT

Kent State University (OKentU)
University Libraries
Department of Special Collections &
  Archives
Kent, OH 44242-0001
phone: 216-672-2270
fax: 216-672-4811
contact: Dean Keller, Associate Dean of
  Libraries
e-mail: dkeller@KentVM
Internet: catalyst.kent.edu
catalog status: OCLC, online catalog

### Special Collections

Within the Special Collections Department
are a variety of materials pertinent to children's literature. The Saalfield Publishing
Company Archive contains books, games,
puzzles, activity books, manuscripts, artwork, correspondence, and business
records. More than 1,500 volumes dating
from the nineteenth century include 200
dime novels published from 1850 to 1900.
In addition, holdings include representative collections of published books and
manuscripts by Ohio authors Virginia
Hamilton and Cynthia Rylant. (Subjects:
Dime Novels; Hamilton, Virginia; Historical; Manuscript/Illustration Material; Rylant, Cynthia; Saalfield Publishing Company)

## OXFORD

Miami University (OOxM)
Miami University Libraries
Walter Havighurst Special Collections
  Library
Oxford, OH 45056
phone: 513-529-3324
fax: 513-529-3110
contact: C. Martin Miller, Head Special
  Collections & Archives
e-mail:
  cmmiller@miamiu.acs.muohio.edu
catalog status: OCLC

### E. W. and Faith King Juvenile Collection of Juvenile Literature

The collection, primarily English-language,
consists of 11,000 volumes of children's
literature dating from 1536 to the present,
with over 750 volumes published prior to
1801 and 1,550 published between 1802
and 1836. Other languages in the collection are primarily French and German.
Complete or long runs of 128 titles of
nineteenth-century periodicals and fourteen titles of twentieth-century periodicals
are in the collection. Original materials are
held for Kate Seredy and Mary M. Sherwood. (Subjects: Abbott, Jacob; Darton,
William; Harris, John; Historical; Manu-
script/Illustration Material; Periodicals;
Seredy, Kate; Sherwood, Mary Martha
Butt)

### McGuffey Collection of Readers and Spellers

This collection of 480 McGuffey readers
and spellers is the most complete collection known. It includes numerous issues
within each year, as well as foreign-language editions. The manuscript collection
of letters and sermons by William Holmes
McGuffey and his family includes a letter
from Noah Webster to McGuffey's
younger brother, Alexander. (Subjects:
Manuscript/Illustration Material; Mc-
Guffey, William; Textbooks)

### School Book Collection

The School Book Collection comprises
5,500 books, printed from 1774 to 1901,
that were used in educating American
schoolchildren. Subjects include Greek,
Latin, elocution, debate and oratory, gram-
mar and composition, readers (excluding
McGuffey readers), mathematics, etiquette, and botany, among others. The
collection provides a broad view of education primarily in the nineteenth century,
as well as the social history of education.
(Subject: Textbooks)

## SIDNEY

**Amos Memorial Public Library (OSiA)**
230 E. North St.
Sidney, OH 45365
phone: 513-492-8354
fax: 513-492-9229
contact: Bonnie Banks, Children's
Librarian
catalog status: uncataloged

### Bessie Schiff Collection

A collection of books and manuscripts created by local author Bessie Schiff (1889–1973). Included are copies of her published children's titles, unpublished works, and bound volumes of manuscripts, letters clippings, and autobiographical information. (Subjects: Manuscript/Illustration Material; Schiff, Bessie)

### Lois Lenski Collection

This collection consists of both published books and original manuscripts and illustrations. Included are ninety-three published books, sixty-four of which are autographed; more than 100 pen-and-ink illustrations, lithographs, linoleum prints, and woodcuts; eighty pieces of correspondence to, from, and about Lenski; and a variety of ephemeral items. (Subjects: Lenski, Lois; Manuscript/Illustration Material)

## SPRINGFIELD

**Warder Literacy Center (OS)\*\***
**Branch of Clark County Public Library**
137 E. High St.
Springfield, OH 45501
phone: 513-323-8617

### Library

Collection holds materials on Lois Lenski, including ninety-two published books, manuscripts, drawings, and ephemera. (Subjects: Lenski, Lois; Manuscript/Illustration Material)

# Oklahoma

## ALVA

**Northwestern Oklahoma State**
**University (OkAlvN)\*\***
**J. W. Martin Library**
601 Oklahoma Blvd.
Alva, OK 73717
phone: 405-327-1700, ext. 219

### Library

Within the library's holdings are fifteen volumes written by Harold Keith, as well as a collection of his correspondence. (Subject: Keith, Harold)

## NORMAN

**University of Oklahoma (OkU)**
**University Libraries**
401 West Brooks, Room 521
Norman, OK 73019
phone: 405-325-2741
fax: 405-325-7618
contact: Marcia M. Goodman,
Librarian; Marilyn B. Ogilvie,
Curator, History of Science
Collections
e-mail: qd3305@uokmvsa

### Lois Lenski Collection

This is an extensive collection of materials by and about Lois Lenski, containing autographed books, manuscripts, illustrations, proofs, photographs, correspondence, speeches, and related ephemeral items. (Subjects: Lenski, Lois; Manuscript/Illustration Material)

*Publication:* The Lois Lenski Collection in the University of Oklahoma Library, compiled by Esther G. Witcher. Norman: University of Oklahoma Library and the School of Library Science, 1963.

## OKLAHOMA CITY

**Metropolitan Library System in Oklahoma County (OkOk)\*\***
131 Dean A. McGee Ave.
Oklahoma City, OK 73102-6499
phone: 405-235-0571
fax: 405-236-5219

### Juvenile Special Collection

Included in this collection are books about Oklahoma, as well as those created by Oklahoma authors and illustrators. (Subjects: Oklahoma; Oklahoma—Authors and Illustrators)

**Oklahoma Department of Libraries (Ok)\*\***
200 N. E. 18th St.
Oklahoma City, OK 73105-3298
phone: 405-521-2502
fax: 405-525-7804

### Juvenile Book Evaluation Collection

This collection contains all titles listed in *Wilson's Children's Catalog* and the *Junior High School Catalog*. (Subject: Historical—20th Century)

## STILLWATER

**Oklahoma State University (OkS)**
University Library
Stillwater, OK 74078
phone: 405-744-6310
fax: 405-744-5183
contact: Jo Ann Bierman
catalog status: OCLC, NOTIS

### Curriculum Materials Laboratory

The library includes print and nonprint materials representative of a school library collection, including professional materials for teachers, textbooks, curriculum guides, audiovisual materials, journals, and posters. Special features include 355 books in seven foreign languages and a Native American collection that includes historical books about various tribes, their customs, and folklore. Also included are the winning titles for the Sequoyah Children's Book Award. (Subjects: Award Books; Foreign Languages; Native Americans)

## TULSA

**Tulsa City-County Library (OkT)**
400 Civic Center
Tulsa, OK 74103
phone: 918-596-7971
fax: 918-596-7882
Internet: aDM_lib8@VAX1.UTulsa.edu
catalog status: OCLC, NOTIS

### Children's Department Research Collection

This collection of 2,500 volumes dating from the late 1800s is maintained to provide examples of the historical development of books written for children and about children's literature. Included is a Marguerite Henry manuscript. (Subjects: Children's Literature, Study of; Henry, Marguerite; Historical; Manuscript/Illustration Material)

# Oregon

## EUGENE

**Northwest Christian College (OrENC)\*\***
Library
828 E. 11th St.
Eugene, OR 97401-9983
phone: 503-343-1641 ext. 40
fax: 503-343-9159

### Kendall Memorial Collection

This collection contains 900 titles of general and religious literature from 1888 to 1976, produced by Disciples of Christ and Churches of Christ denominations. (Subject: Bibles and Books of Religious Instruction)

**University of Oregon (OrU)**
University Libraries
Special Collections
Eugene, OR 97403-1299
phone: 503-346-3068
fax: 503-346-3094
contact: Victoria Jones, Manuscripts
  Curator
Internet: janus.uoregon.edu
catalog status: finding aids; JANUS

*Special Collections*

The Special Collections Department has extensive holdings of original materials. Materials included manuscripts, illustrations, correspondence, and related materials for 200 authors, illustrators, agents, and publishing companies. (Subjects: Too numerous to list)

**PORTLAND**

**Library Association of Portland (OrP)\*\***
801 S. W. 10th Ave.
Portland, OR 97205
phone: 503-223-7201

*Library*

Holdings include 1,000 volumes dating from 1864, including textbooks from 1834 to 1920 and books about Oregon dating from 1884 to 1937. An additional 800 volumes held by the Junior Historical Collection include eighty titles by George A. Henty. (Subjects: Henty, George Alfred; Historical; Oregon; Textbooks)

**Oregon Historical Society (OrHi)\*\***
Library
1230 S. W. Park Ave.
Portland OR 97205
phone: 503-222-1741

*Play and Leisure Collection*

Contained in this collection are toys and educational and outdoor games, representative of all periods of Oregon history, 1840 to the present. They also hold 1,500

artifacts such as games, dolls, miniatures, and puzzles. (Subjects: Games and Pastimes; Toys)

**Portland State University (OrPS)\*\***
**Bransford Price Millar Library**
934 SW Harrison
P.O. Box 1151
Portland, OR 97207-1151
phone: 503-725-4521
fax: 503-725-4524

*Library*

Included in the holdings at Portland State University are 107 volumes in Arabic and 300 titles in Hebrew, as well as several in Yiddish. Winners of the Young Readers Choice Award of the Pacific Northwest are also held. (Subjects: Arabic Language; Award Books; Hebraic Language)

# Pennsylvania

## BALA-CYNWYD

**Bala-Cynwyd Library (PBal)\*\***
Old Lancaster Rd. and North Highland
  Ave.
Bala-Cynwyd, PA 19004-3095
phone: 215-664-1196
fax: 215-664-5534

*Library*

Included are more than 2,000 volumes, dating primarily from 1850 to 1930. (Subject: Historical)

## MEADVILLE

**Crawford County Historical Society
  (PMCHi)**
848 North Main St.
Meadville, PA 16335
phone: 814-724-6080
contact: Robert D. Ilisevich

*Children's Collection*

This collection of some 200 volumes includes textbooks, series books, and folk and fairy tales, dating mainly from the mid-1800s. (Subjects: Historical; Textbooks)

## NORRISTOWN

**Montgomery County-Norristown Public Library (PNo)**
1001 Powell St.
Norristown, PA 19401-3817
phone: 610-278-5100
fax: 610-278-5110
contact: Barbara Gross, Children's Consultant/Head of Children's Services

*Carolyn Wicker Field Collection*

A noncirculating collection of children's books representing the personal collection of Carolyn Wicker Field, retired head of the Office of Work with Children of the Free Library of Philadelphia. Included are 244 children's books, many first editions and autographed, as well as nearly 200 volumes about children's literature. Also included are postcards received by Mrs. Field from the 1950s to 1990s from children's authors and illustrators. (Subjects: Award Books; Children's Literature, Study of; Historical—20th Century)

*Children's Special Collection*

Noncirculating collection of children's books meeting one or more of the following criteria: fiction series, published 1939 or earlier, school readers, complete collection of an author, first editions and second printings, autographed editions, works by significant children's authors or illustrators, Philadelphia publishers, or books of local interest. The collection also includes original illustrations by Katherine Milhous and Rosemary Wells, and manuscripts by Harriet May Savitz. (Subjects: Historical; Manuscript/Illustration Material; Milhous, Katherine; Philadelphia Im-

prints; Savitz, Harriet May; Wells, Rosemary)

## PHILADELPHIA

**Drexel University (PPD)**
**W. W. Hagerty Library**
33rd & Market Sts.
Philadelphia, PA 19104
phone: 215-895-2750
fax: 215-895-2070
contact: Ken Garson, Information Services Librarian
Internet: dulib@library.drexel.edu
(username: PAC)
catalog status: OCLC, online catalog

*Library*

Included in Drexel University's holdings is a selective collection of award-winning books, including the Newbery and Caldecott, ALA Notables, and the Coretta Scott King awards. (Subject: Award Books)

**Free Library of Philadelphia (PP)**
**Central Children's Department**
1901 Vine St.
Philadelphia, PA 19103-1189
phone: 215-686-5370
fax: 215-563-3628
contact: DianeJude L. McDowell, Head Children's Special Collections
catalog status: OCLC, CLSI

*Children's Special Collections*

These are noncirculating research collections totalling over 50,000 books, periodicals, and other items. Materials date from 1837 to the present, most being in English. The collections are divided into several distinct areas: Historical covers the broad scope of the past to today's finest books; Series include the Stratemeyer syndicate works as well as other fiction and nonfiction titles; Folklore is representative of myths, folktales, legends, Mother Goose, and other nursery rhymes from around the world; Illustrators include books revealing the changing patterns of children's book illustration; Historical Bibliography encompasses adult-level resources about children's literature; Framed Illustrations include the original artwork by well-known children's book illustrators. (Subjects: Too numerous to list)

*Publication: Checklist of Children's Books, 1837–1876*, compiled by Barbara Maxwell. Philadelphia: Special collections, Central Children's Department, Free Library of Philadelphia, 1975.

**Free Library of Philadelphia (PP-Rb)**
**Rare Book Department**
1901 Vine St.
Philadelphia, PA 19103-1189
phone: 215-686-5417
fax: 215-563-3628
contact: Cornelia S. King, Technical
    Services Librarian Supervisor I
e-mail: bm.y01@rlg
catalog status: OCLC and RLIN; CLSI

### A. B. Frost Collection

This collection contains 100 volumes of works illustrated by Frost as well as fifty illustrations. (Subjects: Frost, A. B.; Manuscript/Illustration Material)

### A. S. W. Rosenbach Collection of Early American Children's Books

The Free Library's interest in historical children's books was established with the gift by A. S. W. Rosenbach of his personal collection. Ranging in date from 1682 to 1836, the gift includes 816 volumes and encompasses the full range of books produced for children. Through gift and purchase, the collection has increased in size to 13,000 volumes. (Subjects: Abbott, Jacob; Alphabet Books; Bibles and Books of Religious Instruction; Edgeworth, Maria; Etiquette Books; German Language; Historical; Natural History; Parley, Peter; Periodicals; Sherwood, Mary Martha Butt; Textbooks; Watts, Isaac)

### American Sunday-School Union

Founded in Philadelphia in 1824, the American Sunday-School Union was the most prolific publisher of juvenile literature in nineteenth-century America. Their publications cover a wide range of subjects including history, geography, biography, natural and physical sciences, poetry, catechisms, primers, and hymn books. This collection consists of the many file copies retained by the union's Committee of Publication. Many of the 20,000 volumes in the collection, which the union presented to the Free Library in 1962, bear evidence of the committee's editorial work for subsequent editions. (Subjects: American Sunday-School Union; Bibles and Books of Religious Instruction)

### Arthur Rackham Collection

This collection embraces the entire working life of Arthur Rackham, from a guidebook in 1893 to the illustrations for *The Wind in the Willows* published in 1940, a year after his death. Included are fifty original watercolors and drawings; 500 first, limited, and variant editions; 100 manuscripts; periodical appearances; and autograph letters and ephemera. The original collection was assembled by Grace Clark Haskell, one of Rackham's bibliographers. (Subjects: Manuscript/Illustration Material; Rackham, Arthur)

### Beatrix Potter Collection

This collection includes the autograph manuscript, with the original watercolors, of *The Tailor of Gloucester*, the autograph manuscript and drawings for *Little Pig Robinson*, first editions, presentation copies, piracies, adaptations, ephemera, and over 140 watercolors and drawings from Potter's own portfolio, plus more than 75 autographed letters. (Subjects: Manuscript/Illustration Material; Potter, Beatrix)

*Publication: Beatrix Potter: A Guide to the Collection of the Rare Book Depart-*

*ment, The Free Library of Philadelphia*, by Karen J. Lightner, 1992.

### Foreign Language Collection

This is a circulating collection containing over 6,000 volumes representing fifty-four languages published in the twentieth century. Emphasis is on books in the language in which they were written, as well as translations of classics. Extensive holdings in Spanish, French, and German, as well as the Asian languages of Chinese, Japanese, Vietnamese, and Korean are included. (Subject: Foreign Languages)

### Howard Pyle and His Students Collection

Assembled by Thornton Oakley and presented to the Free Library in 1951, this collection focuses on the work of Howard Pyle and his students of the "Brandywine School." Included are first editions and periodical appearances of works by Pyle and his students, as well as some letters and notebooks. Contained in the collection are 1,000 manuscripts and 150 drawings by Pyle, N. C. Wyeth, Maxfield Parish, Elizabeth Shippen Green, Jessie Willcox Smith, Thornton Oakley, and other students. (Subjects: Green, Elizabeth Shippen; Manuscript/Illustration Material; Oakley, Thornton; Parrish, Maxfield; Pyle, Howard; Smith, Jessie Willcox; Wyeth, N. C.)

### Kate Greenaway Collection

This collection includes some 100 published volumes, twenty manuscripts, and eighty original drawings. A complete set of her Almanacks are held, as well as autographed letters and ephemera. (Subjects: Greenaway, Kate; Manuscript/Illustration Material)

### Munro Leaf Collection

The archives of Munro Leaf, Robert Lawson's colleague and frequent collaborator, is complementary to the Free Library's Robert Lawson Collection. Included are some 200 published works, twenty-five manuscripts, photographs, and other memorabilia. (Subjects: Leaf, Munro; Manuscript/Illustration Material)

### Robert Lawson Collection

Robert Lawson's work as an illustrator and author is thoroughly documented in this collection of 1,100 original drawings, dummies, early etchings, first and later editions (including his personal copies of the books), and his papers. (Subjects: Lawson, Robert; Manuscript/Illustration Material)

---

**Historical Society of Pennsylvania (PHi)**
1300 Locust St.
Philadelphia, PA 19107
phone: 215-732-6201
fax: 215-732-2680
contact: Lee Arnold, Library Director

### Library

The library holds 500,000 volumes with strengths in Pennsylvania, New Jersey, and Delaware, but primary and secondary source materials for all thirteen original states are held as well. Children's literature titles comprise 200 titles from 1790 to the early 1900s, including schoolbooks and religious tales. (Subject: Historical)

---

**Library Company of Philadelphia (PPL)**
1314 Locust St.
Philadelphia, PA 19107
phone: 215-546-3181
fax: 215-546-5167
contact: Mary Anne Hines, Chief of
   Reference
e-mail: bm.lpl@rlg.bitnet
catalog status: RLIN

### Library

The entire holdings of the library encompass 400,000 volumes representing the history and background of American culture in the eighteenth and nineteenth centuries. Children's books and works of education are included. (Subject: Historical)

**Rosenbach Museum and Library (PPRF)**
2010 DeLancey Pl.
Philadelphia, PA 19103
phone: 215-732-1600
contact: Constance Kimmerle, Assistant Curator

*Maurice Sendak Collection*

The Sendak Collection includes 400 editions of his books in various languages, 2,100 finished drawings, 800 preliminary drawings, and 700 articles tracing his career since 1947. (Subjects: Manuscript/Illustration Material; Sendak, Maurice)

**Temple University (PPT)**
Samuel Paley Library
Philadelphia, PA 19122
phone: 215-204-8230
contact: Thomas Whitehead, Head Special Collections

*Walter De La Mare Collection*

This collection includes more than 500 volumes from 1902 to date, 1,000 letters, and manuscripts with illustrations by Dorothy Lathrop. Also held are filmstrips, recordings, and portraits. (Subjects: de la Mare, Walter; Lathrop, Dorothy Pulis; Manuscript/Illustration Material)

**PITTSBURGH**

**Carnegie Library of Pittsburgh (PPi)**
4400 Forbes Ave.
Pittsburgh, PA 15213
phone: 412-622-1932
fax: 412-622-6278
e-mail: PrioreG@CLP2.ClPgh.org
contact: Gregory M. Priore, Archivist
catalog status: OCLC

*Children's Historical Collection*

This collection consists of 2,200 volumes of late nineteenth- and early twentieth-century children's books. A special strength of the collection is the folk and fairy tale literature. The Alice Wirth Wirsing Collection includes 200 volumes of illustrated children's books. (Subjects: Folk and Fairy Tales; Historical; Illustration of Children's Books)

**Carnegie-Mellon University (PPiC)**
University Libraries
4825 Frew St.
Pittsburgh, PA 15213-3890
phone: 412-268-6622
fax: 412-268-6944
contact: Mary Catharine Johnsen, Special Collections Librarian
e-mail: mjog+@andrew.cmu.edu
Internet: andrew.library.cmu.edu
catalog status: OCLC

*Anne Lyon Haight Collections of 'Twas the Night before Christmas*

Included are American editions of Clement Clarke Moore's famous poem from the earliest (in facsimile) to the present. Parodies are excluded. Emphasis is on historic editions, illustrators, and printers. Also held are collector's notes, dealer records, provenance records, and ephemera. (Subjects: Christmas; Moore, Clement Clarke)

*Publication: "The Night before Christmas": An Exhibition Catalogue,* compiled by George H. M. Lawrence. Pittsburgh: Pittsburgh Bibliophiles, 1964.

*Frances Hooper Kate Greenaway Collection*

This collection contains 230 published volumes, including duplicate and variant copies. Holdings include 200 pieces of original art, sketchbooks, woodblocks, 600 letters, sales receipts, ephemera, and an unpublished manuscript of autobiographical notes. (Subjects: Greenaway, Kate;

Manuscript/Illustration Material; Wood-blocks)

*Publication: Kate Greenaway: Catalogue of an Exhibition of Original Artworks...*, edited by Robert Kiger. Pittsburgh: Hunt Institute for Botanical Documentation, Carnegie-Mellon University, 1980.

**University of Pittsburgh (PPiU)**
**363 Hillman Library**
Bigalow & Forbes Ave.
Pittsburgh, PA 15260
phone: 412-648-8190
fax: 412-648-1245
contact: Charles E. Aston, Jr., Head
Special Collections
Internet: cea@vms.cis.pitt.edu
catalog status: OCLC

*John A. Nietz Old Textbook Collection*
This collection contains more than 15,000 American textbooks published prior to 1900, many as early as the sixteenth century. Also held are books on the history and theory of education, and writings by the key figures in the field of education. (Subjects: Education; Textbooks)

**University of Pittsburgh (PPiU-LS)**
**School of Library and Information**
**Science**
135 N. Bellefield Ave.
305 SLIS Building
Pittsburgh, PA 15260
phone: 412-624-4708
fax: 412-624-4062
contact: Elizabeth Tillapaugh Mahoney;
Perry Recker
e-mail: etm@vms.cis.pitt.edu and
pdr@vms.cis.pitt.edu
Internet: gate.cis.pitt.edu or
search.library.pitt.edu
catalog status: OCLC; PITTCAT/NOTIS

*Elizabeth Nesbitt Room*
Approximately 10,000 volumes from 1695 through the twentieth century, emphasiz-ing representative works of British and North American authors and illustrators. Included are chapbooks, nineteenth-century illustrated and color picture books, periodicals, series books, award winners, and works by Pennsylvania authors and illustrators. Also held is a small collection of manuscripts and original illustrations as well as the complete archival videotape collection of "Mister Rogers' Neighborhood." (Subjects: Abbott, Jacob; Andersen, Hans Christian; Caldecott, Randolph; Carroll, Lewis; Chapbooks; Evernden, Margery; Fadiman, Clifton; Historical; Hodges, Margaret Moore; Illustration of Children's Books; Manuscript/Illustration Material; Pennsylvania—Authors and Illustrators; Rogers, Fred; Series Books; Ward, Lynd)

## SWARTHMORE

**Swarthmore College (PSC)\*\***
**McCabe Library**
500 College Ave.
Swarthmore, PA 19081-1399
phone: 215-328-8477

*Library*
Among the holdings are 200 volumes and pamphlets published by the Society of Friends, as well as children's periodical titles. (Subjects: Periodicals; Society of Friends)

## UNIVERSITY PARK

**Pennsylvania State University (PSt)**
**Pattee Library W342**
University Park, PA 16802
phone: 814-865-1793
fax: 814-865-3665
contact: Sandra Stelts, Rare Books
Specialist
e-mail: sks@psulias.psu.edu
Internet: psulias.psu.edu
catalog status: OCLC and RLIN; LIAS

*The Allison-Shelley Collection*

Included in the holdings of the Allison-Shelley Collection are 1,000 titles translated from German, including works by the Brothers Grimm and their imitators, Heinrich Hoffmann's *Struwwelpeter*, Wilhelm Busch, Baron Munchausen, and Christmas titles. (Subjects: Christmas; Gag, Wanda; German Language; Grimm, Jacob and Wilhelm; Hoffmann, Heinrich; Manuscript/Illustration Material)

# Rhode Island

## PROVIDENCE

**Brown University (RPB-JH)**
**John Hay Library**
Box A
Providence, RI 02912
phone: 401-863-1514
fax: 401-863-1272
contact: Rosemary L. Cullen, Curator
e-mail: ap201034@brownum
catalog status: RLIN

*Harris Collection of American Poetry and Plays*

Children's materials are included among the 225,000 volumes of poetry, plays, and music in the Harris Collection. Holdings date from 1609, with the children's materials primarily published prior to 1940. (Subjects: Drama; Hymn Books; Moore, Clement Clarke; Mother Goose; Poetry)

**Providence Athenaeum Library (RPA)**
251 Benefit St.
Providence, RI 02903-2799
phone: 401-421-6972
contact: Mary Green

*Library*

Holdings include nineteenth-century children's books as well as several complete runs of children's periodical titles of the nineteenth and twentieth centuries. (Subjects: Historical; Periodicals)

**Providence Public Library (RP)**
225 Washington St.
Providence, RI 02917
phone: 401-455-8021
fax: 401-455-8080
contact: Philip J. Weimerskirch, Special Collections Librarian
e-mail: philwh@dsl.rhilinet.gov
catalog status: OCLC

*Edith Wetmore Collection of Children's Books*

The collection contains 2,000 volumes from the fifteenth century to the mid-twentieth century, with the greatest strength being in the nineteenth-century materials. Some twenty languages are represented, with 200 titles in French, but the majority are in English. Also held are eighty ABC books and several manuscripts and illustrations. (Subjects: Alphabet Books; Foreign Languages; Historical)

## WESTERLY

**Westerly Public Library (RWe)\*\***
38 Broad St.
Westerly, RI 02891
phone: 401-596-2877
fax: 401-596-5600

*Library*

Held by the Westerly Public Library are 106 items created by Margaret Wise Brown, including manuscripts and illustrations. (Subjects: Brown, Margaret Wise; Manuscript/Illustration Material)

# South Carolina

## CLEMSON

**Clemson University (ScCleU)**
**University Libraries**
**Special Collections**
P.O. Box 343001
Clemson, SC 29634-3001
phone: 803-656-3031

Alphabet cards [ca. 1820].

fax: 803-656-0233
contact: Michael Kohl, Head of Special
  Collections
catalog status: NOTIS

### Betsy Cromer Byars Collection

The Byars Papers consist of typescripts
and galleys, correspondence, clippings, reviews, videocassettes, videotapes, and
other materials related to her writing career. Also included are 130 volumes of her
published works. (Subjects: Byars, Betsy;
Manuscript/Illustration Material)

## COLUMBIA

**Columbia College (ScCoC)**
**J. Drake Edens Library**
1301 Columbia College Dr.
Columbia, SC 29203

phone: 803-786-3716
fax: 803-786-3700
contact: John C. Pritchett, Library
  Director
catalog status: OCLC

### Library

Within the holdings at Columbia College
are 183 volumes of religious literature for
children published from 1800 to 1850.
Most of the works are Sunday school
tracts and moral tales. (Subject: Bibles and
Books of Religious Instruction)

**University of South Carolina (ScU)\*\***
**Thomas Cooper Library**
Columbia, SC 29208-0103
phone: 803-777-3142
fax: 803-777-9503

*Library*

Holdings include some 3,000 volumes of children's literature published in the eighteenth and nineteenth centuries. The Education Library contains over 10,000 volumes for children published from 1916 to the present. (Subjects: Historical; Historical—20th Century)

## FLORENCE

Francis Marion University (ScFlM)
James A. Rogers Library
P.O. Box 100547
Florence, SC 29501-0547
phone: 803-661-1310
fax: 803-661-1309
contact: Roger Hux, Reference Librarian
catalog status: OCLC

*George Alfred Henty Books*

The Henty Collection contains 150 volumes dating from 1881 to 1961. A variety of editions and publishers are represented. (Subject: Henty, George Alfred)

## ROCK HILL

Winthrop University (ScRhW)**
Ida Jane Dacus Library
810 Oakland Ave.
Rock Hill, SC 29733-0001
phone: 803-323-2131
fax: 803-323-3285

*Eleanor Burts Children's Book Collection*

The Burts Collection contains 200 volumes dating from 1776. Along with the classic historical titles, this collection also includes fifty miniature books. (Subjects: Historical; Miniature Books)

## SPARTANBURG

Wofford College (ScSpW)**
Sandor Teszler Library
429 N. Church St.
Spartanburg, SC 29303-3663
phone: 803-597-4000
fax: 803-597-4329

*Children's Literature Collection*

This collection holds a miscellany of titles dating from 1830 to the present. Also included is a small collection of book dealer catalogs. (Subjects: Book Dealer Catalogs; Historical)

# South Dakota

## ABERDEEN

Northern State University (SdAbN)**
William Library & Learning Resources
   Center
14th Ave. & S. Washington
Aberdeen, SD 57401-7198
phone: 605-622-2645
fax: 605-622-2473

*Library*

Included in their holdings are 2,000 volumes of historical children's literature, as well as 100 volumes written by South Dakota authors. Also included are five illustrations and proof sheets done by Lois Lenski. (Subjects: Historical; Lenski, Lois; South Dakota—Authors and Illustrators)

# Tennessee

## MEMPHIS

Memphis State University (TMM)
Library Special Collections
Memphis, TN 38152
phone: 901-678-2210
contact: Ed Frank, Interim Curator
catalog status: OCLC

## *Baldwin Collection*

The nucleus of this 1,600-volume collection was formed by a schoolteacher/collector and has been augmented by gifts and transfers from other library collections. Included are textbooks, readers, and picture and storybooks published from 1850 to 1920, all in English. (Subjects: Historical; Textbooks)

## RUGBY

**Thomas Hughes Free Public Library (TRuT)\*\***
P.O. Box 8 Highway 52
Rugby, TN 37733
phone: 615-628-2441

### *Library*

Included are more than 1,000 volumes of children's books published from 1880 to 1889. (Subject: Historical)

# Texas

## AUSTIN

**University of Texas (TxU)\*\***
University Library
Special Collections
Sid Richardson Hall 1.109
Austin, TX 78713-7330
phone: 512-495-4520
fax: 512-495-4568

### *Barker Texas History Center*

Holdings include 870 volumes about Texas and by Texas authors. (Subjects: Texas; Texas—Authors and Illustrators)

### *Library*

Within the holdings of the library, there are 34,000 United States textbooks, dating from 1800. Emphasis is on those volumes used in Texas schools since 1900. (Subject: Textbooks)

**University of Texas at Austin (TxU-Hu)**
P.O. Drawer 7219
Austin, TX 78713-7219
phone: 512-471-9119
contact: R.W. Oram, Librarian
e-mail: hmab151@utxvm.cc.utexas.edu
Internet: utcat.utexas.edu
catalog status: OCLC for books and
    RLIN for manuscripts

### *Harry Ransom Humanities Research Center*

Although the Humanities Research Center does not have an emphasis on collecting children's authors per se, they do have 10,000 volumes related to children's literature and manuscript collections of twenty authors. They hold 4,000 volumes of *Alice in Wonderland* in fifty-eight languages, including parodies, photographs, manuscripts, and ephemera. Also held are the manuscripts of George Macy, relating to the juvenile titles of the Limited Edition Club. (Subjects: Ballantyne, Robert Michael; Baum, Lyman Frank; Burroughs, Edgar Rice; Carroll, Lewis; Church, Richard; Dahl, Roald; Dickens, Charles; Henty, George Alfred; Ireland, Leslie Daiken; Limited Editions Club; Manuscript/Illustration Material; Moore, Ruth; Reeves, James; Stevenson, Robert Louis)

*Publications: Lewis Carroll at Texas.* Austin: Humanities Research Center, 1985. *Catalog of the VanderPoel Dickens Collection*, by L. Carr. Austin: Humanities Research Center, 1968?.

## DALLAS

**Dallas Public Library (TxDa)**
J. Erik Jonsson Central
1515 Young St.
Dallas, TX 75201
phone: 214-670-1671
fax: 214-670-7839
contact: Kathy Toon, Division Manager
catalog status: OCLC, local online
    catalog

*Children's Center Collection*

The Children's Center includes 33,000 reference volumes, 4,000 of which comprise the Siddie Jo Johnson Rare Book Collection. Books in both collections range through the nineteenth and twentieth centuries, with an emphasis on British and American titles. Included are many award-winning titles, signed and first editions, series books, old textbooks, Mother Goose, ABC books, and books about Texas or by Texans. They also hold the original manuscript for *Sarah Crewe* and thirty-eight pieces of original art. (Subjects: Award Books; Historical; Manuscript/Illustration Material; Mother Goose; Series Books; Texas; Texas—Authors and Illustrators; Textbooks)

### DENTON

**Texas Women's University (TxDW)\*\***
**Mary Evelyn Blagg-Huey Library**
P.O. Box 23715, TWU Station
Denton, TX 76204-1715
phone: 817-898-2665
fax: 817-898-3764

*Library*

Within the 10,000-volume collection of children's literature, the emphasis is on series books. Most books are from the nineteenth and twentieth centuries. (Subjects: Historical; Series Books)

**University of North Texas (TxDN)**
**Willis Library**
**Rare Book & Texana Collections**
P.O. Box 5188
Denton, TX 76203-0188
phone: 817-565-2769
fax: 817-565-2599
contact: Dr. Kenneth Lavender, Curator
catalog status: OCLC

*Weaver Collection of Children's Literature*

This collection of 1,700 volumes dating from 1750 has strengths in the following areas: nineteenth- and early twentieth-century educational works and fiction, books about dolls and games, early Newbery/Caldecott winners, illustrated books and substantial holdings of *Heidi* and *Pinocchio*. Also included are miniature books and thumb Bibles. (Subjects: Award Books; Bibles and Books of Religious Instruction; Collodi, Carlo; Dolls; Education; Historical; Miniature Books; Spyri, Johanna)

### EL PASO

**El Paso Public Library (TxE)**
501 N. Oregon St.
El Paso, TX 79901
phone: 915-543-5422
fax: 915-543-5410
contact: Beverly Bixler, Youth Services Coordinator
catalog status: OCLC, online catalog

*Spanish Language*

The purpose of this collection is to provide Spanish-language materials for patrons who wish to read in Spanish. It consists of 63,000 volumes from the twentieth century, including picture books, juvenile fiction and nonfiction, and juvenile reference. (Subject: Spanish Language)

### FORT WORTH

**Fort Worth Public Library (TxF)**
300 Taylor St.
Fort Worth, TX 76102
phone: 817-871-7745
fax: 817-871-7734
contact: Jaye McLaughlin, Children's Unit Manager

### Little Truths Better than Great Fables

This collection encompasses 437 items dating from 1798 to the 1940s, including works in a variety of languages and genres. Periodicals, textbooks, denominational works, and paperbacks are represented. (Subject: Historical)

*Publication: Little Truths Better than Great Fables: A Collection of Old and Rare Books for Children in the Fort Worth Public Library*, compiled by Jim Roginski. Fort Worth: Branch-Smith, 1976.

## HOUSTON

**Houston Public Library (TxH)**
500 McKinney St.
Houston, TX 77002
phone: 713-247-2700
fax: 712-247-3531
contact: Lou Caldwell, Chief, Central
    Services

### Harriet Dickson Reynolds Room

This collection of 900 volumes emphasizes illustrators of the eighteenth through twentieth centuries, including Kate Greenaway, Arthur Rackham, Howard Pyle, Jessie Willcox Smith, Beatrix Potter, and Marcia Brown. (Subject: Illustration of Children's Books)

### Historical Juvenile Collection

This collection contains examples of early classics from the American Sunday School Union publications and other books published prior to the nineteenth century. (Subjects: American Sunday School Union; Historical)

### Norma Meldrum Children's Room Collection

A collection of 6,700 books suitable for children preschool to age fifteen. The collection represents the finest literature and includes winners of most distinguished awards. (Subjects: Award Books; Historical; Series Books)

## WACO

**Baylor University (TxWB)**
**Armstrong Browning Library**
P.O. Box 97152
Waco, TX 76798-7152
phone: 817-755-3566
fax: 817-755-3843
contact: Cynthia A. Burgess, Curator of
    Books and Printed Material
Internet: telnet to baylor.edu (choose
    BU2 at the menu; Username=
    BAYLIS)
catalog status: OCLC, BAYLIS

### The Pied Piper of Hamelin

The library holds an extensive collection of material associated with Robert Browning's poem "The Pied Piper of Hamelin." Holdings include copies of the first publication of the work in Browning's *Dramatic Lyric*, the third pamphlet of his Bells and Pomegranates series, the poem as it first appeared in book form in 1880, and numerous illustrated editions and adaptations. Numerous articles and newspaper clippings about the poem or the Pied Piper motif, musical scores, various types of artwork, and other associational items are included in the collection. (Subjects: Browning, Robert; Hodges, Cyril Walter; Manuscript/Illustration Material)

*Publication: The Pied Piper of Hamelin in the Armstrong Browning Library.* Baylor Browning Interest, Number Twenty, Baylor University, 1969.

# Utah

## LOGAN

**Utah State University (ULA)**
**Merrill Library**
Logan, UT 84322-6700
phone: 801-797-3093
fax: 801-797-3668
contact: Deborah Boutwell, Media
    Director

### Anne Carroll Moore Library

Included in the holdings of this library are 300 volumes of short stories from the early 1900s to the present. (Subject: Short Stories)

## PROVO

**Brigham Young University (UPB)**\*\*
**Harold B. Lee Library**
3080 HBLL
Provo, UT 84602
phone: 801-378-2905
fax: 801-378-3221

### Special Collections

Holdings include about 300 volumes of books and periodicals produced by the Church of Jesus Christ of the Latter Day Saints from the late nineteenth century to the present. The Victorian Collection includes 1,000 volumes. (Subjects: Bibles and Books of Religious Instruction; Historical; Periodicals)

# Virginia

## CHARLOTTESVILLE

**University of Virginia (ViU)**
**Alderman Library**
**Special Collections**
Charlottesville, VA 22903-2498
phone: 804-924-3025
fax: 804-924-3143
contact: Heather Moore, Associate
    Curator for American History &
    American Literature
e-mail: mhm8m@virginia.edu
Internet: telnet 128.143.70.101 (then
    type: c virgo)
catalog status: OCLC, VIRGO

### Clifton Waller Barrett Library of American Literature

This entire collection numbers 35,000 volumes, some of which are children's literature titles. Many notable American authors are represented. (Subjects: Abbott, Jacob; Alcott, Louisa May; Alger, Horatio; Baum, Lyman Frank; Burnett, Frances Hodgson; Castlemon, Harry; Historical; Optic, Oliver; Parley, Peter; Pyle, Howard; Twain, Mark)

### Rare Books Collection

The Rare Books Collection contains works by many of the same authors listed above as well as a substantial collection of works by George A. Henty. (Subject: Henty, George Alfred)

## RICHMOND

**Richmond Public Library (ViR)**
101 E. Franklin St.
Richmond, VA 23219
phone: 804-783-2531
fax: 804-643-1516
contact: Martha Davenport, Friends of
    the Library Volunteer

### Rare Children's Books Room

Opening in 1974 with the gift of 375 early English children's books from Josephine Tucker, former English professor at Richmond's Westhampton College, the collection has expanded to well over 5,000 titles. Tucker's collection included eight battledores, more than 50 chapbooks, and a harlequinade. Holdings also include a number of periodical titles, series books, and numerous editions of *Alice in Wonderland*. A gift of 325 scarce Russian children's books, mainly post-Revolutionary, augment the basic collection. (Subjects: Carroll, Lewis; Chapbooks; Historical; Hornbooks and Battledores; Periodicals; Russian Language; Series Books)

# Washington

## CHENEY

Eastern Washington University
(WaChenE)**
John F. Kennedy Memorial Library
Cheney, WA 99004-2495
phone: 509-359-6263
fax: 509-359-6456

### Almeron T. Perry Science Fiction Collection

Included in the holdings are 1,200 volumes of paperbacks by Andre Norton, Ursula LeGuin, Isaac Asimov, and Robert Heinlein, among others. Also included is an extensive collection of science fiction periodical titles. (Subjects: Periodicals; Science Fiction)

## ELLENSBURG

Central Washington University (WaElC)
University Library
Ellensburg, WA 98926-7591
phone: 509-963-2101
contact: Patrick McLaughlin

### Amanda Hebler Memorial Collection

This collection contains 109 volumes published from 1785 to the early twentieth century. (Subject: Historical)

## OLYMPIA

Washington State Library (Wa)**
Olympia, WA 98926
phone: 206-753-5590
fax: 206-586-7575

### Library

Included in the library's holdings are 1,000 volumes written or illustrated by Washingtonians and sixty volumes about the Pacific Northwest. (Subjects: Pacific Northwest; Washington—Authors and Illustrators)

## SEATTLE

Historical Society of Seattle & King
County (WaSHi)**
Sophie Frye Bass Library of Northwest
Americana
2700 24th Ave. E.
Seattle, WA 98112
phone: 206-324-1126
fax: 206-324-1346

### Library

The Historical Society holdings include 1,800 North American and Western European dolls from the mid-nineteenth century to the 1920s. Models and miniatures of the same period are included. Holdings also include 300 textbooks from 1850 to 1930. The Robbins Collection contains 1,200 volumes about storytelling and puppetry. (Subjects: Dolls; Puppetry; Storytelling; Textbooks)

Seattle Pacific University (WaSPC)**
Weter Memorial Library
3307 Third Ave. W.
Seattle, WA 98119
phone: 206-281-2228
fax: 206-281-2936

### Library

Holdings include 110 volumes of Bible stories and anthologies published in the twentieth century. (Subject: Bibles and Books of Religious Instruction)

Seattle Public Library (WaS)**
1000 Fourth Ave.
Seattle, WA 98104-1193
phone: 206-386-4100
fax: 206-386-4108

### Library

Holdings include 1,500 volumes of children's literature dating from the mid-1700s to the 1920s. Also held are 1,000 volumes in thirty-four languages, with strengths in French, German, and Spanish. (Subjects: Foreign Languages; Historical)

**University of Washington (WaU)**
**Allen Library, FM-25**
Seattle, WA 98195
phone: 206-543-1929
fax: 206-689-8045
contact: Gary L. Menges, Head Special
    Collections
e-mail: speccoll@u.washington.edu
Internet: uwin.u.washington.edu (From
    opening menu, press "J", then enter
    LCAT)
catalog status: OCLC, local online
    catalog

### Special Collections and Preservation Division

The collection includes about 2,200 titles dating from 1650 to the present, with emphasis on the works of nineteenth-century American women authors and on Hans Christian Andersen, illustrated books, and the Pacific Northwest. The latter include biographies and fiction set in the Pacific Northwest from the early 1800s to the 1960s, many by local authors. Works by nineteenth-century American women are being actively collected. (Subjects: Andersen, Hans Christian; Historical; Pacific Northwest; Women Authors and Illustrators)

**University of Washington (WaU-CM)**
**Suzzalo Library, FM-25**
Seattle, WA 98195
phone: 206-543-2725
fax: 206-685-8049
contact: Loretta K. Lopez,
    Reference/Education Librarian
e-mail: lorey@u.washington.edu
Internet: uwin.u.washington.edu
catalog status: OCLC, local online
    catalog

### Curriculum Materials and Children's Literature Section

This is a historical and current collection of over 34,000 volumes, including the following: 7,000 current and out-of-print historical titles dating from the mid-nineteenth century to 1946; titles that have won awards, including the Newbery, Caldecott, Greenaway, Carnegie, Guardian, and Pacific Northwest Young Readers' Choice; 1,800 volumes of folkore; 350 textbooks from 1863 to 1946; and current periodical titles. Fifteen hundred volumes of textbooks for primary through secondary schools dating from the mid-nineteenth century to the 1930s are held by the Main Library Education division. (Subjects: Award Books; Folk and Fairy Tales; Historical; Textbooks)

## SPOKANE

**Spokane Public Library (WaSp)\*\***
West 906 Main Ave.
Spokane, WA 99201-0976
phone: 509-838-3361
fax: 509-625-6794

### George Washington Fuller Collection of Rare and Exhibit Books

This collection consists of 140 volumes published from the eighteenth to early twentieth centuries. Included are fifty-three toy books, thirty-two chapbooks, cheap repository tracts, miniature books from the nineteenth century, and eighteenth- and nineteenth-century textbooks. (Subjects: Chapbooks; Historical; Miniature Books; Textbooks; Toy and Moveable Books)

## TACOMA

**Tacoma Public Library (WaT)**
1102 Tacoma Ave. S.
Tacoma, WA 98498
phone: 206-591-5622
fax: 206-591-5740

### Handforth Collection

This is Thomas Handforth's personal collection of his works. Starting with boyhood sketches in 1912 and concluding with work done just before his death, the collection includes pen-and-ink, watercolors, oils, sketchbooks, prints, and copper plates from his books. Letters to his family, especially from China, describe his work and activities. His own scrapbooks and those of his family are included, as well as artwork and text for two unpublished books. (Subjects: Handforth, Thomas; Manuscript/Illustration Material)

# West Virginia

## ELKINS

**Davis and Elkins College (WvED)\*\***
Library
Sycamore Street
Elkins, WV 26241
phone: 304-636-1900, ext. 244
fax: 304-636-0650

*Myron and Ura Mae Anderson Appalachian Literature Collection*

Within the Anderson Collection are eighty-three volumes of children's literature. (Subject: Appalachia)

# Wisconsin

## MADISON

**University of Wisconsin-Madison (WU)\*\***
General Library System & Memorial Library
600 North Park St.
Madison, WI 53706
phone: 608-263-3193
fax: 608-265-2754

*Foreign Children's Literature Collection*

Contains 500 titles, including 150 German, 125 French, and 75 Russian and Spanish. The remainder are in Swedish,

Norwegian, Italian, and Japanese. The collection is available for research only. (Subject: Foreign Languages)

**University of Wisconsin - Madison (WU-CC)**
School of Education
600 North Park St.
Helen C. White Hall Room 4290
Madison, WI 53706
phone: 608-263-3720
fax: 608-262-4933
contact: Ginny Moore Kruse, Director

*Cooperative Children's Book Center*

This is a general collection of current, retrospective, and historical trade books for children and young adults. There is a special emphasis on multicultural literature, small-press publishing, and Wisconsin authors and illustrators. Included are the complete manuscript materials for Ellen Raskin's *Westing Game*, as well as audio- and videotapes of Raskin describing her writing process. (Subjects: Alternative Press Books; Award Books; Burgess, Thornton Waldo; Children's Literature, Study of; Historical; Periodicals; Wisconsin—Authors and Illustrators)

## MILWAUKEE

**Milwaukee Public Library (WM)**
814 W. Wisconsin Ave.
Milwaukee, WI 53233-2385
phone: 414-286-3078
fax: 414-286-2794
contact: Jane Botham, Coordinator of Children's Services

*Library*

The Brewton Poetry Collection includes 700 volumes of poetry that are listed in Brewton's *Index to Children's Poetry* and supplements. The Children's Popular Literature Reference Collection contains 5,000 volumes of popular children's literature published between 1850 and 1940. The emphasis is on series books such as Horatio Alger and the Bobbsey Twins. The Eastman Folk and Fairy Tale Collection has 1,300 volumes that are indexed in Eastman's *Index to Fairy Tales* and supplements. A collection of 2,000 titles represents 350 authors and illustrators who live or have lived in Wisconsin. (Subjects: Folk and Fairy Tales; Historical; Poetry; Series Books; Wisconsin—Authors and Illustrators)

**University of Wisconsin at Milwaukee (WMUW)**
**Golda Meir Library**
P.O. Box 604
Milwaukee, WI 53201
phone: 414-229-4074
fax: 414-229-5687
contact: Mary Jo Aman, Head, Curriculum Collection
e-mail: ipaman@csd4.csd.uwm.edu
Internet: telnet 129.89.32.6
catalog status: OCLC; NLS

*Curriculum Collection*
This collection contains materials of special interest to students and faculty in preschool, elementary, secondary and adult educational programs. Its 45,550 volumes include curriculum guides, juvenile and young adult literature, a historical collection of juvenile literature and textbooks, and kindergarten through twelfth-grade texts. (Subjects: Education; Historical; Textbooks)

# Wyoming

## SHERIDAN

**Sheridan County Fulmer Public Library (WyShF)**
335 W. Alger St.
Sheridan, WY 82801
phone: 307-674-9898
fax: 307-674-7374
contact: Michelle Havenga, Children's Librarian

*Spellspinner Collection*
A collection of monographs, audiovisual materials, realia, and periodicals. The 1,600 titles cover various aspects of children's literature, from detailed studies to its sharing via storytelling and puppetry. The core of the collection contains books of street songs, rhymes, games, chants, and stories. The focus of this collection is to preserve and share children's literature for present and future generations. (Subjects: Award Books; Folk and Fairy Tales; Games and Pastimes; Historical; Puppetry; Storytelling; Toys)

*Wyoming Room Children's Collection*
This collection contains fifty monographs published from 1900 by Wyoming-based authors such as Will James, Peggy Curry, and E. D. Mygatt. (Subject: Wyoming—Authors and Illustrators)

*Mother Goose: The Old Nursery Rhymes*, illustrated by Arthur Rackham; New York: Century, 1913.

# Subject Listing

## ABBREVIATIONS

| | | | |
|---|---|---|---|
| ca. | approximately | li.ft. | linear feet |
| corr. | correspondence | ms. | manuscript(s) |
| cu.ft. | cubic feet | vols. | volumes |
| il. | illustration(s) | | |

A complete listing of the institutional holding symbols can be found on page xv. The codes are arranged alphabetically using the following system: each code consists of units, with each unit containing an uppercase letter or an uppercase and lowercase letter. A code may have as few as one or as many as five units. As an example, the **Ohioana Library** is represented by the single uppercase letter "**O**," while the **Northern State University** in **Aberdeen, South Dakota,** is represented by "**SdAbN**." Using the "**SdAbN**" code as an example, "**Sd**" is the first unit, representing South Dakota; "**Ab**" is the second unit, representing the city of Aberdeen; and "**N**" is the third unit, representing Northern State University. Alphabetization is by units, not individual letters, therefore the code "**MoIRC**" follows "**MWiW**" due to the combination of upper- and lowercase letters.

**Aardema, Verna**
MnU ms. for 8 titles. MsHaU .50 cu.ft. of ms./il.

**Aaron, Chester**
MnU ms. for 2 titles.

**Aas, Tonje Strom**
MnU il. for 1 title.

**Abbe, Elfriede Martha**
MnU il. for 3 titles.

**Abbott, Jacob**
CoU Substantial book holdings. DLC Extensive book holdings. FTS 200 vols. FU Extensive book holdings. INS 250 vols. MWA 373 vols. MeB 900 vols.; 26 li.ft. of ms. MeWC 703 vols. MiMtpT 89 vols. MnU ms. for 1 title. MsHaU 150+ vols. NhC 120+ vols. OAU 196 vols. OOxM 100 vols. PP-Rb 300 vols. PPiU-LS 120 vols. ViU 134 vols.

**ABC Books** *see* **Alphabet Books**

**Abisch, Roslyn Kroop**
MnU ms. for 3 titles.

**Adams, Adrienne**
MnU il. for 14 titles. MsHaU .60 cu.ft. of ms./il. NjR-Z il. materials.

**Adams, William Taylor** *see* **Optic, Oliver**

**Addams, Charles Samuel**
MnU ms. for 1 title.

**Ade, George**
ICN 230+ vols.; ms. material.

**Adler, C. S.**
MoWarbT ms. and il. materials.

**Adler, David A.**
MsHaU 10 cu.ft. of ms./il.

**Adler, Irving**
MnU ms. for 70 titles; il. for 4 titles. MsHaU 6.6 cu.ft. of ms./il.

**Adler, Larry**
MsHaU .6 cu.ft. of ms./il.

**Adler, Peggy**
MnU il. for 5 titles.

**Adshead, Gladys**
OrU 1.5 li.ft. of ms.

**Aesop** *see* **Fables**

**African American Books** *see* **Multiculturalism**

**Afrikaan Language**
MnU 92 vols.

**Ageton, Arthur**
MnU .30 cu.ft. of ms./il.

**Agle, Nan Hayden**
MnU .90 cu.ft. of ms./il.

**Aiken, Joan**
MnU .90 cu.ft. of ms./il.

**Akino, Fuku**
NjR-Z il. materials.

**Alaska**
AkFSD 300+ 20th-century vols. about or set in Alaska.

**Alcock, Gudrun**
MnU ms. for 2 titles.

**Alcorn, John**
MnU il. for 6 titles.

**Alcott, Louisa May**
CSmH-A 3 ms. and 2 corr. items. DLC Extensive book holdings. FU Extensive book holdings. ICN Book holdings. MCoA 150 vols., 35 periodicals; corr., sketchbooks, and related materials. MsHaU 75 vols. ViU 93 vols.

**Alderman, Clifford Lindsey**
MsHaU 7.8 cu.ft. of ms./il.

**Aldis, Dorothy**
MsHaU .30 cu.ft. of ms./il.

**Aleichem, Sholem**
MnU il. for 1 title.

**Alexander, Charles**
OrU 11.5 li.ft. of ms.

*Ride a Cock-Horse to Banbury Cross and a Farmer Went Trotting upon His Grey Mare* by Randolph Caldecott; London: Routledge [1884].

**Alexander, Joycelyn Arundel** *see* **Arundel, Joycelyn**

**Alexander, Lloyd**
PP-Rb ms., notes, corr. for 40 titles.

**Alexander, Sue**
MsHaU .50 cu.ft. of ms./il.

**Alger, Horatio**
CSmH-A ms. and 88 corr. items. DLC 150+ vols. FU Extensive book holdings. IDeKN 108 vols. MiMtpT 500 vols. MsHaU 200+ vols. NhD Extensive book holdings. OAU 89 vols. PP 150 vols. ViU 87 vols.

**Alger, Leclair Gowans**
MnU ms. for 1 title.

*Alice in Wonderland see* **Carroll, Lewis**

**Aliki** *see* **Brandenberg, Aliki Liacouras**

**Allan, Mabel Esther**
MsHaU 1.8 cu.ft. of ms./il.

**Allen, J. A.**
MsHaU .60 cu.ft. of ms./il.

**Allen, Agnes and Jack**
MnU ms. for 3 titles; il. for 1 title.

**Allen, Elizabeth**
MsHaU .30 cu.ft. of ms./il.

**Allen, Leroy**
MnU ms. for 1 title.

**Allen, Marjorie**
MnU ms. for 2 titles.

**Allen, Terril Diener**
OrU 11 li.ft. of ms.

**Allison, Linda**
MsHaU .60 cu.ft. of ms./il.

**Aloise, Frank E.**
MsHaU 8.2 cu.ft. of ms./il.

**Alphabet Books**
DLC Extensive book holdings. FU Extensive book holdings. HH 175 vols. from 1929 in the Igoe Collection. ICN Extensive holdings in 40 languages from the 15th century; ms. materials. IRoC 800 vols. 16th–20th centuries in 15 languages. IU-Ed 400 vols. InU-Li 300+ vols. 16th–20th centuries. MBAt Substantial book holdings. MiDW Substantial book holdings in the Ramsey Collection. MnU 127 vols. MoWarbT 140 vols. MsHaU 250+ vols. NBuBE 500 vols. from 1790. NNC Substantial book holdings in the Plimpton Library. PP-Rb 200 vols. RP 80 vols.

**Alternative Press Books**
WU-CC 9,500 vols.

**Altman, Elaine Joan**
MnU il. for 1 title.

**Amateur Periodicals**
MWA 5,500 titles. MsHaU 100+ titles.

**Ambrus, Victor G.**
MnU il. for 1 title. MsHaU .6 cu.ft. of ms./il.

**American Book Company**
NSyU 522 li.ft. and 691 cu.ft. of company records, papers, and published books dating from 1840.

**American Sunday School Union**
CSfSt 100+ vols. DLC Extensive book holdings. FU Extensive book holdings. MBCn 5 li.ft. of materials. MiDW Book holdings in the Ramsey Collection. MsHaU 100+ vols. PP-Rb 20,000 vols. TxH Substantial book holdings.

*see also* **Bibles and Books of Religious Instruction**

**American Tract Society**
FU Extensive book holdings. MBCn 27 li.ft. of materials. MsHaU 50+ vols.
*see also* **Bibles and Books of Religious Instruction**

**Ames, Lee J.**
MnU il. for 4 titles. MsHaU 40 cu.ft. of ms./il. OrU 3 li.ft. of ms. and il.

**Ames, Mildred**
MsHaU 5.1 cu.ft. of ms./il.

**Amorosi, Nicholas**
MnU il. for 1 title.

**Amory, Cleveland**
MnU ms. for 1 title.

**Amoss, Berthe**
MnU ms. for 1 title; il. for 1 title. MsHaU 1.5 cu.ft. of ms./il.

**Anckarsvard, Karin**
MnU ms. for 1 title.

**Andersen, Hans Christian**
DLC Hersholt Collection contains ms., corr., and first editions. FU Extensive book holdings. ICN 27+ vols. from 19th–20th centuries. InU-Li 50+ vols. in various languages. MnU 320 vols. NBuBE Significant book holdings. NN-Don 75 vols.; 2 original paper cuttings. PP 250 vols. PPiU-LS 60 vols. WaU 325 vols.
*see also* **Award Books**

**Anderson, Clarence William**
MnU ms. for 1 title; il. for 3 titles. MsHaU .60 cu.ft. of ms./il. OrU 3 li.ft. of ms. and il.

**Anderson, Isabel**
MBAt ms. materials.

**Anderson, John Lonzo**
MnU ms. for 4 titles.

**Anderson, Joy**
MnU ms. for 2 titles.

**Anderson, Walter**
MsHaU 1.2 cu.ft. of ms./il.

**Anderson, William T.**
MoWarbT ms. and il. materials.

**Andre, Richard**
MsHaU .30 cu.ft. of ms./il.

**Andrews, Mary Evans**
MsHaU 1.2 cu.ft. of ms./il.

**Andrews, Michael F.**
MsHaU .30 cu.ft. of ms./il.

**Andrews, Regina M.**
NN-Sc 1 box of ms.

**Angelo, Valenti**
MnU ms. for 3 titles; il. for 16 titles. NGuP il.

**Anglund, Joan Walsh**
MBU 80 vols.; 60 li.ft. of ms. and il. MnU il. for 1 title.

**Annixter, Paul** *see* **Sturtzel, Howard Allison**

**Anno, Mitsumasa**
MnU il. for 1 title. MsHaU .60 cu.ft. of ms./il.

**Annuals and Gift Books**
CtHi Extensive book holdings in the Hewins Collection. DLC Extensive book holdings. FTaSU 500+ vols. FU Extensive book holdings. ICN 200+ vols. NNU-F 500 vols.

**Appalachia**
WvED 83 vols.

**Appel, Benjamin**
OrU 8.5 li.ft. of ms.

**Appleton, Victor**
DLC Extensive book holdings. FU Extensive book holdings. PP 120 vols.

*Arabian Nights*
OCl-RB 761 vols. in 57 languages.

**Arabic Language**
DLC 100+ vols. MnU 32 vols. OrPS 107 vols.

**Archer, Jules**
OrU 42 li.ft. of ms.

**Archer, Marguerite**
CSfSt 6 li.ft. of professional papers.

**Archibald, Joseph Stopford**
MsHaU .30 cu.ft. of ms./il. OrU 1 li.ft. of ms.

**Ardizzone, Aingelda**
MnU ms. for 1 title.

**Ardizzone, Edward**
IDeKN 172 British and American editions. InU-Li 80 vols.; 34 il. for 2 titles. MnU il. for 9 titles. MsHaU .30 cu.ft. of ms./il.

**Arizona**
AzU Collection of books with Arizona as a setting.

**Arizona—Authors and Illustrators**
AzTeS 65 li.ft. of ms. and corr. for Shaaron Cosner, Phyllis Leonard, Marion T. Place, and Glendon and Kathryn Swarthout.

**Arkin, Alan**
MnU ms. for 1 title.

**Armer, Alberta**
MsHaU 2.1 cu.ft. of ms./il.

**Armour, Richard**
CCSc 77 vols.; ms., corr. and drawings for 44 titles. CSmH-A 2 pieces of corr. MnU ms. for 3 titles. MsHaU .30 cu.ft. of ms./il.

**Armstrong, Gerry Breen**
MnU ms. for 1 title.

**Armstrong, William H.**
MnU ms. for 13 titles.

**Arno, Enrico**
MnU il. for 2 titles.

**Arnold, Danny**
MsHaU 1.2 cu.ft. of ms./il.

**Arnold, Olga**
MnU ms. for 1 title.

**Arnold, Pauline**
MnU ms. for 1 title.

**Arntson, Herbert Edward**
OrU 15 li.ft. of ms.

**Art**
NNMMA-U 800 vols.

**Art Education**
NNMMA-U 800 vols. and curriculum guides.

**Arthur, King**
ICN 300+ vols.

**Arthur, Timothy Shay**
CSmH-A 1 ms. and 2 pieces of corr. FTS 125 vols. FU Extensive book holdings.

**Artzybasheff, Boris**
MnU il. for 9 titles. NSyU 4.5 li.ft. of ms. and il.

**Aruego, Jose**
MnU il. for 2 titles.

**Arundel, Jocelyn**
MnU ms. for 5 titles. MsHaU .30 cu.ft. of ms./il.

**Asch, Frank**
NjR-Z il. materials.

**Asher, Sandy**
MsHaU 8.2 cu.ft. of ms./il.

**Ashley, Bernard**
MsHaU .30 cu.ft. of ms./il.

**Asimov, Isaac**
MBU 225 vols.; 400+ boxes of ms. materials.

**Atwater, Montgomery Meigs**
OrU 3 li.ft. of ms.

**Atwood, Ann**
MnU ms. for 1 title.

**Auerbach, Marjorie**
MnU il. for 3 titles.

**Austin, Margot**
MnU il. for 2 titles.

**Austin, Oliver L., Jr.**
MnU ms. for 1 title.

**Averill, Esther Holden**
MnU ms. for 2 titles; il. for 3 titles. MsHaU .30 cu.ft. of ms./il.

**Award Books**
AkA 250 vols. of Young Readers Choice, Newbery, Caldecott, and British and Canadian award winners. ArCCA Collection of award winners. CCCla Recognition of Merit Award winners. CL FOCAL (Friends of Children and Literature) Award winners. CLU-S/C Newbery and Caldecott winners. CSd Newbery and Caldecott winners. CoU Substantial number of award winners. CUEDUC 350 vols. and other documentation for the 1992 Andersen nominees. DeWI 110 vols.; 280 il. and corr. of illustrators, with emphasis on Caldecott recipients. FTS Newbery and Caldecott winners. HH Autographed copies of Nene Award winners. IC 300 vols. of Newbery and Caldecott winners. IEN Award-winning titles. INS Award-winning titles. IU-Ed Extensive holdings of award-winning titles. KEmU 590 vols. and related materials for William Allen White Award. MiDW Extensive book holdings. MnU Extensive book holdings; ms. and il. for many award-winning titles. MoWarbT Depository for the Mark Twain Reading Award winners. MsHaU Extensive book holdings; ms. and il. for many award-winning titles. NNCbc Holdings of Newbery, Caldecott, National Book Award, and IBBY Honor List winners. NcCU Winners of the North Carolina American Association of University Women Juvenile Literature Award. NhC Complete holdings of Newbery and Caldecott winners. OkS Holdings of Sequoyah Children's Book Award winners. OrPS Winners of the Young Readers Choice Award. PNo Newbery and Caldecott winners in Field Collection. PP Newbery, Caldecott, ALA No-

tables. PPD Newbery, Caldecott, and other award winners. TxDa Award-winning titles. TxDN Newbery and Caldecott winners. TxH Holdings of award books. WU-CC 600 vols. of various award winners. WaU-CM Substantial holdings of award-winning books. WyShF Winners of the Indian Paintbrush Award.

**Ayars, James Sterling**
MnU ms. for 8 titles. MsHaU .30 cu.ft. of ms./il.

**Ayer, Jacqueline**
MnU il. for 1 title.

**Ayer, Margaret**
MsHaU .60 cu.ft. of ms./il. OrU 4.5 li.ft. of ms. and il.

**Aylesworth, Jim**
MnU ms. for 6 titles.

**Aylesworth, Thomas G.**
MsHaU 6.3 cu.ft. of ms./il.

**Babbitt, Natalie**
CtU Complete papers.

**Babcock, John and Sidney** (publishers)
CtHi Extensive holdings of Babcock imprints in Connecticut Imprints Collection. CtNhHi 150 vols. printed by S. Babcock and Sidney's Press. CtY-BR 350 vols.

**Bach, Alice**
MsHaU 1.2 cu.ft. of ms./il.

**Bachmann, Evelyn Trent**
MsHaU .9 cu.ft. of ms./il.

**Bacon, Frances A.**
MsHaU .30 cu.ft. of ms./il.

**Bacon, Paul**
MnU il. for 1 title.

**Bacon, Peggy**
MnU ms. for 1 title; il. for 1 title.

**Baerg, Harry John**
MsHaU .30 cu.ft. of ms./il.

**Bagert, Brod**
MsHaU .30 cu.ft. of ms./il.

**Bahr, Howard**
MsHaU .30 cu.ft. of ms./il.

**Bailey, Alice Cooper**
MsHaU 2.1 cu.ft. of ms./il.

**Bailey, Carolyn Sherwin**
CtNhN 78 vols. and memorabilia.

**Baker, Betty**
MnU ms. for 11 titles.

**Baker, Charlotte**
MnU ms. for 1 title.

**Baker, Laura Nelson**
MnU ms. for 12 titles. MsHaU .60 cu.ft. of ms./il.

**Baker, Margaret J.**
MsHaU .30 cu.ft. of ms./il.

**Baker, Mary Elizabeth**
MsHaU 2.4 cu.ft. of ms./il.

**Baker, Sanna**
MnU ms. for 1 title.

**Balch, Glenn**
MsHaU .30 cu.ft. of ms./il.

**Baldridge, Cyrus LeRoy**
MnU il. for 6 titles.

**Balian, Lorna**
MnU ms. for 11 titles; il. for 8 titles.

**Ball, Zachary**
MoWarbT ms./il. materials. MsHaU 2.7 cu.ft. of ms./il.

**Ballantyne, Robert Michael**
DLC Extensive book holdings. FU Extensive book holdings. TxU-Hu 175 vols.

**Ballard, Lowell Clyne**
MsHaU 1.5 cu.ft. of ms./il.

**Bannerman, Helen**
NNC 35 editions of *Little Black Sambo*.

**Bannon, Laura**
ICN 26+ vols.; ms.

**Barber, Elizabeth**
MsHaU .30 cu.ft. of ms./il.

**Barbour, Ralph Henry**
DLC Extensive book holdings. FU Extensive book holdings. NhD Extensive book holdings.

**Bare, Arnold Edwin**
MnU il. for 7 titles.

**Barker, Will**
MnU ms. for 2 titles.

**Barlowe, Dorothea and Sy**
MnU il. for 1 title.

**Barnes, Culmer**
MsHaU .60 cu.ft. of ms./il.

**Barnett, Rainey**
MsHaU .30 cu.ft. of ms./il.

**Barnouw, Victor**
MnU ms. for 1 title.

**Barnstone, Aliki**
MnU ms. for 1 title.

**Barnum, Jay Hyde**
MnU il. for 1 title.

**Baron, Virginia Olsen**
MnU ms. for 1 title.

**Barr, Amelia Edith**
CSmH-A 5 pieces of corr.

**Barr, George**
MsHaU 2.4 cu.ft. of ms./il.

**Barr, Jene**
MsHaU 1.8 cu.ft. of ms./il.

**Barres, Catherine J.**
MnU il. for 1 title.

**Barrie, James Matthew**
CSmH-A 1 ms. and 101 pieces of corr. CtY-BR Extensive holdings of material by and about Barrie, including books, ms., diaries, il., photographs, and corr. InU-Li 60+ vols.; ms. for *Peter Pan.*

**Barron, John N.**
MnU il. for 1 title.

**Barry, Edmund**
MsHaU .60 cu.ft. of ms./il.

**Barry, Katharina Maria Watjen**
MnU il. for 3 titles.

**Barry, Robert Everett**
MnU il. for 8 title.

**Barss, William**
MnU il. for 2 titles.

**Barton, Byron**
MnU ms. for 1 title; il. for 7 titles.

**Basque Language**
ICN 25+ primers in Bonaparte Collection. IdU 20 titles published in the mid-20th century.

**Bateman, Robert**
MsHaU .30 cu.ft. of ms./il.

**Batherman, Muriel**
MnU ms. for 3 titles; il. for 8 titles.

**Batten, John**
MnU il. for 1 title.

**Battle, Gerald N.**
MsHaU 1.3 cu.ft. of ms./il.

**Battledores** *see* **Hornbooks and Battledores**

**Bauer, Marion Dane**
MnU ms. for 19 titles.

**Baum, Lyman Frank**
AzTeS 40 vols., 2 periodical titles, and related ephemera for Baum's Oz books. CSt Extensive book holdings. CtY-BR Extensive ms. holdings. DLC 105 vols. InU-Li 21+ vols.; filmscripts and ms. materials. KyLoU 150 vols. MiMtpT 84 vols. NNC 100 vols. and papers related to exhibit. NSyU 250 vols.; 6 li.ft. of ms., corr., biographical and genealogical materials. PP 75 vols. TxU-Hu 1 box of ms. ViU 80 vols.

**Bawden, Edward**
MnU il. for 1 title.

**Bawden, Nina**
MsHaU .60 cu.ft. of ms./il.

**Baylor, Byrd**
MnU ms. for 1 title.

**Baynes, Pauline Diana**
MnU il. for 3 titles. OrU 1 li.ft. of il.

**Beach, Edward L.**
MsHaU 5.4 cu.ft. of ms./il.

**Beadle and Adams** (publisher)
IDeKN 7500 vols. and periodicals. NCooHi 100 vols. and ms.

**Bealer, Alex Winkler, III**
MnU ms. for 1 title; il. for 1 title.

**Beard, Charles**
DLC 110 pieces of artwork.

**Beatty, Hetty Burlingame**
OrU 9.5 li.ft. of ms. and il.

**Beatty, John and Patricia**
MnU ms. for 1 title.

**Bechdolt, Jack**
MsHaU .30 cu.ft. of ms./il.

**Bechtel, Louise Seaman**
MnU ms. for 1 title.

**Beery, Mary**
MsHaU 3.3 cu.ft. of ms./il.

**Behn, Harry**
MnU ms. for 15 titles; il. for 9 titles. MsHaU .30 cu.ft. of ms./il. OrU 2 li.ft. of ms.

**Belden, Wilanne**
MnU ms. for 5 titles.

**Bell, Anthea**
MnU ms. for 3 titles.

**Bell, Corydon and Thelma**
MnU ms. for 2 titles; il. for 5 titles. MsHaU .90 cu.ft. of ms./il. NcGU ms. and il. for 5 titles.

**Bell, Gertrude**
MoWarbT ms. and il. materials.

**Bellairs, John**
MnU ms. for 4 titles.

**Belting, Natalia**
MnU ms. for 1 title. MsHaU 2.4 cu.ft. of ms./il.

**Bemelmans, Ludwig**
MiD il. MnU il. for 1 title.

**Benary-Isbert, Margot**
MnU ms. for 3 titles. MsHaU 3.6 cu.ft. of ms./il. OrU 4.5 li.ft. of ms. and il.

**Bendick, Jeanne**
MnU ms. for 2 titles; il. for 5 titles. MsHaU 4.2 cu.ft. of ms./il. OrU 13 li.ft. of ms. and il.

**Bendick, Robert**
OrU 1.5 li.ft. of ms.

**Benet, Laura**
MsHaU .30 cu.ft. of ms./il.

**Bengali Language**
MnU 43 vols.

**Bennett, Charles**
NNPM il.

**Bennett, John**
MsHaU .50 cu.ft. of ms./il.

**Bennett, Richard**
MnU il. for 1 title.

**Berelson, Howard**
NjR-Z il. materials.

**Berenstain, Michael**
MsHaU .60 cu.ft. of ms./il.

**Berger, Josef**
OrU 22.5 li.ft. of ms.

**Berger, Terry**
MnU ms. for 2 titles.

**Bernard, Jacqueline de Sieyes**
MnU ms. for 1 title.

**Bernstein, Zena**
NjR-Z il. materials.

**Berry, Erick** *see* **Best, Allena Champlin**

**Berson, Harold**
MnU ms. for 4 titles; il. for 10 titles. MsHaU 3.0 cu.ft. of ms./il.

**Berta, Hugh**
MnU il. for 1 title.

**Best, Allena Champlin**
MnU il. for 1 title. MsHaU 10.6 cu.ft. of ms./il.

**Best, Herbert**
MsHaU .60 cu.ft. of ms./il.

**Beston, Henry**
MeB 205 vols.; 14.5 li.ft. of ms. materials.

**Bethancourt, T. Ernesto**
MoWarbT ms. and il. materials.

**Bethell, Jean**
MsHaU .30 cu.ft. of ms./il.

**Bethers, Ray**
MsHaU .30 cu.ft. of ms./il.

**Bewick, John and Thomas**
CSmH-A 28 pieces of corr. of Thomas Bewick. DLC Extensive book holdings. ICN Extensive book holdings.

**Beyer, Ernestine Cobern**
MnU ms. for 1 title.

**Bianco, Pamela**
MnU il. for 2 titles. MsHaU .30 cu.ft. of ms./il.

**Bibles and Books of Religious Instruction**
AB 40 vols. DLC Extensive book holdings. FU Extensive book holdings. ICN 200+ vols. especially strong in North American Indian languages. MBCn 650+ li.ft. of materials for a number of religious publishers and societies. MiMtpT 250 vols. MoIRC 70 vols. MsHaU 500 vols. NBuBE Significant holdings, including hieroglyphic Bibles. NNC Religious Tract Society publications. NhC Substantial holdings of tract publications. OBlC-M 125 vols. OCH Significant holdings on the Bible and Judaism. OrENC 900 vols. by Disciples of Christ and Churches of Christ. PP-Rb 20,000 vols. of the American Sunday School Union; 500 general vols. ScCoC 183 vols. TxDN Holdings of thumb Bibles. UPB 300 vols. of The Church of Jesus Christ of the Latter Day Saints. WaSPC 110 vols.
*see also* **American Sunday School Union, American Tract Society, Congregational Publishing Society, Congregational Sunday School Curricula, Hymn Books, Massachusetts Sabbath School Society, and Pilgrim Press.**

**Biddle, George**
MsHaU .30 cu.ft. of ms./il.

**Bierhorst, John W.**
MnU ms. for 2 titles.

**Big Little Books**
CFlS 856 vols. from the 1920s–1970s. DLC 534 vols. from the 1930s and 1940s. MiEM Extensive holdings. MnU 604 vols. MsHaU 50 vols. OBgU 115 vols.

**Billings, Henry**
MnU il. for 1 title.

**Binder, Otto O.**
MsHaU .90 cu.ft. of ms./il.

**Bindings**
CFlS 5000 vols. with illustrated or decorative bindings from the late 19th to the early 20th centuries.

**Birch, Reginald Bathurst**
DLC 29 pieces of artwork. MnU il. for 1 title.

**Birnbaum, Uriel**
MnU il. for 1 title.

**Bishop, Claire Huchet**
MnU ms. for 1 title.

**Bixby, William**
MsHaU .90 cu.ft. of ms./il.

**Black, Algernon**
MsHaU .30 cu.ft. of ms./il.

*Black Beauty see* **Sewell, Anna**

**Blackburn, Joyce**
GEU-S 7.5 li.ft. of ms., il., and corr.; 6 published books.

Blackwood, Gary
MoWarbT ms. and il. materials.

Blaine, Margery Kay
MnU ms. for 2 titles.

Blaisdell, Elinore
MnU il. for 11 titles.

Blake, Quentin
MsHaU .40 cu.ft. of ms./il.

Blanchard, Amy E.
DLC 62 vols. FU Extensive book holdings.

Blandford, Percy W.
MsHaU .90 cu.ft. of ms./il.

Blassingame, Lurton
OrU 33 li.ft. of ms.

Blassingame, Wyatt R.
MsHaU 3.9 cu.ft. of ms./il.

Blatter, Dorothy
MsHaU .30 cu.ft. of ms./il.

Blazek, Scott R.
MsHaU .60 cu.ft. of ms./il.

Blecher, Lone and George
MnU ms. for 1 title.

Bleeker, Sonia
MnU ms. for 9 titles. MsHaU 1.2 cu.ft. of ms./il.

Blegvad, Erik
MnU il. for 5 titles. NjR-Z il. materials.

Bleifeld, Stanley
MnU il. for 1 title.

Bloch, Lucienne
MnU il. for 3 titles.

Bloch, Marie Halun
MnU ms. for 20 titles.

Blocklinger, Jeanne
OrU 15 li.ft. of ms.

Blood, Charles and Link
MnU ms. for 1 title.

Blos, Joan W.
MnU ms. for 7 titles.

Blough, Glenn Orlando
MnU ms. for 2 titles. MsHaU .60 cu.ft. of ms./il. OrU 2 li.ft. of ms.

Blumberg, Rhoda
MnU ms. for 1 title.

Blume, Judy
MnU ms. for 11 titles.

Blust, Earl R.
MnU il. for 1 title.

Boardman, Fon Wyman
MsHaU 1.5 cu.ft. of ms./il.

Bobbs Merrill Company
InU-Li Company records from 1885–1957 consists of 130,000 items and corr.

Bock, Vera
MnU il. for 9 titles.

Bodecker, Niels
MnU ms. for 10 titles; il. for 27 titles.

Bodker, Arne
MnU il. for 1 title.

Boegehold, Betty
MsHaU .60 cu.ft. of ms./il.

Boggs, Ralph S.
MsHaU .30 cu.ft. of ms./il.

Bohnanon, Eunice Blake
OrU .5 li.ft. of ms.

Bombova, Viera
MnU il. for 1 title.

Bond, Carrie Jacobs
MsHaU .30 cu.ft. of ms./il.

Bond, Michael
MBU 150 vols. and 40 boxes of ms. materials. MsHaU .30 cu.ft. of ms./il.

Bonehill, Ralph
DLC Extensive book holdings. FU Extensive book holdings.

Bonham, Frank
MnU ms. for 31 titles.

Bonin, Jane
MsHaU .60 cu.ft. of ms./il.

Bonsall, Crosby
MnU ms. for 1 title; il. for 2 titles.

Bontemps, Arna
MnU ms. for 1 title. NSyU 30 li.ft. of ms.
materials.

Boodell, Patricia
MnU il. for 1 title.

Book Dealer Catalogs
MsHaU Extensive holdings. ScSpW Small
holdings of catalogs.

Booz, Elisabeth Benson
MnU ms. for 1 title.

Borten, Helen Jacobson
MnU il. for 3 titles.

Bossom, Naomi
MsHaU .60 cu.ft. of ms./il.

Botany
CoDDB 1000 vols. on botany and related
topics.

Bothwell, Jean
MBU 92 vols.; 50 boxes of ms. materials.

Bottner, Barbara
MnU ms. for 1 title.

Bouchard, Lois Kalb
MnU ms. for 1 title.

Bougere, Marguerite
MsHaU .60 cu.ft. of ms./il.

Bowden, Joan
MnU ms. for 1 title.

Bowen, Joshua David
MsHaU .60 cu.ft. of ms./il.

Bower, Louise
MnU ms. for 2 titles.

Boxer, Devorah
MnU il. for 1 title.

Boyle, Mildred
MiD il.

Bozzo, Frank
MnU il. for 1 title.

Bracker, Charles Eugene
MnU il. for 2 titles.

Bradfield, Margaret
MnU il. for 8 titles.

Bradfield, Roger
MnU ms. for 1 title; il. for 2 titles.

Brady, Lillian
MnU ms. for 1 title.

Bragdon, Elspeth
MnU ms. for 1 title.

Brancato, Robin
NjR ms. materials.

Brandenberg, Aliki Liacouras
MnU ms. for 1 title; il. for 17 titles.
MsHaU 2.4 cu.ft. of ms./il. NjR-Z il.
materials. PP 50 vols.; il.

Brandon, Frances Sweeney
MsHaU .90 cu.ft. of ms./il.

Branfield, John Charles
MnU ms. for 4 titles.

Branley, Franklyn Mansfield
MnU ms. for 2 titles. MsHaU 2.7 cu.ft. of
ms./il.

Brann, Esther
OrU .5 li.ft. of ms.

Branscum, Robbie
MnU ms. for 1 title.

Brantley, Lucille
MsHaU .30 cu.ft. of ms./il.

Bratton, Helen
OrU 1.5 li.ft. of ms.

Braun, Kathy
MnU ms. for 1 title.

Braymer, Marjorie
MnU ms. for 2 titles; il. for 2 titles.

Breck, Vivian
MsHaU .90 cu.ft. of ms./il.

Breckenfeld, Vivian *see* Breck, Vivian

Breen, Else
MnU ms. for 2 titles.

Brelis, Nancy
MnU ms. for 1 title.

Brennan, J. H.
MnU ms. for 1 title.

Brenner, Barbara Johnes
MnU ms. for 7 titles. MsHaU 3.6 cu.ft. of
ms./il.

Brett, Jan
MsHaU .60 cu.ft. of ms./il.

Briard, Cheryl
NjR-Z il. materials.

Bridgman, Elizabeth Klein
MnU ms. for 1 title.

Bridwell, Norman
MsHaU .60 cu.ft. of ms./il.

Briggs, Katharine M.
MsHaU 1.5 cu.ft. of ms./il.

Bright, Robert
MsHaU .60 cu.ft. of ms./il.

Brink, Carol Ryrie
MnM 20 vols. and corr. MnU ms. for 1
title. MsHaU .30 cu.ft. of ms./il.

Brock, Emma Lillian
MnM 50 vols., dolls, and corr. MnU ms.
for 17 titles; il. for 51 titles. MsHaU .60
cu.ft. of ms./il.

Broderick, Dorothy M.
MnU ms. for 1 title.

Broekel, Ray
MsHaU .30 cu.ft. of ms./il.

Bromhall, Winifred
MsHaU .30 cu.ft. of ms./il.

Bronson, Wilfrid Swancourt
MnU ms. for 5 titles; il. for 18 titles.
MsHaU .30 cu.ft. of ms./il.

Brooks, Anne Tedlock
OrU 3 li.ft. of ms.

Brown, Goold
MWA 12 octavo vols. of ms. materials.

Brown, Judith Gwyn
MnU il. for 6 titles. MsHaU 2.1 cu.ft. of
ms./il.

Brown, Lloyd Arnold
MnU ms. for 1 title.

Brown, Marcia
MnU il. for 4 titles. MsHaU 3 cu.ft. of
ms./il. NAIU 27 li.ft. of ms. and il. materials.

Brown, Margaret Wise
MnU ms. for 7 titles. RWe 106 items of
ms. and il.

Brown, Margery
NjR-Z il. materials.

Brown, Marice
MsHaU .3 cu.ft. of ms./il.

Brown, Palmer
MnU ms. for 1 title; il. for 3 titles.

Brown, Paul
MnU ms. for 5 titles; il. for 24 titles.
MsHaU .60 cu.ft. of ms./il. NGuP il.

Brown, Virginia Pounds
MsHaU .30 cu.ft. of ms./il.

Brown, William Louis
OrU 2.5 li.ft. of ms.

Browne, Dik
MnU ms. for 1 title.

Browning, Colleen
MnU il. for 2 titles.

Browning, Robert
TxWB 95 vols., il.

Brudi, Theresa
MsHaU .60 cu.ft. of ms./il.

Bruhl, Edelgard von Heydekamph
MnU ms. for 1 title.

Bruner, Paul
NjR-Z il. materials.

Brunhoff, Jean de
MnU il. for 1 title.

**Brunhoff, Laurent de**
MnU il. for 1 title.

**Brustlein, Janice Tworkov**
MnU ms. for 1 title.

**Bryan, Ashley**
MnU ms. for 1 title. MsHaU .30 cu.ft. of ms./il.

**Bryant, Bernice**
MsHaU 2.1 cu.ft. of ms./il.

**Buba, Joy**
MnU il. for 4 titles.

**Buchenholz, Bruce**
MnU ms. for 1 title.

**Buchheimer, Naomi B.**
MsHaU .30 cu.ft. of ms./il.

**Buchwald, Emilie**
MnU ms. for 1 title.

**Buck, Margaret Waring**
CtU ms. and il. for 10 titles.

**Buckels, Alec**
MnU il. for 1 title. MsHaU .30 cu.ft. of ms./il.

**Buckley, Helen Elizabeth**
MnU ms. for 15 titles. MsHaU .30 cu.ft. of ms./il.

**Buckley, Peter**
MnU ms. for 1 title.

**Buckmaster, Henrietta**
MsHaU 2.7 cu.ft. of ms./il.

**Buehr, Walter**
MsHaU .30 cu.ft. of ms./il.

**Bufano, Remo**
MsHaU .60 cu.ft. of ms./il.

**Buff, Conrad and Mary**
CP il. materials. MnU ms. and il. for 5 titles. MsHaU .30 cu.ft. of ms./il.

**Bulla, Clyde Robert**
MnU ms. for 20 titles. MoWarbT ms. and il. materials. OrU .5 li.ft. of ms.

**Bullock, Judy**
MsHaU .30 cu.ft. of ms./il.

**Bunting, Eve**
MnU ms. for 28 titles.

**Bunyan, John**
FU Extensive book holdings. ICN Extensive book holdings.

**Bunyan, Paul** *see* **Paul Bunyan**

**Burch, Robert**
GU 135 folders of ms., galleys, and related materials.

**Burchard, Peter**
MsHaU .60 cu.ft. of ms./il.

**Burger, Carl**
MnU il. for 2 titles. MsHaU .30 cu.ft. of ms./il. OrU 3 li.ft. of ms. and il.

**Burgess, Barbara Hood**
MnU ms. for 1 title.

**Burgess, Christopher Victor**
MsHaU .30 cu.ft. of ms./il.

**Burgess, Gelett**
CSmH-A 2 ms. and 15 pieces of corr.

**Burgess, Thornton Waldo**
DLC Extensive book holdings. FU 79 vols. MSanB 1,700 vols. and il. by Harrison Cady and Phoebe Erickson that were used in his books. MsHaU .30 cu.ft. of ms./il. WU-CC 150 vols.

**Burgwyn, Mebane H.**
NcGU ms, il. and corr. for 6 titles.

**Burnett, Frances Hodgson**
CSmH-A 1 ms. and 10 pieces of corr. DLC Extensive book holdings. FU Extensive book holdings. ICN 26 vols.; 2 ms. MBU 64 pieces of corr. PP 60 vols. ViU 85 vols.

**Burns, Catherine**
MnU ms. for 1 title.

**Burroughs, Edgar Rice**
DLC 159 vols. InU-Li 30+ vols.; filmscript. KyLoU 50,000 vols. and 10,000

periodical vols. in the Burroughs Collection. TxU-Hu 350 vols.

**Burt, Olive**
MsHaU .30 cu.ft. of ms./il.

**Burton, Virginia Lee**
MnU il. for 2 titles. OrU 3 li.ft. of il.

**Busch, Phyllis**
MnU ms. for 1 title.

**Busoni, Rafaello**
MnU il. for 25 titles.

**Butler, Francelia**
MnU ms. for 1 title.

**Butler, Roger**
MsHaU .30 cu.ft. of ms./il.

**Butterworth, Hezekiah**
CSmH-A 2 pieces of corr. DLC Extensive book holdings. FU 44 vols.

**Byars, Betsy**
MnU ms. for 2 titles. MsHaU .30 cu.ft. of ms./il. ScCleU 130 vols. and 4 cu.ft. of ms.

**Byers, Irene**
MsHaU .30 cu.ft. of ms./il.

**Cady, Harrison**
MSanB 350 il. used in Thornton Waldo Burgess books.

**Caines, Jeanette**
MnU ms. for 1 title.

**Caldecott, Randolph**
CSmH-A 2 pieces of corr. DLC 47 vols.

FU Extensive book holdings. InU-Li 50+ vols.; 9 il. for 2 titles. MiKW Woodblocks engraved by Edmund Evans after designs by Caldecott. MnU ms. for 1 title; il. for 3 titles. MsHaU Substantial book holdings, woodblocks and .60 cu.ft. of ms./il. NN-Don 55 vols.; 6 il. NNPM il. PPiU-LS 60 vols.

**Caldecott Medal** *see* **Award Books**

**Calhoun, Mary Huiskamp**
MnU ms. for 34 titles. MsHaU .60 cu.ft. of ms./il.

**California**
CL 2,500 titles with California settings from 1850. CSd 180 vols. on California history with emphasis on San Diego County.

**California—Authors and Illustrators**
CL 12,000 titles by California authors and illustrators from 1850. CSd 100 vols. by San Diego County authors and illustrators.

**Call, Hughie**
MsHaU .30 cu.ft. of ms./il. OrU 3 li.ft. of ms.

**Calvert, Patricia**
MnU ms. for 1 title.

**Cameron, Eleanor Butler**
MnU ms. for 17 titles. MsHaU .30 cu.ft. of ms./il.

**Campbell, Virginia**
MnU il. for 1 title.

*The Brownies: Their Book*, by Palmer Cox; London: Unwin [1887?].

**Campion, Nardi**
MnU ms. for 1 title.

**Canfield, Jane White**
MnU ms. for 1 title.

**Caple, Kathy**
MnU il. for 1 title.

**Capron, Jean**
MsHaU .30 cu.ft. of ms./il.

**Caras, Roger**
MnU ms. for 3 titles.

**Carew, Dorothy**
OrU 1.5 li.ft. of ms.

**Carle, Eric**
MnU il. for 5 titles.

**Carlisle, Norman**
MsHaU .30 cu.ft. of ms./il.

**Carlsen, Ruth Christoffer**
MnU ms. for 9 titles.

**Carlson, Bernice Wells**
MsHaU 2.1 cu.ft. of ms./il.

**Carlson, Natalie Savage**
MnU ms. for 16 titles. MsHaU 2.1 cu.ft. of ms./il.

**Carmer, Elizabeth Black**
MnU il. for 3 titles.

**Carona, Philip**
MsHaU .30 cu.ft. of ms./il.

**Carr, Mary Jane**
MnU ms. for 1 title. OrU .5 li.ft. of ms. and il.

**Carrick, Carol**
MnU ms. for 1 title.

**Carrick, Donald**
MnU ms. for 2 titles; il. for 11 titles.

**Carrington, Richard**
MsHaU .30 cu.ft. of ms./il.

**Carroll, Lewis**
CSmH-A 2 ms. and 94 pieces of corr. DLC 265 vols. FU Extensive book holdings. ICN 70+ vols. InU-Li 100+ vols.; ms.

and il. materials. MiD 63 vols. MiDW Various editions of *Alice in Wonderland*. MsHaU Substantial book holdings; .30 cu.ft. of ms./il. NNPM Books, letters, photographs and objects. NNU-F 650 vols. and other materials. OCl 50 vols. *Alice in Wonderland*. PPiU-LS 60 vols. TxU-Hu 4,000 vols., ms., ephemera. ViR Significant holdings.

**Carroll, Ruth and Latrobe**
MsHaU .30 cu.ft. of ms./il. NcGU ms. and il. for 3 titles. OrU 13.5 li.ft. of ms. and il.

**Carse, Robert**
MsHaU .30 cu.ft. of ms./il.

**Carson, John F.**
MsHaU .30 cu.ft. of ms./il.

**Carter, Helene**
MnU il. for 11 titles.

**Carter, James**
MnU ms. for 1 title.

**Carter, Katharine**
MsHaU .30 cu.ft. of ms./il.

**Cartwright, Sally**
MsHaU .30 cu.ft. of ms./il.

**Case, Victoria**
OrU 5 li.ft. of ms.

**Casewit, Curtis**
MsHaU 3.3 cu.ft. of ms./il.

**Cass, Joan E.**
MsHaU .30 cu.ft. of ms./il.

**Cassel-Wronker, Lili**
MnU il. for 27 titles.

**Cassidy, Vincent**
MsHaU .30 cu.ft. of ms./il.

**Castlemon, Harry**
DLC Extensive book holdings. FU 86 vols. InU-Li 400+ vols.; corr. NhD Extensive book holdings. PP 75 vols. ViU 82 vols.

**Castor, Henry**
OrU .5 li.ft. of ms.

**Catherall, Arthur**
MsHaU .30 cu.ft. of ms./il.

**Catherwood, Mary**
ICN 28 vols.; ms. collection.

**Caudill, Rebecca**
KyU 13 boxes of ms. materials. MnU ms. for 1 title; il. for 7 titles. MsHaU .30 cu.ft. of ms./il.

**Cauley, Lorinda Bryan**
MsHaU .90 cu.ft. of ms./il.

**Cavanah, Frances**
MnU ms. for 3 titles. MsHaU .30 cu.ft. of ms./il. OrU 1.5 li.ft. of ms.

**Cavanna, Betty**
MsHaU 11.5 cu.ft. of ms./il.

**Ceder, Georgiana**
MsHaU .9 cu.ft. of ms./il.

**Cellini, Joseph**
MsHaU .30 cu.ft. of ms./il.

**Chafetz, Henry**
MnU ms. for 1 title.

**Chaikin, Miriam**
MnU ms. for 14 titles. MsHaU 1.2 cu.ft. of ms./il.

**Chalmers, Audrey**
MnU ms. for 3 titles; il. for 6 titles.

**Chalmers, Mary**
MsHaU 1.2 cu.ft. of ms./il. NjR-Z il. materials.

**Champney, Elizabeth W.**
MDeeP 40+ vols.

**Champney, J. Wells**
MsHaU .30 cu.ft. of ms./il.

**Chandler, Edna Walker**
MnU ms. for 1 title.

**Chandler, Ruth Forbes**
MsHaU .30 cu.ft. of ms./il.

**Chanslor, Marjorie Torrey Hood**
MnU il. for 1 title.

**Chapbooks**
CLU-S/C Significant holdings. CtY-BR 350 vols. from 18th–19th centuries. FTS 350 vols. primarily 1830–1850. FU 300 vols. from 1800–1840. ICN 200+ British and American, 18th–19th centuries. InU-Li 2,000+ vols. from 19th century. MBAt Significant holdings. MBWS Small holdings. MiMtpT 500 vols. British and American. MnU 88 vols. MoS 100+ vols. from 1780–1860. MsHaU 250+ vols. NCooHi 500 vols. from 19th century. NHyF 268 vols. NjP-C Substantial holdings. NN-Don 75 vols. NWe 70 vols. NhD 275 vols. NjR 300 vols. OCl-RB 3,000 vols. PPiU-LS 250 vols. ViR 50+ vols. WaSp 32 vols.

**Chapman, Allen**
DLC 18 vols.

**Chapman, Frederick Trench**
MnU il. for 2 titles.

**Chapman, Maristan**
OrU 36 li.ft. of ms.

**Chappell, Warren**
MnU il. for 4 titles.

**Charlip, Remy**
MnU il. for 9 titles.

**Charlot, Jean**
MnU il. for 20 titles. MsHaU 1.2 cu.ft. of ms./il.

**Charlot, Martin**
MsHaU .60 cu.ft. of ms./il.

**Chartier, Normand**
CtU ms. and il. for 6 titles.

**Chase, Mary Coyle**
OrU 1 li.ft. of ms.

**Chase, Richard**
MnU ms. for 20 titles.

**Chastain, Madye Lee**
MnU il. for 1 title. MsHaU .30 cu.ft. of ms./il. OrU .5 li.ft. of ms. and il.

**Chee, Cheng-Khee**
MnU il. for 1 title.

**Cheesman, Lilian**
MnU ms. for 1 title.

**Chen, Tony**
MnU il. for 19 titles. MsHaU 4.9 cu.ft. of ms./il. NjR ms. materials. NjR-Z il. materials.

**Cheney, Cora**
MnU ms. for 3 titles. MsHaU 1.5 cu.ft. of ms./il.

**Chess, Victoria**
CtU il. for 15 titles.

**Chessare, Michele**
NjR-Z il. materials.

**Chew, Ruth**
MsHaU .60 cu.ft. of ms./il.

**Children's Book Week Posters**
CRiv Complete collection from 1919 to date. NNCbc Complete collection from 1919 to date. PP Complete collection from 1919 to date.

**Children's Literature, Study of**
AkA 1,000 vols. of texts, histories, and reference works. CCCla Reference collection. CoU References in Westerberg Collection. DLC Comprehensive, growing reference collection of over 2,000 items. FU Collection of 500 reference works. GS 500 vols. ICN 750+ vols. IEN Reference collection. IU-LS 800 vols. NBPu 2,000+ vols. MBSi Archives of the *Horn Book* magazine provides information on this topic. MiDW Extensive collection. MnU 1,222 vols. and 3,089 vertical files. MoS Extensive collection. MoWarbT 600 vols. MsHaU Extensive book holdings and vertical files. NN-Don 70 vols. NNC 200 vols. NNCbc Extensive holdings. OU Extensive holdings. OkT Substantial holdings. PNo 200 vols. in Field Collection. PP Extensive holdings. WU-CC 850 vols.

**Chinese Language**
DLC 300+ vols. MnU 46 vols. NjP-C 124 vols. NN-BrC 3,000 vols.

**Chittum, Ida**
MoWarbT ms. and il. materials.

**Christensen, Nadia**
MnU ms. for 1 title.

**Christgau, Alice Erickson**
MnU ms. for 3 titles.

**Christmas**
MsHaU 300+ vols. NcU 1,000 vols. NNMus 70 vols. PPiC "'Twas the Night before Christmas" collection. PSt 250 vols.

**Christopher, Matt**
MnU ms. for 9 titles.

**Church, Richard**
CSmH-A 8 pieces of corr. TxU-Hu 7 ms.

**Church of Jesus Christ of the Latter Day Saints** *see* **Bibles and Books of Religious Instruction**

**Chute, Beatrice Joy**
MnU ms. for 1 title.

**Chute, Marchette Gaylord**
MnU ms. for 2 titles; il. for 1 title. MsHaU .30 cu.ft. of ms./il.

**Cinderella**
FU Extensive book holdings. MsHaU Substantial book holdings.

**Circus**
INS 660 vols.

**Clapp, Patricia**
MnU ms. for 2 titles. MsHaU .30 cu.ft. of ms./il.

**Clark, Ann Nolan**
AzU ms. MsHa .60 cu.ft. of ms./il.

**Clark, Frank James**
MsHaU .30 cu.ft. of ms./il.

**Clark, Margaret Goff**
MsHaU 8.4 cu.ft. of ms./il.

**Clark, Willard**
MnU il. for 1 title.

**Clarke, Arthur Charles**
MnU ms. for 1 title. MsHaU .30 cu.ft. of
ms./il.

**Clarke, Rebecca Sophia**
MePW 50 vols.

**Clarke, Tom Eugene**
MsHaU .60 cu.ft. of ms./il.

**Cleary, Beverly**
MnU ms. for 1 title.

**Cleaver, Vera and Bill**
MnU ms. for 1 title.

**Clemens, Samuel L.** *see* **Twain, Mark**

**Cleveland, Philip**
MsHaU .60 cu.ft. of ms./il.

**Cleven, Kathryn Seward**
MsHaU 1.8 cu.ft. of ms./il.

**Clewes, Dorothy**
MsHaU .30 cu.ft. of ms./il.

**Clifford, Eth**
MnU ms. for 7 titles.

**Clifford, Harold B.**
MsHaU .60 cu.ft. of ms./il.

**Climo, Shirley**
MnU ms. for 1 title.

**Clymer, Eleanor**
MnU ms. for 36 titles. MsHaU .9 cu.ft. of
ms./il.

**Coates, Belle**
MnU ms. for 1 title.

**Coates, Ruth Allison**
MsHaU .30 cu.ft. of ms./il.

**Coatsworth, Elizabeth**
MeB 205 vols.; 14.5 li.ft. of ms. materials. MePW Books and ms. materials.
MnU ms. for 57 titles. MsHaU .30 cu.ft.
of ms./il.

**Cobb, Vicki**
MsHaU 6.0 cu.ft. of ms./il.

**Cober, Alan E.**
MnU il. for 2 titles.

**Cock Robin**
DLC 20 versions. FU 65 versions.

**Coen, Rena**
MnU ms. for 1 title.

**Coerr, Eleanor**
MnU ms. for 1 title. MsHaU .30 cu.ft. of
ms./il.

**Coggins, Jack**
MsHaU 3.0 cu.ft. of ms./il.

**Cohen, Barbara**
MnU ms. for 1 title. NjR ms. materials.

**Cohen, Daniel**
MsHaU 12.3 cu.ft. of ms./il.

**Cohen, Miriam**
MnU ms. for 3 titles. MsHaU .30 cu.ft. of
ms./il.

**Cohen, Robert Carl**
MnU ms. for 1 title.

**Cohn, Angelo**
MnU ms. for 2 titles.

**Colby, Carroll B.**
MsHaU .30 cu.ft. of ms./il.

**Colby, Jean Poindexter**
MsHaU 1.2 cu.ft. of ms./il.

**Cole, Martin**
MsHaU 1.8 cu.ft. of ms./il.

**Coleman, Harry**
MsHaU .30 cu.ft. of ms./il.

**Collier, James Lincoln**
MnU ms. for 12 titles.

**Collier, Julia**
MsHaU .30 cu.ft. of ms./il.

**Collins, Frederica Joan Hale**
MsHaU .60 cu.ft. of ms./il.

**Collins, Robert**
MnU ms. for 1 title.

**Collodi, Carlo**
FU Extensive book holdings. TxDN Substantial holdings of *Pinocchio*.

**Colman, Hila**
MsHaU .30 cu.ft. of ms./il. OrU 2.5 li.ft. of ms.

**Colorado—Authors and Illustrators**
CoU Collection of books written by Colorado authors.

**Colum, Padraic**
MnU ms. for 1 title.

**Comfort, Claudette**
MnU ms. for 1 title.

**Comfort, Mildred**
MsHaU .30 cu.ft. of ms./il.

**Comic Books**
CFlS 4,000 issues from 1938. CNoS 720 comic books from 1937–1960 and other related material. CSfACA Extensive holdings. IDeKN 800 comic books and strips. InU-Li Extensive holdings of books and strips; 74 il. KyLoU Tarzan comic books and strips. MiEM Comic art. MnU 1,534 issues. NcCU 160 titles. OBgU 42,000 issues; ms. materials for Allen and John Saunders. OC 550 issues.

**Cone, Molly**
MsHaU 7.5 cu.ft. of ms./il.

**Confederate Imprints**
GU Collection of children's books published in the Confederacy during the Civil War.

**Conford, Ellen**
MnU ms. for 2 titles.

**Congregational Publishing Society**
MBCn 54 li.ft. of materials.

**Congregational Sunday School Curricula**
MBCn 400 li.ft. of materials.

**Connecticut Imprints**
CtH 518 vols. printed by Kellogg & Bulkeley. CtHi 500 vols. printed in Connecticut from 1750 in Connecticut Imprints Collection; 1,200 vols. printed by Connecticut Printers, Inc., between 1955–1969 in Connecticut Printers Archive. CtNhHi 200 vols. published 1777–1875, most published in Connecticut.

**Connecticut Printers, Inc.**
CtHi 1,200 vols.

**Connolly, Jerome Patrick**
MnU il. for 1 title.

**Connor, Eva G.**
MsHaU 1.2 cu.ft. of ms./il.

**Conrad, Pam**
MsHaU .30 cu.ft. of ms./il.

**Cook, Howard**
MnU il. for 2 titles.

**Cook, Joseph J.**
MsHaU 2.1 cu.ft. of ms./il.

**Cook, Olive Rambo**
MsHaU 3.3 cu.ft. of ms./il.

**Cooke, David C.**
MsHaU 3.9 cu.ft. of ms./il.

**Cooke, Donald E.**
MnU ms. for 2 titles. MsHaU .30 cu.ft. of ms./il. PP ms. and il.

**Cooley, Donald**
MnU ms. for 1 title.

**Coolidge, Olivia Ensor**
MnU ms. for 20 titles.

**Coombs, Charles**
MsHaU 18.6 cu.ft. of ms./il.

**Coombs, Patricia**
MnU ms. for 5 titles; il. for 7 titles. MsHaU 1.2 cu.ft. of ms./il.

**Cooney, Barbara**
CtU il. for 20 titles. MnU il. for 42 titles. MsHaU 4.5 cu.ft. of ms./il. NjR-Z il. materials.

**Cooper, Lee Pelham**
MsHaU .30 cu.ft. of ms./il.

**Copy Books**
ICN Extensive collection of calligraphy and writing books. MStuO Collection of ms. exercise books.

**Corbett, Scott**
MnU ms. for 16 titles. MsHaU 4.2 cu.ft. of ms./il.

**Corcoran, Barbara**
MnU ms. for 13 titles. MoWarbT ms. and il. materials. MsHaU 12 cu.ft. of ms./il.

**Corcos, Lucille**
MnU ms. for 1 title; il. for 3 titles.

**Corey, Bob**
MnU il. for 2 titles.

**Cormack, Maribelle**
OrU 13 li.ft. of ms.

**Cormier, Robert**
MFiT ms. materials.

**Cornwall, Ian Wolfran**
MnU ms. for 1 title.

**Cosby, Willi, Jr.**
MnU ms. for 2 titles.

**Cosgrave, John O'Hara, II**
MnU il. for 3 titles. OrU 12.5 li.ft. of il.

**Cosgrove, Margaret**
MnU il. for 1 title. MsHaU 3.3 cu.ft. of ms./il.

**Cosner, Shaaron**
AzTeS ms. MsHaU .30 cu.ft. of ms./il.

**Cotton, Morris** (publisher)
MWA 2 folio vols. of ms. materials and records.

**Courlander, Harold**
MsHaU .60 cu.ft. of ms./il.

**Coville, Bruce**
MsHaU 18 cu.ft. of ms./il.

**Cowell, Vi**
MnU il. for 1 title.

**Cox, Donald William**
MsHaU 2.7 cu.ft. of ms./il.

**Cox, Miriam**
MsHaU .30 cu.ft. of ms./il.

**Cox, Palmer**
FU 28 vols. MnU il. for 1 title. PP 100 vols. PP-Rb 90 il. and corr.

**Cox, William Robert**
MsHaU 3 cu.ft. of ms./il. OrU 29.5 li.ft. of ms.

**Coy, Harold**
MsHaU .60 cu.ft. of ms./il.

**Craig, Chase**
CNoS Comic book collection.

**Craig, M. Jean**
MsHaU .60 cu.ft. of ms./il.

**Craig, Mary Francis Shura**
OrU 8 li.ft. of ms.

**Cramer, Rita**
MnU il. for 1 title.

**Crane, Walter**
CSmH-A 5 pieces of corr. CtY-BR 200 books written and/or illustrated by Crane, with proofs, drawings, and ms. DLC 93 vols. FU 73 vols. ICN 30+ vols. InU-Li 100+ vols.; ms. materials. MiD 350+ items including il., wallpaper, and related materials. MnU il. for 1 title. MsHaU il. NN-Don 80 vols.; il. PP 50 vols.

**Crary, Margaret**
MsHaU 1.2 cu.ft. of ms./il.

**Crawford, Mel**
MnU il. for 1 title.

**Crayder, Dorothy**
MnU ms. for 8 titles.

**Credle, Ellis**
MnU il. for 1 title. OrU 1 li.ft. of ms. and il.

**Creekmore, Raymond**
MnU il. for 4 titles.

**Cresswell, Helen**
MnU ms. for 2 titles.

**Cretan, Gladys Yessayan**
MnU ms. for 1 title.

**Cretien, Paul D.**
MnU il. for 1 title.

**Crews, Donald**
MnU ms. for 1 title; il. for 1 title.

**Crist, Richard**
MsHaU .30 cu.ft. of ms./il.

**Croatian Language**
MnU 12 vols.

**Crofford, Emily**
MnU ms. for 3 titles.

**Cromie, Robert**
MsHaU .30 cu.ft. of ms./il.

**Crosby, Alexander**
OrU 30 li.ft. of ms.

**Cross, Helen Reeder**
MsHaU .30 cu.ft. of ms./il.

**Crossley-Holland, Kevin**
MnU ms. for 1 title.

**Crowell, Pers**
MnU il. for 1 title. MsHaU 1.3 cu.ft. of ms./il. OrU 7 li.ft. of ms. and il.

**Cruikshank, George**
DLC Extensive book holdings. FU 38 vols. ICN 60+ vols.; 1 piece of corr. InU-Li Extensive holdings in Starling Collection; il. for several titles. MnU il. for 2 titles. MsHaU .30 cu.ft. of ms./il. NNU-F 2 li.ft. of letters, drawings, and prints. OC 206 vols. and proofs.

**Cruse, Laurence**
MnU il. for 1 title.

**Cruz, Ray**
MnU il. for 1 title. MsHaU 4.4 cu.ft. of ms./il.

**Cuffari, Richard**
MnU il. for 4 titles. MsHaU .60 cu.ft. of ms./il.

**Cullen, Charles**
MnU il. for 1 title.

**Cummings, Betty Sue**
MnU ms. for 3 titles.

**Cunningham, Julia Woolfolk**
MnU ms. for 16 titles. OrU 1.5 li.ft. of ms.

**Curren, Polly**
MsHaU .90 cu.ft. of ms./il. OrU 1.5 li.ft. of ms.

**Curry, Jane Louise**
MnU ms. for 15 titles.

**Cykler, Edmund**
MsHaU .30 cu.ft. of ms./il.

**Dahl, Borghild**
MnU ms. for 8 titles. MsHaU .30 cu.ft. of ms./il.

**Dahl, Roald**
TxU-Hu 1 box of ms.

**Dalgliesh, Alice**
MnU ms. for 2 titles; il. for 1 title.

**Dalke, Susan**
MnU il. for 1 title.

**Daly, Maureen**
OrU 7.5 li.ft. of ms.

**Dalziel, Edward**
MnU il. for 1 title.

**Daniel, Hawthorne**
MsHaU 3.3 cu.ft. of ms./il.

**Danish Language**
MnU 510 vols.

**Danziger, Paula**
MnU ms. for 12 titles.

**Darling, Lois and Louis**
MnU ms. for 12 titles; il. for 38 titles.

**Darrow, Whitney**
MnU ms. for 2 titles.

**Darton, William** (publisher)
FU Extensive book holdings. InU-Li Extensive book holdings. OOxM 184 vols.

**Daugherty, Charles Michael**
OrU .5 li.ft. of ms. and il.

**Daugherty, Harry R.**
MnU il. for 2 titles.

**Daugherty, James Henry**
KEmU ms. and il. MnU ms. for 3 titles; il. for 29 titles. OrU 20.5 li.ft. of ms. and il.

**d'Aulaire, Edgar Parin and Ingri**
KWi il. MnU il. for 12 titles. MsHaU .30 cu.ft. of ms./il. OrU 3 li.ft. of il.

**Davis, Anne Pence**
KyBgW 1.5 li.ft. of corr., clippings, reviews, and photographs.

**Davis, Arthur Kennard**
MsHaU .30 cu.ft. of ms./il.

**Davis, Edward**
MnU ms. for 1 title.

**Davis, Hubert J.**
MsHaU .30 cu.ft. of ms./il.

**Davis, Julia**
MsHaU .90 cu.ft. of ms./il.

**Davis, Mary Gould**
MnU ms. for 1 title.

**Davis, Paul**
MnU il. for 2 titles.

**Davis, Russell G.**
MnU ms. for 2 titles.

**Dawson, Carley Robinson**
OrU 16.5 li.ft. of ms.

**Day, Beth**
MsHaU 1.8 cu.ft. of ms./il.

**Day, Mahlon** (publisher)
NRU Substantial holdings.

**Day, Thomas**
FU 110 vols.; 87 editions of *Sanford and Merton.*

**de Angeli, Marguerite Lofft**
KWi il. MiD il. MnU ms. for 2 titles; il. for 9 titles. MsHaU .50 cu.ft. of ms./il. PP 40 vols., ms., il.

**De Beque, Maurice**
MnU il. for 2 titles.

**Decker, Duane**
MsHaU .30 cu.ft. of ms./il.

**Defoe, Daniel**
CSmH-A 2 ms. CtY-BR 300+ editions of *Robinson Crusoe.* FU 300+ editions of *Robinson Crusoe.* ICN 46+ editions of *Robinson Crusoe.* InU-Li Extensive holdings with 175 editions of *Robinson Crusoe.* MiD 40 editions of *Robinson Crusoe.*

**DeGering, Etta**
MsHaU .60 cu.ft. of ms./il.

**De Groat, Diane**
MsHaU .60 cu.ft. of ms./il.

**de Grummond, Lena Y.**
MsHaU 10 cu.ft. of ms./il.

**DeJong, Meindert**
MiMtpT Published vols. and ms. materials. MnU ms. for 6 titles.

**de la Mare, Walter**
CSmH-A 358 pieces of corr. MnU ms. for 1 title. PPT 500 vols., 1,000 pieces of corr.

**de Larrea, Victoria**
NjR-Z il. materials.

**Delaune, Lynn de Grummond**
MsHaU .60 cu.ft. of ms./il.

**De Leeuw, Adele and Cateau**
MsHaU 35.1 cu.ft. of ms./il.

**Delton, Judy**
MnU ms. for 60 titles. MsHaU .30 cu.ft. of ms./il.

**Dengel, Dianne**
MsHaU .60 cu.ft. of ms./il.

**Dennis, Wesley**
KWi il. MnU il. for 18 titles. MsHaU .60 cu.ft. of ms./il.

**Denslow, William Wallace**
MnU il. for 3 titles. MsHaU .40 cu.ft. of ms./il. NNC 42 il.

**de Paola, Tomie**
MnU ms. for 99 titles; il. for 158 titles.

**DePauw, Linda Grant**
MnU ms. for 1 title.

**Deraney, Michael J.**
MnU il. for 2 titles.

**de Regniers, Beatrice**
MnU ms. for 1 title. MsHaU 1.5 cu.ft. of ms./il. PP 40 vols., ms.

**Derleth, August**
MsHaU .30 cu.ft. of ms./il.

**Desmond, Alice Curtis**
OrU 3 li.ft. of ms. and il.

**DeTerra, Rhoda Hoff**
MsHaU .30 cu.ft. of ms./il.

**Detmold, Edward Julius**
MnU il. for 1 title.

**DeVault, M. Vere**
MsHaU .30 cu.ft. of ms./il.

**Devlin, Harry**
NjR-Z il. materials.

**DeWeese, Gene**
MsHaU 9.9 cu.ft. of ms./il.

**DeWeese-Wehen, Joy**
MsHaU .90 cu.ft. of ms./il.

**Dewey, Ariane**
NjR-Z il. materials.

**DeWit, Dorothy**
MnU ms. for 2 titles.

**DeWitt, Cornelius**
MnU il. for 2 titles. OrU 9 li.ft. of il.

**Deyhle, Nancy**
MsHaU .60 cu.ft. of ms./il.

**Diaz, Abby Morton**
CSmH-A 49 pieces of corr. FU Extensive book holdings.

**Dick, Trella Lamson**
MnU ms. for 1 title. MsHaU .30 cu.ft. of ms./il.

**Dickens, Charles**
CLU-C 350 early and fine published edition. CSmH-A 12 ms.; 1,000 pieces of corr. CtY-BR Gimbel Dickens Collection includes books, ms., il., and corr. FU Extensive book holdings. ICN 300+ vols. NNU-F 1,800 vols. and ms. TxU-Hu 1,100 vols., corr.

**Dietmeier, Mel**
MsHaU .30 cu.ft. of ms./il.

**Dillon, Leo and Diane**
MnU il. for 2 titles.

**Dime Novels**
ArU 1,630 vols. CSd 779 vols. CSfACA Extensive holdings of published works. DLC 50,000 vols. FTS 8,000 vols. ICN 63+ vols. IDeKN 7,500 vols. in the Johannsen Collection. INS 60 vols. about the circus. IaU 360 vols. InU-Li 350+ vols. MWalB 4,000 vols. MiEM 10,500 vols. MnU 50,000 vols. MsHaU 300 vols. NCooHi 100 vols.; ms. materials. NNU-F 15,000 vols. OC 245 vols. OKentU 200 vols.

**Dines, Carol**
MnU ms. for 1 title.

**Dines, Glen**
MnU il. for 2 titles. MsHaU .60 cu.ft. of ms./il.

**Disney, Walt**
CAna Extensive holdings of books, periodicals, and ms. materials. CBbWDA 8,000 Disney books dating from 1930 in 40 languages; 435 li.ft. of ms. and il. IC 85 vols. MnU ms. for 2 titles; il. for 5 titles.

**Divers, Dorothy**
MnU il. for 1 title.

**Dixon, Franklin W.**
DLC 81 vols. FU Extensive book holdings.

**Dixon, Jeanne**
MsHaU .30 cu.ft. of ms./il.

**Doane, Pelagie**
MnU ms. for 3 titles.

**Dobie, James Frank**
MsHaU .30 cu.ft. of ms./il.

**Dobson, Austin**
MsHaU .30 cu.ft. of ms./il.

**Dodd, Mead and Company** (publisher)
MWA 2 boxes of company records and papers.

**Dodds, Andrea**
MsHaU .30 cu.ft. of ms./il.

**Dodge, Bertha S.**
MsHaU .30 cu.ft. of ms./il.

**Dodge, Mary Mapes**
CSmH-A 1 ms.; 76 pieces of corr.

**Dodgson, Charles Lutwidge** *see* **Carroll, Lewis**

**Dolls**
CL 450 dolls from 40+ countries. MsHaU 600 international dolls. TxDN Books about dolls. WaSHi 1,800 dolls.
*see also* **Toys**

**Domanska, Janina**
MnU ms. for 1 title; il. for 14 titles. MsHaU 4.6 cu.ft. of ms./il.

**Domjan, Joseph**
MnU ms. for 2 titles.

**Donovan, John**
MnU ms. for 6 titles.

**Doremus, Robert**
MsHaU 2.40 cu.ft. of ms./il.

**Dorian, Edith**
MsHaU 1.2 cu.ft. of ms./il.

**Dorliae, Peter G.**
MnU ms. for 1 title.

**Dorros, Arthur**
MnU ms. for 3 titles.

**Doty, Jean Slaughter**
MsHaU .90 cu.ft. of ms./il.

**Dougherty, Joanna Foster**
OrU 1.5 li.ft. of ms.

**Douglass, Ralph**
MsHaU .90 cu.ft. of ms./il.

**Douty, Esther M.**
MsHaU .30 cu.ft. of ms./il.

**Dowd, Helen** *see* **Lietta**

**Dowden, Anne Ophelia**
MnU ms. for 2 titles; il. for 2 titles.

**Downer, Marion**
MnU ms. for 3 titles; il. for 1 title.

**Downey, Fairfax**
MsHaU .60 cu.ft. of ms./il.

**Doyle, Arthur Conan**
MnU ms. for 1 title.

**Doyle, Richard**
FU Extensive book holdings. NNPM il.

**Drama**
AzTeS 800 vols., periodicals, and ms. RPB-JH 800 vols.

**Draper, Cena Christopher**
MoWarbT ms. and il. materials.

**du Bois, William Pene**
MnU il. for 1 title. NjR-Z il. materials.

**Duffy, Joseph**
MnU il. for 1 title.

**Dulac, Edmund**
CSmH-A 6 pieces of corr.

**Duncan, Lois**
MnU ms. for 6 titles.

**Duncombe, Frances**
MsHaU .60 cu.ft. of ms./il.

**Durant, John**
MsHaU .60 cu.ft. of ms./il.

**Dutch Language**
CtNbT 329 vols. from 1758 to 1890. ICN 50+ vols. MnU 209 vols. MsHaU 50+ vols.

**Dutton, E. P.** (publisher)
NSyU 89 li.ft. of company records and papers.

**Duvoisin, Roger A.**
MnU ms. for 5 titles; il. for 88 titles. MsHaU 1.8 cu.ft. of ms./il. NjR ms.

materials. NjR-Z il. materials. OrU .5 li.ft. of ms. and il.

**Dyer, Jane**
CtU ms. and il. for 6 titles.

**Earle, Olive L.**
MnU il. for 2 titles.

**Eaton, Jeanette**
MnU ms. for 1 title.

**Eberle, Irmengarde**
MnU ms. for 2 titles. MsHaU .60 cu.ft. of ms./il. OrU 1.5 li.ft. of ms.

**Ecke, Wolfgang**
MnU ms. for 1 title.

**Ede, Janina**
MsHaU .30 cu.ft. of ms./il.

**Edgeworth, Maria**
CLU-S/C Extensive book holdings; 100 letters. CSmH-A 1 ms.; 76 pieces of corr. DLC 104 vols. FU Extensive book holdings. PP-Rb 200 vols.

**Edmonds, Walter D.**
MnU ms. for 3 titles.

**Education**
InTI 2,000 vols. from the 18th century. MHi 24 boxes of ms. materials in the Horace Mann Papers. PPiU Substantial holdings. TxDN 250 vols. WMUW 45,550 vols.

**Edwards, Leo**
DLC 29 vols. FU 22 vols.

**Egyptian Language**
MnU 101 vols.

**Ehlert, Loi**
MnU il. for 3 titles.

**Ehrlich, Bettina**
MnU il. for 3 titles. MsHaU .30 cu.ft. of ms./il. OrU .5 li.ft. of ms. and il.

**Eichenberg, Fritz**
MnU il. for 17 titles. NBuBE 20 il.

**Eicke, Edna**
MnU ms. for 1 title.

**Eifert, Virginia S.**
MsHaU .90 cu.ft. of ms./il.

**Eiseman, Alberta**
MsHaU .60 cu.ft. of ms./il.

**Eisenberg, Phyllis**
MnU ms. for 1 title.

**Elliott, Margaret**
MsHaU .30 cu.ft. of ms./il.

**Elliott, Mary Belson**
FU Extensive book holdings.

**Ellis, Edward**
DLC Extensive book holdings. FU Extensive book holdings. MnU 1,400 vols., 57 periodicals, and 60 dime novels. NhD Extensive book holdings. PP 100 vols.

**Ellis, Leo R.**
MsHaU .30 cu.ft. of ms./il.

**Emberley, Ed**
ICN 160+ vols. MnU il. for 2 titles. MoWarbT ms. and il. materials. MsHaU 1 cu.ft. of ms./il.

**Emerson, Alice**
DLC Extensive book holdings. FU Extensive book holdings.

**Emery, Anne**
OrU 21 li.ft. of ms.

**Emrich, Duncan Black Macdonald**
MnU ms. for 2 titles.

**Engelbrecht, Trientja**
MnU il. for 1 title.

**Engle, Eloise**
MsHaU 1.2 cu.ft. of ms./il.

**Epp, Margaret**
MsHaU .30 cu.ft. of ms./il.

**Epstein, Anne Merrick**
MsHaU .30 cu.ft. of ms./il.

**Epstein, Sam and Beryl**
MnU ms. for 1 title. MsHaU 2.4 cu.ft. of ms./il.

**Equinox Cooperative Press**
DGU Records of the press founded by Lynd Ward in 1932.

**Erdman, Loula Grace**
MoWarbT ms. and il. materials. MsHaU .30 cu.ft. of ms./il.

**Erdoes, Richard**
MnU ms. for 1 title.

**Erickson, Phoebe**
MSanB 30 il. used in Burgess books. MnU ms. for 8 titles; il. for 25 titles. MsHaU .30 cu.ft. of ms./il.

**Ernst, Kathryn**
MnU ms. for 1 title.

**Esbensen, Barbara J.**
MnU ms. for 7 titles.

**Escourido, Joseph**
MnU il. for 2 titles.

**Espenscheid, Gertrude Elliott**
MnU il. for 3 titles.

**Estes, Eleanor**
MnU ms. for 10 titles; il. for 17 titles. MsHaU .60 cu.ft. of ms./il.

**Etiquette Books**
DLC Extensive book holdings. FU Extensive book holdings. ICN Very extensive holdings of courtesy books from the Renaissance to 1900. PP-Rb 400 vols.

**Ets, Marie Hall**
MnU ms. for 12 titles; il. for 32 titles. MsHaU .60 cu.ft. of ms./il.

**Eubank, Mary**
MnU il. for 1 title.

**Evanoff, Vlad**
MsHaU 5.1 cu.ft. of ms./il.

**Evans, Edmund** (printer)
CLU-S/C Extensive holdings of books engraved and printed by Evans. MiKW Woodblocks engraved by Evans after Caldecott designs. MsHaU Collection of books and woodblocks engraved by Evans.

**Evans, Ethel M.**
MsHaU .60 cu.ft. of ms./il.

**Evans, Katherine Floyd**
MnU il. for 3 titles.

**Evans, Reginald E. (grandson of Edmund Evans)**
MsHaU 2 pieces of correspondence.

**Evans, Sarah**
MnU ms. for 1 title.

**Evarts, Hal George**
OrU 6 li.ft. of ms.

**Evernden, Margery**
PPiU-LS 11 vols., 4 cu.ft. of ms.

**Everton, Macduff**
MsHaU .90 cu.ft. of ms./il.

**Ewing, Juliana Horatia**
DLC 79 vols. FU 85 vols. InU-Li 14+ vols. OAU 53 vols. PP 75 vols.

**Ewing, Kathryn**
MsHaU .30 cu.ft. of ms./il.

**Eyerly, Jeannette Hyde**
IaU Books and ms. MnU ms. for 12 titles.

**Faber, Doris**
MnU ms. for 10 titles.

**Fables**
CCSc 63 vols. dating from 1554 of Aesop, Gay, and Fontaine. DLC Extensive book holdings. FU Extensive book holdings. ICN 300+ vols. IU-Ed 250 vols. MsHaU Extensive holdings dating from 1530. PP Extensive holdings.

**Fadiman, Clifton**
PPiU-LS 1,893 vols. with annotations; 7 cu.ft. of ms. notes.

**Fairy Tales** *see* **Folk and Fairy Tales**

**Falls, C. B.**
KEmU ms. and il. materials.

**Farber, Norma**
MnU ms. for 19 titles.

**Farley, Carol**
MsHaU .30 cu.ft. of ms./il.

**Farley, Walter**
NNC 21 boxes of ms. materials.

**Farquhar, Margaret Cutting**
MnU ms. for 2 titles.

**Fast, Julius**
MnU il. for 1 title.

**Fatio, Louise**
MnU ms. for 2 titles. OrU .5 li.ft. of ms.

**Faulkner, Nancy**
MsHaU 1.8 cu.ft. of ms./il.

**Faulknor, Cliff V.**
MnU ms. for 2 titles.

**Fax, Elton C.**
MnU il. for 1 title.

**Fay, Helen**
MsHaU .3 cu.ft. of ms./il.

**Feague, Mildred H.**
MnU ms. for 2 titles.

**Feaser, Daniel David**
MnU il. for 4 titles.

**Fehrenbach, T. R.**
MnU ms. for 1 title.

**Feiffer, Jules**
MnU il. for 1 title.

**Feil, Hila**
MnU ms. for 11 titles.

**Feldman, Anne**
MsHaU .60 cu.ft. of ms./il.

**Felsen, Henry Gregor**
IaU Books and ms.

**Felt, Sue**
MsHaU .30 cu.ft. of ms./il.

**Felton, Harold William**
NbU 400 vols.; ms. and il. materials.

**Fenisong, Ruth**
MnU ms. for 1 title.

**Fenn, Eleanor**
FU Extensive book holdings.

**Fenn, George Manville**
CSmH-A 4 pieces of corr. DLC 87 vols.
    FU Extensive book holdings.

**Fenner, Carol**
MnU ms. for 5 titles; il. for 5 titles.

**Fenton, Carroll Lane**
MsHaU 7.2 cu.ft. of ms./il.

**Fenton, Edward**
MnU ms. for 3 titles. MsHaU 3 cu.ft. of
    ms./il.

**Fenton, Sophia H.**
MsHaU .30 cu.ft. of ms./il.

**Feravolo, Rocco V.**
MsHaU .60 cu.ft. of ms./il.

**Ferguson, Evelyn Nevin**
OrU 1.5 li.ft. of ms.

**Fern, Eugene**
MsHaU .30 cu.ft. of ms./il.

**Ferris, Helen**
MsHaU .30 cu.ft. of ms./il.

**Fetz, Ingrid**
MnU il. for 1 title.

**Fiammenghi, Gioia**
MnU il. for 56 titles. MsHaU 2.4 cu.ft. of
    ms./il.

**Fichter, George S.**
MsHaU 5.4 cu.ft. of ms./il.

**Field, Eugene**
CSmH-A 52 ms.; 73 pieces of corr. CoD
    300 vols.; 350 ms., corr., and photo-
    graphs. ICN 120+ vols.; 2 ms. and 1
    letter. MnU ms. for 2 titles. MoSFi 200
    vols.; ms. materials. MoSHi 46 vols.
    and 2 boxes of ms. materials. MoSW
    100 vols. and ms. materials.

**Fife, Dale**
MnU ms. for 7 titles. MsHaU 2.1 cu.ft. of
    ms./il.

**Figurines**
MnU 500 figurines of children's literature subjects.

**Fine, Aaron**
MnU il. for 2 titles.

**Finlay, Campbell K.**
MsHaU .30 cu.ft. of ms./il.

**Finlay, Ian**
MnU ms. for 1 title; il. for 1 title.

**Finley, Martha**
DLC 39 vols. FU Extensive book holdings. OAU 72 vols. PP 50 vols.

**Finn, Francis J.**
OCX 683 items of books, short stories, diaries, and other ms. materials.

**Finnish Language**
MnU 114 vols.

**Fischer, Hans Erich**
MnU il. for 1 title.

**Fisher, Aileen**
MnU ms. for 3 titles. MsHaU .30 cu.ft. of ms./il.

**Fisher, Leonard Everett**
CtU Personal papers from 1968 to present. MnU ms. for 7 titles; il. for 44 titles. MsHaU 6.1 cu.ft. of ms./il. OrU 15 li.ft. of ms. and il.

**Fitzgerald, John D.**
MnU ms. for 6 titles.

**Fitzhugh, Percy**
DLC 50 vols.

**Flack, Marjorie**
OrU 3 li.ft. of ms. and il.

**Flaherty, Robert**
MnU ms. for 1 title.

**Fleischman, Paul**
MnU ms. for 1 title.

**Fleischman, Sid**
MnU ms. for 2 titles.

**Fleishman, Seymour**
MnU il. for 1 title. MsHaU 3.6 cu.ft. of ms./il.

**Floethe, Louise**
FTS 10 li.ft. ms. and il. MnU ms. for 4 titles. MsHaU 1 cu.ft. of ms./il. OrU 3.5 li.ft. of ms. and il.

**Floethe, Richard**
FTS 10 li.ft. ms. and il. MnU il. for 14 titles. MsHaU 1.8 cu.ft. of ms./il. OrU 3.5 li.ft. of ms. and il.

**Flora, James Royer**
MnU ms. for 5 titles; il. for 10 titles.

**Florida**
FTS 250 vols.

**Florida—Authors and Illustrators**
FTS 250 vols.

**Flower, Jessie**
DLC 23 vols.

**Foley, Louise Munro**
MsHaU 3 cu.ft. of ms./il.

**Folger, Joseph**
MsHaU .90 cu.ft. of ms./il.

**Folk and Fairy Tales**
CB 1,100 vols. CL 6,000 vols. from the late 19th century. CP 400 vols. CoU Substantial holdings in the Epsteen and Bloch Collections. DLC Extensive book holdings. DeU 6,000 vols. from 1955–1980. FU Extensive book holdings. IC 2,000 vols. ICN 2,000+ vols. InU-Li Extensive book holdings, some ms. MB 4,500 vols. MSanP 15 original il. by children illustrating Grimm fairy tales. MeWC 50 vols. of Irish folklore. MiD 600 vols. MnM 300 vols. from 1867. MnU Extensive holdings. MoS 2,500 vols. MoWarbT 360 vols. MsHaU Extensive holdings. NBPu 1,000+ vols. NGuP 800 vols. in the American Juvenile Collection; 100 vols. in Gilbert Collection. NJQ Substantial holdings. NN-BrR Sizable holdings. NN-Don 3,000 vols. OCl-RB Substantial holdings. PP

Extensive holdings. PPi Sizable holdings. WM 1,300 vols. WaU-CM 1,800 vols. WyShF 400 vols.

**Folk Tales** *see* Folk and Fairy Tales

**Folklore** *see* Folk and Fairy Tales

**Follett Publishing Co.**
OrU 13.5 li.ft. of ms. and il.

**Fontane, Theodor**
MnU ms. for 1 title.

**Fontenot, Mary Alice**
MsHaU 1.2 cu.ft. of ms./il.

**Forberg, Ati**
MnU il. for 1 title.

**Forbus, Ina B.**
MsHaU .3 cu.ft. of ms./il. NcGU ms. for 1 title.

**Ford, Henry Justice**
MnU il. for 1 title.

**Ford, Lauren**
MsHaU .30 cu.ft. of ms./il.

**Foreign Languages**
CL 5,000 titles from the 1850s published in 50+ countries. CtH Foreign picture books of the 1920s and 1930s. DLC Over 50,000 vols. in 60 languages. ICN Extensive holdings. MB 45,000 vols. in 50 languages from 100 countries. MiD 1,000 vols. in 20 languages. MiDW 500 vols. in Ramsey Collection. MnM 1,800 vols. in 44 languages. MnSP 1,000 vols. with strength in Spanish, French, and German. MnU 8,700 vols. in 68 languages. MoWarbT 355 vols. MsHaU Extensive holdings. NHem 2,500 vols. NNC Over 600 vols. from Japan, China, Indonesia, Czechoslovakia, and Russia. NN-Don 7,000 vols. in French, German, Japanese, Russian, and Spanish. NjP 100 vols. from a variety of countries in the Graphic Arts Collection. OCl-FL 9,000 vols. in 34 languages. OkS 355 vols. in 7 languages. PP-Rb 6,000 vols. in 54 languages. RP

20 languages represented. WU 500 vols. WaS 1,000 vols. with strength in French, German, and Spanish.
*see also* Bengali; Croatian; Danish; Dutch; Egyptian; Finnish; French; German; Greek; Hebraic; Hindi; Hungarian; Icelandic; Italian; Japanese; Korean; Latin; Latvian; Middle Eastern Languages; Native American Languages; Norwegian; Polish; Portuguese; Russian; Samoan; Scandinavian; Serbian; Slavic Languages; Slovenian; Southeast Asian Languages; Spanish; Swedish; Turkish; Ukrainian; Urdu; and Yugoslavian

**Forman, James**
MnU ms. for 1 title.

**Forsee, Frances Aylesa**
MsHaU .30 cu.ft. of ms./il.

**Fortnum, Peggy**
MsHaU .30 cu.ft. of ms./il.

**Fosdick, Charles Austin** *see* Castlemon, Harry

**Foster, Doris Van Liew**
MnU ms. for 1 title.

**Foster, Elizabeth**
MnU il. for 1 title.

**Foster, Genevieve Stump**
MnU il. for 6 titles. MsHaU .60 cu.ft. of ms./il. OrU 9.5 li.ft. of ms. and il.

**Foster, George Allen**
MsHaU 1.2 cu.ft. of ms./il.

**Foster, John T.**
MsHaU 1.2 cu.ft. of ms./il.

**Foster, Marian Curtis**
MnU il. for 3 titles. MsHaU 1.50 cu.ft. of ms./il.

**Foulds, Elfrida Vipont**
MnU ms. for 20 titles.

**Fox, Frances**
MiMtpT 34 boxes and scrapbook ms. materials.

**Fox, Michael Wilson**
MnU il. for 1 title.

**Fox, Paula**
MnU ms. for 1 title.

**Fraelich, Richard O.**
MsHaU .30 cu.ft. of ms./il.

**Frame, Paul**
MnU il. for 8 titles.

**Franchere, Ruth Myers**
OrU 2 li.ft. of ms.

**Francis, Dorothy Brenner**
MsHaU 5.7 cu.ft. of ms./il.

**Francois, Andre**
MnU il. for 1 title.

**Franke, Joseph**
MsHaU .30 cu.ft. of ms./il.

**Frankenberg, Robert Clinton**
MnU il. for 1 title. OrU 3 li.ft. of il.

**Fraser, Conon**
MsHaU .3 cu.ft. of ms./il.

**Frazier, Neta Lohnes**
MnU ms. for 1 title.

**Freeman, Barbara**
MsHaU 1.5 cu.ft. of ms./il.

**Freeman, Don**
KEmU ms. and il. materials. MnU ms. for 2 titles; il. for 17 titles. MsHaU 1.2 cu.ft. of ms./il.

**Freeman, Jean Todd**
MsHaU .60 cu.ft. of ms./il.

**Freeman, Ruth**
NWat ms. materials.

**Freeman, Terence R.**
MsHaU .30 cu.ft. of ms./il.

**French, Laura**
MnU ms. for 3 titles.

**French Language**
DLC Growing collection of 1,300+ vols. ICN 500+ vols. MnU 676 vols. MsHaU 200+ vols. NjP-C 347 vols. NNFI 1,500 vols. NNPM Books from the Gordon N. Ray bequest.

**Freschet, Berniece**
MnU ms. for 1 title. MsHaU .30 cu.ft. of ms./il.

**Freund, Rudolf**
MnU il. for 1 title.

**Fribourg, Marjorie**
MnU ms. for 1 title.

**Friedman, Anne Nathan**
MsHaU .30 cu.ft. of ms./il.

**Friermood, Elisabeth Hamilton**
MsHaU 2.4 cu.ft. of ms./il. OrU 1.5 li.ft. of ms.

**Frisch, Otto R.**
MsHaU .30 cu.ft. of ms./il.

**Fritz, Jean**
MnU ms. for 12 titles. MsHaU 1.5 cu.ft. of ms./il. OrU .5 li.ft. of ms.

**Froman, Elizabeth Hull**
MnU ms. for 1 title.

**Frost, A. B.**
DLC Extensive book holdings; 68 pieces of artwork. GEU-S il. in Joel Chandler Harris Collection. PP-Rb 100 vols. and 50 il.

**Fry, Guy**
MsHaU .30 cu.ft. of ms./il.

**Fry, Rosalie K.**
MsHaU .30 cu.ft. of ms./il.

**Fuller, Catherine L.**
MnU ms. for 1 title; il. for 1 title.

**Funai, Mamoru**
MnU il. for 1 title.

**Funk, Clothilde Embree**
MnU il. for 1 title.

**Gackenbach, Dick**
CtU ms. and il. for 21 titles. MsHaU 1.80 cu.ft. of ms./il. NjR-Z il. materials.

**Gag, Flavia**
MnU il. for 11 titles. MsHaU .30 cu.ft. of ms./il.

**Gag, Howard**
MnU ms. for 1 title.

**Gag, Wanda**
MiD il. MnU ms. for 8 titles; il. for 15 titles. MsHaU .30 cu.ft. of ms./il. PSt il. for 1 title.

**Gagliardo, Ruth Garver**
KEmU corr. between Gagliardo and authors, illustrators, and editors. KU 1.5 li.ft. of personal papers, corr., and clippings.

**Galdone, Paul**
MnU ms. for 1 title; il. for 110 titles.

**Gallant, Roy**
MsHaU 20.2 cu.ft. of ms./il.

**Galloway, Lyle**
MnU il. for 1 title.

**Galt, Thomas**
MsHaU .60 cu.ft. of ms./il.

**Gambino, Robert**
MnU ms. for 1 title.

**Games and Pastimes**
CtY-BR Cary Collection of Playing Cards includes 2,600 packs, 460 sheets, 150 woodblocks, and 200 books representing the last 500 years of production throughout the world. DLC 30 19th-century games and 100 20th-century games. DeWint Extensive holdings from the 17th–20th centuries. ICN 44+ vols. InU-Li Extensive holdings from 17th–20th centuries. MnM Folklore Collection has games and songs. MsHau Substantial book holdings. NN-Don 50 vols. OrHi Educational and outdoor games from 1840 to the present. Wy-ShF Volumes on street songs, games, rhymes, and chants.

**Gannett, Ruth Stiles**
MnU il. for 11 titles.

**Gannon, Robert**
MsHaU 1.2 cu.ft. of ms./il.

**Gans, Roma**
MnU ms. for 1 title.

**Gantos, Jack**
MnU ms. for 1 title.

**Garden, Nancy**
MnU ms. for 15 titles.

**Gardener, Martin**
MnU ms. for 1 title.

**Gardner, Richard**
MsHaU 1.2 cu.ft. of ms./il.

**Garelick, May**
MsHaU .30 cu.ft. of ms./il.

**Garis, Howard R.**
DLC Extensive book holdings. FU Extensive book holdings. NSyU 4 li.ft. of ms. and il. PP 100 vols.

**Garrison, Barbara**
MsHaU .30 cu.ft. of ms./il.

**Garrison, Christian**
MnU ms. for 1 title.

**Gates, Doris**
CF 18 vols., some autographed. MnU ms. for 1 title. OrU 27 li.ft. of ms.

**Gauch, Patricia**
MnU ms. for 1 title. NjR ms. materials.

**Gay, Zhenya**
MnU il. for 1 title. MsHaU .30 cu.ft. of ms./il.

**Gaze, Harold**
CCSc 6 watercolor paintings.

**Gehr, Mary**
MnU il. for 3 titles.

**Geisel, Theodor Seuss** *see* **Seuss, Dr.**

**Geisert, Arthur**
MnU il. for 2 titles.

**Gekiere, Madeleine H.**
MnU il. for 3 titles.

**Gemmill, Jane**
MsHaU .30 cu.ft. of ms./il.

**Gentry, Helen**
CCSc 78 vols. designed by Helen Gentry, items printed by her, corr. and ephemera.

**George, Jean Craighead**
MnU ms. for 59 titles; il. for 6 titles. MsHaU .30 cu.ft. of ms./il.

**Gergely, Tibor**
MnU il. for 7 titles. MsHaU 1.2 cu.ft. of ms./il. NNC 7 li.ft. of ms. and illustrative materials.

**Gerhard, Mae**
MsHaU .60 cu.ft. of ms./il.

**German Language**
DLC Growing collection of over 2,000 titles in German from Germany, Austria, and Switzerland. ICN 300+ vols. MnU 1,259 vols. NjP-C 1,000 vols. NN-Rb 700 vols. in the Schatski Collection. PP-Rb 800 vols. PSt 1,200 vols. in translation.

**Gersh, Harry**
MsHaU .60 cu.ft. of ms./il.

**Giacoia, Frank**
MnU il. for 1 title.

**Gibbons, Faye**
MsHaU .60 cu.ft. of ms./il.

**Giblin, James Cross**
MnU ms. for 1 title. MsHaU 4 cu.ft. of ms./il.

**Gibson, Gertrude**
MsHaU .30 cu.ft. of ms./il.

**Gidal, Sonia and Tim**
MsHaU 1.2 cu.ft. of ms./il.

**Giff, Patricia Reilly**
MsHaU 1.2 cu.ft. of ms./il.

**Gilchrist, Theo E.**
MnU ms. for 1 title.

**Gill, Margery**
NjR-Z il. materials.

**Gillett, Mary**
NcCU ms. for 1 title.

**Gillham, Charles Edward**
MnU ms. for 1 title.

**Ginsburg, Mirra**
MnU ms. for 32 titles.

**Giovanopoulos, Paul**
MnU il. for 9 titles.

**Girion, Barbara**
NjR ms. materials.

**Girls' Series Books** *see* **Series Books**

**Glaser, William and Lillian**
OrU 96 li.ft. of ms. and il.

**Glendining, Marion**
MnU ms. for 1 title.

**Glubok, Shirley**
MsHaU 12.4 cu.ft. of ms./il.

**Glynne-Jones, William**
MsHaU .60 cu.ft. of ms./il.

**Gnoli, Domenico**
MnU il. for 1 title.

**Gobbato, Imero**
MnU il. for 12 titles.

**Goble, Paul**
MnU ms. for 4 titles; il. for 10 titles.

**Godden, Rumer**
MBU 17 vols. and 12 li.ft. of ms. materials.

**Godwin, Edward Fell and Stephanie Mary**
MnU ms. for 4 titles; il. for 11 titles.

**Goetz, Lee Garrett**
MnU ms. for 1 title; il. for 12 titles.

**Goff, Lloyd Lozes**
MnU il. for 1 title.

**Goins, Ellen**
MsHaU 1.2 cu.ft. of ms./il.

**Goldsmith, Howard**
MsHaU .60 cu.ft. of ms./il.

**Goll, Reinhold W.**
MsHaU .90 cu.ft. of ms./il.

**Gollomb, Joseph**
MsHaU .30 cu.ft. of ms./il.

**Goode, Diane**
MnU il. for 1 title.

**Goodenow, Earle**
MnU ms. for 3 titles; il. for 3 titles.

**Goodman, Elaine**
MnU ms. for 1 title.

**Goodman, Walter**
MnU ms. for 1 title.

**Goodrich, Samuel Griswold** *see* **Parley, Pe-ter**

**Goodwin, Harold L.**
MBU 43 vols. by John Blaine (pseud-onym) and 23 boxes of ms. materials.

**Gordon, Ayala**
MnU il. for 1 title.

**Gordon, Lesley**
MsHaU .30 cu.ft. of ms./il.

**Gordon, Sheila**
MsHaU .6 cu.ft. of ms./il.

**Gordon, Shirley**
MsHaU .30 cu.ft. of ms./il.

**Gorey, Edward**
InU-Li 145+ vols.; ms. MnU il. for 2 titles.

**Gorog, Judith**
NjR ms. materials.

**Gorsline, Douglas**
MnU il. for 1 title. MsHaU 1.8 cu.ft. of ms./il.

**Gottshall, Franklin**
MsHaU .60 cu.ft. of ms./il.

**Goudey, Alice E.**
MnU ms. for 2 titles.

**Gould, Jean R.**
MnU ms. for 1 title.

**Gould, Marilyn**
MnU ms. for 1 title.

**Govan, Christine**
MsHaU .9 cu.ft. of ms./il.

**Graber, Richard**
MnU ms. for 4 titles.

**Graham, Frank and Ada**
MsHaU 3.9 cu.ft. of ms./il.

**Graham, Janette Sargeant**
MnU ms. for 2 titles.

**Graham, John**
MsHaU .30 cu.ft. of ms./il.

**Graham, Lorenz Bell**
MnU ms. for 6 titles.

**Graham, Margaret Bloy**
MnU ms. for 1 title; il. for 25 titles.

**Gramatky, Hardie**
CtU ms. and il. for 1 title. InU-Li ms. for 1 title. MnU ms. for 2 titles; il. for 11 titles. MsHaU 3.8 cu.ft. of ms./il. OrU 9 li.ft. of ms. and il.

**Granahan, David and Lolita**
MnU il. for 1 title.

**Grassini, Carl**
NjR-Z il. materials.

**Graves, Charles P.**
MsHaU .30 cu.ft. of ms./il.

**Gray, Nigel**
MnU ms. for 1 title.

**Grayland, Valerie**
MsHaU .30 cu.ft. of ms./il.

**Greek Language**
MnU 19 vols. NjP-C 132 vols.

**Green, Elizabeth Shippen**
PP-Rb ms. and il.

**Green, Roger Lancelyn**
MnU ms. for 1 title.

**Greenaway, John**
MsHaU .30 cu.ft. of ms./il.

**Greenaway, Kate**
CSmH-A 2 pieces of corr. FU Extensive book holdings. ICN 25+ vols.; 3 il.

InU-Li 60+ vols.; 9 il. MiD Extensive holdings of ms., il., and related materials. MnU il. for 5 titles. MsHaU 200+ vols. and 15 cu.ft. of ms./il. PP-Rb 100 vols., 20 ms., and 80 il. PPiC 230 vols., 200 il., ms.

**Greenberg, Barbara**
MsHaU .30 cu.ft. of ms./il.

**Greenberg, Polly**
MnU ms. for 1 title.

**Greene, Bette**
MnU ms. for 5 titles.

**Greene, Carla**
MnU ms. for 30 titles.

**Greene, Constance**
MnU ms. for 7 titles.

**Greene, Ellin**
MnU ms. for 1 title.

**Greenfield, Eloise**
MnU ms. for 1 title.

**Greenwald, Sheila**
MsHaU .30 cu.ft. of ms./il.

**Greenwillow Books**
OrU 158 li.ft. of ms.

**Greer, Blanche**
MnU il. for 1 title.

**Greeting Cards**
DeWint Collection of historical valentines and Christmas cards. ICN 23 19th-century valentines. MsHaU Extensive holdings of 19th-century cards.

**Gretzer, John**
MsHaU .60 cu.ft. of ms./il. NjR-Z il. materials.

**Grice, Frederick**
MsHaU .3 cu.ft. of ms./il.

**Grider, Dorothy**
KyBgW .2 li.ft. of il.

**Griese, Arnold A.**
MnU ms. for 1 title. MsHaU .3 cu.ft. of ms./il.

**Grifalconi, Ann**
MsHaU .30 cu.ft. of ms./il.

**Grimm, Jacob and Wilhelm**
DLC Extensive book holdings. FU Extensive book holdings. ICN 150 vols. InU-Li 60+ vols. NN-Don 75 vols. PSt 200 vols.

**Grinder, Marshall**
MsHaU .30 cu.ft. of ms./il.

**Gringhuis, Richard H.**
MsHaU 2.1 cu.ft. of ms./il.

**Griset, Ernest**
MsHaU .60 cu.ft. of ms./il.

**Grohskopf, Bernice**
MsHaU 1.2 cu.ft. of ms./il.

**Groom, Arthur W.**
MsHaU .30 cu.ft. of ms./il.

**Gropper, William**
MnU il. for 1 title.

**Gross, Ruth Belov**
MnU ms. for 1 title.

**Grossman, Nancy**
MsHaU .60 cu.ft. of ms./il.

**Guenberg, Sid**
MnU il. for 1 title.

**Guernsey, JoAnn**
MnU ms. for 3 titles.

**Guggenheim, Hans**
MnU il. for 1 title.

**Gulliver's Travels** *see* **Swift, Jonathan**

**Gustafson, Anita** *see* **Larsen, Anita**

**Gutman, Ilene**
NjR-Z il. materials.

**Guy, Anne Welsh**
MsHaU .30 cu.ft. of ms./il.

**Gwynne, Fred**
MnU ms. for 3 titles.

**Haas, Carolyn**
MsHaU 2.7 cu.ft. of ms./il.

**Haas, Dorothy**
MsHaU 14 cu.ft. of ms./il.

**Haas, Irene**
MnU il. for 1 title. MsHaU .30 cu.ft. of ms./il.

**Habeck, Fritz**
MsHaU .3 cu.ft. of ms./il.

**Hader, Berta and Elmer**
KWi il. MnU il. for 11 titles. MsHaU 3 cu.ft. of ms./il. OrU 54 li.ft. of ms. and il.

**Haenigsen, Harry**
OrU 18.5 li.ft. of ms. and il.

**Hager, Alice Rogers**
MsHaU .60 cu.ft. of ms./il.

**Hahn, Mary Downing**
MnU ms. for 5 titles.

**Halacy, Daniel S.**
MsHaU 11.4 cu.ft. of ms./il.

**Hale, Kathleen**
MnU il. for 1 title.

**Haley, Gail E.**
MnU ms. for 9 titles; il. for 18 titles. MsHaU .90 cu.ft. of ms./il.

**Hall, Anna Gertrude**
MnU ms. for 1 title.

**Hall, Barb**
MnU ms. for 1 title.

**Hall, Elvajean**
MnU il. for 1 title. MsHaU .60 cu.ft. of ms./il.

**Hall, Gordon Langley**
MnU ms. for 13 titles.

**Hall, Lynn**
MnU ms. for 16 titles.

**Hall, Marjory**
MsHaU .30 cu.ft. of ms./il.

**Hall, Natalie Watson**
MnU ms. for 1 title.

**Hall, Robin**
NjR-Z il. materials.

**Hall, Rosalys Haskell**
OrU 1 li.ft. of ms.

**Hallman, Ruth**
MsHaU .60 cu.ft. of ms./il.

**Hamil, Tom**
MsHaU .3 cu.ft. of ms./il.

**Hamilton, Katharine Parr**
MnU ms. for 1 title.

**Hamilton, Virginia**
OKentU Books and ms. materials.

**Hamm, Jack**
MsHaU .30 cu.ft. of ms./il.

**Hammontree, Marie**
MsHaU .30 cu.ft. of ms./il.

**Hample, Stoo**
MnU ms. for 1 title.

**Hamre, Leif**
MnU ms. for 1 title.

**Hancock, Sibyl**
MsHaU .30 cu.ft. of ms./il.

**Handforth, Thomas**
MnU il. for 1 title. WaT 50 vols. and ms., il., corr., and scrapbooks.

**Hands, Nancy**
MsHaU 1.2 cu.ft. of ms./il.

**Hansen, Joyce**
MnU ms. for 2 titles.

**Hanson, Joan**
MnU ms. for 1 title; il. for 6 titles.

**Harayda, Marel**
MsHaU .60 cu.ft. of ms./il.

**Harbin, Robert**
MsHaU .60 cu.ft. of ms./il.

**Hardendorff, Jeanne B.**
MnU ms. for 1 title.

Harlequinades *see* Toy and Movable Books

**Harness, Cheryl**
MnU il. for 1 title.

**Harper, Wilhelmina**
CSfSt 6 li.ft. of professional papers.

**Harris, Dorothy Joan**
MsHaU .9 cu.ft. of ms./il.

**Harris, Joel Chandler**
CSmH-A 6 ms.; 2 pieces of corr. DLC Extensive book holdings. FU 36 vols. GEU-S 300 vols., ms., corr., and il. by others. ICN 40+ vols.

**Harris, John** (publisher)
CLU-S/C Extensive holdings of Harris imprints. InU-Li Extensive book holdings. OOxM 153 vols.

**Harrison, David**
MoWarbT ms. and il. materials.

**Harvey, George**
MsHaU .3 cu.ft. of ms./il.

**Harvey, Lois**
MnU ms. for 1 title.

**Harwood, Pearl A.**
MsHaU 9.6 cu.ft. of ms./il.

**Hassler, Jon**
MnU ms. for 2 titles.

**Haugaard, Erik Christian**
MnU ms. for 8 titles. MsHaU .60 cu.ft. of ms./il.

**Haugaard, Kay**
MsHaU .9 cu.ft. of ms./il.

**Hauman, George and Doris**
MnU il. for 1 title. MsHaU .60 cu.ft. of ms./il.

**Hautzig, Esther**
MnU ms. for 12 titles.

**Havighurst, Walter, and Marion M. Boyd**
MnU ms. for 1 title.

**Havill, Juanita**
MnU ms. for 5 titles.

**Hawaii**
ICN 30+ vols.

**Hawkins, Quail**
OrU 4.5 li.ft. of ms. and il.

**Hayes, Geoffrey**
MnU ms. for 2 titles. MsHaU .60 cu.ft. of ms./il.

**Hayes, William D.**
MsHaU 2.4 cu.ft. of ms./il.

**Haynes, Betsy**
MoWarbT ms. and il. materials. MsHaU .30 cu.ft. of ms./il.

**Haynes, Bob**
MnU il. for 1 title.

**Haynes, James**
MoWarbT ms. and il. materials.

**Hays, Mattie Sue**
MsHaU .60 cu.ft. of ms./il.

**Hays, Wilma Pitchford**
MnU ms. for 7 titles. MsHaU 1.8 cu.ft. of ms./il.

**Haywood, Carolyn**
MnU ms. for 3 titles; il. for 16 titles. MsHaU .60 cu.ft. of ms./il. PP 50 vols., ms. and il.

**Headstrom, Richard**
MsHaU 2.4 cu.ft. of ms./il.

**Heal, Edith**
MsHaU .60 cu.ft. of ms./il.

**Healey, Lawrence**
MsHaU 1.8 cu.ft. of ms./il.

**Hearn, Lafcadio**
CCSc 150 vols. CSmH-A 3 ms.; 40 pieces of corr. ICN 100+ vols. InU-Li *Japanese Fairy Tale* series in 18 parts. NSyU 104 vols.

**Hebraic Language**
DLC 500+ vols. ICN 50+ vols. MBrH 5,000 vols. MnU 152 vols. NjP-C 135 vols. OCH Significant holdings. OrPS 300 vols.

Heck, Bessie
MsHaU 1.8 cu.ft. of ms./il.

Heiderstadt, Dorothy
MnU ms. for 1 title. MsHaU .3 cu.ft. of ms./il.

*Heidi see* Spyri, Johanna

Heine, Helme
MsHaU .30 cu.ft. of ms./il.

Helfman, Elizabeth S.
MsHaU 2.1 cu.ft. of ms./il.

Helfman, Harry
MsHaU .30 cu.ft. of ms./il.

Heller, Ruth
MnU ms. for 1 title; il. for 2 titles.

Hemphill, Josephine
MnU ms. for 1 title.

Henderson, LeGrand
OrU 12 li.ft. of ms. and il.

Hendrickson, David
OrU 16.5 li.ft. of ms. and il.

Henry, Joanne Landers
MnU ms. for 1 title.

Henry, Marguerite
MnU ms. for 23 titles; il. for 2 titles. OkT ms. for 1 title.

Henstra, Friso
MnU il. for 2 titles.

Henty, George Alfred
DLC 138 vols. FTS 500 vols. FU Extensive holdings. GU 179 vols. InU-Li 400+ vols.; ms. materials. KyLoU 200 vols. MsHaU 200+ vols. NIC Significant holdings. NNU-F Extensive holdings. OAU 76 vols. OrP 80 vols. PP 100 vols. ScFlM 150 vols. TxU-Hu 150 vols. ViU 350 vols.

Herford, Oliver
CCSc 67 vols.

Herman, George
MsHaU .30 cu.ft. of ms./il.

Hermann, Max R.
MsHaU .60 cu.ft. of ms./il.

Herric, Pru
MnU il. for 1 title.

Herron, Edward
MsHaU .60 cu.ft. of ms./il.

Hess, Lowell
MnU il. for 2 titles.

Heuman, William
MsHaU 1.8 cu.ft. of ms./il.

Heyer, William
MnU il. for 1 title.

Hicks, Clifford B.
MsHaU .30 cu.ft. of ms./il.

Hieroglyphic Bibles *see* Bibles and Books of Religious Instruction

Hightower, Florence
MnU ms. for 2 titles.

Hill, Donna
MsHaU 3.3 cu.ft. of ms./il.

Hill, Jeff
MnU il. for 1 title.

Hill, Margaret O.
MsHaU .30 cu.ft. of ms./il.

Hill, Robert
MsHaU .30 cu.ft. of ms./il.

Hiller, Catherine
MsHaU .30 cu.ft. of ms./il.

Hillert, Margaret
MsHaU .60 cu.ft. of ms./il.

Hillier, Jack
MsHaU .60 cu.ft. of ms./il.

Hillman, Priscilla
MsHaU .30 cu.ft. of ms./il.

Hilton, Suzanne
MsHaU 4.5 cu.ft. of ms./il.

Hindi Language
MnU 14 vols.

**Hirawa, Yasuko**
MnU ms. for 1 title.

**Hirsch, Miriam**
MnU il. for 1 title.

**Hirsch, S. Carl**
MnU ms. for 8 titles.

**Hirsh, Marilyn**
MsHaU 16 cu.ft. of ms./il.

**Hirshberg, Albert**
MBU 54 vols.; 52 boxes of ms. materials.

**Historical (19th Century and Earlier)**
AB 700 vols. from the 19th century. ArCCA 18,000 vols. from the 19th–20th centuries. AzTeS 1,000 vols. from 1708–1900. AzU 400 vols. from 1727. CB 700 vols. CCCla 30,000 vols. from 19th–20th centuries. CCSc 425 vols. from 1554. CFlS 5,000 vols. from the late 19th to early 20th centuries with illustrated or decorative bindings. CLUS/C 22,000 vols. from 1564. CNoS 250 vols. of 19th- to 20th-century English language imprints. CRiv 1,360 vols. from 1801. CSf 2,100 vols. from 18th–19th centuries. CSfACA Extensive holdings of published works. CSfSt 5,000 vols. from 1790. CSj 8,000 vols. from 1880–1930. CSmH-A Collection of 19th-century English and American imprints. CSt 10,148 vols. from the 18th–20th centuries. CoD 1,550 vols. CoU 2,000 vols. of 19th- to early 20th-century imprints in Bloch Collection; 2,900 vols. of 19th- to early 20th-century imprints in Epsteen Collection.

CtH 1,000 vols. CtHSD 300 vols. from 1800–1900. CtHT 1,500 vols. of 18th–20th century American and English imprints. CtHi 2,500 vols. in Bates Collection; 3,500 vols. in Hewins Collection; 500 vols. printed in Connecticut in Connecticut Imprints Collection; 250 vols. in Juveniles Collection. CtNbT 1,700 vols. CtNhHi 200 vols. published 1777–1875, mostly in Connecticut. CtNhN 2,450 vols. from 1800–1930. CtNlC 3,000 vols. from 18th–20th centuries in the Gildersleeve Collection. CtU 14,000 vols. from 1780. CtY-BR Extensive holdings of books, ms., il., and related materials for many prominent American and English children's authors and illustrators.

DLC Collection of over 18,000 old and rare books, including American children's books from the early 18th century; 16,000+ vols. of American juveniles. DWP 13,000 vols. from 1800. DeWint 500 vols. and a wide variety of paper toys from the 17th to 20th centuries. FTS 40,000 vols. from 18th century. FTaSU 25,000+ vols. FU 40,000 vols., English and American, published before 1900, 800 of which are pre-1821 American imprints. GU Historical books include George Alfred Henty and Confederate imprints. HH 600 vols. from 1855. ICN 10,000+ vols. from the Middle Ages to the early 20th century, in many languages. ICarbS 6,000 vols. IDeKN 2,000 vols. INS 2,000 vols. up to 1900. IQ 200 vols. IU-Ed Extensive holdings from 1800. IaU 1,200 vols. from the 19th century.

InI 1,500+ vols. from the 19th century. InMuB 670 vols. from 1890–1910. InTI Substantial holdings from 1472. InU-Li 15,000 vols. IWW 12,000 vols. KEmU 1,291 vols. in Massee Collection; 1,804 vols. in Gagliardo Collection; 436 vols. in Historical Children's Literature Collection. KU 6,500 vols. from 18th–20th centuries. KyBgW 600 vols. dating from 1850. KyLoU Collection of 19th-century titles. LN 150 vols. from 1787. MAJ 1,000 vols. from the 17th–18th centuries in the Johnson Collection. MB Extensive holdings of 19th–20th-century vols. MBAt 4,000 vols. from 1790. MBSi The Knapp Collection contains 1,200 vols. of 19th-century titles. MBWS 500 vols., British and American, 19th century. MBrH Extensive holdings of books with a Jewish theme.

MCot 2,000 vols. MDeeP Substantial holdings of 18th–20th-century imprints. MHi 600 vols. MNS 1,000 vols. from the 17th–20th centuries. MSaA 326 vols. MSaP 5,000 vols. MStuO 350 vols. MWA 17,000 vols. from 1700–1899. MWelC 800 vols. MWelF 1,680 vols. MWiW 400 vols. MdBE 2,000+ vols. from the 19th century. MeB Substantial holdings of 19th-century imprints. MeP 600 vols., primarily 19th century, in the Children's Antique Collection. MeWC 1,500 vols. from the 19th–20th centuries. MiD Substantial holdings from the 18th century. MiDW 14,000 vols. from 1601. MiDbH Collection from the 19th century. MiKW 1,000 vols. MiMtpT 8,000 vols. from 1648. MiU 900 vols. published before 1900. MnM 4,400 vols. from 1792. MnSP Nearly 2,000 vols. MnU 2,700 vols. MoK 7,200 vols. from 1800.

MoS 6,000 vols. MoSW 2,000 vols. in Hochschild Collection. MoWarbT 12,000 vols. dating from 1799. MsHaU 15,000 vols. from the 17th–20th centuries. NAlU 7,000 vols. NBPu 3,000+ vols. from 1741–1920. NBuBE 800 vols. NCooHi Collection from the 19th century. NEaHi 1,500 vols. from 1790. NGuP 1,000 vols. NHemH 1,000 vols. from 1825–1940. NHi 2,300 vols. NHyF 500 vols. NIC Significant holdings of 18th–19th-century titles. NJQ 200 vols. NN-Don 2,000 vols. NN-Rb 700 vols. in the Schatski Collection; 427 vols. in the Darton Collection; illustrated works in the Spencer Collection; 11,000 titles in the general collection. NNC 3,100 vols. in the Henne Collection; 950 vols. in the Plimpton Library; 10,000 vols. in the Historical Collection of Children's Literature.

NNMus 1,000 vols. NNPM 10,000 vols. from the 3rd–20th centuries. NNStJ 550 vols. NNU-F Extensive collection of 19th- and 20th-century authors in the Fales Collection; 500 vols. in the Adkins Collection. NPV 8,000 vols. NRU 3,750 vols. NSyU Extensive holdings of 19th-century English and American titles. NWat 3,700 vols. NWe 1,500 vols. NbSeT 12,500 vols. in the Koschman Collection. NcCU 1,000 vols. NcD 500+ vols. NcGU 1,800 vols. NhC 5,600 vols. NhU 1,200 vols. NjN 900 vols. in the Stone Collection. NjP-C Extensive holdings. OAU 1,400 vols. OBgU 1,000 vols. OC Several collections have historical items. OCl-RB 1,500+ vols. from 19th–20th centuries. ODaWU 500 vols.

OFH Collection of books used by Rutherford B. Hayes' children. OHirC 200 vols. OKentU 1,500 vols. OOxM 11,000 vols. OU 800 vols. OkT 2,500 vols. OrP 1,800+ vols. PBal 2,000 vols. PHi 200 vols. PMCHi 200 vols. PNo Collection of books published before 1939. PP 50,000 vols. PP-Rb 13,000 vols. PPL 18th–19th-century holdings. PPi 2,200 vols. PPiULS 10,000 vols. RP 2,000 vols. RPA 19th-century holdings. ScRhW 200 vols. ScSpW Holdings from 1830. ScU 3,000 vols. SdAbN 2,000 vols. TMM 1,600 vols. TRuT 1,000 vols. TxDN 1,700 vols. TxDW 10,000 vols. TxDa 33,000 vols. TxF 437 vols. TxH 6,700 vols. UPB 1,000 vols. ViR 5,000 vols. ViU Extensive holdings. WM 5,000 vols. WMUW Substantial holdings. WU-CC 4,000 vols. WaElC 109 vols. WaS 1,500 vols. WaSp 140 vols. WaU 2,200 vols. WaUCM 7,000 vols. WyShF 700 vols.

### Historical— 20th Century

AkA Extensive holdings from the 1960s to date. CP 1,400 vols. from 1900–1950. CoU 6,000 vols. in Westerberg Collection. CtHi 1,200 vols. in Connecticut Printers Archive. DeU 6,000 vols. IC 50,000 vols. from 1900–1970. IEN 14,000 vols. INS 400 trade books, many autographed, from 1930–1950 in the Johnson Collection. IU-LS 14,000 vols. from 1945 to date. KEmU 1,291 vols. MBChM 10,000 vols. MBSi Ar-

*Hey Diddle Diddle and Baby Bunting* by Randolph Caldecott; London: Routledge [1882].

chives of the *Horn Book* magazine provides information on this topic. MWW 11,000 vols. from 1950 to date. NGuP 4,000 vols. from 1910–1960. NN-Don 30,000 vols. NNCbc 7,000 vols. OCl 8,000 vols. from 1900–1960. Ok Collection of 20th-century books. PNo 244 vols. in Field Collection. ScU 10,000 vols. from 1916.

**History and Criticism of Children's Literature** *see* **Children's Literature, Study of**

**Hnizdovsky, Jacques**
MnU il. for 1 title.

**Hoare, Robert J.**
MsHaU .30 cu.ft. of ms./il.

**Hoban, Lillian**
CtU 11 boxes of il. MnU ms. for 5 titles; il. for 4 titles. MsHaU .5 cu.ft. of ms./il.

**Hoban, Tana**
MnU il. for 9 titles. MsHaU 5.7 cu.ft. of ms./il.

**Hoban, Russell**
MsHaU .5 cu.ft. of ms./il.

**Hobart, Lois**
MsHaU 1.5 cu.ft. of ms./il.

**Hobbs, Barbara**
MnU ms. for 2 titles; il. for 2 titles.

**Hobbs, Morris**
MsHaU .90 cu.ft. of ms./il.

**Hobson, Burton**
MsHaU 1.5 cu.ft. of ms./il.

**Hodges, Cyril Walter**
MnU il. for 3 titles. TxWB 31 il. for *Pied Piper of Hamelin*.

**Hodges, Margaret Moore**
MnU ms. for 23 titles. MsHaU 6.3 cu.ft. of ms./il. PPiU-LS 44 vols.; 4 cu.ft. of ms.

**Hoff, Sydney**
MnU ms. for 23 titles; il. for 49 titles. MsHaU 11.4 cu.ft. of ms./il.

**Hoffine, Lyla**
MnU ms. for 4 titles; il. for 1 title.

**Hoffman, Margaret**
MsHaU .3 cu.ft. of ms./il.

**Hoffman, Miriam**
MsHaU .3 cu.ft. of ms./il.

**Hoffman, Rosekrans**
CtU il. for 1 title. MnU il. for 5 titles. MsHaU 1.5 cu.ft. of ms./il.

**Hoffmann, Heinrich**
PSt 200 vols. of *Struwwelpeter* and parodies.

**Hofland, Barbara**
FU 158 vols.

**Hofsinde, Robert**
MnU ms. for 6 titles; il. for 5 titles. MsHaU 1.2 cu.ft. of ms./il.

**Hogan, Inez**
MnU il. for 2 titles. OrU 7 li.ft. of ms.

**Hogner, Nils**
MnU il. for 2 titles. MsHaU 1.8 cu.ft. of ms./il. OrU 8 li.ft. of ms. and il.

**Hogrogrian, Nonny**
MnU il. for 1 title. MsHaU 10 cu.ft. of ms./il.

**Hohn, Hazel**
MsHaU .3 cu.ft. of ms./il.

**Holberg, Ruth and Richard**
MsHaU .30 cu.ft. of ms./il. OrU 12 li.ft. of ms.

**Holden, Edith**
MnU ms. for 1 title.

**Holding, James**
MnU ms. for 2 titles.

**Holl, Adelaide Hinkle**
MnU ms. for 1 title. MsHaU .60 cu.ft. of ms./il.

**Holl, Kristi**
MnU ms. for 2 titles.

**Holland, Isabelle**
MnU ms. for 10 titles. MsHaU 5.1 cu.ft. of ms./il.

**Holland, Janice**
MnU ms. for 8 titles; il. for 28 titles.

**Holland, Joyce**
MsHaU .30 cu.ft. of ms./il.

**Holland, Marion**
MnU ms. for 2 titles; il. for 5 titles.

**Hollands, Hulda Theodate**
MiMtpT ms. materials and published books.

**Holling, Holling Clancy and Lucille**
CLU-S/C Depository for books, il., ms., and woodcarvings by the Hollings. CP il. materials. MnU il. for 1 title. OrU .5 li.ft. of ms. and il.

**Holman, Felice**
MnU ms. for 21 titles.

**Holmes, Bea**
MnU ms. for 1 title.

**Holmes, Marjorie**
IaU Books and ms.

**Holmes, Thomas J., Jr.**
MsHaU .30 cu.ft. of ms./il.

**Holtan, Gene**
MnU il. for 1 title.

**Homar, Lorenzo**
NjR-Z il. materials.

**Hooks, William H.**
MsHaU .30 cu.ft. of ms./il.

**Hoover, H. M.**
MnU ms. for 13 titles.

**Hoover, Helen**
MnU ms. for 6 titles.

**Hope, Laura Lee**
DLC Extensive book holdings. FU Extensive book holdings. PP 100 vols.

**Hopkins, Lee Bennett**
MnU ms. for 6 titles. MsHaU 21.7 cu.ft. of ms./il.

**Hopkins, Lila**
NcCU 79 ms. items for 2 titles.

**Hopkins, Livingston**
MsHaU .30 cu.ft. of ms./il.

**Horn, George F.**
MsHaU .3 cu.ft. of ms./il.

*Horn Book* **Magazine**
MBSi Archives of the *Horn Book* magazine provide information on this topic.

**Hornbooks and Battledores**
CtY-BR 15+ items. ICN 10+ items. InU-Li Several battledores and 20+ hornbooks. NNC Holdings in the Plimpton Library. ViR 8 battledores.

**Horticulture**
CoDDB 1,000 vols. on horticulture and related topics.

**Horwitz, Sylvia**
MsHaU .60 cu.ft. of ms./il.

**Houck, Carter**
MnU ms. for 1 title.

**Hough, Richard Alexander**
MnU ms. for 1 title.

**Houser, Lowell**
MnU il. for 1 title.

**Hovey, Tamara**
MsHaU .60 cu.ft. of ms./il.

**Howard, Robert West**
MnU il. for 2 titles.

**Howe, Caroline**
MnU ms. for 1 title.

**Huffman, Tom**
MsHaU 4.3 cu.ft. of ms./il.

**Hughes, Dean**
MoWarbT ms. and il. materials.

**Hull, Eleanor Means**
MnU ms. for 1 title.

**Hummel, Arthur W.**
MnU ms. for 1 title.

**Humphrey, Henry**
MnU ms. for 1 title; il. for 1 title. MsHaU .60 cu.ft. of ms./il.

**Humphries, Stella**
MnU ms. for 1 title.

**Hungarian Language**
MnU 153 vols.

**Hunt, Irene**
MnU ms. for 2 titles. MsHaU .60 cu.ft. of ms./il.

**Hunt, Mabel Leigh**
MnU ms. for 4 titles. MsHaU 1.5 cu.ft. of ms./il.

**Hunt, Sarah E.**
MsHaU 1.5 cu.ft. of ms./il.

**Hunter, Frances Tipton**
MnU il. for 1 title.

**Hunter, James A. H.**
MsHaU .30 cu.ft. of ms./il.

**Hunter, Mollie**
MsHaU .30 cu.ft. of ms./il.

**Hunter, Ted, Mark and Richard**
MnU il. for 1 title.

**Huntington, Harriet Elizabeth**
OrU 9 li.ft. of ms.

**Hurd, Clement**
MnU ms. for 2 titles; il. for 76 titles.

**Hurd, Edith Thacher**
MnU ms. for 30 titles; il. for 1 title.

**Hurmence, Belinda**
MsHaU .60 cu.ft. of ms./il. NcCU 22 ms. items for 2 titles.

**Hurwitz, Johanna**
MnU ms. for 2 titles.

**Hussey, Betty A.**
MsHaU .60 cu.ft. of ms./il.

**Hutchings, Margaret J.**
MsHaU 2.1 cu.ft. of ms./il.

**Hutchinson, Paula**
MsHaU 1.2 cu.ft. of ms./il.

**Hyde, Margaret O.**
MsHaU 4.2 cu.ft. of ms./il.

**Hyman, Trina Schart**
CtU ms. for 1 title. MnU il. for 7 titles. MsHaU .60 cu.ft. of ms./il. OrU 6 li.ft. of il.

**Hymn Books**
CtHT 100+ 18th- and 19th-century American song and hymn books. FTaSU 300 vols. ICN 600+ 19th-century American hymnals. RPB-JH Substantial holdings.

**Icelandic Language**
MnU 327 vols.

**Ichikawa, Satomi**
MnU il. for 1 title.

**Illustration of Children's Books**
CRiv Illustrated books from 1900–1950. CSf Illustrated books from 18th and 19th centuries. CtNlC Extensive holdings. CtU 8,000 vols. in the Levy Collection. DLC Extensive book holdings. DWP 13,000 vols. from 1800 to date. DeWI 280 il., 110 vols., and corr. for authors and illustrators with emphasis on Caldecott Medal recipients. DeWint Extensive holdings. FTS 8,000 vols. of 20th-century American picture books. FTaSU Extensive holdings. FU Extensive book holdings. GS 500 vols. ICN Extensive book holdings. InI 870 vols. InU-Li Extensive holdings from 17th–20th centuries. MBAt Extensive book holdings. MBSi Archives of the *Horn Book* magazine provide information on this topic. MdBE 500 vols. in Holme Collection; 114 vols. in the Peabody Collection. MiKW Illustrated books. MnU Extensive holdings. MsHaU Extensive holdings. NjP-C Extensive holdings. NN-Don Extensive holdings. NN-Rb Extensive holdings in the Spencer Collection. NNPM Extensive holdings of illustrated books. NNStJ 300 vols. NWat 1,000 vols. in the Freeman Collection. NhD 1,400 vols. in the Illustrated Books Collection and 2,400 vols. in the 1926 Memorial Collection. NjP 100 vols. in the Graphic Arts Collection and outstanding American examples in the Hamilton Collection. OC Substantial holdings in several collections. OFiC 300 pieces of original art from children's books. PP 10,000+ vols. PPi 200 vols. PPiU Extensive holdings. TxH 900 vols.

**Ilsley, Velma Elizabeth**
MnU il. for 24 titles.

**Indiana**
InI 435 vols.

**Indiana—Authors and Illustrators**
InI 435 vols. InTI Collection of books by Indiana authors.

**Iowa—Authors and Illustrators**
IaU Books and ms. materials for Iowa authors and illustrators.

**Ipcar, Dahlov Zorach**
MnU ms. for 34 titles; il. for 40 titles. MsHaU 1.3 cu.ft. of ms./il.

**Ipsen, D. C.**
MsHaU .90 cu.ft. of ms./il.

**Ireland, Leslie Daiken**
TxU-Hu 5 boxes of ms.

**Ireland, Thelma**
MsHaU .30 cu.ft. of ms./il.

**Irving, James Gordon**
MnU il. for 4 titles.

**Irving, Washington**
NBuBE 250 books and other items relating to Rip Van Winkle.

**Irwin, Hadley**
MnU ms. for 9 titles.

**Italian Language**
MnU 150 vols.

**Ivan, Martha Miller Pfaff**
MnU ms. for 2 titles.

**Ivanov, Anatoly**
NjR-Z il. materials.

**Ivanovsky, Elizabeth**
MnU il. for 3 titles.

**Jackson, Caary Paul and O. B.**
MsHaU 6.3 cu.ft. of ms./il.

**Jackson, Jacqueline**
MnU ms. for 2 titles.

**Jackson, Reggie**
MnU ms. for 1 title.

**Jackson, Robert Blake**
MnU ms. for 1 title. MsHaU .90 cu.ft. of ms./il.

**Jacobs, David**
MsHaU .30 cu.ft. of ms./il.

**Jacobs, Leslie**
MnU il. for 1 title.

**Jacques, Florence Page**
MnU ms. for 1 title.

**Jacques, Francis**
MnU il. for 2 titles.

**Jacques, Robin**
MsHaU .90 cu.ft. of ms./il.

**Jagendorf, Moritz Adolf**
MsHaU .60 cu.ft. of ms./il. OrU 9 li.ft. of ms.

**James, G. O.**
MsHaU .60 cu.ft. of ms./il.

**James, Harry Clebourne**
MsHaU .30 cu.ft. of ms./il.

**Jane, Mary Childs**
MsHaU .30 cu.ft. of ms./il.

**Japanese Language**
CLob 350 vols. CU-EDUC 200 late 20th-century vols. for grades K–3 in Japanese. DLC 1500+ vols., mostly published in Japan during the U.S. occupation; 3,000 issues of a dozen different periodical titles. MnU 350 vols. MsHaU Substantial collection. NjFoP 1,500 vols. NjP-C 250 vols.

**Jaquith, Priscilla**
MnU ms. for 1 title.

**Jauss, Anne Marie**
MnU ms. for 3 titles; il. for 47 titles. MsHaU 3.3 cu.ft. of ms./il.

**Jeffries, Roderic**
MnU ms. for 5 titles.

**Jemne, Elsa Laubach**
MnU il. for 4 titles.

**Jenkyns, Chris**
MnU il. for 1 title. MsHaU .60 cu.ft. of ms./il.

**Jennings, Gary**
MsHaU 14.7 cu.ft. of ms./il.

**Jensen, Henning**
MnU il. for 1 title.

**Jensen, Virginia Allen**
MnU ms. for 4 titles.

**Jeschke, Susan**
MnU ms. for 1 title; il. for 1 title.

**Jessen, Bubi**
MnU il. for 1 title.

**Johnson, Annabell Jones and Edgar**
MnU ms. for 14 titles. MsHaU .30 cu.ft.of ms./il.

**Johnson, Crockett**
CtU ms. and il. for 15 titles. MsHaU .30 cu.ft. of ms./il.

**Johnson, Dorothy Marie**
MsHaU 1.2 cu.ft. of ms./il.

**Johnson, Elizabeth**
MnU ms. for 3 titles.

**Johnson, Harper**
MsHaU .30 cu.ft. of ms./il.

**Johnson, Holly**
MsHaU 1.25 cu.ft. of ms./il.

**Johnson, James Ralph and Burdetta Faye**
MsHaU 5.7 cu.ft. of ms./il.

**Johnson, Lois Smith**
MsHaU .9 cu.ft. of ms./il.

**Johnson, Shirley K.**
MsHaU .30 cu.ft. of ms./il.

**Johnston, Dorothy**
OrU 6 li.ft. of ms.

**Johnston, Tony**
MnU ms. for 4 titles.

**Jones, Elizabeth Orton**
MnU il. for 3 titles. OrU 10 li.ft. of ms. and il.

**Jones, Harold**
MnU il. for 1 title. MsHaU 1 cu.ft. of ms./ il. OrU .5 li.ft. of il.

**Jones, Helen Hinckley**
MsHaU 1.5 cu.ft. of ms./il.

**Jones, Henrietta**
MnU il. for 1 title.

**Jones, Jessie Orton**
OrU 10 li.ft. of ms.

**Jones, Toeckey**
MsHaU .9 cu.ft. of ms./il.

**Jones, Weyman B.**
MnU ms. for 1 title.

**Jonk, Clarence**
MnU ms. for 3 titles.

**Joseph, Nannine**
OrU 10.5 li.ft. of ms.

**Judah, Aaron**
MnU ms. for 4 titles.

**Judaica**
MBrH 5,000 vols. OCH Significant holdings.

**Jupo, Frank**
MsHaU 2.1 cu.ft. of ms./il.

**Justus, May**
MsHaU .30 cu.ft. of ms./il.

**Kahl, Ann**
MnU il. for 1 title.

**Kamen, Gloria**
MnU ms. for 4 titles; il. for 13 titles. MsHaU .90 cu.ft. of ms./il.

**Kaminsky, Basia**
MnU il. for 1 title.

**Kamm, Josephine**
MsHaU .30 cu.ft. of ms./il.

**Kane, Robert W.**
MsHaU .60 cu.ft. of ms./il.

**Kansas**
KHi 250 vols.

**Kansas—Authors and Illustrators**
KHi 250 vols.

**Kantrowitz, Mildred**
MnU ms. for 2 titles.

**Kaplan, Boone**
MnU il. for 2 titles.

**Kapp, Paul**
MsHaU .30 cu.ft. of ms./il.

**Karalus, Karl E.**
MsHaU .30 cu.ft. of ms./il.

**Karl, Jean**
MnU ms. for 5 titles.

**Kashiwagi, Isami**
MnU il. for 1 title.

**Kassirer, Norma**
MnU ms. for 1 title.

**Katzoff, Sy**
MnU il. for 1 title.

**Kauffman, Henry C.**
MsHaU .30 cu.ft. of ms./il.

**Kaufmann, Helen**
MsHaU 2.4 cu.ft. of ms./il.

**Kaufmann, John**
MsHaU .30 cu.ft. of ms./il.

**Kaula, Edna**
MsHaU .60 cu.ft. of ms./il.

**Kavaler, Lucy**
MnU ms. for 1 title. MsHaU .60 cu.ft of ms./il.

**Kaye, Gertrude**
MnU il. for 1 title.

**Kaye, Marilyn**
MnU ms. for 1 title.

**Keane, Marie**
NjR-Z il. materials.

**Keats, Ezra Jack**
MnU il. for 5 titles. MsHaU Substantial book holdings and 130 cu.ft. of ms./il. NBPu Working file of source material for his writings and il.

**Keeler, Katherine Southwick**
MnU il. for 6 titles.

**Keeping, Charles**
MnU il. for 1 title.

**Keith, Harold**
MnU ms. for 1 title. MsHaU .30 cu.ft. of ms./il. OkAlvN 15 vols. and corr.

**Kellogg, Elijah**
MeB 92 vols. and 4.5 li.ft. of ms. materials.

**Kellogg, Jean**
MnU ms. for 1 title. MsHaU .30 cu.ft. of ms./il.

**Kellogg & Bulkeley** (publishers)
CtH 518 vols.

**Kelly, Eric Philbrook**
MnU il. for 1 title.

**Kelly, Regina Z.**
MsHaU .90 cu.ft. of ms./il.

**Kelly, Rosalie**
MsHaU .30 cu.ft. of ms./il.

**Kelsey, Vera**
MnU ms. for 1 title.

**Kemble, Edward**
DLC 32 pieces of artwork.

**Kennedy, Richard S.**
MsHaU .30 cu.ft. of ms./il.

**Kenoyer, Natlee**
MsHaU .30 cu.ft. of ms./il.

**Kent, Jack**
MnU ms. for 9 titles; il. for 54 titles.

**Kent, Jennifer**
MnU il. for 1 title.

**Kentucky—Authors and Illustrators**
KyBgW 400 books and several ms. collections.

**Kepes, Juliet Appleby**
MnU ms. for 3 titles; il. for 9 titles.

**Kerlan Award** *see* **Award Books**

**Kerr, M. E.**
MnU ms. for 17 titles; il. for 1 title. MsHaU .30 cu.ft. of ms./il.

**Kerwin, Doris Boody**
MsHaU .60 cu.ft. of ms./il.

**Kessler, Leonard P.**
MnU ms. for 8 titles; il. for 30 titles. MsHaU 12.6 cu.ft. of ms./il. NjR-Z il. materials.

**Kettelkamp, Larry**
NjR ms. materials. NjR-Z il. materials.

**Key, Alexander**
MsHaU 7.5 cu.ft. of ms./il.

**Kiddell-Monroe, Joan**
MnU ms. for 3 titles; il. for 15 titles.

**Killilea, Marie**
MsHaU 8.4 cu.ft. of ms./il.

**Killion, Bette**
MsHaU .30 cu.ft. of ms./il.

**Kilner, Dorothy**
FU Extensive book holdings.

**Kindred, Wendy**
MnU il. for 1 title.

King, Cynthia
MsHaU .30 cu.ft. of ms./il.

King, Edna Knowles
MnU ms. for 1 title; il. for 1 title.

King, Joseph T.
MnU il. for 1 title.

King, Marian
MsHaU 3.6 cu.ft. of ms./il.

King, Robin
MsHaU .30 cu.ft. of ms./il.

King Arthur *see* Arthur, King

Kingman, Lee
MnU ms. for 4 titles. MsHaU .90 cu.ft. of ms./il.

Kingsland, Leslie William
MnU ms. for 3 titles.

Kingston, William Henry Giles
FU 200+ vols.

Kipling, Rudyard
CSmH-A 12 ms.; 19 pieces of corr. NIC Large collection of books and ms. materials.

Kirk, Ruth Kratz
MnU ms. for 1 title; il. for 1 title. MsHaU .30 cu.ft. of ms./il.

Kirmse, Marguerite
MsHaU .30 cu.ft. of ms./il.

Kirn, Ann Minette
MnU il. for 3 titles.

Kismaric, Carole
MnU il. for 4 titles.

Kissin, Eva H.
MnU ms. for 1 title.

Kissin, Rita
MsHaU 6 cu.ft. of ms./il.

Kjelgaard, James Arthur
MnU ms. for 17 titles.

Klein, H. Arthur and Mina C.
MsHaU 3 cu.ft. of ms./il.

Klein, Norma
MnU ms. for 10 titles.

Klemin, Diana
MsHaU 15 cu.ft. of ms./il.

Knight, Clayton
MsHaU .60 cu.ft. of ms./il.

Knight, David C.
MsHaU .30 cu.ft. of ms./il.

Knight, Hilary
CtU ms. for 1 title. MnU il. for 2 titles.

Knight, Ruth Adams
OrU 7 li.ft. of ms.

Knowles, Anne
MnU ms. for 8 titles.

Knudson, R. R.
MsHaU 2.7 cu.ft. of ms./il.

Kobs, Ruth Lowrey
MsHaU .30 cu.ft. of ms./il.

Koertge, Ron
MnU ms. for 1 title.

Koffler, Camilla
MnU ms. for 1 title.

Kolb, Avery
MsHaU .60 cu.ft. of ms./il.

Komoda, Beverly
NjR-Z il. materials.

Komoda, Kiyo
NjR-Z il. materials.

Konkle, Janet
MsHaU .60 cu.ft. of ms./il.

Konzal, Theresa S.
MsHaU 1.2 cu.ft. of ms./il.

Korach, Mimi
MsHaU .60 cu.ft. of ms./il.

Korean Language
DLC 500+ vols. MnU 24 vols.

Koren, Ed
MnU ms. for 1 title.

**Kotzwinkle, William**
MnU ms. for 1 title.

**Krahn, Fernando**
MnU il. for 1 title.

**Kraner, Florian**
MnU il. for 9 titles.

**Krantz, Hazel**
MsHaU .60 cu.ft. of ms./il.

**Kraus, Richard**
MsHaU .30 cu.ft. of ms./il.

**Kraus, Robert**
MnU ms. for 41 titles; il. for 39 titles.

**Krauss, Ruth**
CtU Complete papers. MnU ms. for 1 title.
   MsHaU .30 cu.ft. of ms./il.

**Krautter, Elisa Bialk**
OrU 4.5 li.ft. of ms.

**Kredel, Fritz**
ICN 69+ vols.; ms. and woodblocks. MnU
   il. for 14 titles.

**Krensky, Stephen**
MnU ms. for 8 titles.

**Kroll, Edite**
MnU ms. for 1 title.

**Kroll, Steven**
MsHaU .30 cu.ft. of ms./il.

**Krueger, Bob**
MsHaU .60 cu.ft. of ms./il.

**Krush, Beth**
MnU il. for 9 titles.

**Krush, Joe**
MnU il. for 4 titles.

**Kruss, James**
MnU ms. for 2 titles.

**Kubinyi, Laszlo**
MsHaU .30 cu.ft. of ms./il.

**Kullman, Harry**
MnU ms. for 1 title.

**Kumin, Maxine W.**
MsHaU .30 cu.ft. of ms./il.

**Kuskin, Karla**
MnU ms. for 2 titles; il. for 3 titles.
   MsHaU .30 cu.ft. of ms./il.

**La Farge, Sheila**
MnU ms. for 2 titles.

**Laklan, Carli**
MnU ms. for 1 title. MsHaU .30 cu.ft. of
   ms./il.

**Lamb, Beatrice Pitney**
MnU ms. for 1 title.

**Lamb, Cecile**
MsHaU .90 cu.ft. of ms./il.

**Lambie, Laurie Jo**
MnU il. for 1 title.

**Lambo, Don**
MnU ms. for 1 title. MsHaU .60 cu.ft. of
   ms./il.

**Lamplugh, Lois**
MsHaU .60 cu.ft. of ms./il.

**Lampman, Evelyn Sibley**
OrU 9 li.ft. of ms.

**Land, Mary**
MsHaU 1.5 cu.ft. of ms./il.

**Landau, Jacob**
MnU il. for 8 titles.

**Landshoff, Ursula**
MsHaU 1.2 cu.ft. of ms./il.

**Lane, Rose Wilder**
IaWbH 1.3 cu.ft. of ms. and corr.

**Lang, Andrew**
CSmH-A 12 ms.; 65 pieces of corr. DLC
   Extensive book holdings. FU 32 vols.
   ICN 175+ vols. InU-Li 600+ vols.; ms.,
   corr. NN-Don 75 vols. PP 50 vols.

**Langstaff, John**
MnU ms. for 2 titles.

**Langton, Jane**
MnU ms. for 10 titles.

**Languages** *see* **Foreign Languages**

La Palme, Robert Andree
MnU il. for 1 title.

Lardner, Ring
ICN 50+ vols. and ms. collection.

Larsen, Anita
MsHaU 3 cu.ft. of ms./il.

Larson, Jean R.
MsHaU .30 cu.ft. of ms./il.

Lasell, Fen
MsHaU .90 cu.ft. of ms./il.

Lasker, Joe
MnU ms. for 13 titles; il. for 26 titles.
   MsHaU .60 cu.ft. of ms./il.

Lasky, Kathryn
MnU ms. for 42 titles.

Latham, Barbara
MnU ms. for 6 titles; il. for 16 titles.
   MsHaU .60 cu.ft. of ms./il.

Latham, Donald
MsHaU .30 cu.ft. of ms./il.

Latham, Jean Lee
MnU ms. for 26 titles. MsHaU 1.8 cu.ft.
   of ms./il.

Latham, Peter
MsHaU .30 cu.ft. of ms./il.

Lathrop, Dorothy Pulis
MnU il. for 5 titles. PPT il.

Latimer, James
MnU ms. for 1 title.

Latin America
ICN Extensive holdings.

Latin Language
MnU 19 vols.

Lattimore, Eleanor F.
MnU il. for 9 titles. MsHaU .9 cu.ft. of
   ms./il.

Latvian Language
MnU 14 vols.

Lauber, Patricia
MnU ms. for 9 titles.

Laughlin, Florence
MsHaU .60 cu.ft. of ms./il.

Lavine, Sigmund A.
MsHaU 6.9 cu.ft. of ms./il.

Lawler, Pat
MsHaU .60 cu.ft. of ms./il.

Lawrence, Isabelle
MsHaU 1.8 cu.ft. of ms./il.

Lawrence, Jacob
MnU ms. for 2 titles.

Lawrence, James Duncan
MnU ms. for 2 titles.

Lawrence, Judith Ann
MsHaU 1.5 cu.ft. of ms./il.

Lawrence, Mildred
MsHaU 2.4 cu.ft. of ms./il.

Lawson, Donald
MsHaU 6.3 cu.ft. of ms./il.

Lawson, Marie Abrams
MnU il. for 1 title.

Lawson, Robert
MnU ms. for 8 titles; il. for 12 titles.
   MsHaU .50 cu.ft. of ms./il. NNPM il.
   PP 25 vols. PP-Rb 100 vols. and 1,100
   drawings, etchings, and papers.

Laycock, George Edwin
MnU ms. for 11 titles; il. for 1 title.
   MsHaU .90 cu.ft. of ms./il.

Lazarevich, Mila
MsHaU .30 cu.ft. of ms./il.

Leaf, Munro
PP-Rb 200 vols. and 25 ms.

Lear, Edward
CSmH-A 2 ms.; 85 pieces of corr. DLC
   Extensive book holdings. FU 22 vols.
   InU-Li 35+ vols.

Leavitt, Jerome E.
MsHaU 2.1 cu.ft. of ms./il.

Lebenson, Richard
NjR-Z il. materials.

**Lee, Doris Emrick**
MnU il. for 3 titles.

**Lee, Manning de Villeneuve**
MnU il. for 1 title. MsHaU .60 cu.ft. of ms./il. OrU 10.5 li.ft. of ms. and il.

**Lee, Marie G.**
MnU ms. for 2 titles.

**Lee, Mildred**
MnU ms. for 3 titles.

**Lee and Shepard** (publisher)
MWA 12 boxes of company records.

**Leeper, Clare**
MsHaU .30 cu.ft. of ms./il.

**Le Galliene, Eva**
MnU ms. for 1 title.

**Leighton, Margaret**
MnU ms. for 1 title. MsHaU .30 cu.ft. of ms./il. OrU 3 li.ft. of ms.

**Leisk, David Johnson** *see* **Johnson, Crockett**

**Lemke, Horst**
MnU il. for 1 title.

**Le Moult, Adolph**
MsHaU .60 cu.ft. of ms./il.

**Lenard, Alexander**
MnU ms. for 3 titles.

**L'Engle, Madeleine**
IWW Extensive holdings of books and ms. MnU ms. for 10 titles. MsHaU 2.4 cu.ft. of ms./il.

**Lenniger Literary Agency**
OrU 70.5 li.ft. of ms.

**Lenski, Lois**
ArStC 345 vols. from 1924–1987; 27 li.ft. of ms., il., and corr. FTaSU 250 vols. and 1,011 ms., proofs, corr., il., scrapbooks, and other materials. INS 200 vols.; ms., il., corr. KWS Autographed vols. and ink etchings. KWi il. MiD il. MnU ms. for 9 titles; il. for 48 titles. MsHaU 2.4 cu.ft. of ms./il. NBuC 241 vols., ms., dummies, and il. NSyU 35 vols.; 9 li.ft. of ms. and il. NcGU 230 vols.; 12 li.ft. of ms. and il. NjR-Z il. materials. O Books and il. OS 92 vols., ms., il. OSiA 93 vols., 100 il., and 80 pieces of corr. OkU Autographed books, ms., il., corr. and related items. SdAbN 5 il. and proofs.

**Lent, Blair**
MnU ms. for 5 titles; il. for 23 titles.

**Leonard, Phyllis**
AzTeS ms.

**Lerner, Sharon Ruth**
MnU il. for 1 title.

**LeShan, Eda**
MsHaU .90 cu.ft. of ms./il.

**Leslie, Robert Franklin**
MsHaU 2 cu.ft. of ms./il.

**Le Sueur, Meridel**
MnU ms. for 3 titles.

**Levin, Betty**
MnU ms. for 13 titles.

**Levine, Betty K.**
MsHaU .60 cu.ft. of ms./il.

**Levinger, Elma Ehrlich**
OrU 1.5 li.ft. of ms.

**Levinson, Nancy**
MnU ms. for 2 titles.

**Levitin, Sonia**
MnU ms. for 1 title. MsHaU 6.6 cu.ft. of ms./il.

**Lewin, Ted and Betsy**
CtU 1 box of ms. and il. MoWarbT ms. and il. materials. MsHaU .30 cu.ft. of ms./il.

**Lewis, Allen**
MnU il. for 1 title.

**Lewis, C. S.**
IWW Extensive holdings of books and ms.

**Lewis, Claudia**
MsHaU 1.2 cu.ft. of ms./il.

**Lexau, Joan M.**
MnU ms. for 6 titles. MsHaU .30 cu.ft. of ms./il.

**Ley, Willy**
MsHaU .30 cu.ft. of ms./il.

**Leydenfrost, Robert**
NjR-Z il. materials.

**Lietta**
MsHaU 2.9 cu.ft. of ms./il.

**Likhanov, Albert**
MnU ms. for 1 title.

**Lilly, Charles**
MsHaU .30 cu.ft. of ms./il.

**Limited Editions Club**
TxU-Hu 20 ms. relating to juvenile titles.

**Lindgren, Astrid**
MnU ms. for 2 titles.

**Lindstrom, Sister E.**
MnU il. for 1 title.

**Linkletter, Arthur**
MsHaU .60 cu.ft. of ms./il.

**Lionni, Leo**
MnU il. for 2 titles.

**Lipkind, William**
MnU ms. for 15 titles.

**Lippman, Peter**
MnU ms. for 1 title.

**Lipsyte, Robert**
MnU ms. for 4 titles. MsHaU 3 cu.ft. of ms./il. NjR ms. materials.

**Lisowski, Gabriel**
MsHaU .30 cu.ft. of ms./il.

**Liss, Howard**
MsHaU 1.5 cu.ft. of ms./il.

**Liston, Robert A.**
MsHaU .90 cu.ft. of ms./il.

**Little, Jean**
MnU ms. for 4 titles.

***Little Black Sambo*** *see* **Bannerman, Helen**

**Little Golden Books**
MnU Extensive holdings. MsHaU 200+ titles. OrU 37.5 li.ft. of ms. and il.

**Liu, Beatrice**
MnU ms. for 1 title.

**Lively, Penelope**
MnU ms. for 5 titles.

**Livingston, Myra Cohn**
MnU ms. for 82 titles.

**Lobel, Anita**
MnU ms. for 5 titles; il. for 3 titles.

**Lobel, Arnold Stark**
MnU ms. for 9 titles; il. for 45 titles.

**Lobsenz, Norman M.**
MsHaU 3.6 cu.ft. of ms./il.

**Locker-Lampson, Frederick**
MsHaU .30 cu.ft. of ms./il.

**Loeffler, Gisella**
MnU il. for 1 title.

**Loeper, John J.**
NjR ms. materials. NjR-Z il. materials.

**London, Jack**
CGlen 100 vols. COPL 375 vols. and 2 periodical titles. CSmH-A Extensive collection of 30,000 pieces including literary ms., corr., photographs, broadsides, and ephemera. ICN 87+ vols.

**Lopshire, Robert**
MnU il. for 2 titles. MsHaU 1.3 cu.ft. of ms./il.

**Lord, D. Douglas**
MsHaU .3 cu.ft. of ms./il.

**Lorenzini, Carlo** *see* **Collodi, Carlo**

**Lorenzo, Carol Lee**
MnU ms. for 1 title.

**Lorraine, Walter**
MnU il. for 1 title.

**Lostutter, Robert**
MnU il. for 1 title.

**Louisiana**
L Several hundred vols.

**Louisiana—Authors and Illustrators**
L Several hundred vols.

**Louw, Juliet M.**
MsHaU .30 cu.ft. of ms./il.

**Lovelace, Maud Hart**
MsHaU .30 cu.ft. of ms./il. OrU 3 li.ft. of
il.

**Low, Alice**
MnU ms. for 5 titles.

**Low, Joseph**
MsHaU 2 cu.ft. of ms./il.

**Lowrey, Janette Sebring**
MnU ms. for 2 titles.

**Lowry, Lois**
MnU ms. for 7 titles.

**Lubell, Winifred Milius**
MnU il. for 12 titles. MsHaU 3.8 cu.ft. of
ms./il.

**Lund, Doris Herold**
MsHaU .3 cu.ft. of ms./il.

**MacDonald, George**
CSmH-A 1 ms.; 42 pieces of corr. CtY-BR
First editions and personal papers, with
3,500+ pieces of corr. IWW Extensive
holdings of books and ms.

**Machetanz, Sara Burleson and Frederick**
MsHaU .90 cu.ft. of ms./il. OrU .5 li.ft. of
ms.

**MacIntyre, Elisabeth**
MsHaU .60 cu.ft. of ms./il.

**MacKellar, William**
CtU 1 box of ms. MsHaU .30 cu.ft. of
ms./il.

**MacKenzie, Garry**
MnU il. for 1 title.

**MacKinstry, Elizabeth**
MnU il. for 1 title.

**MacKnight, Ninon**
MnU il. for 1 title.

**MacLeod, Ellen Jane**
MsHaU 1.2 cu.ft. of ms./il.

**Madden, Donald**
MsHaU 1.2 cu.ft. of ms./il.

**Maddox, Harry**
MsHaU .30 cu.ft. of ms./il.

**Madison, Arnold**
MsHaU 3 cu.ft. of ms./il.

**Maestro, Giulio**
CtU ms. for 4 titles. MnU il. for 8 titles.
MsHaU .30 cu.ft. of ms./il.

**Maguire, Gregory**
MnU ms. for 3 titles.

**Mahlmann, Lewis**
MsHaU .30 cu.ft. of ms./il.

**Maine**
MeU 2,000 vols.

**Maine—Authors and Illustrators**
MePW ms. and other materials for Sophie
May, Elizabeth Coatsworth, and Kate
Douglas Wiggin. MeU 2,000 vols.

**Malcolmson, David**
MsHaU .60 cu.ft. of ms./il.

**Malkus, Alida Wright Sims**
MnU ms. for 2 titles. MsHaU .90 cu.ft. of
ms./il.

**Malvern, Corinne**
MnU il. for 5 titles.

**Manley, Seon**
MsHaU .30 cu.ft. of ms./il.

**Mann, Horace**
MHi 24 boxes and 10 vols. of ms. materials on education.

**Mannheim, Grete Salomon**
MnU ms. for 1 title; il. for 1 title.

**Mannix, Daniel**
MsHaU 10.8 cu.ft. of ms./il.

**Mansfield, Norma Bicknell and Robert
Stuart Mansfield**
OrU 5.5 li.ft. of ms.

## Manuscript/Illustration Material

ArStC 27 li.ft. of ms., il., and corr. for Lois Lenski. AzT 12 il. by Grace Moon. AzTeS 65 li.ft. of ms., galleys, and corr. for five Arizona authors; 200 li.ft. of playwright ms. AzU ms. for Ann Nolan Clark. CBbWDA 435 li.ft. of Walt Disney ms. and il. CCSc ms. and il. for several authors and illustrators. CFLp 2 li.ft. of il. of Leo Politi. CL 190 il. dating from 1924–1958 in the English Collection; 27 il. in Politi Collection. CLSU ms. materials for Leonard Wibberley. CLU-S/C ms., corr., and il. for a number of authors and illustrators. CP il. materials for Mary and Conrad Buff, Holling Clancy Holling, Grace and Carl Moon, and Leo Politi. CPom ms., corr., and related materials.

CSfACA Extensive holdings of art and ms. CSfSt Professional papers of Marguerite Archer and Wilhelmina Harper. CSmH-A ms., corr., and related materials for nearly 50 children's authors and illustrators. CStoC ms. for Howard Pease. CoD 350 ms., corr., and photographs for Eugene Field. CtH 50 il. by a variety of artists. CtU ms. and il. for 29 authors and illustrators. CtY-BR ms., il., corr., and related materials for numerous children's authors and illustrators; 370 li.ft. of ms. and il. of Peter Newell and family. DGU ms. and il. of Lynd Ward and May McNeer Ward. DeU ms., corr., photographs of Howard Pyle and Katharine Pyle. DeWA Extensive holdings of il., scrapbooks, corr. relating to Howard Pyle and his students Frank Schoonover, Katharine Pyle, and N. C. Wyeth.

DeWI 280 il., 110 vols. and 15 binders of corr. for illustrators. FTS 300 li.ft. of ms. and il. FTaSU Significant holdings of ms. Also 1,011 ms., proofs, corr., il., and related materials of Lois Lenski. GEU-S ms. and il. in Harris Collection and the Blackburn Papers. GU 135 folders of ms. materials for Robert Burch. ICN ms. and il. for numerous authors and illustrators. INS ms. for Lois Lenski. IWW ms. and il. for C. S. Lewis, George MacDonald, Dorothy L. Sayers, and J. R. R. Tolkien. IaU ms. and il. for Jeannette Hyde Eyerly, Henry Gregor Felsen, Marjorie Holmes, Edward L. Sabin, and Nancy Veglahn. IaWbH 1.3 cu.ft. of ms. and corr. for Rose Wilder Lane and Laura Ingalls Wilder.

InU-Li Extensive holdings of ms. and il. KEmU ms. and il. for authors and illustrators in the Massee Collection and the Yates Collection; corr. in the Gagliardo Collection. KU Papers of Ruth Garver Gagliardo. KWi ms., il., sketchbooks, and related items for 10 author/illustrators. KyBgW ms. and il. for Anne Pence Davis, Dorothy Grider, and Alice Hegen Rice. KyLoU 50 li.ft. of il. and corr. for Arthur Rackham. KyU 13 boxes of ms. materials for Rebecca Caudill. MAA 1.5 li.ft. of ms. and related items of Peter Parley. MBAt ms. materials for Isabel Anderson. MBU ms., il., corr., and related materials for 14 authors and illustrators.

MCo ms. and related materials for Concord, Massachusetts, authors and illustrators. MCoA corr., sketchbooks, and notebooks for Louisa May Alcott. MFiT ms. materials for Robert Cormier. MHi 24 boxes and 20 vols. of ms. materials of Horace Mann. MSanB 380 il. used in Thornton W. Burgess books. MSanP 15 paintings of fairy tales by children. MWA ms. holdings for author Goold Brown and publishers Morris Cotton; Dodd, Mead & Co.; and Lee and Shepard. MWiW 35 li.ft. of ms. materials for several authors. MeB ms. materials for Jacob Abbott, Henry Beston, Elizabeth Coatsworth, Elijah Kellogg, Charles Asbury Stephens, and Kate Douglas Wiggin. MeGar 70 li.ft. of ms. materials of Laura E. Richards. MePW ms. and other materials for Sophie May, Elizabeth Coatsworth, and Kate Douglas Wiggin. MiD ms. and il.

for Kate Greenaway, Laura Ingalls Wilder, Helen Sewell, and Mildred Boyle. MiMtpT ms. materials for four authors. MnM il. and corr. for Carol Ryrie Brink and Emma Brock.

MnSSC ms., il., and corr. for Ruth Sawyer. MnU ms., il., and corr. for 1,300+ authors and illustrators. MoHM ms. for Mark Twain. MoSFi corr., photographs, royalty reports for Eugene Field. MoSHi Papers from 1855–1940 and corr. MoSW ms. and corr. for Eugene Field and William Jay Smith. MoStoM ms. for Mark Twain. MoWarbT ms., il., corr., interviews, and related materials for nearly 200 authors and illustrators. MsHaU ms. il., corr., and related materials for 1,200 authors and illustrators. NAiU ms. and il. for Marcia Brown and Maud and Miska Petersham. NBuC ms. and il. for Lois Lenski. NGuP il. for several artists.

NIC ms. for Rudyard Kipling, E. B. White, and Hendrik Willem Van Loon. NN-Rb ms. and il. in Spencer Collection; il. in the Arents Collection. NN-Sc ms. and il. for John L. Steptoe and Regina M. Andrews. NNC ms., corr., il. for Arthur Rackham, L. Frank Baum, W. W. Denslow, Walter Farley, and Tibor Gergely. NNPM ms. and il. for many people. NNU-F ms. and corr. for Lewis Carroll in Berol Collection. NSyU ms. and il. for six authors and illustrators and two publishers. NWe il. of several prominent artists. NbU ms. and corr. for Mari Sandoz and Harold William Felton. NcCU ms. for 5 North Carolina authors. NcGU ms., il. and corr. for 9 authors and illustrators.

NjMF 80 il. of Winsor McCay. NjP-C Substantial holdings. NjR ms. materials for 17 authors. NjR-Z il. materials for 67 illustrators. O ms. and il. for Ohio authors and illustrators. OBgU ms. materials for John and Allen Saunders related to comic books; 6 boxes of ms. materials for Jan Wahl. ODaWU 4 il. of Arthur Rackham. OFiC 300 pieces of art from children's books. OKentU ms. and il. from Saalfield Publishing Co., Cynthia Rylant, and Virginia Hamilton. OOxM ms. for Mary M. Sherwood and William McGuffey; il. for Kate Seredy. OS ms. and il. for Lois Lenski. OSiA ms., il., corr. for Lois Lenski and Bessie Schiff. OkT ms. by Marguerite Henry. OkU ms., il., corr. for Lois Lenski.

OrU ms., il., and corr. for 200+ authors, illustrators, literary agents, and publishing companies. PNo ms. by Harriet May Savitz, il. by Katherine Milhous and Rosemary Wells. PP il. by many artists. PP-Rb 100 ms. and 140 il. for Beatrix Potter; 1,100 il. for Robert Lawson; 50 il. by A. B. Frost; 100 ms. and 50 il. for Arthur Rackham; 1,000 ms. and 150 il. for Howard Pyle and students of the Brandywine School; 20 ms. and 80 il. for Kate Greenaway; 25 ms. for Munro Leaf. PPRF 3,000 il. for Maurice Sendak. PPT ms. and corr. for Walter de la Mare. PPiC 200 il. and ms. for Kate Greenaway. PPiU-LS il. for 17 artists. PSt il. for Wanda Gag and Maud and Miska Petersham.

RWe 106 items of ms. and il. for Margaret Wise Brown. ScCleU 130 vols. and 4 cu.ft. of ms. for Betsy Byars. TxDa ms. for Sarah Crewe and 38 il. TxU-Hu ms. and corr. for 20 authors. TxWB ms. for *Pied Piper of Hamelin*. WaT ms., il., corr., and scrapbooks for Thomas Handforth.

**Marabella, Madeline**
MsHaU .30 cu.ft. of ms./il.

**Margolis, Bette Shula**
NjR-Z il. materials.

**Margolis, Richard**
MnU ms. for 1 title.

**Margules, Gabriele**
MnU ms. for 1 title; il. for 1 title.

**Mariana** *see* **Foster, Marian Curtis**

A shelf of *Fifty Two Stories of . . .*, edited by Alfred H. Miles; London: Hutchinson [ca. 1890–1905].

**Marine, Edmund**
MnU il. for 1 title.

**Mark Twain Reading Award** *see* **Award Books**

**Marks, Mickey Klar**
MsHaU 6.3 cu.ft. of ms./il.

**Marlin, Herb T.**
MsHaU .30 cu.ft. of ms./il.

**Marokvia, Artur**
MnU il. for 1 title.

**Mars, Witold Tadeusz**
MnU il. for 38 titles.

**Marsh, Irving T.**
MsHaU .30 cu.ft. of ms./il.

**Marsh, Susan**
MsHaU .60 cu.ft. of ms./il.

**Marshall, Daniel**
MsHaU 1.3 cu.ft. of ms./il.

**Marshall, Edward** *see* **Marshall, James**

**Marshall, James**
CtU ms. and il. for 25 titles. MnU il. for 11 titles. MsHaU 10.5 cu.ft. of ms./il. OrU .5 li.ft. of ms. and il.

**Marshall, John** (publisher)
InU-Li Extensive book holdings.

**Martin, Ann**
MnU ms. for 10 titles.

**Martin, Dick**
MnU il. for 7 titles.

**Martin, Henry R.**
MnU il. for 2 titles.

**Martin, John**
MsHaU .9 cu.ft. of ms./il.

**Martin, Patricia Miles**
MnU ms. for 11 titles. MsHaU 2.4 cu.ft. of ms./il.

**Martin, Rene**
MnU ms. for 2 titles.

**Martin, Richard**
MnU il. for 1 title.

**Martin, Stefan**
MnU il. for 4 title.

**Martin, William**
MnU ms. for 1 title.

**Mason, Arthur and Mary Frank Mason**
OrU 1.5 li.ft. of ms.

**Mason, George Frederick**
MnU il. for 5 titles. MsHaU .9 cu.ft. of ms./il.

**Mason, Miriam**
MnU ms. for 1 title. MsHaU .3 cu.ft. of ms./il.

**Mason, Theodore**
MsHaU .60 cu.ft. of ms./il.

**Massachusetts—Authors and Illustrators**
MCo Books and ms. materials for Concord, Massachusetts, authors and illustrators.

**Massachusetts Imprints**
MHi Extensive holdings.

**Massachusetts Sabbath School Society**
MBCn 55 li.ft. of materials.

**Massee, May**
KEmU Books from her personal library and books published by her.

**Massey, Clara H.**
MsHaU .30 cu.ft. of ms./il.

**Massie, Diane Redfield**
MnU il. for 1 title.

**Masten, Helen A.**
MsHaU .80 cu.ft. of ms./il. NAlU corr.

**Masterman-Smith, Virginia**
NjR ms. materials.

**Masters, Kelly** *see* Ball, Zachary

**Matson, Emerson Nels**
MnU ms. for 1 title.

**McCarthy, Agnes**
MsHaU .30 cu.ft. of ms./il.

**McCaslin, Nellie**
MsHaU .30 cu.ft. of ms./il.

**McCaw, Jessie Brewer**
MnU ms. for 1 title; il. for 1 title.

**McCay, Winsor**
NjMF 80 il.

**McClelland, Hugh**
MnU il. for 1 title.

**McCloskey, Robert**
KEmU ms. and il. in Massee Collection. OC ms. and il. in Goldsmith Collection.

**McClung, Robert M.**
MnU ms. for 31 titles; il. for 19 titles. MsHaU 4.5 cu.ft. of ms./il.

**McClure, Herbert**
MnU il. for 2 titles.

**McCord, Jean**
MsHaU .30 cu.ft. of ms./il.

**McCorkell, Elsie**
MsHaU .60 cu.ft. of ms./il.

**McCormick, Wilfred**
MBU 22 vols. and 10 li.ft. of ms. materials. MsHaU .60 cu.ft. of ms./il.

**McCrea, James and Ruth**
MnU il. for 3 titles. MsHaU .60 cu.ft. of ms./il.

**McCully, Emily Arnold**
MnU ms. for 16 titles; il. for 70 titles. MsHaU .60 cu.ft. of ms./il.

**McCurdy, Michael**
MnU il. for 2 titles.

**McCutcheon, John T.**
ICN 20+ vols. and ms. collection.

**McDermont, Gerald**
MnU ms. for 2 titles.

**McDonald, Megan**
MnU ms. for 1 title.

**McFall, Christie**
NjR-Z il. materials.

**McGee, Barbara**
MnU il. for 1 title.

**McGee, Myra**
MnU ms. for 1 title.

**McGinley, Phyllis**
MnU ms. for 1 title.

**McGovern, Ann**
MnU ms. for 2 titles.

**McGowen, Tom**
MsHaU .30 cu.ft. of ms./il.

**McGraw, Eloise Jarvis and Lauren McGraw Wagner**
MnU ms. for 1 title.

**McGraw, Eloise Jarvis and William Corbin McGraw**
OrU 22 li.ft. of ms.

**McGuffey, William**
OOxM corr. and sermons.

**McGuffey Readers** *see* **Textbooks**

**McHargue, Georgess**
MnU ms. for 1 title. MsHaU .30 cu.ft. of ms./il.

**McIntyre, Elisabeth**
MnU il. for 1 title.

**McKay, Donald**
MsHaU .30 cu.ft. of ms./il.

**McKee, Alexander**
MsHaU .60 cu.ft. of ms./il.

**McKee, Elizabeth**
MnU ms. for 1 title.

**McKenzie, Ellen Kindt**
MnU ms. for 1 title.

**McKinnon, Lise Somme**
MnU ms. for 4 titles.

**McKown, Robin**
MsHaU 1.2 cu.ft. of ms./il.

**McLean, Susan**
MnU ms. for 1 title.

**McLelland, Isabel Couper**
OrU 1.5 li.ft. of ms.

**McLerran, Alice**
MnU ms. for 2 titles.

**McLoughlin Brothers**
CSf Prints of woodblocks and some blocks. DeWint Extensive holdings of books, paper dolls, paper toys, and games. MWA 1,500 titles. MsHaU Scrapbook of printer's proofs and extensive published book holdings. NNC 820 vols. NHi 136 vols. and woodblocks.

**McMillen, Neil R.**
MsHaU .60 cu.ft. of ms./il.

**McNeer, May Yonge**
DGU Collection of ms. MnU ms. for 3 titles; il. for 1 title. MsHaU .50 cu.ft. of ms./il. OrU .5 li.ft. of ms. and il.

**McPhail, David M.**
MnU ms. for 1 title; il. for 3 titles.

**McQueen, Mildred H.**
MsHaU .30 cu.ft. of ms./il.

**McRae, James and Ruth**
MsHaU .30 cu.ft. of ms./il.

**Meader, Stephen W.**
MsHaU .30 cu.ft. of ms./il.

**Means, Carroll**
MsHaU .30 cu.ft. of ms./il.

**Meeks, Bernard**
MsHaU .60 cu.ft. of corr. with authors and illustrators.

**Meigs, Cornelia**
MsHaU .30 cu.ft. of ms./il.

**Meilach, Dona Z.**
MsHaU 9 cu.ft. of ms./il.

**Melcher, Marguerite**
MsHaU .30 cu.ft. of ms./il.

**Meltzer, Milton**
MsHaU 1.5 cu.ft. of ms./il. OrU 17 li.ft. of ms.

**Melville, Herman**
CCSc 175 vols. in the Ament Collection. CSmH-A 1 piece of correspondence. ICN One of the preeminent collections of Melville editions.

**Mendelowitz, Daniel**
MsHaU 1.2 cu.ft. of ms./il.

**Mendoza, George**
MnU il. for 1 title.

**Meretzky, S. Eric**
MnU il. for 1 title.

**Merida, Carlos**
MnU il. for 1 title.

**Merriam, Eve**
MnU ms. for 47 titles. MsHaU .30 cu.ft. of ms./il.

**Merrill, Frank Thayer**
MnU il. for 1 title.

**Merrill, Jean**
MsHaU .60 cu.ft. of ms./il.

**Merwin, Decie**
MnU il. for 1 title.

**Metz, Lois L.**
MsHaU .30 cu.ft. of ms./il.

**Meyer, Edith Patterson**
MsHaU .60 cu.ft. of ms./il.

**Michigan**
MiMtpT 500 vols. by Michigan residents and with Michigan as a setting.

**Michigan—Authors and Illustrators**
MiMtpT 500 vols. by Michigan residents and with Michigan as a setting.

**Middle Eastern Languages**
DLC 50 vols. of Turkish, Persian, and Central Asian titles.

**Migdalski, Edward C.**
MsHaU .30 cu.ft. of ms./il.

**Miklowitz, Gloria D.**
MsHaU 10 cu.ft. of ms./il.

**Mikolaycak, Charles**
MnU ms. for 2 titles; il. for 67 titles.

**Miles, Betty**
MnU ms. for 20 titles.

**Miles, Miska** *see* **Martin, Patricia Miles**

**Milhous, Katherine**
KWi il. MnU ms. for 4 titles; il. for 20 titles. MsHaU .30 cu.ft. of ms./il. PNo il. PP 25 vols. and il.

**Miller, Albert**
MsHaU .30 cu.ft. of ms./il.

**Miller, Helen M.**
MsHaU .30 cu.ft. of ms./il.

**Miller, Jane Judith**
MnU il. for 2 titles.

**Miller, Teresa**
MnU ms. for 1 title.

**Mills, Lauren**
CtU ms. and il. for 10 titles.

**Milne, A. A.**
NN-Don 35 vols. and the original toys from *Winnie the Pooh*.

**Mincieli, Rose Laura**
MnU ms. for 1 title.

**Miner, Lewis S.**
MsHaU .30 cu.ft. of ms./il.

**Miniature Books**
CSfSt 100+ vols. CSmH-A Weber Miniature Book Collection. FTS 500 vols. from 17th century to present, with emphasis on 19th century. ICN 110+ vols. InU-Li Growing collection of several hundred vols. MBWS Collection of miniatures in the Ingraham Collection. MiKW 315 vols. from 1780. MiMtpT 50 vols. NBPu 200+ vols. from the 19th century to present. NBuBE 150 vols. NCooHi 50 vols. ScRhW 50 vols. TxDN 150 vols. WaSp 19th-century holdings.

**Minich, Newell R.**
MnU il. for 2 titles.

**Minnesota**
MnM 1,400 vols.

**Minnesota—Authors and Illustrators**
MnM 1,400 vols. MnSP 200 vols.

**Minnich, Helen Benton**
MnU il. for 1 title.

**Minor, Wendell**
MnU il. for 1 title.

**Miret, Gil**
MnU il. for 2 titles.

**Mirsky, Reba Paeff**
MsHaU .30 cu.ft. of ms./il.

**Mississippi—Authors and Illustrators**
MsHaU 100 vols.

**Missouri**
MoHI 1,000+ vols. by Missourians and
about Missouri.

**Missouri—Authors and Illustrators**
MoHI 1,000+ vols. by Missourians and
about Missouri. MoWarbT 4,000 items
of books, and ms. materials.

**Mitchell, Jerry**
MsHaU .30 cu.ft. of ms./il.

**Moche, Dinah**
MsHaU 5.5 cu.ft. of ms./il.

**Mocniak, George**
MnU il. for 1 title.

**Molesworth, Mary Louisa Stewart**
DLC Extensive book holdings. FU Extensive book holdings.

**Monath, Elizabeth**
NjR-Z il. materials.

**Monjo, Ferdinand N.**
MnU ms. for 17 titles.

**Monk, Marvin Randolph**
MnU il. for 1 title.

**Monsell, Helen A.**
MsHaU .30 cu.ft. of ms./il.

**Montgomery, Elizabeth R.**
MsHaU 1.8 cu.ft. of ms./il.

**Montgomery, Rutherford G.**
MnU il. for 1 title. MsHaU .90 cu.ft. of
ms./il. OrU 28.5 li.ft. of ms.

**Montgomery, Vivian**
MsHaU .30 cu.ft. of ms./il.

**Montressor, Beni**
MnU il. for 3 titles.

**Moon, Grace and Carl**
AzT 12 il. CP il. materials.

**Moon, Sheila Elizabeth**
MnU ms. for 1 title.

**Moore, Alma C.**
MsHaU .30 cu.ft. of ms./il.

**Moore, Clement Clarke**
CSmH-A 1 ms. of "A Visit from St. Nicho-
las"; 3 pieces of corr. FU Extensive book
holdings. InU-Li 100+ vols. NAlU 200
editions of "A Visit from St. Nicholas."
NcU 1,000 vols. PPiC 300 vols. of
"'Twas the Night before Christmas."
RPB-JH 300 vols.

**Moore, Lilian**
OrU 1.5 li.ft. of ms.

**Moore, Rosalie**
OrU 6 li.ft. of ms.

**Moore, Ruth**
TxU-Hu 9 boxes of ms.

**Moore, Wilfred G.**
MsHaU .30 cu.ft. of ms./il.

**Mooser, Stephen**
MnU ms. for 1 title.

**Mordvinoff, Nicolas**
MnU il. for 16 titles.

**Morey, Walt**
OrU 30 li.ft. of ms.

**Morgan, Alison**
MnU ms. for 3 titles.

**Morris, Loverne**
MnU ms. for 1 title.

**Morrison, Dorothy**
OrU .5 li.ft. of ms.

**Morrison, Lillian**
MsHaU 2.7 cu.ft. of ms./il.

**Morrow, Barb**
MnU il. for 1 title.

**Morrow, Suzanne Stark**
MnU ms. for 1 title.

**Morse, Evangeline**
MnU ms. for 1 title.

**Moseley, Elizabeth R.**
MsHaU .30 cu.ft. of ms./il.

**Moser, Barry**
CtU ms. for all of his children's books. GEU-S il. in the Harris Collection.

**Moskin, Marietta D.**
MsHaU .30 cu.ft. of ms./il.

**Mother Goose**
CF 170 vols. dating from 1899. CL 1,000+ vols. of 19th–20th-century editions published in the United States and England. FU 200+ vols. IC 135 vols. from 1900. InU-Li 100+ vols. MiD 135 vols. from 1878. MiGrA 55 vols. in a variety of languages. MnU 266 vols. MoS 50+ vols. from 1878. MoWarbT 120 vols. MsHaU 200+ vols. NN-Don 100 vols. NmAl 90 vols. PP Extensive holdings. RPB-JH 450 vols. TxDa 150 vols.

**Moy, Evangeline**
MnU ms. for 1 title.

**Moy, Seong**
MnU il. for 2 titles.

**Moyers, William**
MnU il. for 12 titles.

**Mozley, Charles**
MnU il. for 1 title.

**Mueller, Hans Alexander**
MnU il. for 1 title.

**Mulac, Margaret E.**
MsHaU 1.2 cu.ft. of ms./il.

**Multiculturalism**
CSf 600 vols. on various ethnic groups in the United States. CSmar 11,000+ vols. in Spanish and in English about Latinos. DeU 6,000 vols. from 1955–1985. MBChM Extensive book holdings. MiDW 1,500 vols. MsHaU Extensive holdings. NAlU 900 vols. NJQ 400 vols. of African-American titles. NN-BrCo 2,000 vols. of African-American books. NmU 1,000 print and 100 non-print items in Spanish and Native American languages.

**Munroe, Kirk**
CSmH-A 1 piece of corr.

**Munsinger, Lynn**
MsHaU .60 cu.ft. of ms./il.

**Murphy, Barbara Beasley**
MsHaU 6 cu.ft. of ms./il.

**Murphy, Emmett Jefferson**
MnU ms. for 1 title.

**Murphy, Marjorie C.**
MsHaU 1.2 cu.ft. of ms./il.

**Murphy, Shirley Rousseau**
MnU ms. for 1 title. MsHaU 5.4 cu.ft. of ms./il.

**Musgrave, Florence**
MsHaU .30 cu.ft. of ms./il.

**Music** *see* **Performing Arts**

**Myers, Elisabeth Perkins**
MsHaU 1.2 cu.ft. of ms./il.

**Myers, Steven**
MsHaU .30 cu.ft. of ms./il.

**Myller, Rolf**
MsHaU 2.8 cu.ft. of ms./il.

**Nagy, Al**
MnU il. for 1 title.

**Naidoo, Beverley**
MsHaU .30 cu.ft. of ms./il.

**Nankivell, Joice M.**
MnU ms. for 2 titles.

**Naprstek, Joel**
NjR-Z il. materials.

**Nash, Mary H.**
MsHaU .30 cu.ft. of ms./il.

**Nast, Thomas**
MsHaU .60 cu.ft. of ms./il.

**Nathan, Dorothy G.**
OrU .5 li.ft. of ms.

**Native American Languages**
ICN Extensive holdings of published works dating from 1600 to the present. NmU 1,000 print and 100 nonprint items in Spanish and Native American languages.

**Native Americans**
AzU Collection of published works. ICN 400+ vols. OkS 275 vols.

**Natti, Susanna**
MsHaU .60 cu.ft. of ms./il.

**Natural History**
ICN 40+ vols. PP-Rb 500 vols.

**Naylor, Phyllis Reynolds**
MnU ms. for 18 titles. MsHaU 9 cu.ft. of ms./il.

**Nazi Literature**
NcD Substantial holdings.

**Nebel, Gustave E.**
MnU il. for 1 title.

**Negri, Rocco**
MnU il. for 3 titles.

**Neill, John R.**
MsHaU .40 cu.ft. of ms./il.

**Nelson, Marg**
MsHaU .30 cu.ft. of ms./il.

**Nelson, Mary Carroll**
MnU ms. for 3 titles.

**Nene Award** *see* **Award Books**

**Nesbit, E.**
DLC Extensive book holdings. FU 50 vols.

**Nesbitt, Esta**
MnU ms. for 1 title; il. for 9 titles.

**Ness, Evaline**
MiD il. MnU ms. for 2 titles; il. for 20 titles. MsHaU 1.2 cu.ft. of ms./il. NjR-Z il. materials. PP 15 vols. and il. for 5 titles.

**Neufeld, John**
MnU ms. for 9 titles.

**Nevil, Susan R.**
MnU il. for 1 title.

**Neville, Emily Cheney**
MnU ms. for 5 titles.

**New England**
InTI Walker Collection features New England titles. MHi 600 vols. MStuO 350 vols. MeWC 1,500 vols. NhD 2,400 vols. published throughout New England states.

**New England Primer** *see* **Textbooks**

**New England Round Table of Children's Librarians**
MB 30 boxes of the organization's archives.

**New Hampshire**
NhC Substantial holdings.

**New Hampshire—Authors and Illustrators**
NhC Substantial holdings. NhU Growing collection of books by New Hampshire authors and illustrators.

**New Jersey**
NjSoCo 285 vols.

**New Jersey—Authors and Illustrators**
NjR ms. and corr. for many New Jersey residents.

**New York**
NAlU 225 vols. NN-Don 200 vols. NNMus 50 vols.

**New York—Authors and Illustrators**
NBPu Growing collection of titles written by Brooklyn residents. NHas Books by Hastings authors and illustrators.

New York Imprints
NCooHi 19th-century upstate New York and Cooperstown.

**Newbery, John** (publisher)
CLU-S/C 200+ vols. published by Newbery or his successors. InU-Li 200+ vols. published by Newbery and his successors. NjP-C Extensive holdings published by Newbery.

**Newbery Medal** *see* **Award Books**

**Newberry, Clare Turlay**
KWi il. MnU il. for 5 titles. MsHaU .30 cu.ft. of ms./il. OrU 6 li.ft. of ms. and il.

**Newell, Peter**
CtY-BR 370 li.ft. of ms., il., sketches, proofs, corr., and books. DLC 15 pieces of artwork.

**Newhall, Beaumont**
MsHaU 1.8 cu.ft. of ms./il.

**Newman, Shirlee**
MsHaU .60 cu.ft. of ms./il.

**Newsom, Carol**
NjR-Z il. materials.

**Ney, John**
MnU ms. for 3 titles.

**Nichols, Ruth**
MnU ms. for 1 title.

**Nickless, Will B.**
OrU .5 li.ft. of il.

**Nielson, Jon**
NjR-Z il. materials.

**Nixon, Joan Lowery**
MnU ms. for 42 titles.

**Noad, Frederick**
MsHaU .30 cu.ft. of ms./il.

**Noble, Iris**
MsHaU 5.1 cu.ft. of ms./il.

**Noble, Trinka Hakes**
NjR-Z il. materials.

**Nodjoumi, Nickzad**
MnU il. for 1 title.

**Nolan, Jeannette Covert**
MsHaU .60 cu.ft. of ms./il.

**Nolan, Paul T.**
MsHaU 2.4 cu.ft. of ms./il.

**Norris, Gunilla Brodde**
MnU ms. for 1 title.

**North Carolina—Authors and Illustrators**
NcCU books and ms. of several authors. NcGU books, ms., il., and corr. for 10 authors and illustrators.

**North Carolina Imprints**
NcCU 30 19th-century vols.

**North, Sterling**
MBU 58 vols. and 27 boxes of ms. materials.

**Norwegian Language**
MnU 654 vols.

**Oakley, Thornton**
PP-Rb ms. and il.

**Obligado, Lilian**
MnU il. for 6 titles.

**O'Brien, Frank**
MsHaU .30 cu.ft. of ms./il.

**O'Brien, Robert C.**
MnU ms. for 2 titles.

**O'Clery, Helen**
MsHaU 1.2 cu.ft. of ms./il.

**O'Connell, Alice Louise**
MnU ms. for 2 titles.

**O'Dell, Scott**
MnU ms. for 28 titles. MsHaU .90 cu.ft. of ms./il. OrU 1 li.ft. of ms.

**Oechsli, Kelly**
MnU ms. for 1 title; il. for 16 titles.

**Offit, Sidney**
MnU ms. for 11 titles.

Ogle, Lucille
OrU 37.5 li.ft. of ms. and il.

O'Hanlon, Jacklyn
MsHaU .30 cu.ft. of ms./il.

Ohio
O Collection of books about Ohio and Ohioans.

Ohio—Authors and Illustrators
O Books, ms., and il. by Ohio authors and illustrators.

Ohlsson, Ib
MnU il. for 8 titles.

Oklahoma
OkOk Collection of books about Oklahoma.

Oklahoma—Authors and Illustrators
OkOk Collection of books by Oklahoma authors and illustrators.

Olds, Elizabeth
MnU il. for 4 titles. MsHaU .50 cu.ft. of ms./il.

Olds, Helen
MsHaU .30 cu.ft. of ms./il.

Olsen, Ib Spang
MnU il. for 6 titles.

Oneal, Zibby
MnU ms. for 3 titles.

O'Neill, Mary LeDuc
MnU ms. for 11 titles.

Optic, Oliver
DLC 96 vols. FU Extensive book holdings. IDeKN 63 vols. MWA 124 vols. NhD Extensive book holdings. PP 100 vols. ViU 71 vols.

Orbaan, Albert F.
MsHaU .60 cu.ft. of ms./il.

Oregon
OrP Volumes about Oregon from 1884–1937.

Orgel, Doris
MnU ms. for 8 titles. MsHaU .30 cu.ft. of ms./il.

Original Artwork see Manuscript/Illustration Materials

Orlob, Helen S.
MsHaU .60 cu.ft. of ms./il.

Ormsby, Virginia
MsHaU .30 cu.ft. of ms./il.

Osborne, Dorothy
MsHaU .30 cu.ft. of ms./il.

Osborne, Edgar
MsHaU .30 cu.ft. of ms./il.

Ottseon, Madalene
MsHaU .60 cu.ft. of ms./il.

Ousley, Odille
MsHaU .30 cu.ft. of ms./il.

Owens, Gail
MsHaU 2.5 cu.ft. of ms./il. NjR-Z il. materials.

Oz see Baum, Lyman Frank

Paca, Lillian G.
MsHaU .60 cu.ft. of ms./il.

Pacific Northwest
Wa 60 vols. WaU 300 vols.

Page, Thornton Leigh and Lou Williams
MsHaU .9 cu.ft. of ms./il.

Palazzo, Tony
MnU il. for 4 titles.

Palestrant, Simon S.
MsHaU 6.6 cu.ft. of ms./il.

Panetta, George
MnU ms. for 1 title.

Pantell, Dora
MsHaU 2.4 cu.ft. of ms./il.

Paradis, Adrian A.
MsHaU .30 cu.ft. of ms./il.

Parish, Peggy
MnU ms. for 4 titles.

**Parker, Edgar**
MnU ms. for 4 titles.

**Parker, John**
MnU ms. for 1 title.

**Parker, Nancy Winslow**
MnU ms. for 3 titles; il. for 7 titles. MsHaU 5.3 cu.ft. of ms./il. NjR-Z il. materials.

**Parker, Richard**
MnU ms. for 1 title. MsHaU .3 cu.ft. of ms./il.

**Parks, Gordon, Jr.**
MnU il. for 1 title.

**Parley, Peter**
DLC 193 vols. FU Extensive book holdings. MAA 700 vols. and 1.5 li.ft. of ms. and related items. MCot 150 vols. MWA 296 titles. PP-Rb 400 vols. ViU 109 vols.

**Parrish, Maxfield**
PP-Rb ms. and il.

**Parsons, Ellen**
MnU ms. for 1 title.

**Partch, Virgil Franklin**
MnU ms. for 2 titles.

**Paterson, Katherine**
MnU ms. for 17 titles.

**Paton Walsh, Jill**
MnU ms. for 11 titles.

**Patterson, Karen Thompson**
MsHaU .30 cu.ft. of ms./il.

**Paul Bunyan**
MnU 145 vols. and 9 li.ft. of ms.

**Pauli, Hertha E.**
MsHaU .3 cu.ft. of ms./il.

**Paull, Grace A.**
MnU il. for 2 titles. MsHaU .3 cu.ft. of ms./il.

**Paulsen, Gary**
MnU ms. for 1 title.

**Paw Oo Thet, U**
MnU il. for 1 title.

**Payne, Joan Balfour**
MnU il. for 2 titles. MsHaU .90 cu.ft. of ms./il.

**Payson, Dale**
MnU il. for 10 titles.

**Payzant, Charles**
MnU il. for 1 title.

**Peare, Catherine Owens**
MsHaU .30 cu.ft. of ms./il.

**Pearl, Richard**
MsHaU 1.8 cu.ft. of ms./il.

**Pearson, Susan**
MnU ms. for 13 titles.

**Pease, Howard**
CStoC 65 vols. and ms.

**Peck, Richard**
MnU ms. for 4 titles. MsHaU 5.5 cu.ft. of ms./il.

**Peet, Bill**
MnU il. for 15 titles.

**Pellowski, Anne**
MnU ms. for 11 titles; il. for 3 titles.

**Pennington, Lillian**
NjR-Z il. materials.

**Pennsylvania**
PP Extensive holdings.

**Pennsylvania—Authors and Illustrators**
PP Extensive holdings. PPiU-LS Extensive holdings.

**Perceval, Don**
MnU il. for 1 title. MsHaU 2.1 cu.ft. of ms./il.

**Percival, Walter**
MsHaU .3 cu.ft. of ms./il.

**Performing Arts**
ICN Extensive holdings. NN-BrR 300 vols. on all aspects of the performing arts.

**Periodicals**

ArU Complete runs of *Tip Top Weekly, New Tip Top Weekly*, and several others. AzTeS Extensive runs of 4 science fiction titles. CAna 11 titles relating to Disneyland and Walt Disney Productions. CCCla Complete runs of *Children's Magazine, St. Nicholas, Harper's Young People, Cricket, Wee Wish Tree.* CL Over 350 titles of British and American periodicals from the 1790s to the present. CLU-C Complete runs of *Bentley's Miscellany and Household Words.* COPL Complete runs of Jack London periodicals. CSfACA Extensive holdings. CSfSt 70+ titles. CtHT 40+ titles of American 19th-century periodicals. CtHi 250 titles in Hewins Collection. CtNbT Complete runs of several 19th-century titles. DLC Extensive holdings of 19th-century titles. FTaSU Complete runs of several titles.

FU 400 titles from 19th century. GU Complete runs of several titles. ICN 32 19th-century and 1 20th-century titles. IDeKN 200 titles from 1905–1955. KEmU Complete runs of several periodical titles. KU Complete runs of numerous titles. KyLoU Complete runs of several titles. MBAt Substantial holdings of 19th-century titles. MBrH Substantial holdings of early 20th-century Zionist titles. MCoA 35 periodicals relating to Louisa May Alcott. MSaA Complete runs of several 19th-century titles. MSaP 30 titles from the 19th century. MWA 357 titles from 1789–1915. MeWC Complete runs of several 19th-century titles.

MnM Complete runs of several titles. MnU 224 titles in Kerlan Collection; 151 titles in Hess Collection. MsHaU 250 titles from 19th–20th centuries. NBPu 80 titles from the 19th and 20th centuries. NCooHi 19th-century titles. NHi 39 titles. NN-Don 75 titles. NNC 450 titles from the 19th century. NNCbc 200 titles from 20th century. OCH Significant holdings of juvenile Jewish periodicals. OCl 20 titles. ODaWU Several 19th-century titles. OHirC Several titles. OOxM 150 titles. PP Extensive holdings. PP-Rb 50 19th-century titles. PSC 10 titles. RPA Complete runs of 19th- and 20th-century titles. UPB Complete runs of several religious titles. ViR 25 titles. WU-CC 40 titles. WaChenE 40 science fiction titles.

**Perkins, Lucy Fitch**
PP 50 vols., ms. and il.

**Perkins, Minnie McCausland**
MsHaU .3 cu.ft. of ms./il.

**Perrault, Charles**
FU Extensive book holdings. NNPM ms.

**Perry, Octavia Jordan**
NcGU ms. and il. for 1 title.

*Peter Pan see* **Barrie, James Matthew**

**Peters, Evelyn**
MsHaU 2.4 cu.ft. of ms./il.

**Peters, Lisa Westberg**
MnU ms. for 3 titles.

**Petersham, Maud and Miska**
MnU ms. for 1 title; il. for 4 titles. MsHaU 12 cu.ft. of ms./il. NAlU ms. and dummy. OrU 3 li.ft. of ms. and il.

**Peterson, Betty Ferguson**
MnU il. for 1 title.

**Peterson, Esther**
MnU ms. for 2 titles.

**Peterson, Harold Leslie**
MnU ms. for 4 titles.

**Peterson, Jeanne Whitehouse**
MnU ms. for 1 title.

**Petie, Haris**
MnU il. for 1 title.

**Pevsner, Stella**
MnU ms. for 4 titles.

**Phelps, Naomi**
OrU 2 li.ft. of ms.

**Philadelphia Imprints**
PNo Collection of books published in Philadephia.

**Philbrook, Clem**
MsHaU .3 cu.ft. of ms./il.

**Philip, Core**
MsHaU .3 cu.ft. of ms./il.

**Phillips, Charles Fox**
MsHaU 2.5 cu.ft. of ms./il.

**Phipson, Joan**
MsHaU .30 cu.ft. of ms./il.

*Pied Piper of Hamelin see* **Browning, Robert**

**Pienkowski, Jan**
MsHaU 40 cu.ft. of ms./il.

**Pierce, Dorothy Mason**
MnU il. for 1 title.

**Pierce, Frank Richardson**
CSmH-A 1 piece of corr.

**Pilgrim Press**
MBCn 100 li.ft. of materials.

**Pincus, Harriet**
MsHaU 1.2 cu.ft. of ms./il.

**Pine, Tillie Schloss**
MnU ms. for 1 title.

**Pinkerton, Robert Eugene and Kathrene**
OrU 4.5 li.ft. of ms.

*Pinocchio see* **Collodi, Carlo**

**Pitz, Henry C.**
MnU il. for 12 titles. MsHaU 1.8 cu.ft. of ms./il. OrU 10.5 li.ft. of ms. and il.

**Piussi-Campbell, Judy**
MnU il. for 2 titles.

**Place, Marian T.**
AzTeS ms.

**Plotz, Helen**
MnU ms. for 2 titles.

**Plowhead, Ruth Gipson**
OrU 3 li.ft. of ms. and il.

**Plowman, Fred**
MsHaU .60 cu.ft. of ms./il.

**Plumb, Beatrice**
MsHaU .30 cu.ft. of ms./il.

**Poe, Edgar Allen**
MnU ms. for 1 title.

**Poetry**
FTaSU 25,000+ vols. in Shaw Collection. ICN Extensive book holdings. MsHaU Substantial holdings. RPB-JH 1,700 vols. WM 700 vols.

**Pogany, Willy**
MsHaU .60 cu.ft. of ms./il. OrU 34.5 li.ft. of ms. and il.

**Pohl, Frederik**
MsHaU .30 cu.ft. of ms./il.

**Pohlmann, Lillian G.**
MsHaU 1.2 cu.ft. of ms./il.

**Polgreen, John**
MnU il. for 1 title.

**Polish Language**
MnU 128 vols.

**Politi, Leo**
CFLp 50 vols. and 2 li.ft. of il. CL 40 vols.; il. for 25 titles. CP il. materials. MnU il. for 10 titles.

**Polseno, Jo**
MnU il. for 2 titles.

**Pomerantz, Charlotte**
MnU ms. for 1 title.

**Pons, Helene**
MsHaU .30 cu.ft. of ms./il.

**Pont, Clarice**
MsHaU .30 cu.ft. of ms./il.

**Ponter, James**
MsHaU .60 cu.ft. of ms./il.

**Poole, Gray and Lynn**
MsHaU 4.5 cu.ft. of ms./il.

Pop-Up Books *see* Toy and Movable Books

**Pope, Clifford**
MsHaU .30 cu.ft. of ms./il.

**Pope, Elizabeth Marie**
MnU ms. for 1 title.

**Popular Culture Materials**
CSfACA Extensive holdings. MnU Extensive holdings in the Hess Collection. NNC 570 vols. OBgU Extensive holdings.

**Porter, Jean Macdonald**
MnU il. for 1 title. MsHaU .30 cu.ft. of ms./il.

**Portuguese Language**
MnU 43 vols.

**Posell, Elsa Z.**
MsHaU 3 cu.ft. of ms./il.

**Posters of Children's Literature**
MnU 800 items. MsHaU 1700+ items.
*see also* Children's Book Week Posters

**Potter, Beatrix**
CSt Extensive book holdings. InU-Li 20+ vols. MnU il. for 2 titles. NNPM ms. and il. materials. PP-Rb 350 vols., 100 ms., and 140 il.

**Potter, Bronson**
MnU ms. for 5 titles.

**Potter, Miriam Clark**
MnU ms. for 1 title; il. for 1 title.

**Potter, Zemas**
MnU il. for 1 title.

**Powers, Richard M.**
MnU il. for 2 titles. MsHaU 1.8 cu.ft. of ms./il.

**Preissler, Audrey**
MnU il. for 1 title.

**Prelutsky, Jack**
MnU ms. for 2 titles.

Press Books *see* individual publisher names.

**Preston, Edna Mitchell**
MnU il. for 1 title.

**Price, Christine**
MnU ms. for 1 title; il. for 9 titles. MsHaU 1.5 cu.ft. of ms./il. OrU 21 li.ft. of ms. and il.

**Price, Edith Ballinger**
MnU il. for 5 titles. OrU 6 li.ft. of ms. and il.

**Price, Garrett**
MnU il. for 1 title.

**Price, Harold**
MsHaU .40 cu.ft. of ms./il.

**Price, Lowi**
MsHaU .30 cu.ft. of ms./il.

**Price, Margaret**
OrU 3.5 li.ft. of il.

**Price, Norman**
OrU 1 li.ft. of il.

**Prieto, Mariana B.**
MnU ms. for 1 title. MsHaU 1.2 cu.ft. of ms./il.

**Provensen, Alice and Martin**
MnU ms. for 1 title. NjR-Z il. materials.

**Pryor, Frances**
MsHaU .30 cu.ft. of ms./il.

**Publishers' Catalogs**
MnU 1,900 catalogs representing 135 publishers. MsHaU Extensive holdings of contemporary publishers.

**Publishing of Children's Books** *see* American Book Company; American Sunday School Union; American Tract Society; Beadle and Adams; Bobbs Merrill Company; Church of Jesus Christ of the Latter Day Saints; Congregational Publishing Society; Connecticut Printers, Inc.; Morris Cotton; William Darton; Mahlon Day; Walt Disney Productions; Dodd, Mead and Co.; E. P. Dutton; Equinox Cooperative Press; Follett Publishing Co.; Greenwillow Books; John Harris; *Horn Book* Magazine; Kellogg

& Bulkeley; Lee & Shepard; Limited Editions Club; Little Golden Books; John Marshall; Massachusetts Sabbath School Society; McLoughlin Brothers; John Newbery; Pilgrim Press; Publishers' Catalogs; Reorganized Church of Jesus Christ of the Latter Day Saints; and Saalfield Publishing Co.

**Pullig, Lois**
MsHaU .30 cu.ft. of ms./il.

**Pulp Novels**
MnU 1,847 issues.

**Puppetry**
MnM 70 vols., pamphlets, journals, and puppets. NN-BrR 100 vols. WaSHi 1,200 vols. WyShF 420 vols.
*see also* Performing Arts

**Putcamp, Luise**
MsHaU .30 cu.ft. of ms./il.

**Pyk, Ann**
MnU ms. for 2 titles.

**Pyle, Howard**
CSmH-A 1 piece of corr. DLC 77 vols. DeU 16 pieces of corr. DeWA Extensive holdings of books, il., scrapbooks, and corr. ICN 31 vols. and 5 il. NN-Don 50 vols., 38 il. PP-Rb 2,000 vols., 1,000 ms., and 150 il. by Pyle and his students of the Brandywine School. ViU 64 vols.

**Pyle, Katharine**
DeU 1.33 li.ft. ms. and corr. DeWA il., scrapbooks, etc.

**Pyne, Mabel**
MsHaU .6 cu.ft. of ms./il.

**Quackenbush, Robert M.**
MnU il. for 2 titles. MsHaU 25.2 cu.ft. of ms./il.

**Quigley, Lillian**
MnU ms. for 1 title.

**Quin, Jeff**
MnU il. for 1 title.

**Rabe, Berniece**
MnU ms. for 11 titles.

**Rackham, Arthur**
AkFSD 100 vols. CSmH-A 2 pieces of corr. KyLoU 283 vols., periodicals, and 50 li.ft. of il. in the Arthur Rackham Memorial Collection. NN-Don 75 vols. NNC 400 vols., corr., sketchbooks, ms., and illustrative materials. ODaWU 100 volumes and 4 pieces of original art. PP-Rb 500 vols., 100 ms., and 50 il.

**Radford, Ruby**
MsHaU .30 cu.ft. of ms./il.

**Ramage, Rosalyn Rikel**
MnU ms. for 1 title.

**Rand, Gloria**
MnU ms. for 1 title.

**Rand, Ted**
MnU il. for 1 title.

**Ransom, Candice**
CtU 4 boxes of ms.

**Ransome, Arthur**
DGU 200+ vols.

**Raskin, Ellen**
MnU ms. for 10 titles; il. for 41 titles.

**Rasmussen, Halfdan**
MnU ms. for 1 title.

**Rathjen, Carl**
MsHaU 1.2 cu.ft. of ms./il.

**Ray, Deborah Kogan**
MnU il. for 1 title.

**Ray, Ralph**
MnU il. for 19 titles.

**Ray, Wade**
MnU il. for 1 title.

**Reading**
NHemH 2,500 vols.

**Reading, J. P.**
MsHaU .60 cu.ft. of ms./il.

**Reck, Franklin Mering**
OrU 4.5 li.ft. of ms.

**Recordings**
MBrH 400 recordings of children's songs with Jewish theme. NNFI French recordings.

**Reed, Philip**
MnU il. for 3 titles.

**Reeder, Russell P.**
MsHaU .30 cu.ft. of ms./il.

**Reeves, James**
MsHaU .30 cu.ft. of ms./il. TxU-Hu 3 boxes of ms.

**Reid, Meta Mayne**
MsHaU .30 cu.ft. of ms./il.

**Reit, Seymour**
MnU ms. for 5 titles. MsHaU 3 cu.ft. of ms./il.

**Remington, Barbara**
MnU il. for 1 title.

**Renfro, Ed**
MsHaU 6.8 cu.ft. of ms./il.

**Reorganized Church of Jesus Christ of Latter Day Saints** *see* **Bibles and Books of Religious Instruction**

**Ressner, Philip**
MnU ms. for 2 titles.

**Rey, Hans Augusto and Margret**
MnU il. for 3 titles. MsHaU 7.0 cu.ft. of ms./il. OrU 2 li.ft. of ms. and il.

**Reyher, Rebecca Hourwich**
MnU ms. for 1 title.

**Reynolds, Marjorie**
MnU ms. for 2 titles.

**Rhead, Louis**
MiD il.

**Rhoads, Dorothy**
MnU ms. for 1 title.

**Ricciuti, Edward**
MsHaU .30 cu.ft. of ms./il.

**Rice, Alice Hegan**
CSmH-A 1 piece of corr. KyBgW 100 items of letters, business, and legal papers.

**Rich, Josephine**
MsHaU .30 cu.ft. of ms./il.

**Richards, Laura E.**
CSmH-A 17 pieces of corr. MeGar 100 vols. and 70 li.ft. of ms. materials. MeWC 91 vols.

**Richardson, Grace Haddon**
MnU ms. for 2 titles.

**Riedman, Sarah R.**
MsHaU 9.0 cu.ft. of ms./il.

**Rieseberg, Harry E.**
MsHaU .30 cu.ft. of ms./il.

**Rietveld, Jane**
MsHaU .90 cu.ft. of ms./il.

**Riggio, Anita**
CtU ms. and il. for 15 titles.

**Rigolo, Stanislao Dino**
MnU il. for 1 title.

**Riley, James Whitcomb**
CSmH-A 16 ms.; 155 pieces of corr. InU-Li 650+ vols.; corr. and ms.

**Rinkoff, Barbara**
MnU ms. for 1 title.

**Riordan, James**
MnU ms. for 1 title.

**Ripper, Charles L.**
MnU ms. for 1 title; il. for 6 titles.

**Rivoli, Mario**
MnU il. for 1 title.

**Roach, Marilynne K.**
MnU ms. for 1 title; il. for 1 title. MsHaU .60 cu.ft. of ms./il.

**Roam, Pearl**
MsHaU .30 cu.ft. of ms./il.

**Robbins, Ruth**
MnU il. for 4 titles.

**Roberts, Howard**
MsHaU .60 cu.ft. of ms./il.

**Roberts, Nancy C. and Bruce**
MsHaU 2.1 cu.ft. of ms./il.

**Roberts, Willo Davis**
MoWarbT ms. and il. materials. MsHaU .30 cu.ft. of ms./il.

**Robertson, Keith**
MsHaU .30 cu.ft. of ms./il.

**Robertson, Lilian**
MnU il. for 2 titles.

**Robin Hood**
FU Extensive book holdings. ICN 50+ vols. OCl-RB 757 vols.

**Robinson, Charles**
MnU il. for 1 title. NjR-Z il. materials.

**Robinson, Irene Bowen**
MnU il. for 10 titles.

**Robinson, Joan**
MsHaU .30 cu.ft. of ms./il.

**Robinson, Marileta**
MsHaU .30 cu.ft. of ms./il.

**Robinson, Thomas Pendleton**
MnU ms. for 1 title.

**Robinson, W. W. and Irena Bowen Robinson**
CCSc 19 vols.; 11 drawings.

**Robinson, William Wilcox**
MnU ms. for 5 titles.

**Robinson Crusoe** *see* **Defoe, Daniel**

**Roche, A. K.** *see* **Abisch, Roslyn Kropp**

**Rochman, Hazel**
MsHaU .60 cu.ft. of ms./il.

**Rocker, Fermin**
MnU il. for 3 titles. NjR-Z il. materials.

**Rockwell, Anne and Harlow**
MnU ms. for 37 titles; il. for 78 titles. MsHaU .30 cu.ft. of ms./il.

**Rodgers, Mary**
MnU ms. for 4 titles. MsHaU .30 cu.ft. of ms./il.

**Rodman, Maia Wojciechowska** *see* **Wojciechowska, Maia**

**Rodowsky, Colby**
MsHaU .60 cu.ft. of ms./il.

**Roetter, Sonia**
MnU il. for 1 title.

**Rogers, Frances**
MsHaU .90 cu.ft. of ms./il.

**Rogers, Fred**
PPiU-LS Complete archival videotape collection of "Mister Rogers' Neighborhood."

**Rogers, John**
MsHaU .60 cu.ft. of ms./il.

**Roginsky, Jim W.**
MsHaU .90 cu.ft. of ms./il.

**Rojankovsky, Feodor S.**
MnU il. for 7 titles. MsHaU .60 cu.ft. of ms./il.

**Roland, Albert**
MnU ms. for 1 title.

**Rollins, Charlemae Hill**
MsHaU .30 cu.ft. of ms./il.

**Rollo Books** *see* **Abbott, Jacob**

**Root, Phyllis**
MnU ms. for 2 titles.

**Rosenberg, Ethel Clifford** *see* **Clifford, Eth**

**Rosenberg, Nancy and Lawrence**
MsHaU 1.2 cu.ft. of ms./il.

**Rosenfield, Bernard**
MsHaU .30 cu.ft. of ms./il.

**Rosier, Lydia**
MnU il. for 2 titles.

**Ross, Anthony**
MsHaU .30 cu.ft. of ms./il.

**Ross, Pat**
MnU ms. for 5 titles.

**Rosselli, Colette**
MnU il. for 1 title.

**Rothman, Joel**
MsHaU .30 cu.ft. of ms./il.

**Rounds, Glen**
MnU ms. for 28 titles; il. for 20 titles.

**Rouse, Donald and David**
MnU ms. for 1 title.

**Rowand, Phyllis**
MnU il. for 1 title.

**Rowlett, Margaret**
NcGU ms., il., and corr. for 12 titles.

**Roy, Ron**
MsHaU 1.8 cu.ft. of ms./il.

**Royal, Denise**
OrU 3 li.ft. of ms.

**Ruchlis, Hyman**
MsHaU .60 cu.ft. of ms./il.

**Ruckman, Ivy**
MoWarbT ms. and il. materials.

**Rudnik, Maryka and Raphael**
MnU ms. for 1 title.

**Rudolph, Marguerita**
MnU ms. for 2 titles. MsHaU .30 cu.ft. of ms./il.

**Rush, Charles Everett and Amy Winslow**
MnU ms. for 1 title.

**Rushmore, Helen**
MsHaU .90 cu.ft. of ms./il.

**Ruskin, John**
CSmH-A 23 ms.; 797 pieces of corr. CtY-BR Extensive holdings of published works with ms. materials and 2,500+ letters. ICN 190+ vols. by him and 115+ about him.

**Russell, Solveig Paulson**
MnU ms. for 1 title.

**Russian Language**
CLU-S/C Significant Russian-language books issued between the two World Wars. MnU 531 vols. ViR 325 vols. NjP-C 485 vols.

**Rutland, Eva**
OrU 1.5 li.ft. of ms.

**Rutledge, Archibald**
MsHaU .30 cu.ft. of ms./il.

**Rutzebeck, Hjalmar**
MsHaU 10.8 cu.ft. of ms./il.

**Rylant, Cynthia**
MnU ms. for 12 titles. OKentU Books and ms. materials.

**Saalfield Publishing Company** (publisher)
OKentU Company archive contains books, ms., il., corr., and business records.

**Sabin, Edwin L.**
ICN 10 vols. and corr. IaU Books and ms.

**Sachs, Marilyn**
MnU ms. for 33 titles.

**Sage, Michael**
MnU ms. for 1 title.

**St. George, Judith**
MnU ms. for 1 title. NjR ms. materials.

**St. John, Wylly Folk**
MnU ms. for 1 title.

***St. Nicholas Magazine***
MsHaU 1.2 cu.ft. of corr. and ms. materials.
*see also* **Periodicals**

**St. Tamara**
NjR ms. materials. NjR-Z il. materials.

**Salem, James**
MsHaU 1.8 cu.ft. of ms./il.

**Salem, Mary Miller**
MnU ms. for 1 title.

**Sallis, Susan**
MnU ms. for 1 title. MsHaU 1.8 cu.ft. of ms./il.

**Salmon, Annie Elizabeth**
MsHaU .60 cu.ft. of ms./il.

**Salomon, Julian Harris**
MnU ms. for 1 title.

**Salvs, Naomi Punush**
MnU ms. for 1 title.

**Samoan Language**
MnU 17 vols.

**Samuels, Eva**
MsHaU .30 cu.ft. of ms./il.

**Sancha, Sheila**
MsHaU .30 cu.ft. of ms./il.

**Sandberg, Lasse**
MnU il. for 1 title.

**Sanderlin, George**
MsHaU 1.2 cu.ft. of ms./il.

**Sanderlin, Owenita**
MsHaU .30 cu.ft. of ms./il.

**Sandin, Joan**
MnU il. for 2 titles.

**Sandoz, Mari**
NbU 450 vols.; ms. and corr. materials. NSyU 1 li.ft. of manuscripts.

**Sanford and Merton** *see* **Day, Thomas**

**Sargent, J. W.**
MsHaU .30 cu.ft. of ms./il.

**Saroyan, William**
MnU ms. for 1 title.

**Sarton, May**
MsHaU .30 cu.ft. of ms./il.

**Sauer, Julia Lina**
MnU ms. for 1 title.

**Saunders, Allen and John**
OBgU ms. materials for comic books.

**Savage, George**
MsHaU .30 cu.ft. of ms./il.

**Savery, Constance W.**
MsHaU 1.2 cu.ft. of ms./il.

**Saviozzi, Adrianna Mazza**
MnU il. for 1 title.

**Savitt, Sam**
MsHaU 3.1 cu.ft. of ms./il.

**Savitz, Harriet May**
PNo ms. for 7 titles.

**Sawyer, Ruth**
MnSSC 2,550 vols., ms., and corr. with Anne Carroll Moore and others.

**Saxe, John Godfrey**
MnU ms. for 1 title.

**Sayers, Dorothy L.**
IWW Extensive holdings of books and ms.

**Scandinavian Languages**
DLC Extensive holdings in Danish, Norwegian, and Swedish. ICN 180+ vols.

**Scanlon, Marion S.**
MsHaU .30 cu.ft. of ms./il.

**Scarry, Richard**
CtU 1,100 pieces of original artwork. MnU il. for 3 titles. MsHaU .30 cu.ft. of ms./il.

**Schachner, Erwin**
MnU il. for 1 title.

**Schakell, Rodney**
NjR-Z il. materials.

**Scheib, Ida**
MnU il. for 1 title.

**Scherf, Margaret**
OrU 1.5 li.ft. of ms.

**Schick, Eleanor**
MnU ms. for 2 titles.

**Schiff, Bessie**
OSiA Books and ms.

**Schiller, Barbara**
MnU ms. for 1 title.

**Schlein, Miriam**
MnU ms. for 8 titles.

**Schloat, G. Warren, Jr.**
MnU ms. for 12 titles; il. for 13 titles.

**Schmidt, Harvey**
MnU il. for 1 title.

**Schneider, Leo**
MsHaU .90 cu.ft. of ms./il.

**Schoenherr, John**
MnU il. for 2 titles. MsHaU .60 cu.ft. of ms./il. NjR-Z il. materials.

**Scholberg, Henry**
MnU ms. for 1 title.

**Scholz, Jackson V.**
MsHaU .30 cu.ft. of ms./il.

**Schoonover, Frank**
DeWA Extensive holdings of books, il., scrapbooks and corr. of Schoonover and his teacher, Howard Pyle.

**Schreiber, Georges**
MnU il. for 5 titles.

**Schwandt, Stephen**
MnU ms. for 2 titles.

**Schwartz, Charles and Elizabeth**
MsHaU 2.6 cu.ft. of ms./il.

**Schwartz, Julius**
MsHaU .30 cu.ft. of ms./il.

**Schwebell, Gertrude C.**
MsHaU .30 cu.ft. of ms./il.

**Science**
CoDDB 1,000 vols. FSpSC 15,000 vols. for grades 4-12. MBChM Extensive book holdings.

**Science Fiction**
AzTeS 800 vols. of 20th-century publications. CSmH-A Collection of over 2,000 ms. and corr. items for Robert Silverberg and other science fiction authors. InU-Li Extensive book and periodical holdings; scripts for "Star Trek" and general corr. WaChenE 1,200 vols. and 40 periodical titles.

**Scoppettone, Sandra**
MnU ms. for 3 titles. MsHaU .30 cu.ft. of ms./il.

**Scott, Alma Olivia Schmidt**
MnU ms. for 2 titles.

**Scott, Arthur Finley**
MsHaU .30 cu.ft. of ms./il.

**Scott, Frances Gruse**
NjR-Z il. materials.

**Scovel, Frederick Gilman and Myra Scott Scovel**
OrU 2 li.ft. of ms.

**Searcy, Margaret**
MsHaU .60 cu.ft. of ms./il.

**Sears, Paul McCutcheon**
MnU ms. for 2 titles.

**Sebestyen, Ouida**
MnU ms. for 4 titles. MsHaU 1.2 cu.ft. of ms./il.

**Sechrist, Elizabeth H.**
MsHaU 1.2 cu.ft. of ms./il.

**Sedgwick, Paulita**
NjR-Z il. materials.

**Segal, Lore**
MnU ms. for 1 title.

**Seiden, Art**
MnU il. for 6 titles. MsHaU .4 cu.ft. of ms./il. NjR-Z il. materials.

**Seifert, Shirley L.**
MsHaU .9 cu.ft. of ms./il.

**Seignobosc, Françoise**
MnU ms. for 12 titles; il. for 19 titles.

**Selden, Bernice**
MsHaU 1.2 cu.ft. of ms./il.

**Self, Margaret C.**
MsHaU .30 cu.ft. of ms./il.

**Selsam, Millicent Ellis**
MnU ms. for 1 title. MsHaU 1.8 cu.ft. of ms./il. OrU 2.5 li.ft. of ms.

**Sendak, Jack**
MnU ms. for 1 title.

**Sendak, Maurice**
InU-Li 75+ vols.; portfolio of il. MnU ms. for 1 title; il. for 22 titles. PPRF 400 vols., 3,000 il., related material.

**Sequoyah Children's Book Award** *see* **Award Books**

**Serbian Language**
MnU 17 vols.

**Seredy, Kate**
KEmU ms. and il. in May Massee Collection. MnU il. for 1 title. MsHaU .60 cu.ft. of ms./il. OOxM 22 vols. and il. OrU 3 li.ft. of il.

**Series Books**
AB 150 vols. CSj Holdings of popular series writers. DLC Extensive holdings of 19th- and 20th-century girls' and boys' series. FTS 7,000 vols. of 19th- and 20th-century boys', girls', and animal series books. FU Extensive holdings of 19th- and 20th-century girls' and boys' series. IDeKN Substantial holdings. InNd 545 vols. by Burt Standish. InU-Li Extensive holdings. MBSi Substantial holdings of girls' series books. MCot Boys' series books. MnU 9,000 vols. MsHaU Extensive holdings. NAlU 2,500 vols. NJQ Substantial holdings. NcCU Boys' series books. NcGU 1,350 girls' series books. NhC Substantial holdings. NhD 900 vols. of boys' series books. OAU Substantial holdings. OBgU 750+ vols. OC Extensive holdings. PP Extensive holdings. PPiU-LS Substantial holdings. TxDW Substantial holdings. TxDa 500 vols. TxH Substantial holdings. ViR Substantial holdings. WM Substantial holdings.

**Seroff, Victor Ilyitch**
MnU ms. for 2 titles.

**Servello, Joe**
MnU il. for 21 titles.

**Seton, Ernest Thompson**
CSmH-A 4 ms.; 29 pieces of corr.

**Seuling, Barbara**
MoWarbT ms. and il. materials. MsHaU 13.8 cu.ft. of ms./il.

**Seuss, Dr.**
CLU-S/C Extensive holdings of published works; early ms. CSd 70 vols. and 3

notebooks of biographical information. MnU ms. for 1 title; il. for 3 titles.

**Severn, David**
MsHaU .6 cu.ft. of ms./il.

**Severn, William**
MsHaU 16.2 cu.ft. of ms./il.

**Sewall, Marcia**
MnU il. for 2 titles.

**Sewell, Anna**
CtU 500 editions of *Black Beauty*.

**Sewell, Helen**
KWi il. MiD il. MnU il. for 13 titles.

**Seymour, Alta H.**
MsHaU .30 cu.ft. of ms./il.

**Shackelford, Shelby**
OrU 3 li.ft. of ms. and il.

**Shannon, George**
MnU ms. for 20 titles.

**Shannon, Terry**
MnU ms. for 1 title.

**Shapiro, Milton**
MsHaU .30 cu.ft. of ms./il.

**Sharmat, Marjorie Weinman**
MsHaU 1.2 cu.ft. of ms./il.

**Sharp, William**
MnU il. for 2 titles.

**Shaw, Evelyn**
MnU ms. for 5 titles.

**Shaw, Richard**
MnU ms. for 4 titles.

**Shecter, Ben**
MnU ms. for 1 title; il. for 1 title.

**Sheldon, Muriel** *see* **Batherman, Muriel**

**Shell, Richard**
NjR-Z il. materials.

**Shenton, Edward**
MnU il. for 16 titles.

**Shepard, Ernest H.**
MnU il. for 2 titles. MsHaU .60 cu.ft. of
ms./il.

**Shepard, Steve**
MsHaU .60 cu.ft. of ms./il.

**Sherburne, Zoa**
MsHaU 1.5 cu.ft. of ms./il.

**Sherman, Diane Finn**
MsHaU .30 cu.ft. of ms./il.

**Sherwan, Earl**
MsHaU .30 cu.ft. of ms./il.

**Sherwood, Mary Martha Butt**
CLU-S/C Extensive holdings of published
works; ms. journals. DLC 47 vols. FU
Extensive book holdings. OOxM 86
vols. and ms. materials. PP-Rb 200 vols.

**Shimin, Symeon**
MnU il. for 13 titles. MsHaU 1.3 cu.ft. of
ms./il.

**Shinn, Everett**
MnU il. for 1 title.

**Shipley, Nan**
MsHaU .60 cu.ft. of ms./il.

**Shippen, Katherine Binney**
MsHaU .90 cu.ft. of ms./il.

**Short Stories**
ULA 300 vols.

**Showalter, Jean B.**
MnU ms. for 1 title.

**Showers, Paul C.**
MnU ms. for 1 title.

**Shub, Elizabeth**
MnU ms. for 8 titles.

**Shulevitz, Uri**
MnU il. for 2 titles. MsHaU .30 cu.ft. of
ms./il.

**Shuttlesworth, Dorothy**
MsHaU 1.5 cu.ft. of ms./il. NjR ms. materials.

**Siberell, Anne**
MnU ms. for 1 title; il. for 1 title. MsHaU
1.8 cu.ft. of ms./il.

**Sibley, Don**
MnU il. for 3 titles.

**Sicotte, Virginia**
MsHaU .30 cu.ft. of ms./il.

**Sidjakov, Nicolas**
MnU il. for 3 titles. MsHaU .60 cu.ft. of
ms./il.

**Sidney, Margaret**
FU Extensive book holdings; 2 boxes of
letters and ms.

**Siebel, Fritz**
MnU il. for 1 title.

**Siegal, Aranka**
MnU ms. for 2 titles.

**Siegl, Helen**
MnU il. for 2 titles.

**Silverberg, Robert**
MsHaU 1.5 cu.ft. of ms./il.

**Silverman, Fritz**
MnU il. for 1 title.

**Silverstein, Shel**
MnU il. for 1 title.

**Simister, Florence Parker**
MsHaU 2.1 cu.ft. of ms./il.

**Simmons, Dawn Langley**
MnU ms. for 1 title.

**Simon, Charlie May**
ArL 23 vols.

**Simon, Howard and Mina Lewiton Simon**
MsHaU .30 cu.ft. of ms./il. OrU 4.5 li.ft.
of ms. and il.

**Simon, Nancy**
MsHaU .30 cu.ft. of ms./il.

**Simon, Norma**
MnU ms. for 1 title. MsHaU 8 cu.ft. of
ms./il.

*Mother Goose: The Old Nursery Rhymes,* illustrated by Arthur Rackham; New York: Century, 1913.

**Simon, Shirley Schwartz**
MsHaU .6 cu.ft. of ms./il.

**Simont, Marc**
MnU il. for 5 titles. NjR-Z il. materials.

**Singer, Arthur**
MnU il. for 1 title.

**Singer, Isaac Bashevis**
MnU ms. for 1 title.

**Singer, Marilyn**
MnU ms. for 19 titles.

**Skurzynski, Gloria**
MnU ms. for 12 titles; il. for 1 title.

**Slavic Languages**
DLC Growing collection of over 1,000 titles. ICN 150+ vols.

**Sleator, William**
MoWarbT ms. and il. materials.

**Slepian, Janice B.**
MnU ms. for 1 title.

**Slobodkin, Louis**
MnU ms. for 1 title; il. for 16 titles. MsHaU .30 cu.ft. of ms./il. OrU 9 li.ft. of ms.

**Slobodkina, Esphyr**
MnU il. for 6 titles. MsHaU 2.7 cu.ft. of ms./il.

**Slotberg, Doris**
MsHaU .30 cu.ft. of ms./il.

**Slote, Alfred**
MnU ms. for 20 titles.

**Slovenian Language**
MnU 65 vols.

**Smaridge, Norah**
MsHaU .9 cu.ft. of ms./il.

Smith, Allen Field
MiMtpT ms. materials.

Smith, Datus Clifford
NjR ms. materials.

Smith, Doris
MnU ms. for 6 titles.

Smith, E. Boyd
GEU-S il. in Joel Chandler Harris Collection.

Smith, Eunice Young
MsHaU 1.5 cu.ft. of ms./il.

Smith, Glanville Wynkoop
MnU ms. for 1 title.

Smith, Howard Jerome
MnU il. for 1 title.

Smith, Jay
MnU il. for 1 title.

Smith, Jessie Willcox
DLC 13 pieces of artwork. MiD il. PP-Rb
ms. and il.

Smith, Lee
MsHaU .90 cu.ft. of ms./il.

Snyder, Joel
NjR-Z il. materials.

Snyder, Zilpha Keatley
MnU ms. for 12 titles.

Sobol, Donald J.
MnU ms. for 2 titles. MsHaU .30 cu.ft. of
ms./il.

Society of Friends
PSC 200 vols.

Soderhjelm, Kai
MnU ms. for 1 title.

Sokol, William
MnU il. for 1 title. MsHaU .60 cu.ft. of
ms./il.

Solbert, Ronni G.
MnU il. for 20 titles. MsHaU .30 cu.ft. of
ms./il.

Someren, Liesje Van
MsHaU .30 cu.ft. of ms./il.

Song Books
MsHaU 150 vols.

Sootin, Harry and Laura
MsHaU 1.8 cu.ft. of ms./il.

Sorel, Edward
MnU il. for 2 titles.

Sorensen, Virginia
MnU ms. for 7 titles.

Sotomayor, Antonio
MnU il. for 1 title.

Soule, Jean Conder
MsHaU .30 cu.ft. of ms./il.

South Dakota—Authors and Illustrators
SdAbN 100 vols.

Southeast Asian Languages
DLC Collection of over 200 titles. IDeKN
350 vols.

Southwestern United States
AzT 2,000 vols. dating from 1890 to date
concerning the Southwest.

Spain, Frances Lander
MsHaU .60 cu.ft. of ms./il.

Spanish Language
CSmar 8,000+ vols. CoU Strength in Spanish materials. DLC 300+ vols. ICN
300+ vols. MnU 338 vols. NjP-C 293
vols. NN-BrH 750 vols. NmU 1,000
print and 100 nonprint items in Spanish and Native-American languages.
TxE 63,000 vols.

Spear, Daisy
MsHaU .60 cu.ft. of ms./il.

Spear, Margaret
MsHaU .60 cu.ft. of ms./il.

Sperry, Armstrong W.
MnU ms. for 2 titles; il. for 8 titles.
MsHaU .30 cu.ft. of ms./il.

Spielmann, M. H.
MsHaU .30 cu.ft. of ms./il.

**Spier, Peter**
MnU il. for 4 titles. MsHaU 2.5 cu.ft. of ms./il.

**Spilka, Arnold**
MnU il. for 10 titles. MsHaU .30 cu.ft. of ms./il.

**Sprague, Gretchen**
MsHaU .30 cu.ft. of ms./il.

**Springer, Harriett**
MsHaU .60 cu.ft. of ms./il.

**Spyri, Johanna**
TxDN Substantial holdings of *Heidi.*

**Srivastava, Jane**
MnU ms. for 1 title.

**Stackpole, Edward**
MsHaU .30 cu.ft. of ms./il.

**Stahl, Benjamin Albert**
MnU ms. for 1 title; il. for 1 title.

**Stallybrass, Oliver**
MnU ms. for 1 title.

**Stamaty, Mark**
MnU ms. for 1 title.

**Stambler, Irwin**
MsHaU .9 cu.ft. of ms./il.

**Stampone, John**
MsHaU .60 cu.ft. of ms./il.

**Standish, Burt L.**
InNd 545 vols.

**Stanley, Fay**
MnU ms. for 1 title.

**Stapp, Emilie and Marie**
MsHaU 20 cu.ft. of ms./il.

**Starkey, Marion Lena**
MnU ms. for 1 title.

**Steele, Mary Q.**
MnU ms. for 2 titles.

**Steele, William O.**
MnU ms. for 2 titles.

**Steen, Vagn**
MnU ms. for 2 titles.

**Steffan, Alice**
OrU 2 li.ft. of ms.

**Steichen, Edward**
MnU il. for 1 title.

**Steig, William**
MnU ms. for 5 titles; il. for 2 titles.

**Stein, Harve**
MnU il. for 5 titles. MsHaU .60 cu.ft. of ms./il. OrU 3 li.ft. of ms. and il.

**Steiner, Charlotte**
MnU il. for 1 title.

**Stephens, Charles Asbury**
MeB 40 vols. and 10 li.ft. of ms. materials.

**Steptoe, John L.**
NN-Sc Professional papers including ms. and il.

**Sterling, Dorothy**
MsHaU 1.6 cu.ft. of ms./il. OrU 3 li.ft. of ms.

**Sterling, Philip**
OrU 5 li.ft. of ms.

**Stern, Madeleine**
MnU ms. for 1 title. MsHaU 4.8 cu.ft. of ms./il.

**Stern, Marie**
MnU ms. for 7 titles.

**Sterne, Emma Gelders**
OrU 9 li.ft. of ms.

**Stevens, Leslie**
MnU il. for 1 title.

**Stevenson, Janet**
OrU 8.5 li.ft. of ms.

**Stevenson, Robert Louis**
CLU-C 100+ early and fine editions. CSahS 8,000 items related to Stevenson. CSmH-A 60 ms.; 91 pieces of corr. CtY-BR Extensive holdings of books, ms., and letters. ICN 200+ vols. TxU-Hu 1,025 vols.

**Stewart, Arvis L.**
NjR-Z il. materials.

**Stewart, Jeannette**
MsHaU .30 cu.ft. of ms./il.

**Stewart, Katharine**
MsHaU .60 cu.ft. of ms./il.

**Stewig, John Warren**
MnU ms. for 1 title.

**Stiles, Martha Bennett**
MnU ms. for 9 titles. MsHaU 2.1 cu.ft. of ms./il.

**Still, C. Henry**
MsHaU .9 cu.ft. of ms./il.

**Stinetorf, Louise A.**
MnU ms. for 2 titles.

**Stirling, Nora**
MsHaU 3.3 cu.ft. of ms./il.

**Stivers, Don**
MsHaU .60 cu.ft. of ms./il.

**Stobbs, William**
MnU il. for 2 titles.

**Stock, Catherine**
MsHaU .60 cu.ft. of ms./il.

**Stockton, Frank R.**
MnU ms. for 1 title.

**Stoiko, Michael**
MsHaU 1.3 cu.ft. of ms./il.

**Stokes, Jack**
MsHaU .60 cu.ft. of ms./il.

**Stolz, Mary**
MnU ms. for 36 titles. MsHaU 4.8 cu.ft. of ms./il.

**Stone, Eugenia**
MsHaU .30 cu.ft. of ms./il.

**Stone, Helen V.**
MnU ms. for 3 titles.

**Stone, Wilbur Macey**
NcCU 63 ms. items.

**Stoops, Herbert**
MsHaU .30 cu.ft. of ms./il.

**Stopple, Libby**
MsHaU .30 cu.ft. of ms./il.

**Storr, Catherine**
MnU ms. for 10 titles.

**Story Papers**
MnU 23,150 items.

**Storytelling**
InI 1,170 vols. in the Harding Memorial Storytelling Collection. MoS 550+ vols. NN-Don 55 vols. WaSHi 1,200 vols. WyShF 420 vols.

**Stoutenburg, Adrien**
MnU ms. for 20 titles. MsHaU .9 cu.ft. of ms./il.

**Stover, Jo Ann**
MnU il. for 1 title.

**Stowe, Harriet Beecher**
CSmH-A 45 ms.; 162 pieces of corr. CtHSD Collection of published children's adaptations and translations of *Uncle Tom's Cabin*. FU Extensive book holdings. ICN 80+ vols.

**Strachan, Margaret**
MnU ms. for 1 title. MsHaU 3 cu.ft. of ms./il.

**Stradler, John**
MnU il. for 1 title.

**Strang, Ruth**
MsHaU .30 cu.ft. of ms./il.

**Stratemeyer Syndicate**
DLC 131 vols. FU Extensive book holdings. OrU .5 li.ft. of ms. PP Extensive holdings.

**Streatfeild, Noel**
MnU ms. for 1 title.

**Street, Julia Montgomery**
NcGU ms., il. and corr. for 17 titles.

**Street Cries**
ICN 16+ vols. InU-Li 350+ vols.

**Strong, Barbara Nolen**
OrU 4.5 li.ft. of ms.

***Struwwelpeter*** *see* **Hoffmann, Heinrich**

**Stubis, Talivaldis**
MnU il. for 3 titles.

**Stull, Betty**
MnU il. for 1 title.

**Sturm, M. Rowell**
MsHaU .3 cu.ft. of ms./il.

**Sturtzel, Howard Allison and Jane Levington Sturtzel**
MsHaU 1.2 cu.ft. of ms./il. OrU 1 li.ft. of ms.

**Suba, Susanne**
MnU il. for 12 titles. MsHaU 2.8 cu.ft. of ms./il.

**Suckling, Eustace Edgar**
MnU ms. for 1 title.

**Suggs, William W.**
MnU ms. for 1 title.

**Suhl, Jan**
MsHaU .30 cu.ft. of ms./il.

**Summers, James Levingston**
MsHaU 2.7 cu.ft. of ms./il. OrU 12 li.ft. of ms.

**Sussman, Susan**
MsHaU .60 cu.ft. of ms./il.

**Sutcliff, Rosemary**
MnU ms. for 5 titles. MsHaU .30 cu.ft. of ms./il.

**Sutton, Margaret**
MnU ms. for 2 titles.

**Svenson, Andrew**
MsHaU 2.4 cu.ft. of ms./il.

**Swain, SuZan**
MsHaU .90 cu.ft. of ms./il.

**Swarthout, Glendon and Kathryn**
AzTeS ms.

**Swayne, Samuel and Zoa**
MsHaU .30 cu.ft. of ms./il.

**Sweat, Lynn**
MsHaU .30 cu.ft. of ms./il.

**Swedish Language**
MnU 964 vols.

**Sweeney, James**
MsHaU .30 cu.ft. of ms./il.

**Swenson, Allan**
MsHaU .30 cu.ft. of ms./il.

**Swift, Jonathan**
FU 55 vols. of *Gulliver's Travels*.

**Swinford, Betty**
MsHaU 1.8 cu.ft. of ms./il.

*Swiss Family Robinson see* **Wyss, Johann**

**Syme, Neville Ronald**
MsHaU .30 cu.ft. of ms./il.

**Szekeres, Cyndy**
CtU ms. and il. for 13 titles. MnU il. for 1 title.

**Taback, Simms**
MnU il. for 4 titles.

**Takakjian, Portia**
MnU il. for 2 titles.

**Talbot, Charlene**
MsHaU .3 cu.ft. of ms./il.

**Tamarin, Alfred**
MsHaU 4.2 cu.ft. of ms./il.

**Tanner, Louise Stickney**
MnU ms. for 1 title.

**Tanz, Chris**
MnU ms. for 1 title.

*Tarzan see* **Burroughs, Edgar Rice**

**Tate, Eleanora**
MsHaU .30 cu.ft. of ms./il.

**Tate, Joan**
MnU ms. for 6 titles.

**Tauschinski, Oskar Jan**
MsHaU .60 cu.ft. of ms./il.

**Taylor, Ann and Jane**
DLC Extensive book holdings. FU Extensive book holdings. InU-Li 80+ vols.

**Taylor, Florance**
MsHaU 1.2 cu.ft. of ms./il.

**Taylor, Mark**
MnU ms. for 1 title.

**Taylor, Sydney Brenner**
MnU ms. for 5 titles.

**Taylor, Theodore**
MnU ms. for 22 titles.

**Tee-Van, Helen Damrosch**
OrU 3 li.ft. of il.

**Teibl, Margaret**
MnU ms. for 1 title.

**Telemaque, Eleanor**
MnU ms. for 1 title.

**Temperance**
DLC Extensive book holdings. ICN 200+ vols.

**Tenggren, Gustaf**
MnU il. for 38 titles.

**Tenniel, John**
ICN 37+ vols.; 6 drawings and woodblocks. NNU-F Etchings, prints, and drawings.

**Tensen, Ruth M.**
MsHaU .30 cu.ft. of ms./il.

**Terris, Susan**
MnU ms. for 16 titles.

**Texas**
TxDa 400 vols. TxU 870 vols.

**Texas—Authors and illustrators**
TxDa 400 vols. TxU 870 vols.

**Textbooks**
AkA 280 vols. AzTeS Group of early textbooks. AzU Collection of 19th-century textbooks. CLU-S/C Primary and secondary American textbooks. CSfSt 1,100 vols. CSmH-A Collection of early American and English primers. CoD Nearly complete collection of McGuffey readers and spellers. CoU 600 vols. in the Epsteen Collection. CtHT 7,000 vols. of 18th- and 19th- century American imprints. DLC 35 vols. of New England primers; 300 vols. of McGuffey readers. FTS 10,000 vols. of pre–Civil War American schoolbooks. FU 23 vols. of New England primers. ICN 400+ vols. from the Middle Ages to 1900; 24+ editions of the New England primer. ICarbS Extensive collection.

INS 1,000 vols. from late 1700s to 1900. IU-Ed 47,800 vols. InTI 1,500 vols. in the Floyd Family Collection; 900 vols. in the Walker Collection, and early textbooks in the Cunningham Collection. LN 23 vols. of McGuffey readers. MAJ Early readers and spellers in the Johnson Collection. MBWS Collection of primers and early textbooks. MCot Substantial holdings of textbooks. MDeeP Extensive holdings from the 19th–20th centuries. MH-Ed 35,000 vols. dating from 1800–1950. MHi 1,750 vols. from 1700. MStuO Good holdings of primers and elementary and secondary textbooks. MiDbH McGuffey readers, New England primers, and Websteriana in the Geesy Collection.

MiMtpT 600 vols. MsHaU 2,000 vols. NEaHi 1,500 vols. from 1790. NHemH 2,500 vols. from 1620–1950. NNC 5,000 vols. in the Plimpton Library. NNStJ Good selection of educational vols. NSyU Collection of textbooks in the American Book Company records. NbU 450 vols. from 1820–1960. NcCU 300 vols. NcGU American imprints before 1850. NjR 550 vols. OAU 78 McGuffey readers. OC Substantial holdings of textbooks published in Cincinnati. OFH Schoolbooks from the latter 19th century. OHi 800 19th-century vols., including McGuffey readers. OOxM 5,500 textbooks; 480 McGuffey readers. OrP Textbooks dating from 1834–1920. PMCHi Textbooks from the mid-1800s. PP-Rb 500+ vols. of grammars and New England primers. PPiU 15,000 vols. TMM Volumes from 1850–1920. TxDa Substantial holdings. TxU 34,000 vols. since 1800. WMUW Substantial holdings of historical and contemporary textbooks. WaSHi 300 vols. WaSp 18th- and 19th-century textbooks. WaU-CM 1,850 vols.

**Thatcher, Dora**
MsHaU .30 cu.ft. of ms./il.

**Thayer, Marjorie**
MsHaU .30 cu.ft. of ms./il.

**Theater** *see* **Drama**

**Thiele, Colin**
MnU ms. for 2 titles. MsHaU 2.7 cu.ft. of ms./il.

**Thollander, Earl**
MnU il. for 1 title.

**Thomas, Jane Resh**
MnU ms. for 6 titles.

**Thomas, Shirley**
MsHaU .60 cu.ft. of ms./il.

**Thompson, Blanche Jennings**
MnU ms. for 1 title.

**Thompson, George Selden**
MsHaU .30 cu.ft. of ms./il.

**Thompson, John**
NjR-Z il. materials.

**Thompson, Mozelle**
MnU il. for 1 title.

**Thompson, Vivian L.**
MsHaU 1.2 cu.ft. of ms./il.

**Thomson, Peter**
MsHaU .30 cu.ft. of ms./il.

**Thorne-Thomsen, Gudrun**
MnU ms. for 1 title.

**Thrasher, Crystal**
MnU ms. for 5 titles.

**Tiegreen, Alan**
MsHaU 2.7 cu.ft. of ms./il.

**Tillett, Leslie**
MnU il. for 2 titles.

**Tinkelman, Murray**
MnU il. for 3 titles. MsHaU .30 cu.ft. of ms./il.

**Tinker, Bill**
MsHaU 1.2 cu.ft. of ms./il.

**Tinker, Edward**
MsHaU .3 cu.ft. of ms./il.

**Tippett, James S.**
MnU ms. for 1 title. NcGU ms., notes, and artifacts for 17 titles.

**Titler, Dale**
MsHaU .30 cu.ft. of ms./il.

**Titus, Eve**
MiDW ms. materials in Ramsey Collection. MnU ms. for 3 titles.

**Tobias, Ann**
MsHaU .30 cu.ft. of ms./il.

**Todd, Herbert**
MsHaU .30 cu.ft. of ms./il.

**Tolford, Joshua**
MnU il. for 1 title.

**Tolkien, J. R. R.**
IWW Extensive holdings of books and ms.

**Tomei, Lorna**
NjR-Z il. materials.

**Tomes, Margot**
MnU il. for 54 titles. MsHaU 1.8 cu.ft. of ms./il.

**Tompert, Ann**
MoWarbT ms. and il. materials.

**Tonn, Martin**
MsHaU .30 cu.ft. of ms./il.

**Torbert, Floyd**
MsHaU .3 cu.ft. of ms./il.

**Torjesen, Elizabeth Fraser**
MnU ms. for 1 title.

**Torre, Vincent**
MnU il. for 6 titles.

**Torrey, Helen**
MsHaU .30 cu.ft. of ms./il.

**Toschik, Larry**
MnU il. for 1 title.

**Townsend, John Rowe**
MnU ms. for 5 titles.

**Toy and Movable Books**
CLU-S/C Collection of 2,000+ early games, pop-up, and movable books that includes one of the most extensive groups of harlequinades extant. CSfSt 100+ vols. DLC 40+ vols. from the 19th–20th centuries. DeWint Extensive holdings of movable and pop-up books, peep shows, panoramas, and toy theaters. FTS Extensive book holdings. FU Extensive book holdings. ICN Small holdings. IU-Ed 150+ vols. InU-Li Extensive holdings from 18th–20th centuries, including harlequinades and peepshows; il. and ms. materials. MiMtpT Extensive holdings. MoWarbT 665 vols. MsHaU Extensive holdings. NN-Don 221 vols. NNPM Extensive holdings in the Wightman Collection. WaSp 53 toy books.

**Toys**
CSahS Toys and lead soldiers of Robert Louis Stevenson. CSfACA Holdings of fiction-related toys. DeWint Extensive holdings of paper toys, toy soldiers, and board and card games. INS Toys in Circus Collection; toys used as models in

The *"Pop-Up" Pinocchio*, with illustrations by Harold Lentz; New York: Blue Ribbon Books, 1932.

Lenski Collection. MnM 135 items related to children's books. NN-Don Stuffed animals that inspired *Winnie the Pooh*. NWe Large holdings of toys, dolls, and models. NcGU Toys belonging to Lois Lenski. OC Toys, figurines, and dolls. OrHi Games, toys, puzzles, and dolls. WyShF Large collection of dolls, puppets, figurines, and character animals.

**Translators' Manuscripts**
MnU 60 items.

**Travel and Geography**
DLC Extensive book holdings. ICN 300+ vols. NAlU 200 vols.

**Traylor, Sarah M.**
MsHaU .30 cu.ft. of ms./il.

**Trease, Geoffrey**
MnU ms. for 3 titles.

**Tredez, Alain and Denise**
MsHaU .60 cu.ft. of ms./il.

**Trelease, Allen W.**
MnU ms. for 1 title.

**Tresselt, Alvin**
MnU ms. for 4 titles.

**Trevelyan, Julian Otto**
MsHaU .30 cu.ft. of ms./il.

**Trotter, Grace V.**
MsHaU .30 cu.ft. of ms./il.

**Tubby, I. M.** *see* **Kraus, Robert**

**Tucker, Bruce**
NcCU 2 ms. items for 1 title.

**Tudor, Tasha**
CSt Extensive book holdings. MnU il. for 9 titles. MsHaU .60 cu.ft. of ms./il. NhC Complete published works.

**Tunis, Edwin Burdett**
MnU il. for 1 title. OrU 12 li.ft. of ms.

**Tunis, John R.**
MBU 60 vols. and 88 boxes of ms. materials.

**Turkish Language**
MnU 84 vols.

**Turngren, Annette**
OrU 1.5 li.ft. of ms. and il.

**Turngren, Ellen**
MnU ms. for 2 titles.

**Twain, Mark**
CSmH-A 18 ms.; 200 pieces of corr. CtY-BR Morse Collection contains ms., first editions, and letters. ICN 300+ vols. IDekn Significant holdings. InU-Li 450+ vols. and corr. MeWC 159 vols. MiMtpT Extensive holdings of books and pamphlets. MoHM 1,200 vols. and ms. materials. MoS 85 items of broadsides, pamphlets, and monographs. MoStoM 275 vols. and ms. materials. NBuBE 500 vols., ms., and other items. NSyU 110 vols. ViU 700 vols.

**"'Twas the Night before Christmas"** *see* **Moore, Clement Clarke**

**Uchida, Yoshiko**
MnU ms. for 2 titles. MsHaU .40 cu.ft. of ms./il. OrU 4.5 li.ft. of ms.

**Udry, Janice May**
MsHaU .30 cu.ft. of ms./il.

**Uhl, Melvin J.**
MsHaU .60 cu.ft. of ms./il.

**Ukrainian Language**
MnU 45 vols.

**Ulreich, Edward**
MnU il. for 1 title.

**Uncle Remus** *see* **Harris, Joel Chandler**

**Uncle Tom's Cabin** *see* **Stowe, Harriet Beecher**

**Underhill, Jill**
MnU ms. for 1 title.

**Ungerer, Tomi**
MnU il. for 8 titles.

University of Southern Mississippi Medallion *see* Award Books

Unnerstad, Edith
MnU ms. for 1 title.

Unwin, Nora Spicer
MnU il. for 9 titles. MsHaU 1.2 cu.ft. of ms./il. OrU 15 li.ft. of ms. and il.

Urdu Language
MnU 10 vols.

Uttley, Alison
MnU ms. for 65 titles.

Valens, Evans G., Jr.
MnU ms. for 3 titles.

Valentine, Deborah
MsHaU .60 cu.ft. of ms./il.

Valentines *see* Greeting Cards

Van Allsburg, Chris
MnU il. for 4 titles.

Van Coevering, Jan Adrian
MsHaU .30 cu.ft. of ms./il.

Van Loon, Hendrik Willem
MnU ms. for 1 title; il. for 1 title. NIC il. and ms.

Van Riper, Guernsey
MsHaU .30 cu.ft. of ms./il.

Van Stockum, Hilda
MnU ms. for 2 titles. MsHaU 2.5 cu.ft. of ms./il.

Van Woerkom, Dorothy O.
MnU ms. for 12 titles. MsHaU .30 cu.ft. of ms./il.

Vance, Eleanor Graham
MnU ms. for 1 title. MsHaU .30 cu.ft. of ms./il.

Vasiliu, Mircea
MnU ms. for 2 titles; il. for 2 titles. MsHaU 4.9 cu.ft. of ms./il.

Vaughan-Jackson, Genevieve
MsHaU .30 cu.ft. of ms./il.

Veglahn, Nancy
IaU Books and ms.

Vidrine, Mercedes
MsHaU .30 cu.ft. of ms./il.

Viel, D.
MsHaU .30 cu.ft. of ms./il.

Viereck, Ellen
MnU il. for 1 title.

Villarejo, Mary
MsHaU .30 cu.ft. of ms./il.

Vining, Elizabeth Gray
MsHaU .30 cu.ft. of ms./il.

Viorst, Judith
MnU ms. for 3 titles. NjR ms. materials.

"A Visit from St. Nicholas" *see* Moore, Clement Clarke

Vizenor, Gerald
MnU ms. for 2 titles; il. for 1 title.

Vogel, Ilse-Margret
MnU ms. for 5 titles; il. for 11 titles.

Voight, Virginia
MsHaU .3 cu.ft. of ms./il.

Vosburgh, Leonard
MsHaU .60 cu.ft. of ms./il.

Voss, Carroll
MnU ms. for 1 title.

Voute, Kathleen
MnU il. for 5 titles.

Waber, Bernard
MnU ms. for 1 title; il. for 1 title.

Wagner, Jane
MnU ms. for 1 title.

Wahl, Jan
MnU ms. for 19 titles. OBgU 6 boxes of ms., il., and corr.

Walker, Barbara K.
MnU ms. for 11 titles.

Walker, Charles
MnU il. for 1 title.

*The Brownies: Their Book* by Palmer Cox; London: Unwin [1887?].

**Walker, Donald S.**
MsHaU .9 cu.ft. of ms./il.

**Walker, Kathrine Sorley**
MsHaU 1.2 cu.ft. of ms./il.

**Walker, Michael J.**
MsHaU .30 cu.ft. of ms./il.

**Walker, Mort**
MnU ms. for 1 title; il. for 1 title.

**Wallace, Barbara Brooks**
MnU ms. for 6 titles. MsHaU 1.5 cu.ft. of ms./il.

**Wallace, Bill**
MsHaU .30 cu.ft. of ms./il.

**Walsh, Ellen Stoll**
MnU ms. for 1 title; il. for 2 titles.

**Walter, Mildred Pitts**
MnU ms. for 2 titles.

**Waniek, Marilyn**
MnU ms. for 1 title.

**Ward, Cindy**
MnU ms. for 1 title.

**Ward, Lynd**
DGU Extensive holdings of ms. and il. MsHaU 1.8 cu.ft. of ms./il. NjR-Z il. materials. PP 100 vols. and il. PPiU-LS 17 vols., il.

**Ward, May McNeer** *see* McNeer, May

**Ward, William**
MsHaU .30 cu.ft. of ms./il.

**Warner, Edythe Records**
MnU ms. for 5 titles; il. for 9 titles.

**Warner, Gertrude Chandler**
MsHaU .9 cu.ft. of ms./il.

**Warner, Priscilla M.**
MsHaU .90 cu.ft. of ms./il.

**Warner, Sunny B.**
MnU il. for 1 title.

**Warren, Betsy**
MsHaU .3 cu.ft. of ms./il.

**Warren, Ed**
MnU il. for 1 title.

**Warren, Robert Penn**
MnU ms. for 1 title.

**Wartik, Herschel**
MnU il. for 3 titles.

**Wartski, Maureen Crane**
MnU ms. for 1 title. MsHaU .30 cu.ft. of ms./il.

**Washburne, Heluiz**
MsHaU .9 cu.ft. of ms./il.

**Washington—Authors and Illustrators**
Wa 1,000 vols.

**Waters, Tony**
MnU ms. for 1 title; il. for 1 title.

**Watkins, Arthur M.**
MsHaU .30 cu.ft. of ms./il.

**Watson, Aldren Auld**
MnU il. for 8 titles.

**Watson, Jane Werner**
OrU 4 li.ft. of ms.

**Watson, Pauline**
MsHaU .60 cu.ft. of ms./il.

**Watson, Wendy**
MnU il. for 1 title.

**Watts, Isaac**
DLC 18 vols. FU Extensive book holdings. ICN 150+ vols. InU-Li 90+ vols. PP-Rb 200 vols.

**Watts, Mabel Pizzey**
MsHaU .30 cu.ft. of ms./il.

**Weaver, Harriet**
MsHaU 1.2 cu.ft. of ms./il.

**Weaver, Robert G.**
MnU ms. for 1 title.

**Webber, Irma Eleanor Schmidt**
MnU ms. for 2 titles; il. for 6 titles.

**Weddle, Ethel**
MsHaU .60 cu.ft. of ms./il.

**Weidt, Maryann N.**
MnU ms. for 1 title.

**Weihs, Erika**
MnU il. for 4 titles.

**Weik, Mary Hays**
MnU ms. for 5 titles.

**Weil, Ann**
MsHaU 2.1 cu.ft. of ms./il.

**Weil, Lisl**
MnU ms. for 6 titles; il. for 26 titles. MsHaU 3.4 cu.ft. of ms./il. OrU 3 li.ft. of ms. and il.

**Weiner, Sandra**
MnU ms. for 2 titles; il. for 3 titles.

**Weisburd, Ida**
MnU il. for 1 title.

**Weisgard, Leonard Joseph**
MnU ms. for 1 title; il. for 18 titles. NGuP il.

**Weiss, Emil**
MnU il. for 22 titles.

**Wellman, Alice**
MnU ms. for 1 title.

**Wells, Jane McC. B.**
MsHaU .60 cu.ft. of ms./il.

**Wells, Luther Coleman**
MnU il. for 1 title.

**Wells, Rosemary**
CtU 2 pieces of artwork. PNo il.

**Welskopf-Henrich, Liselotte**
MnU ms. for 1 title.

**Werner, Vivian Lescher**
OrU 2 li.ft. of ms.

**Werstein, Irving**
MsHaU 3.9 cu.ft. of ms./il.

**Werth, Kurt**
MnU ms. for 4 titles; il. for 36 titles. MsHaU 2.4 cu.ft. of ms./il. OrU 21 li.ft. of ms. and il.

**Wexler, Jerome**
MsHaU 9.7 cu.ft. of ms./il.

**Weygant, Noemi**
MnU ms. for 2 titles; il. for 2 titles.

**Wheeler, Candace T.**
MsHaU .30 cu.ft. of ms./il.

**Whipple, Dorothy**
MsHaU .30 cu.ft. of ms./il.

**White, Anne Terry**
MsHaU .60 cu.ft. of ms./il. OrU 1.5 li.ft. of ms.

**White, Bessie Felstiner**
MnU ms. for 4 titles.

**White, David Omar**
MnU il. for 1 title. NjR-Z il. materials.

**White, E. B.**
NIC Principal collection of ms. and published books.

**White, Frank**
MsHaU corr.

**White, JoAnn**
MsHaU .30 cu.ft. of ms./il.

**White, Laurence B.**
MsHaU 1.8 cu.ft. of ms./il.

**White, Robb**
MsHaU .30 cu.ft. of ms./il.

**White, Thelma V. Bounds**
MsHaU .30 cu.ft. of ms./il.

**Whitmore, Arvella**
MnU ms. for 1 title.

**Whitney, Alex**
MsHaU 1.2 cu.ft. of ms./il.

**Whitney, Phyllis**
MsHaU .30 cu.ft. of ms./il.

**Whitney, Thomas P.**
MnU ms. for 2 titles.

**Wibberley, Leonard**
CLSU ms. materials.

**Wier, Ester**
MnU ms. for 14 titles. MsHaU 1.8 cu.ft. of ms./il.

**Wiese, Kurt**
MnU ms. for 3 titles; il. for 43 titles. MsHaU .30 cu.ft. of ms./il. OrU 12 li.ft. of ms. and il.

**Wiesner, William**
MnU ms. for 3 titles; il. for 8 titles.

**Wiggin, Kate Douglas**
CSmH-A 1 ms.; 6 pieces of corr. FU Extensive book holdings. MeB 450 vols., 3.5 li.ft. of ms. materials. MePW 44 vols. MeWC 78 vols.

**Wilcox, Eleanor**
MnU ms. for 1 title.

**Wilder, Cherry**
MsHaU 1.2 cu.ft. of ms./il.

**Wilder, Laura Ingalls**
CPom 51 vols.; 2 ms. and related ephemera. IaWbH 1.3 cu.ft. of ms. and corr. KWPu 8 autographed books, scrapbook, photographs, and corr. MiD ms. NMalo corr. of the James Wilder family in the Alice Wilder and the Eliza Jane Wilder Collections.

**Wildsmith, Brian**
MnU il. for 5 titles.

**Wilkie, Katharine E.**
MsHaU .30 cu.ft. of ms./il.

**Wilkin, Eloise B.**
OrU 3 li.ft. of ms. and il.

**Wilkinson, Brenda**
MnU ms. for 1 title.

**Willard, Nancy**
MnU ms. for ms. for title; il. for 13 titles.

**Willett, John**
MnU ms. for 1 title.

**William Allen White Children's Book Award** *see* **Award Books**

**Williams, Berkeley, Jr.**
MnU il. for 9 titles.

**Williams, Garth**
MnU il. for 2 titles.

**Williams, Jay**
MBU 24 vols. and 33 boxes of ms. materials. MnU ms. for 1 title.

**Williams, Vera B.**
MnU il. for 1 title.

**Willimson, Hamilton**
MnU ms. for 1 title.

**Wilson, Charles Morrow**
OrU 7.5 li.ft. of ms.

**Wilson, Dagmar**
MnU il. for 7 titles.

**Wilson, Edward Arthur**
MnU il. for 3 titles. OrU 21 li.ft. of ms. and il.

**Wilson, Hazel Hutchins**
MnU ms. for 2 titles. MsHaU .30 cu.ft. of
ms./il. OrU .5 li.ft. of ms.

**Wilson, W. N.**
MsHaU 4 cu.ft. of ms./il.

**Wilwerding, Walter Joseph**
MnU ms. for 2 titles; il. for 2 titles.

**Winchester, Linda**
MsHaU .60 cu.ft. of ms./il.

**Winders, Gertrude H.**
MsHaU .30 cu.ft. of ms./il.

**Windsor, Patricia**
MnU ms. for 1 title.

**Winfield, Arthur**
DLC 49 vols.

**Winslow, Amy**
MnU ms. for 1 title.

**Winslow, Earle**
MnU il. for 1 title.

**Winsor, Robert**
MnU ms. for 1 title; il. for 2 titles.

**Winter, Ginny Linville**
MnU ms. for 1 title; il. for 1 title.

**Winter, Paula**
MsHaU .60 cu.ft. of ms./il.

**Winter, William**
MnU il. for 1 title.

**Winthrop, Elizabeth**
MnU ms. for 3 titles.

**Wisa, Louis**
MnU il. for 1 title.

**Wisbeski, Dorothy**
MsHaU .90 cu.ft. of ms./il.

**Wisconsin — Authors and Illustrators**
WM 2,000 vols. WU-CC 500 vols.

**Wise, Lu Celia**
MsHaU .40 cu.ft. of ms./il.

**Wise, William**
MBU 80 vols. and 178 li.ft. of ms. materials. MnU ms. for 1 title.

**Witheridge, Elizabeth P.**
MnU ms. for 2 titles.

**Wohlberg, Meg**
MnU il. for 20 titles.

**Wohlrabe, Raymond A.**
MsHaU 3.6 cu.ft. of ms./il.

**Wojciechowska, Maia**
MnU ms. for 29 titles. MsHaU 10 cu.ft.
of ms./il.

**Wolcott, Elizabeth Tyler**
MnU il. for 1 title.

**Wolfson, Evelyn**
MsHaU .60 cu.ft. of ms./il.

**Wolters, Richard A.**
MsHaU 1.8 cu.ft. of ms./il.

**Women Authors and Illustrators**
WaU 200 vols.

**Wong, Jeanyee**
MnU il. for 1 title.

**Wood, James Playsted**
MsHaU 2.1 cu.ft. of ms./il.

**Wood, Leslie**
MsHaU .30 cu.ft. of ms./il.

**Woodblocks**
CSf McLoughlin Brothers woodblocks and
prints. MiKW Randolph Caldecott
woodblocks engraved by Edmund
Evans. MsHaU Randolph Caldecott
and Kate Greenaway woodblocks engraved by Edmund Evans. NHi
McLoughlin Brothers woodblocks.
PPiC Kate Greenaway woodblocks.

**Woods, George A.**
MnU ms. for 1 title.

**Woods, Joan**
MsHaU .30 cu.ft. of ms./il.

**Woodson, Jacqueline**
MnU ms. for 4 titles.

**Woodward, Hildegard**
MnU il. for 5 titles. MsHaU .60 cu.ft. of
ms./il.

**Woolley, Catherine**
OrU 9 li.ft. of ms.

**Wooton, Carl**
MsHaU .30 cu.ft. of ms./il.

**Worcester, Donald Emmet**
MnU ms. for 3 titles.

**Worth, Valerie**
MnU ms. for 1 title.

**Wright, Betty Ren**
MoWarbT ms. and il. materials.

**Wright, Frances**
MsHaU .30 cu.ft. of ms./il.

**Wrightson, Patricia**
MnU ms. for 2 titles. MsHaU .30 cu.ft. of
ms./il.

**Wronker, Lili Cassell** *see* **Cassel-Wronker,
Lili**

**Wyeth, N. C.**
DeWA Extensive holdings of books, il.,
scrapbooks, and corr. of Wyeth and his
teacher, Howard Pyle. NN-Don 40 vols.
and 20 original il. PP-Rb ms. and il.

**Wyndham, Lee**
MsHaU 1.2 cu.ft. of ms./il. OrU 21 li.ft.
of ms.

**Wyoming — Authors and Illustrators**
WyShF 50 vols.

**Wyss, Johann**
FU Extensive holdings of *Swiss Family
Robinson*. InU-Li 36 pre-1865 editions
of *Swiss Family Robinson* in various
languages.

**Yager, Rosemary**
MsHaU .60 cu.ft. of ms./il.

**Yamaguchi, Marianne**
MnU il. for 3 titles.

**Yashima, Taro**
MnU il. for 5 titles. MsHaU 3.5 cu.ft. of
ms./il.

**Yates, Elizabeth**
KEmU ms. materials. MBU 85 vols. and
23 boxes of ms. materials. MnU ms. for
1 title. MsHaU .30 cu.ft. of ms./il. NhC
Complete published works.

*Jack and the Bean-Stalk* by W. W. Denslow;
New York: Dillingham, 1903.

**Yaukey, Grace Sydenstricker**
MsHaU .30 cu.ft. of ms./il. OrU 4.5 li.ft. of ms. and il.

**Yeo, Wilma**
MoWarbT ms. and il. materials.

**Yolen, Jane H.**
MnU ms. for 17 titles.

**Yonge, Charlotte Mary**
CSmH-A 37 pieces of corr. DLC Extensive book holdings. FU Extensive book holdings. MsHaU .30 cu.ft. of ms./il. NNU-F 300 vols.

**Young, Ed**
MnU il. for 1 title.

**Young, Janet and Robert**
MsHaU 10 cu.ft. of ms./il.

**Young, Scott**
MsHaU .30 cu.ft. of ms./il.

**Young Adult Literature**
IaU 400+ vols. in G. Robert Carlsen Collection.

**Young Readers Choice Award** *see* **Award Books**

**Yugoslavian Language**
MnU 42 vols.

**Yurka, Blanche**
MnU ms. for 1 title.

**Zacharias, Thomas**
MnU ms. for 1 title.

**Zagoren, Ruby**
MnU ms. for 1 title.

**Zallinger, Jean Day**
CtU 1 box of ms. and il. MnU il. for 3 titles. MsHaU 2.1 cu.ft. of ms./il. NjR-Z il. materials.

**Zehrnfennig, Gladys**
MnU ms. for 2 titles.

**Zemach, Harve**
MnU ms. for 1 title. MsHaU .30 cu.ft. of ms./il.

**Zemach, Margot**
MnU ms. for 1 title; il. for 28 titles.

**Zim, Herbert Spencer**
MnU ms. for 12 titles. MsHaU 3.6 cu.ft. of ms./il. OrU 30 li.ft. of ms. and il.

**Zimnik, Reiner**
MnU ms. for 1 title.

**Ziner, Florence Feenie**
MsHaU .30 cu.ft. of ms./il.

**Zolotow, Charlotte S.**
MnU ms. for 13 titles. MsHaU 1 cu.ft. of ms./il.

**Zuraw, Elizabeth**
MsHaU .90 cu.ft. of ms./il.

**Zweifel, Frances**
MsHaU .30 cu.ft. of ms./il. NjR-Z il. materials.

# Directory of International Collections

## Albania

### TIRANA

National Library
Shashi "Skenderbej"
Tirana, Albania
phone: 243-73
fax: ++355.42.23843
contact: Mrs. Forfuri Xhaja, Librarian

This special collection of children's literature contains nearly 20,000 volumes of books and magazines dating from 1969 to the present day, mostly in Albanian. The collection is cataloged, and a bibliography of Albanian children's books is available.

## Argentina

### BUENOS AIRES

Centro de Documentacion e Informacion
    sobre Medios de Comunicacion
    (CEDIMICO)
Venezuela 3031
Buenos Aires, Argentina
phone: 97-5461
contact: Pablo Medina, Director

Primarily a pedagogical collection, CED-IMICO provides resources for librarians and teachers. Holdings include works about the history of children's literature in Argentina, original illustrations and published works of contemporary Argentine illustrators, books about games and team sports, scholarly periodicals, and works on children's rights. Featured is a 200-volume collection of the works of Carlo Collodi, including various editions of *Pinocchio*.

## Australia

## New South Wales

### SYDNEY

National Trust of Australia
The Merchants' House
43 George St.
The Rocks
Sydney
New South Wales 2000, Australia
phone: 02-241-5099
fax: 02-241-5320
contact: Jim Logan, Curator

The Australian Childhood Collection consists of 4,000 volumes, dating from 1840. Holdings include rare children's books, illustrations, board games, toys, and ephemera. Also held are original comic illustrations and drawings of Ginger Meggs and the well-known characters of Norman Lindsays' *Magic Pudding*.

## South Australia

### UNDERDALE

**University of South Australia Library**
Holbrooks Rd.
Underdale
South Australia 5032, Australia
phone: 08 302 6254
fax: 08 302 6699
contact: Anne Marie Lynch, Library
  Liaison, Education

The HOPE (History of Primary Education) Collection focuses on textbooks used in the state of South Australia from earliest times to the 1960s. The collection is currently being reorganized and added to the University of South Australia Library's database.

## Tasmania

### HOBART

**State Library of Tasmania**
91 Murray St.
Hobart
Tasmania, Australia 7000
phone: 002 33 7467
fax: 002 33 7902
contact: Ray Bartle, Senior Librarian,
  Collection Development

The Children's Literature Collection at the State Library of Tasmania consists of approximately 6,000 volumes dating from the 1890s, with the bulk of the collection post-1940. They have a representative collection of Australian authors and illustrators; award-winning books from Austra-lia, the United Kingdom, and the United States; and a folktale collection.

## Victoria

### MELBOURNE

**State Library of Victoria**
328 Swanston St.
Melbourne
Victoria 3001, Australia
phone: 03 66 99822
fax: 03 6631480
contact: Juliet O'Conor, Librarian
e-mail: j.oconor@slv950.slv.vic.gov.au
Internet: slv950.slv.vic.gov.au

The Children's Literature Research Collection consists of 22,000 volumes, mainly from the nineteenth and twentieth centuries, reflecting Australian and overseas trends in children's literature. The emphasis is on Australian material, including picture books, fiction, poetry, folktales, and legends, as well as a reference collection of bibliographies and reference tools relating to children's literature. Australia's rich heritage of Aboriginal legends is represented in publications from the 1890s to the present day.

### PARKVILLE

**University of Melbourne**
**Baillieu Library**
Parkville
Victoria 3052, Australia
phone: 03 3446636
fax: 61-3-348-1142
contact: Merete Smith, Curator of Rare
  Books
e-mail: m.smith@lib.unimelb.edu.au
Internet: library.unimelb.edu.au

The nucleus of the Morgan Collection of Children's Books was donated in 1954 by Frederick Morgan and has been augmented through gifts and library funds. It now comprises more than 4,000 items, primarily English imprints published prior to 1900, a few toys, and some manuscript materials. Collection strengths include early fiction for children, poetry, chapbooks, boys' books, religious school prizes, and instructional materials.

### RIDDELL'S CREEK

**Dromkeen Children's Literature Collection**
Main Rd.
Riddell's Creek
Victoria 3431, Australia
phone: 054-286701
fax: 054-28630
contact: Kaye Keck

The Dromkeen Collection is recognized worldwide as being of major significance in the field of children's literature. Collection holdings of 3,000 volumes dating from 1890 are complemented by original illustrations and manuscripts representing more than 500 Australian authors and illustrators.

## Western Australia

### PERTH

**Library and Information Service of Western Australia**
**Alexander Library**
Perth Cultural Centre
Perth
Western Australia 6000, Australia
phone: 09 427 3205
fax: 09 427 3256
contact: Kate Eckersley or Marilyn Cacavas

The bulk of the Research Collection of Children's Literature consists of 7,000 volumes of Australian juvenile fiction, poems, and plays dating from the 1840s, as well as a small collection of manuscripts by Australian authors. The reference collection contains books, journals, and a small grouping of annuals and fiction from the Pacific area, primarily New Zealand.

The collection is cataloged and accessible through LIBERTAS, their online catalog.

## Azerbaijan

### BAKU

**Republic Children's Library named after F. Kercharli**
104, S. Vurgun St.
370022 Baku, Azerbaijan
phone: 953926/953934
contact: Gasinova Fizura, Director

This library's children's collection contains a small number of Azerbaijan children's books. Included are folktales, fairy tales, poetry anthologies, and encyclopedias.

## Belarus

### MINSK

**National Library of Belarus**
9, Chyrvonaarmejskaja St.
220636 Minsk, Belarus
phone: 27-54-63
fax: 27-54-63
contact: Tatyana I. Roshtchina, Head Manuscripts and Rare Books Dept.; Ludmila N. Rabok, Head, Belarusian Literature Dept.

Within the holdings of the National Library are two special collections of children's literature. One is the Belarusian Children's Literature Collection consisting of 11,520 volumes of children's books published from 1767 to the present day in the territory of Belarus. All items are in Belarusian, Russian, and other European languages, as well as Arabic. The other is the ABC Books, Primers and Other Educational Material for Children Collection. Included are 30 primers, alphabet books, and related materials published outside of the present territory of Belarus in Russian, Polish, and other European languages, dating from the seventeenth through the nineteenth centuries.

# Belgium

## ANTWERP

**National Centre of Children's Literature**
Minderbroedersstraat 22
2000 Antwerp, Belgium
phone: 03/234.16.67
fax: 03/226.64.55
contact: Greet Spaepen, Director

Located in the Archives and Museum of Flemish Culture, the National Centre was founded in 1976. Its purposes are to catalog and preserve the archives of Flemish children's literature, to collect Flemish children's books published in Belgium or translated into other languages, to operate as a research and reference library for the study of Flemish children's literature, and to promote Flemish children's books. Currently, the center houses more than 1,400 volumes published from 1960 to the present.

## BRUSSELS

**Centre Belge Francophone de Litterature Jeunesse**
**Bibliothèque Principale de Bruxelles II (Laeken)**
246 Boulevard Emile Bockstael
1020 Brussels, Belgium
phone: 428.92.73
fax: 426.06.90
contact: Luc Battieuw,
    Bibliothécaire-Responsable

This is a consulting center for researchers and specialists in children's literature. Holdings include 3,000 volumes created by Belgian authors and illustrators.

**Nos Enfants et Leurs Livres (NELL)**
45 Rue François Stroobant
1060 Brussels, Belgium
phone: 02/345.96.06
contact: P. de Viron

NELL is a French-language lending library for children. The library is subsidized by the French community; most of its holdings are gifts from the publishers. In return, the library evaluates the books with the reviews appearing in its quarterly journal. Currently there are approximately 500 books in the collection.

**Ville de Bruxelles**
**Bibliothèque Principale**
**Jeunesse**
24, Rue des Riches-Claires
1000 Brussels, Belgium
phone: 02/512.40.12
fax: 502.59.39
contact: Bertrand Jacques or Beaujean
    Anne

This collection contains 30,000 volumes of works for children and young adults, in French, dating from 1975 to the current time.

## LIÈGE

**Bibliothèque Centrale Chiroux-Croisiers**
**Province de Liège**
15, Rue des Croisiers
B 4000 Liège, Belgium
phone: 32.41.23.19.16
fax: 32.41.21.25.07
contact: Mr. B. Demoulin,
    Bibliothécaire-Directeur Principal

The library for adolescents contains a unique collection of materials for young people from twelve to eighteen years of age. Included are 20,000 volumes dating from 1956 to the present.

# Bulgaria

## SOFIA

**Central Library of Sophia**
4, Slaveikov Square
1000 Sofia, Bulgaria
phone: 80 22 34
fax: 80 22 38
contact: Head of the Children's
Department

Since 1978, the Central Library of Sophia has had depository status for books and periodicals published in Bulgaria. The children's book collection includes 7,000 volumes of classic and contemporary Bulgarian literature, translations of foreign books for children, and Bulgarian children's books published in foreign languages by Bulgarian publishers.

# Canada

# British Columbia

## VANCOUVER

**University of British Columbia**
**Special Collections**
**Main Library**
1956 Main Mall
Vancouver, British Columbia
Canada V6T 1Z1
phone: 604-822-2521
fax: 604-822-9587
contact: Frances Woodward, Reference
Librarian
e-mail: franwood@unixg.ubc.ca
Internet: telnet library.ubc.ca

Holdings of children's literature in the libraries of the University of British Columbia are varied and significant. The early and rare children's book collections comprise some 10,000 volumes in English,

*Mother Goose: The Old Nursery Rhymes*, illustrated by Arthur Rackham; New York: Century, 1913.

most of which were published in Canada, Great Britain, and the United States. Included are all major titles and authors prominent in the development of children's literature from early chapbooks and books of religious instruction to twentieth-century classics. Emphasis is placed on Canadian and illustrated books and on early twentieth-century American series books and school stories. The time span is about 1713–1939.

Other holdings include the Alice Collection, which covers every aspect of Carroll's writing for children and contains more than 200 different editions; the Miriam Morton Collection of 700 Russian children's books from the 1940s to the 1960s; and the Early Textbook Collection, with nearly 4,000 volumes spanning the eighteenth century to 1930.

## New Brunswick

### FREDERICTON

**University of New Brunswick**
**Harriet Irving Library**
Education Resource Centre
Box 7500
Fredericton, New Brunswick
Canada E3B 5H5
phone: 506-453-3516
fax: 506-453-4831
e-mail: johnston@unb.ca
contact: Pat Johnston, Education
    Resource Centre

The Children's Literature Research Collection was established in 1988 and currently contains 7,000 volumes. Strengths of the collection include works by Juliana Horatia Ewing, Mary Grannan, L. M. Montgomery, and Ann and Jane Taylor. In addition, the collection has many of the microfilm sets of rare children's books and periodicals.

## Newfoundland

### ST. JOHN'S

**Memorial University of Newfoundland**
**Curriculum Materials Centre**
**Centre for Instructional Services**
G. A. Hickman Building
St. John's, Newfoundland
Canada A1B 3X8
phone: 709-737-7465
fax: 709 737 2345
contact: Alison Mews, Librarian
e-mail: amews@kean.ucs.mun.ca

The Children's Literature Collection, begun in 1968, is primarily a contemporary collection of English-language children's literature, although it does contain some earlier imprints. Emphasis is placed on critical and bibliographic works about children's literature, as well as collections of poetry, fairy tales, legends, and nursery rhymes. Particular attention is given to quality Canadian children's books, which make up nearly 20 percent of the 24,500-volume collection.

## Ontario

### GUELPH

**University of Guelph**
**McLaughlin Library**
**Archival and Special Collections**
Guelph, Ontario
Canada N1G 2W1
phone: 519-824-4120
fax: 519-824-6931
contact: Nancy Sadek, Section Head,
    Archival and Special Collections
Internet: searchme.uoguelph.ca

The Special Collections Department of the University of Guelph has diverse holdings of materials related to children's literature. They have an extensive collection of Canadian juvenile literature, an apiculture collection that includes books about bees written for children, and the largest collection of Scottish books outside Scotland that includes many children's writers.

The L. M. Montgomery Collection consists of 300 published volumes, dating from 1850 to 1988, as well as journals, scrapbooks, personal papers, and artifacts of the Canadian author. All About Us/Nous Autres is a collection of Canadiana and international children's art and creative writing. It is the archive of a cultural foundation established to encourage the creative abilities of young people ages six through eighteen and includes over 5,000 works of art and 100,000 pieces of creative writing.

## KINGSTON

**Queen's University**
**Douglas Library**
**Special Collections**
Kingston, Ontario
Canada K7L 5C4
phone: 613-545-2528
fax: 613-545-6819
contact: Pamela Thayer, Head of Special
   Collections
Internet: telnet to 130.15.125.20 or
   qline.queensu.ca

The Children's Collection of 2,500 non-Canadian children's books is held in Special Collections. Items in this collection, primarily British imprints, illustrate the genre up to the beginning of the twentieth century and include works that represent the history of publishing, binding, and illustration in children's literature.

## OTTAWA

**National Library of Canada**
395 Wellington St.
Room 468C
Ottawa, Ontario
Canada K1A ON4
phone: 613-996-2300
fax: 613-952-2895
contact: Mary Collis, Children's
   Literature Librarian

e-mail: envoy: 00NL.CLS
Internet: cls@psb.nlc-bnc.ca

The Children's Literature Service of the National Library maintains a separate collection of 44,000 books suitable for children and young adults. Included are books in English, French, and other languages which are published in Canada, books written or illustrated by Canadians, and books about Canada which are published abroad. Books in the collection date from the nineteenth century to the present day and are acquired through legal deposit, purchase, and donation. Also held are original manuscripts and illustrations for 15 authors and illustrators.

## TORONTO

**The Canadian Children's Book Centre**
35 Spadina Rd.
Toronto, Ontario
Canada M5R 2S9
phone: 416-975-0010
fax: 416-975-1839
contact: Nancy Pearson, Administrative
   Director

The center houses a collection of approximately 7,000 English-language children's books, written and/or illustrated by Canadians from 1976 to the present. Included are folk and fairy tales, picture books, fiction, and nonfiction, as well as some rare and out-of-print titles.

**Toronto Public Library**
**Boys and Girls House**
40 St. George St.
Toronto, Ontario
Canada M5S 2E4
phone: 416-393-7753
fax: 416-393-7635
contact: Jill Shefrin, Exhibitions and
   Publications Librarian

The Osborne Collection of Early Children's Books encompasses the development of English children's literature, ranging from a fourteenth-century manuscript of Aesop's fables, through fifteenth-century school texts and courtesy books, godly Puritan works, eighteenth-century chapbooks, moral tales and rational recreations, Victorian classics of fantasy, adventure and school stories, up to 1910—the end of the Edwardian era.

The Lillian H. Smith Collection was established in 1962 to mark the fiftieth anniversary of the inauguration of children's libraries in Toronto by this distinguished pioneer. It comprises creative books published in English since 1910, including picture books, fairy tales, fiction, and poetry, selected on the basis of literary and artistic merit.

The Canadiana Collection is a representative selection of nineteenth- and twentieth-century children's books in English related to Canada, and whose writers, illustrators, and publishers are associated with this country. Important holdings include the manuscript for the first Canadian picture book, *An Illustrated Comic Alphabet* (1859), archives of current Canadian authors and a selection of popular materials and small-press publications.

# Colombia

## BARRANQUILLA

**Comfamiliar del Atlantico**
Calle 48 Carrera 44
Esquina Piso 2
Barranquilla, Colombia
phone: 510722
fax: 958-419961
contact: Carmen Alvarado de Escorcia, Director

Centro Documentacion en Literatura Infantil y Lectura contains 3,000 volumes of children's literature from throughout the world, with an emphasis on Latin American authors. The majority of the works are in Spanish, but some English and Portuguese works are included.

# Cyprus

## NICOSIA

**MAM Publishers**
**The House of the Cyprus and Cypriological Publications**
P.O. Box 1722
Nicosia, Cyprus
phone: 00357-2-465411
contact: M. A. Michaelides

This publisher specializes in Cypriot publications and holds copies of all of the children's books published in Cyprus.

# Czeck Republic

## PRAGUE

**City Library**
Marianske nam. 1,
115 72 Prague 1, Czech Republic
phone: 266 585
fax: 232 82 30
contact: Marcela Machackova, Librarian

The City Library holds 18,000 volumes of children's literature, most published after World War II, written in Czech. Also included are secondary sources about the literature.

**Comenius Library of Education**
Mikulandska 5
116 74 Prague 1, Czech Republic
phone: 29 10 84
contact: Jurai Daubner

Included in the Suk Library of Children's Literature are 49,500 volumes of Czech and Slovak literature dating from 1800. Also held are magazines for children and theoretical studies.

**Pamatnik Narodniho Pisemnictvi**
**(Museum of Czech Literature)**
Strahovske Nadvori c.1

118 38 Prague 1, Hradcany, Czech
   Republic
phone: 538841-7
contact: Dr. Ruzena Hamanova, Deputy
   Director

The Museum of Czech Literature is a specialized institution, whose goal is to collect
all items that document the development of
Czech literature from the nineteenth and
twentieth centuries. While it does not have
a special children's collection, works of children's literature can be found in the three
specialized departments—The Literary Archive, The Study Library, and the Art Collection. The archives have collections of
more than 70 authors who write for children, and the Art Collection has some
8,000 pieces of art created by fifty-five artists whose work is devoted to children's literature. An accurate count is not available
of the numerous children's books held by
the Study Library.

## Czechoslovakia *see* Czeck Republic and Slovakia

## Denmark

### COPENHAGEN

**Danmarks Paedagogiske Bibliotek**
**(National Library of Education)**
Postbox 840
Emdrupvej 101
DK 2400 Copenhagen NV, Denmark
phone: (+45) 39 69 66 33
fax: (+45) 39 66 00 82
contact: Leif Lorring, Head of Library
Internet: bib.dlh.dk (130.225.172.3)
   Login: dpbasen

The National Library of Education's collection includes 76,000 volumes dating
from 1730 to the present time.

## Egypt

### CAIRO

**Documentation and Research Center for**
   **Children's Literature**
15 El-Manial St.
Roda, Cairo, Egypt
phone: 0020-3640312
contact: Mrs. Zeinab El Fawanissy,
   Director

The Documentation and Research Centre
at the General Egyptian Book Organization provides reference and bibliographic
assistance to those interested in the media
world of the child. The center's users are
children's book authors and illustrators,
publishers, librarians, and scholars. The
7,000-volume reference collection is
complemented by an annual book list published by the center, as well as by bibliographies, guides, and catalogs.

## England

### BIRMINGHAM

**Birmingham Library Services**
**Central Library**
Chamberlain Square
Birmingham B3 3HQ, England
phone: 021-235-4227
contact: Librarian, Parker Collection

The Parker Collection of Children's Books
is predominantly books, numbering nearly
12,000 titles, both fiction and nonfiction,
dating from 1538 to the present day. This
is a constantly growing collection with
strengths in illustrated and movable books.
A complement to the books are a collection of 105 nineteenth-century games,
many of them board games and jigsaw
puzzles.

## BRIGHTON

**University of Sussex**
**Education Library**
Education Development Building
Brighton BN1 9RG, England
phone: 0273-678259
contact: Jackie Edgell, Education
 Librarian
e-mail: l.j.nicholls@sussex.ac.uk
Internet: available through NISS gateway

Holdings of the Education Library include children's fiction, poetry, short stories, and picture books for young children. All are in English, most by British authors. They form part of the library's Classroom Materials Collection, which is for use in school by teachers in training.

## DEVON

**Devon Library Service**
Barley House
Isleworth Rd.
Exeter, Devon EX4 1RQ England
phone: 0392-384302
fax: 0392-384316
contact: Kati Vamos, Assistant Lending
 and Special Services

The Early Children's Book Collection consists of approximately 2,300 items, published from 1690 to 1950, including general fiction and nonfiction, chapbooks, movable books, and educational games.

## LEICESTER

**Leicester University Education Library**
21 University Rd.
Leicester LE1 7RF England
phone: 0533523735
fax: 0533523653
contact: R. W. Kirk, Librarian in Charge
e-mail: edlib@uk.ac.leicester

The Winifred Higson Collection consists of 2,600 books and periodicals of children's literature published from 1700 to 1920. Also included are 600 volumes published from 1930 to the present and 500 volumes of criticism and bibliographies about children's literature.

## LONDON

**Bethnal Green Museum of Childhood**
Cambridge Heath Rd.
London E2 9PA England
phone: 081 980 3204/4315 or 081 981
 6789/1711
fax: 081 980 4759
contact: Tessa Chester, Curator of
 Children's Books

The most important collection of children's books held by the Museum is the Renier Collection of Children's Books, built up by Anne and Fernand Renier and given to the Victoria and Albert Museum (of which this Museum is a branch) in 1970. It consists of over 80,000 books, toys, games, and related background materials collected for their value as documents of social history.

Most subject areas are covered, from all periods from 1585 to 1988, including educational material and printed ephemera, such as painting books. All formats are represented, from the chapbook and toy book to comics, movables and annuals. There is a substantial amount of foreign language material and variant editions are a particular strength. The Renier Collection is supported by the Book Trust Collection, which consists of nearly every book published for children in the United Kingdom and dates from 1982, at present numbering around 20,000, with some 3,000 books added annually.

Occasional lists featuring different areas of the Renier Collection are produced regularly. An exhibit catalog, *Trash or Treasure*, was published in 1992. There is no access to any of the above collections at present, although this could change at any time depending on resources becoming available. Please contact the curator for details of the current situation.

**Book Trust**
Book House
45 East Hill Rd.
London SW18 2Q2 England
phone: 081 870 9055
fax: 081 874 4790
contact: Ann Sohn-Rethel, Librarian

The Young Book Trust Children's Library houses a collection of all children's books, excluding educational materials, published in the United Kingdom during the last two years. In addition, there is a cuttings library on current issues in children's literature, periodicals, and reference books. The collection currently numbers 10,000 volumes.

**British Library**
Humanities and Social Sciences
Great Russell St.
London WC1B 3DG England
phone: 071-323 7676
fax: 071-323 7557
contact: Alison Bailey or Morna Daniels, Curators

Although this is a national legal deposit library, the acquisition of children's books was unsystematic until the 1950s. Special collections include the Henry Mayor Lyon collection of chapbooks; nineteenth-century bloods and penny dreadfuls collected by Barry Ono; a collection of chapbooks printed by William and Cluer Dicey; and an uncataloged collection of comics and strip cartoons. Access to these collections is by photographic pass.

**Evangelical Library**
78A Chiltern St.
London W1M 2HB England
phone: 935-6997
contact: Mr. S. J. Taylor, Librarian

The Junior Section of the Evangelical Library contains Christian literature for children in English from the nineteenth and twentieth centuries.

**Holborn Library**
32-38 Theobalds Rd.
London WC1X 8PA England
phone: 071 413 6342
contact: Richard Knight, Local Studies Manager

The Eleanor Farjeon Collection is a grouping of 160 volumes collected by Farjeon and presented by her to the former Hampstead Public Libraries in 1960. The volumes consist of books and music by the author, as well as her collaborative efforts.

**London Borough of Camden**
**Keats House**
Keats Grove
Hampstead, London NW3 2RR England
phone: 071 794 6829
fax: 071 431 9293
contact: Christina M. Gee, Curator

The Kate Greenaway Collection was presented by her brother John to the people of Hampstead. It is perhaps the largest collection of her original pencil sketches and drawings, and scores of her proofs, with holographic notes and text. Currently numbering 1,200 volumes dating from 1870 to date, the collection has an almost complete set of first editions of her books and many of her greeting cards.

**National Art Library**
**Victoria and Albert Museum**
London SW7 2RL England
phone: 071 938 8315
fax: 071 938 8461
contact: Anne Hobbs

The National Art Library has collected children's books from the mid-nineteenth century and now holds a major collection of approximately 6,500 children's books dating from the sixteenth century to the present day. The collection is particularly rich in late eighteenth- and early nineteenth-century British and North West European imprints and illustrated children's books, with a fine collection of Russian (mainly Soviet) material. Included is source material in publishing history, social history, and the art of the book.

Apart from its own acquisitions, the library also holds the following collections: The Guy Little Bequest consisting of 2,400 children's books; the Queen Mary Gift of 100 books formerly belonging to members of the royal family; the Horton Collection of Soviet Children's Books acquired in 1981; and the Harrod Bequest, which includes many children's books by artists of the 1860s.

In addition, the National Library holds several major collections of materials relating to Beatrix Potter: the Linder Bequest, which includes a large selection of drawings, manuscripts, and early editions, with photographs by Rupert Potter and related memorabilia; the Linder Archive of Leslie Linder's letters and other working papers; the Linder Collection of 280 drawings and forty early editions; and the Peter Rabbit picture letter sent to Noel Moore on September 4, 1893, telling for the first time the story of Peter Rabbit. All collections are now housed at the Archive of Art and Design, 23 Blythe Rd., Olympia, London W14 0QF. Appointments may be made with the Frederick Warne Curator of Children's Literature at 071-602-0281, ext. 212. Three days' notice is normally required.

**Poetry Library**
Royal Festival Hall
South Bank Centre
London SE1 8XX England
phone: 071-921-0664
contact: Jacalyn Leedham, Assistant
  Librarian

The Children's Collection consists of poetry books, tapes, and video recordings for children and young people and their parents. The more than 4,000 books are of poetry in English or translated into English and published in the United Kingdom and Ireland. The Teacher's Collection consists of books and materials about and for teaching poetry for ages nursery school through A-level (ages three to eighteen).

**The Polish Library**
238-246 King St.
London W6 0RF England
phone: 081-741 0474
contact: Dr. Z. Jagodrinski, Librarian

This library's holdings include 200 volumes, mostly postwar publications, although some by prewar authors. Books are represented in their bibliography if published outside Poland since 1939, in Polish or by Polish authors and illustrators in other languages.

**Society for Cooperation in Russian and**
  **Soviet Studies**
320 Brixton Rd.
London SW9 6AB England
phone: 071 274 2282
fax: 071 489 0391
contact: Jane Rosen

The Children's Library is a collection of approximately 2,000 volumes of children's books from Russia and the republics of the former Soviet Union. It consists of a full range of materials from ABC books, children's poetry, and folklore to teenage fiction and nonfiction. Included are materials from the pre-revolutionary period to the present in Russian, English translations, and many other languages of the former Soviet Union.

**Society for Promoting Christian**
  **Knowledge (SPCK)**
**Holy Trinity Church**
Marylebone Road
London NW1 4DU England
phone: 071 387 5282
fax: 071 388 2352

contact: Rev. Dr. Gordon Wuelin,
Archivist and Librarian

The collection of eighteenth- and early
nineteenth-century tracts and nineteenth-
and early twentieth-century story books at
the society's headquarters is quite unique,
with many of the volumes still in their
original dust jackets. Holdings are limited
to publications of the society.

**Wandsworth Public Libraries**
**West Hill Library**
West Hill
London SW18 1RZ England
phone: 081 871 6365
contact: Chris Mason, Head of Special
Services

The Wandsworth Collection of Early Children's Books is a representative collection
of 4,500 English children's books, published from 1673 to 1950. Included are
fiction, nonfiction and chapbooks.

## LOUGHBOROUGH

**Loughborough University**
**Department of Information and Library**
**Studies**
Loughborough LE11 3TU England
phone: 0509-223062
fax: 0509-223053
contact: Professor M. Evans

The Mary Ward Collection consists of approximately 6,000 volumes, representative of the eighteenth through twentieth
centuries in children's literature.

## MANCHESTER

**Language and Literature Library**
**Central Library**
St. Peter's Square
Manchester M2 5PD England
phone: 061-234-1972
fax: 061-234-1963

The Early Children's Books Collection at
the Central Library consists of more than
1,000 chapbooks, literary tracts, classic
novels, twentieth-century standards, and
books with the initial teaching alphabet.

**University of Manchester**
**John Rylands University Library**
Oxford Rd.
Manchester M13 9PP England
fax: 061-273 7488
contact: Brenda Scragg

The Rylands Library houses several special collections important to children's literature. The Allison Uttley Collection contains copies of her own works, as well as
presentation copies of other contemporary children's writers and illustrators such
as Arthur Rackham and Edmund Dulac
from 1900 to 1960. The books are supported by a selection of manuscripts, letters, and diaries. The Elfrida Vipont Collection contains books written by Vipont
as well as extensive manuscripts, typescripts, and letters. Materials of Jack Cox,
last editor of the *Boy's Own Paper*, comprise all of his working papers as editor,
as well as a virtually complete run of the
periodical.

## NORTH YORKSHIRE

**Harrogate Library**
**North Yorkshire County Library**
Victoria Ave.
Harrogate
North Yorkshire HG1 1EG England
phone: 0423-502744
fax: 0423-523158
contact: M. Schofield, Special Services
Librarian

The Harrogate Early Children's Books
Collection of 2,500 volumes consists
mainly of English children's books of the
Victorian era, with particular emphasis on
illustrated books which exemplify nineteenth century developments in color

printing. Some late chapbooks are included together with toy books, annuals, school books, and prizes.

## NOTTINGHAM

**University of Nottingham**
**Hallward Library**
**Department of Manuscripts and Special**
   **Collections**
University Park
Nottingham NG7 2RD England
phone: 0602-514565
fax: 0602-514558
contact: Dr. D. B. Johnston, Keeper of
   Manuscripts & Special Collections
e-mail: mss-library@ Nottingham.ac.uk

The Briggs Collection of Educational Literature was established in 1950 as a gift from W. G. Briggs. At that time, the collection numbered some 200 items, dating from the sixteenth to the early nineteenth century, described as "books of instruction for children." The collection now contains more than 1,700 items published prior to 1850. The strength of the collection lies in the eighteenth- and nineteenth-century pedagogic texts, largely in English. Included are fifty copy books of pupils on various subjects and some related manuscripts.

## OXFORD

**University of Oxford**
**Bodleian Library**
Broad St.
Oxford OX1 3BG England
phone: 0865-277000
fax: 0865-277182
contact: Clive Hurst, Head of Special
   Collections
e-mail:
   clive.hurst@bodleian-library.ox.ac.uk

The Bodleian Library is a 400-year-old institution entitled to a copy of all British publications, and as such, holds a great many children's titles. In addition, they

hold the Opie Collection, consisting of approximately 20,000 English children's books in all subjects from the mid-eighteenth century to the present. The greatest strength is the large number of eighteenth- and early nineteenth-century books. There is a small but significant collection of French, German, and Russian children's books as well. The Opie Collection is being microfilmed by UMI, and microfiche sets are available complete with cataloging data. Descriptions of the Opie Collection can be found in Iona and Peter Opie's *Three Centuries of Nursery Rhymes and Poetry for Children* and *Treasures of Childhood* by Iona and Robert Opie and Brian Alderson.

## READING

**University of Reading**
**The Library**
Whiteknights
P.O. Box 223
Reading, Berks RG6 2AE England
phone: 0734-318773
fax: 0734-312335
contact: David Knott, Rare Book
   Librarian
e-mail: library@reading.ac.uk
Internet: NRS address: 00005010002350
   (this may be difficult to access)

The Children's Collection originated in the 1950s in a gift of early nineteenth-century children's books from Sir Frank and Lady Stenton. The collection currently comprises over 6,000 volumes, including runs of periodicals, embracing children's literature primarily up to 1940. Predominantly comprising English titles of the nineteenth century, it includes some 900 pre-1851 titles. Strength lies in school stories and editions of *Robinson Crusoe*. A printed guide, *The Catalogue of the Collection of Children's Books, 1617–1939*, in the library of the University of Reading, is available.

## WAKEFIELD

**Yorkshire and Humberside Joint Library
  Service**
**Library Headquarters, Balne Lane**
Wakefield WF2 0DQ England
phone: (0924) 371231
fax: (0924) 379287
contact: Simon Rice, Honorable
  Secretary

The collection at the Yorkshire and Humberside Joint Library Service (YHJLS) numbers some 20,000 volumes dating from 1930. Included in their holdings are the former WRCL junior fiction reserve and the contents of the bookshop operated by the Yorkshire Purchasing Organization.

## WEST MALLING

**Kent Arts and Libraries**
West Malling Air Station
West Malling, Kent ME19 6QG England
phone: 0622-605213
fax: 0622-605221
contact: Sheila Golden, Stock and
  Promotions Officer

The Marcus Crouch Collection consists of approximately 1,500 children's books published in the United Kingdom from 1830 to 1930. Titles included are mainly English fiction.

# Finland

## ABO

**Abo Akademi University**
**Library**
Domkyrkogatan 2-4
FIN-20500 Abo, Finland
phone: (21) 654183
contact: Marita Rajalin, Deputy
  Librarian
e-mail: mrajalin abo.fi

Gifts from private donors are the core of the collection of 7,000 children's books, mainly from 1700 to 1900, reflecting the reading habits and tastes of Swedish-speaking Finland over a period of 200 years. The books are mainly in Swedish, French, English, German, and Russian. As a national depository library, they receive all children's books printed and published in Finland. The Tove Jansson collection consists of original manuscripts, illustrations, and fan mail and is housed in the department of manuscripts.

## TAMPERE

**Suomen Nuorisokirjallisuuden Instituutti
  (SNI)**
**(Finnish Institute for Children's
  Literature)**
Puutarhakatu 2 D-E
33100 Tampere, Finland
phone: 931-2121 923
fax: 931-2122 178
contact: Paivi Nordling, Librarian

The Finnish Institute for Children's Literature is a documentation, information, and research center, founded in 1978. The institute's main goal is to collect all children's books published in Finland, both original and in translation. The collection consists of nearly 30,000 volumes of children's books and some 2,000 reference books. The institute owns a special collection of ABC books, Estonian children's books, and books donated by Tove Jansson.

# France

## BORDEAUX

**Association Nous Voulons Lire**
**CRALEJ**
**Centre Regional Aquitain du Livre**
**Bibliothèque de Bordeaux**

85 Cours du Marechal Juin
33 075 Bordeaux Cedex, France
phone: 56 99 20 60
fax: 56 99 20 60
contact: Denise Dupont, Escarpit

Holdings of the CRALEJ Collection include 22,000 French children's books which have been sent by publishers to the journal *Nous Voulons Lire* since 1972, as well as books given by libraries and private donors. In addition, holdings include 3,000 books in English, Spanish, Chinese, Japanese, Indian, and other foreign languages. A collection of 900 reference works is representative of many countries.

## NANTES

Centre d'Études Verniennes
Bibliothèque Médiathèque
3 Rue de l'Héronnière
44041 Nantes Cedex 01, France
phone: 40.41.95.95
fax: 40.41.91.33
contact: Mme. Sainlot, Librarian

Created in 1969, the center is dedicated to the study of Jules Verne and his works. They hold first editions published by J. Hetzel, manuscripts, correspondence, translations in other languages, and a variety of other objects and documents.

## NIVELLES

Bibliothèque Publique Centrale de la
    Communauté Française
Place Albert ler, I
1400 Nivelles, France
phone: 067/21 95 91
fax: 067/21 35 03
contact: Jean-Luc Capeue, Chief Youth
    Section

Within this library's holdings are 35,000 volumes of children's literature.

## PARIS

Centre National du Livre Pour Enfants
La Joie par les Livres
8 rue Saint-Bon
75004 Paris, France
phone: (1) 48.87.61.95
fax: (1) 48.87.08.52
contact: Caroline Rives

This collection consists of 75,000 children's books dating from 1965. Included are books and periodicals, both in French and other languages, as well as books about children's literature and children's libraries. In addition, they have a significant collection of folktale anthologies. They receive one copy of each children's book deposited at the Bibliothèque Nationale.

Fonds Historique de Litterature Jeunesse
Bibliothèque de l'Heure Joyeuse
6 Rue des Prêtres-Saint-Severin
75005 Paris, France
phone: 43 25 83 24
fax: 43 54 58 63
contact: Françoise Leveque

L'Heure Joyeuse is the first children's library, opened in France in 1924, and offered by the American Book Committee on Children's Libraries, "in honor of the children's courage during the first world war . . . ." It now operates as a branch of the Paris public library system. The historical collection houses the library's archives and 30,000 old and rare books for children, from the eighteenth century to the present, of French and foreign-language children's literature.

# Germany

## BERLIN

Staatsbibliothek zu Berlin in der Stiftung
  Prebischer Kulturbesitz
(Berlin State Library - Prussian Cultural
  Foundation)
Haus 1
Unter den Linden 8
10102 Berlin, Germany
phone: (030) 20151404
fax: (030) 20151665
contact: Carola Pohlmann

The Children's Book Collection was established in 1951 with the objectives being to build a collection of rare, unusual, or stylistically unique examples of children's books and a collection of corresponding periodicals and journals for the purpose of research. Included in their holdings of more than 125,000 titles are 40,000 German-language children's books published since 1945, 48,000 published before 1945, and 6,000 published before 1861. An additional 30,000 children's books are in foreign languages, and eighty current children's magazine titles are held. Over 7,000 books about children's literature are complemented by forty current periodicals. A collection of more than 4,000 original illustrations by sixty-four artists is also held.

## FRANKFURT

Heinrich Hoffmann Museum
Schubertstrasse 20
D-60325 Frankfurt am Main, Germany
phone: 069/74 79 69
contact: Beate Zekorn, Director

This collection of 900 volumes consists mainly of editions of *Der Struwwelpeter*, including translations, imitations, and parodies in a variety of formats. Other children's titles by Hoffmann are also included. Volumes date from 1847 and are mostly in German, although there are a large number of English translations and *Struwwelpeter* imitators.

Institut fur Jugendbuchforschung
Johann Wolfgang Goethe University
Myliusstrasse 30
6000 Frankfurt am Main 1, Germany
phone: (069) 798-3564
fax: national, (069) 798-2398;
    international:+49/69/798 2398
e-mail: dolle-weinkauff at
    rz.uni-frankfurt.dbp.de

This collection consists of approximately 100,000 volumes, dating from the early 1600s to the present. They hold original manuscripts and illustrations of approximately twenty authors and illustrators. Nearly 78,000 of the volumes are German children's books, and 20,000 volumes of German comic books are held.

## MAINZ

Gutenberg Museum
Liebfrauenplatz 5
D-55116 Mainz, Germany
phone: 06131/122460
fax: 06131/123488
contact: Dr. Cornelia Schneider,
    Custodian

The Gutenberg Museum holdings include a collection of 600 children's books dating from 1850.

## MUNICH

Internationale Jugendbibliothek
  München
(International Youth Library)
Schloss Blutenburg
D-81247 Munich, Germany
phone: +49-89-811-2028
fax: +49-89-811-7553
contact: Dr. Andreas Bode, Library
    Director, or Dr. Barbara Scharioth,
    Executive Director

The International Youth Library holds about 455,000 books (including 60,000 from 1587 to 1950) in more than 100 languages. More than 1,000 publishers from around the world send approximately 10,000 items to the library each year. The reference library offers access to 23,000 volumes of professional literature, including twenty national bibliographies and about 300 subscriptions to professional periodicals. The documentation section consists of 40,000 published and unpublished articles and reports; newspaper clippings on nearly 4,200 children's book authors and 1,350 illustrators; grey literature; and special collections of posters, calendars, manuscripts, autograms, original illustrations, and children's artwork. Three-month research fellowships may be made available upon application. Bibliographic catalogs and literature guides are published regularly in German and English.

# Greece

## ATHENS

**Center for Children's and Adolescents' Books**
56, Hermou St.
105 63 Athens, Greece
phone: 3230 196
fax: 3246 010
contact: Mrs. Elga
   Cavadias-Hatzopoulos

The center holds approximately 18,000 volumes of children's literature from throughout the world. Also included is a collection of old Greek school reading books, as well as children's magazines and newspapers since 1800.

# Hungary

## BUDAPEST

**Orszagos Pedagogiai Konyvtar es
   Muzeum
(National Educational Library and
   Museum)**
Budapest
Honved u. 19, H-1055 Hungary
phone: 112-6862
fax: 112-6862
contact: Zsuzsanna Celler
e-mail: h6049hor@ella.hu

The Gyermek es ifjusagi kulongyujtemeriye (Special Collection for Children's and Youth Literature) consists of 52,000 children's books published in Hungary and abroad. While some of their holdings date back more than 100 years, the majority of titles were published since 1968. Included are historical works of youth literature, theoretical works, bibliographies, and the reviewing of children's and youth literature.

# Iran

## TEHRAN

**The Children's Book Council of Iran**
Engelab Ave Nazari St. no. 69
2nd floor
P.O. Box 13145-133
Tehran, Iran 13156
phone: +9821 640874
fax: +9821 632360
contact: Ms. N. Emad Khorassani

The Children's Research Library Collection contains 14,000 children's books and magazines published in Persian, dating from 1906, but primarily since the 1950s. Also included are documents on children's literature and a large collection of Persian posters.

# Ireland

## DUBLIN

**National Library of Ireland**
Kildare St.
Dublin 2, Ireland
phone: 353 1 6618811
fax: 353 1 6766690

The National Library aims to acquire all editions of children's books by Irish authors, written in Irish or English; all books published in Ireland; or those children's books published abroad which have an Irish theme. The library holds a good collection of early nineteenth-century chapbooks printed in Dublin, mainly evangelical and moralistic in tone. They also hold a good collection of original manuscripts and illustrations.

**Trinity College Library**
**Department of Early Printed Books**
College St.
Dublin 2, Ireland
phone: 353 1 677-2941
fax: 353 1 671-9003
contact: Charles Benson, Keeper of Early
   Printed Books
e-mail: epbooks@lib1.tcd.ie
Internet: library.tcd.ie

The Pollard School-Book Collection consists of 577 volumes, mostly eighteenth and nineteenth century. The works concentrate on Irish publications, especially those published by the Commissioners of National Education from the 1830s onwards, which were widely used in Great Britain and its colonies.

# Israel

## DOAR BEIT BERL

**The Yemima Center for Study and**
   **Teaching of Children's Literature**
**Beit Berl College**

Doar Beit Berl 44905, Israel
phone: 09-906400, 09-906401
fax: 09-454104
contact: Dr. Shlomo Har'el

Holdings of the Yemima Center consist of 15,000 volumes, including rare and ancient books, textbooks, anthologies, and the complete works of Y. Avidar-Tchernovitz, U. Offek, A. Amir, and Devorah Omer. Also included are children's literature stamps from around the world, bookmarkers, miniatures of children's book figures, subject files, and children's magazines from throughout the world.

## JERUSALEM

**Israel Museum**
**Youth Wing Library**
Jerusalem 91710
p.o.b. 71117, Israel
phone: 708952/708835
fax: 02-631833
contact: Tina Litinetsky, Miri Lawfer

The Ben-Yitzhak Collection of Illustrated Children's Books contains nearly 7,200 volumes from throughout the world. Of these, 2,900 are in Hebrew, with 4,200 in a variety of other languages. Two hundred original book illustrations created by sixty artists are also held. The purpose of the collection is to promote high-quality illustrations in children's books. To this end, the collection presents the biennial Ben-Yitzhak Award.

## TEL-AVIV

**Levin Kipnis Center for Children's**
   **Literature**
P.O. Box 48130
61480 Tel-Aviv, Israel
phone +972-3-6902456
fax: +972-3-6993546
contacts: in Hebrew: Mrs. Ziona Kipnis,
   organizer; in other languages, Ms.
   Basmat Even-Zohar, Liaison Officer

*Mother Goose in Silhouettes*, cut by Katharine G. Buffum; Boston: Houghton Mifflin, 1907.

The Levin Kipnis Center for Children's Literature is also the Israeli section of IBBY. It serves as a research center and archive, holding exhibitions, lecture-workshops, and conferences. They also publish a periodical of studies in children's literature. Holdings of the center include a collection of 150 Hebrew readers dating from 1789 to 1994 and a small collection of rare Hebrew children's books from the beginning of the century. An archive of the original materials created by twenty-five prominent Hebrew writers includes manuscripts in Hebrew, drafts, correspondence, and reviews.

### UPPER GALILEE

**Tel-Hai Regional College Library**
Upper Galilee 12210, Israel
phone: 972-6-943731
fax: 972-6-950697
contact: Ruth Gefen-Dotan, Director

The "Books Are Our Friends" collection includes classic children's literature, both in the original Hebrew and in translation from English, French, Russian, Italian, etc. Both preschool and school-age levels are represented. Also included are sixty bound volumes of children's weekly newspapers from 1935 to 1962. These newspapers were instrumental in educating two generations of Israeli children. An extensive collection of didactic materials is included as well, for use by kindergarten and elementary schoolteachers.

## Italy

### GENOVA

**Biblioteca Internazionale per la Gioventu' "E. De Amicus"**
Via Archimede, 44
16142 Genova, Italy
phone: 010/50.91.81
fax: 010/56.67.17
contact: Mr. Francesco Langella, Director

This collection of 31,000 volumes is for use by children, consisting of a full range of children's literature, as well as pedagogical works.

### TRIESTE

**Biblioteca Civica "A. Hortis"**
Piazza Hortis, 4
34123 Trieste, Italy
phone: 0039/40/301214
fax: 0039/40/301108

contact: d.ssa Carmela Apuzza,
  Responsabile Sezione Ragazzi

Although the library was founded in 1793, the children's section is quite recent. Holdings include approximately 2,000 works dating from the 1970s to the present. In addition to children's literature, they have a pedagogical collection as well.

# Japan

### NAGANO

**Little Museum in a Village of Picture Books**
989-5 Osachi
Okaya-shi
Nagano 394, Japan
phone: 0266-28-9877
fax: 0266-28-9866
contact: Shino Sasaki

This museum was established by Japanese author/illustrator, Wakiko Sato, in 1990. Holdings include 1,200 volumes of Japanese and foreign picture books, as well as nearly 250 original illustrations representing twenty-five contemporary Japanese illustrators.

### OSAKA

**International Institute for Children's Literature**
10-6 Bampaku-Koen
Senri Suita-shi
Osaka 565, Japan
phone: 06-876-8800
fax: 06-876-8686
contact: Masafumi Nakagawa, Director

The institute's holdings consist of several special collections. Included are the Torigoe Collection, consisting of 120,000 items published during the Meiji and Taisho eras, as well as in the prewar days in Japan (nineteenth–twentieth centuries), and the Hirokuni Nanbu Collection, which holds 15,000 volumes of nine-

teenth- and twentieth-century Japanese works. Japanese works are also included in the Teru Yokotani Collection, while the Shizuko Kitabatake Collection holds Russian children's literature and the Toru Shinmura Collection has Chinese children's books.

In addition to these collections, the institute contains books and other materials donated by authors, illustrators, scholars, and publishers, or purchased by the institute. This is the first institute in Japan devoted to the study of children's literature. Their hope is to provide a comprehensive collection of materials pertaining to children's literature not only for Japanese, but for foreign researchers as well. Thus, while one important task is to collect as many children's books as possible which have been published in Japan, the institute is also expanding its collection of foreign children's literature.

### TOKYO

**Chihiro Iwasaki Art Museum of Picture Books**
4-7-2, Shimonoshakujii
Nerima-ku
Tokyo 177, Japan
phone: 81 3 3995 0772
fax: 81 3 3995 0680

This museum houses most of the original artwork of artist Chihiro Iwasaki. Built in 1977 on the site of the artist's home, the museum contains the original illustrations and other materials related to her picture books and is dedicated to preserving and exhibiting these works. In addition, the museum has begun to collect the original artwork of other outstanding picture book artists from both Japan and abroad. The collection, now numbering 740 pieces from 10 countries, focuses on works created after World War II and will continue to grow to form an overview of the world of art for children. The twentieth anniversary of the museum will be celebrated in

1997 with the opening of their new museum in Nagano Prefecture.

**National Diet Library**
1-10-1 Nagata-cho
Chiyoda-ku
Tokyo 100, Japan
phone: 3-3581-2331
fax: 3-3597-9104
contact: Mieko Hirano, Chief,
    International Cooperation Division

The National Diet Library inherited the children's book collection of the Imperial Library, which was the predecessor of NDL and a prewar deposit library. Adding to the children's books acquired by the Imperial Library, the NDL has collected a wide range of children's books through the legal deposit system. The collection currently contains 83,000 volumes dating from 1868, mostly in Japanese.

**Shirayuri Women's College Library**
1-25 Midorigaoka
Chofu-shi
Tokyo 182, Japan
phone: 03-3326-5050
fax: 03-3326-4550
contact: Emiko Inoue, Research
    Assistant of the Centre for Children's
    Literature and Culture

The Japanese Picture Book Collection contains twenty-seven Japanese fairy tale books with traditional-style illustrations. The books were published in Japan during the Edo period.

**Suginami Ward Central Library**
3-40-23 Ogikubo
Suginami-ku
Tokyo 167, Japan
phone: 03-3391-5754
fax: 03-3391-7803
contact: Hiroshi Tsukahara

The Japanese Children's Science Book Center was founded by the Japanese Society for Children's Science Books (JSCSB)

in 1979 and transferred to the Suginami Ward Central Library in 1982. The collection consists of 6,000 volumes of Japanese science books for children published from 1927 to date.

**Tokyo Kodomo Toshokan
(Tokyo Children's Library)**
1-9-1-311 Toyotamakita
Nerima-ku
Tokyo 176, Japan
phone: 03-3948-4516
fax: 03-3948-5813
contact: Keiko Harikae, Staff Librarian

The Tokyo Children's Library is a privately run library made up of two "bunko" (home libraries), a lending library for children, and a research library for those who work with children and books. Started in 1974, the research library now has 10,000 volumes of children's books and research materials in English and several other languages. Two special collections have also been added. One is of books that have been awarded children's book prizes in Japan since 1947. Based on this collection, three volumes of Japanese children's book award-winners have been published. The other collection is of folktales both domestic and from abroad which serve as source material for storytellers.

# Kenya

## NAIROBI

**Kenya Children's Book Project**
P.O. Box 38881
Nairobi, Kenya
phone: 747444
fax: 743471
contact: Gachungi Mungau, Project
    Coordinator

The Kenya Children's Book Project (KCBP) was started in 1993 with support from CODE, an agency which supports similar projects in over sixteen countries in the developing world. CODE's mission is to improve literacy through the provision of books and human resource capacity building, and to create a sustainable reading culture among communities. The KCBP currently has 1,200 volumes dating from 1960 to 1993.

# Lebanon

## BEIRUT

**Beirut University College**
Rue Mme. Curie
P.O. Box 13-5053
Beirut, Lebanon
phone: 01/811968
contact: Aida Naaman, Director (475 Riverside Dr., Room 1046, New York, NY 10115)

The Children's Library is part of the Learning Resources Center of Beirut University College. The library was founded in 1968 and has a collection of 5,000 books in Arabic and English, and a few in French. The earliest written books in Arabic by Lebanese authors are held, as are the earliest illustrated works. Included are all of the books published by the Institute for Women's Studies in the Arab World (IWASAW).

# Lithuania

## KAUNAS

**The Museum of Children's Literature**
13 K. Donelaicio Str.
Kaunas 3000, Lithuania
phone: 206488
contact: Birute Glazneriene, Head of the Museum

The Museum of Children's Literature is a branch of Maironis Museum of the Lithuanian Literature. Included are 1,500 books, from the first Lithuanian children's book

in 1867 to the present day. In addition to the books, the museum also holds 1,000 manuscripts, 250 illustrations, 2,000 photographs, correspondence, and personal memorabilia of authors and illustrators. The books are written by Lithuanian residents, as well as by emigrants living in the United States.

## VILNIUS

**National Library of Lithuania**
Gedimino pr. 51,
2635 Vilnius, Lithuania
phone: 61 14 54
fax: 3702 627129
contact: Aldona Augustaitiene, Chair

The Centre of the Children's Literature opened in March 1994 and collects Lithuanian and foreign children's literature and related materials.

# Mexico

## COL. CONDESA

**IBBY Mexico**
Parque Espana 13-A
Col. Condesa
C.P. 06140, Mexico, D.F.
phone: 211-0492
fax: 211-0492
contact: Ma. Antonieta Avila Diaz, Librarian

The center contains several specialized children's book collections, but mainly consists of books published in Mexico, approximately 6,000 volumes covering all subjects and genres. One section contains 2,000 books from throughout the world in German, English, Portuguese, Japanese, and Italian, among other languages.

# Netherlands

## AMSTERDAM

**Openbare Bibliotheek Amsterdam**
**(Public Library of Amsterdam)**
Keizersgracht 440
1016 GD Amsterdam, The Netherlands
phone: 020-52 30 900
fax: 020-52 30 948
contact: Marijke Troelstra, Head of
  Children's Department

The Museum Collection of 20,000 volumes includes some very rare seventeenth–nineteenth-century children's books and a representative collection of modern children's books. Most are in Dutch, although they do have a good collection of English books (mostly obtained through Marshall aid after World War II) and other modern foreign languages.

## THE HAGUE

**Information Centre "Boek en Jeugd"**
**(Dutch Centre for Children's Literature)**
Nederlands Bibliotheek en Lektuur
  Centrum
Post Box 43 300
2504 The Hague, The Netherlands
phone: 070-3090100
fax: 070-3090200
contact: Dr. A. de Vries, Head

The Dutch Centre for Children's Literature contains 60,000 children's books and 700 reference works in children's literature.

**Koninklyke Bibliotheek**
**(National Library of the Netherlands)**
Prins Willem-Alexanderhof 5
P.O. Box 90407
2509 LK The Hague, The Netherlands
phone: +31703140351
fax: +31703140651
contact: Dr. Han van Berkel

The Collection of Children's Books of the National Library contains 17,000 titles dating from the seventeenth to the twentieth centuries. Also included is the 5,000-volume Collection of Comic Books.

# New Zealand

## WELLINGTON

**National Library of New Zealand**
Private Bag
Wellington 1, New Zealand
phone: 04 743000
fax: 04 743035

The National Library houses three separate collections of children's literature. The Dorothy Neal White Collection consists of 6,000 volumes of Victorian and Edwardian books and later titles published up to 1940. The recently donated Susan Price Collection comprises about 7,000 books, chiefly fiction for nine- to eighteen-year-olds, published since 1940. The National Children's Collection consists of volumes published in New Zealand, as well as approximately 50,000 volumes from other countries.

# Norway

## OSLO

**Norsk Barnebokinstitutt (NBI)**
**(The Norwegian Institute for Children's**
  **Books)**
Kristian Augustsgt. 21.
P.O. Box 6719
St. Olavs Plass
N-0130 Oslo, Norway
phone: 22 11 12 80
fax: 22 11 27 02
contact: Karin Beate Vold, Director or
  Anne Kristin Lande, Senior Librarian

The NBI is an information center and document archive of literature for children and young people. Started in 1979, NBI collects all children's and young people's literature published in Norway, as well as Norwegian literature translated into other languages. Currently, the collection numbers 45,000 volumes dating from 1727, of which about 4,000 are reference books.

## Portugal

### LISBON

Instituto da Biblioteca Nacional e do
   Livro
(National Library of Portugal)
Campo Grande, 83
1751 Lisbon, Portugal
phone: 795 01 30/1/2/3/4
fax: 793 36 07
contact: Luisa Cardia

All books published in Portugal are received by the National Library, among them many children's titles. In addition, they have manuscripts, documents, letters, illustrations, and other papers of many Portuguese writers, some of whom are children's authors.

## Republic of South Africa

### POTCHEFSTROOM

Instituut vir Navorsing in Kinderlektuur
(Institute for Research in Children's
   Literature)
Potchefstroom University for Christian
   Higher Education
Private Bag X6001
Potchefstroom 2520, Republic of South
   Africa
phone: 0148-99 2000
fax: 0148-99 2999
contact: Ms. Uca Eiselen, Lecturer
e-mail: fpbcjhl@puknet.puk.ac.za

The institute was founded in 1987 to conduct research in children's and young adult literature, to encourage research by others, and to assist researchers in the field of children's and young adult literature and affiliated subjects. With the assistance of publishers, the institute collects as many as possible of the children's and young adult books published in South Africa, mainly in Afrikaans and English. They currently have 700 volumes dating from 1978, and 2,000 containers of original manuscripts. "Die Afrikaanse Kinderboekgids" (a subject guide to Afrikaans children's books) is compiled and updated biannually.

## Scotland

### EDINBURGH

Book Trust Scotland
Scottish Book Centre
137 Dundee St.
Edinburgh, Scotland
phone: 031 229 3663
fax: 031 228 4293
contact: Lindsey Fraser, Executive
   Director

The Scottish Children's Books Collection consists of approximately 500 volumes dating from the 1950s created by Scottish authors and illustrators. Also included are books that are set in Scotland.

Museum of Childhood
42 High St.
Edinburgh EH1 1TG, Scotland
phone: 031 529 4119
fax: 031 558 3103
contact: John Heyes, Keeper of
   Childhood Collections

This is a mixed collection of some 1,100 volumes, mainly British children's books ranging from seventeenth-century chapbooks to present-day authors. The collection was formed from gifts to libraries and museums in Edinburgh from private donors. The collection is used mainly for museum exhibitions and displays and is accessible by special arrangement only.

National Library of Scotland
George IV Bridge
Edinburgh EH1 1EW, Scotland
phone: 031-226-4531
fax: 031-220-6662
contact: John Morris, Assistant Keeper
e-mail: @uk.nls.admin

Most of the National Library's children's books are in their regular collections. The library has had copyright deposit since the eighteenth century. The Mason Collection consists of 3,600 volumes, and the Hugh Sharp Collection contains manuscripts and first editions of Lewis Carroll and Edward Lear. The library has collected foreign-language children's books since the 1970s.

# Singapore

National Library
Stamford Rd.
Singapore 0617
phone: (65) 3323664
fax: (65) 3371470
contact: Ms. Rashidah Othman,
    Assistant Librarian

The Asian Children's Collection began in the early 1960s with the aim of assembling a comprehensive collection of books pertaining to Asian countries and people, written for children. Today, the collection consists of 22,000 volumes written in the four languages of Singapore—English, Malay, Chinese, and Tamil. Included are picture books and fiction with an Asian setting or characters; nonfiction books and magazines about Asia; books and magazines deposited with the National Library under the Printers and Publishers Act that are either published or printed in Singapore; and guides, bibliographies, and studies on Asian children's literature and reading.

# Slovakia

## KOSICE

Kniznica pre Mladez Mesta Kosice
Tajovskeho 9
043 59 Kosice, Slovakia
phone: 095-62 223 90
fax: 095-62 274 76
contact: Dr. Margita Vargova, Director

The Special Collection of Slovak Literature for Children was begun in 1977 and holds books dating back to Czechoslovakia's beginnings in 1918. A total of nearly 6,200 volumes represent children's literature by Slovak authors, in the Slovak language, or published in Slovakia.

# Spain

## BARCELONA

Biblioteca Infantil i Juvenil "Lola
    Anglada"
c/Rocafort s/n Jardins Montserrat
08029 Barcelona, Spain
phone: 439 41 90
contact: Librarian

This collection consists of 16,000 volumes of children's literature and is used by children and teenagers. They have a special collection of materials created by children's book illustrator Lola Anglada.

Centre de Documentacio del Libre
    Infantil
(Children's Book Documentation Centre)
Biblioteca Infantil Santa Creu
Carrer de l'Hospital, 56
08001 Barcelona, Spain
phone: 93-302 53 48
fax: 93-317 94 92
contact: Ma. Jose Daza, Responsable
    Biblioteca

The Documentation Centre contains 30,000 volumes published since the 1960s; a historical collection of 4,000 volumes, chiefly in Catalan; a documentary archive of unpublished data on children's books; and books about children's literature.

### Xarxa de Biblioteques de la Fundacio "la Caixa"
Serveis Centrals
Jaume 1, 2, 3 planta
08002 Barcelona, Spain
phone: 34-3-3187623
fax: 34-3-3179361
contact: Maria Rossines

The children's section of the library contains works for children and adolescents in the Catalan language.

### MALIANO

### Biblioteca Publica Municipal de Camargo
### Centro Cultural "La Vidriera"
Avda. Cantabria, s/n
39600 Maliano (Cantabria), Spain
phone: 942-253755
fax: 942-253755
contact: Ana Isabel Calvo, Bibliotecaria

This library's holdings include 6,000 volumes of children's literature dating from 1985.

### SALAMANCA

### Centro Internacional del Libro Infantil y Juvenil
### Fundacion German Sanchez Ruiperez
Pena Primera, 14 y 16
37002 Salamanca, Spain
phone: 923-26 96 62
fax: 21 63 17
contact: Dolores Gonzalez
    Lopez-Casero, Director; Raquel Lopez
    Royo, Program Coordinator

Created in 1985, this library has holdings of more 40,000 titles, including 6,000 specialized books. Children's books in all of the languages of Spain, a collection of books published before 1958, a special collection of juvenile books from Latin America, and 130 periodicals from around the world are held.

# Sweden
## STOCKHOLM

### Stockholms Stadsbibliotek Huvudbiblioteket (Stockholm Public Library)
Sveavägen 73 Box 6502
S-113 83 Stockholm, Sweden
phone +4687298700
fax: 4682798680
contact: Gunlog Raihle or Ajta
    Cederholm

The Stockholm Public Library has several collections related to children's literature. The Astrid Lindgren–Elsa Olenius Room is a collection of 1,225 volumes of books written by Astrid Lindgren that were donated by librarian Elsa Olenius. Included are first editions in Swedish and translations in fifty other languages. The Hur Man Hittar Sagor (How to Find Fairy Tales) is a book collection of 750 volumes of folktale collections published in Swedish. An accompanying printed catalog is an index to the stories in collections from 1910 to 1960, with five-year supplements. They also have a collection of Swedish reviews from daily newspapers since 1919.

### Swedish Institute for Children's Books
Odengatan 61
S-113 22 Stockholm, Sweden
phone: +46-8 33 23 23
fax: +46-8 33 24 23
contact: Lena Tornqvist, Head Librarian

The foundation Svenska Barnboksinstitutet, or SBI (The Swedish Institute for Children's Books), is a special library and information center for children's and young people's literature. The aim is to promote this kind of literature in Sweden, as well as Swedish children's and young people's literature abroad. Included in their holdings are 50,000 volumes of children's and young people's literature in both Swedish originals and books translated into Swedish. Also included are 10,000 volumes of theoretical books about children's literature. Several special collections augment the basic collection and are as follows: the Lennart Hellsing Collection of 1,500 volumes published in Swedish from 1601 to 1945, the Gustav Peyron Collection of 1,000 volumes published from 1770 to 1875, and the Olof Hult Collection of 1,000 volumes of adventure stories published from 1850 to 1920. The archives of Barnbiblioteket Saga, published by the Svensk Lararetidning from 1899 to 1954, have been donated and include a complete collection of all work published, as well as original manuscripts, accounts, correspondence, and other documents.

# Switzerland

## BASEL

**Schweizerisches Museum fur Volkskunde**
Munsterplatz 20
CH-4001 Basel, Switzerland
phone: 061 266 5500
fax: 061 266 5605
contact: Konservator
Internet: universitats-bibliothekbasel

The Kinderbuch-sammlung consists of approximately 7,000 volumes of children's literature dating from the seventeenth to the twentieth century.

## LA CHAUX-DE-FONDS

**Bibliothèque des Jeunes**
**(Young People's Library)**
Ronde 9
2300 La Chaux-de-Fonds, Switzerland
phone: 039/276 852
contact: Dominique Thomi Baker,
Manager

Several special collections are in the holdings of the Bibliothèque des Jeunes. The Collection of Books for Children and Young People from the nineteenth and early twentieth centuries comprises over 600 works, mostly by French authors, dating from 1839 to 1945. The Reference Collection of Children's and Young People's Literature contains 1,300 volumes about children's literature, reading, storytelling, child development, and art. This is the most complete reference collection dedicated to children's literature in French-speaking Switzerland. The Reserve Collection of Picture Books consists of more than 1,400 books from fifty countries, mostly from the twentieth century. The collection as a whole provides a world view of illustration and picture books.

## LUZERN

**Bibliotheks-und Medienberatungsstelle**
Sentimatt 1
CH-6003 Luzern, Switzerland
phone: 041/24 6650
fax: 041/24 6656
contact: Dr. Peter Gyr, Leader

The Kinderbuchsammlung has a representative collection of picture books of the German-speaking countries since 1974. In addition, they have a small collection of secondary literature about picture books.

## RENENS

**Globlivres**
**Bibliothèque Interculturelle pour les**
**Jeunes de l'Association Livres sans**
**Frontieres**
Rue Neuve 4 bis
CH-1020 Renens, Switzerland
phone: (21) 635.02.36
contact: Monica Prodon

Globlivres was started in 1988 by a group of bilingual parents and involved teachers in order to create a place of real and concrete exchange. This intercultural library

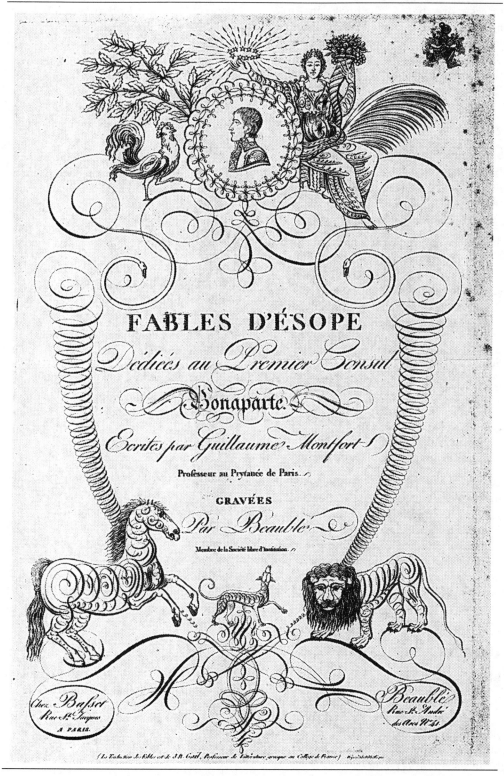

Title page of *Fables D'Esope*, by Guillaume Montfort with illustrations by Beauble; Paris: Basset [1801].

offers more than 6,000 books in Albanian, Croatian, English, French, German, Italian, Kurdish, Persian, and seventy-eight other languages so that foreigners living in the region will have access to books in their mother tongue.

## ZURICH

**Sammlung Elisabeth Waldmann**
Bahnhofstrasse 14
8001 Zurich, Switzerland
phone: ++41 1 211 06 75
contact: Elisabeth Waldmann

This is an international collection, focusing on 12,000 picture books and illustrations, mostly twentieth century, with a small number from the nineteenth century. A collection of more than 500 editions of *Little Red Riding Hood* is also held.

**Schweizerisches Jugendbuch-Institut**
**(Swiss Institute for Children's Books)**
Zeltweg 11
CH-8032 Zurich, Switzerland
phone: ++41 1 261 90 44
fax: ++41 1 261 91 45
contact: Rosmarie Tschirky, Director

Holdings of the Swiss Institute for Children's Books include the Bettina Hurlimann Book Collection. This collection consists of 4,500 titles covering a cross-section of children's books published internationally over three centuries. A 400-page bibliography of this collection is now available.

# Ukraine

## KIEV

**The State Library of the Ukraine for**
**Children**
Bauman St.
60 Kiev, Ukraine 252190
phone: +7-044-442-6587

contact: Anastasia Kobsarenko, Director
e-mail: nata@chlib.adam.kiev.ua

The Fund of the Rare and the Most Valuable Publications for Children is intended for specialists in children's literature. The collection consists of 17,000 volumes in Russian and Ukrainian from 1835 to 1945, books in foreign languages from 1801 to 1945, and the best modern publications for children dating from 1960.

# Wales

## DYFED

**Llyfrgell Genedlaethol Cymru**
**(National Library of Wales)**
Penglais, Aberystwyth
Dyfed SY23 3BU, Wales
United Kingdom
phone: (0970) 623816
fax: (0970) 615709
contact: Menna H. Phillips, Assistant
  Librarian
JANET: 000 1300 0006
e-mail: t-gold (la-net) lla 2092

Holdings of the National Library of Wales include several special collections of children's literature. Children's Books pre-1870 is based on the donation of C. J. Knight in 1937. It now contains 450 items covering the years 1810–1850, including chapbooks, primers, and picture books. The Llanfyllin Collection contains 369 volumes of English fiction and nonfiction and covers 1840–1890 with about one-third being publications of the Society for the Promotion of Christian Knowledge. The D. J. Williams Collection contains 500 volumes in Welsh, dating from 1800 to 1949.

# ❖❖❖❖❖❖❖ *Index*

Collections identified by generic names such as "Library" are indexed under the name of the sponsoring institution. *See also* the detailed Subject Listing, beginning on page 99.

Dee Jones is currently curator of the de Grummond Children's Literature Collection at the University of Southern Mississippi, a position she has held since 1986. She is the editor of *Children's Literature Awards and Winners* (Gale 1994) and the author of *A Bibliography of the Little Golden Books* and *An "Oliver Optic" Checklist*, both published by Greenwood. In addition, Jones has written numerous articles that have appeared in state, regional, and national publications. She holds a B.S. from Pennsylvania State University and an M.L.S. from the University of Southern Mississippi.